Winning a Sports Scholarship

L2   Row 3

Winning A Sports Scholarship

Chris Tenkin

BARRICADE BOOKS / New York

Published by Barricade Books Inc.
150 Fifth Avenue
New York, NY 10011

Printed in the United States of America.

Tenkin, Chris
    Winning a sports scholarship / by Chris Tenkin.
        p.   cm.
    ISBN 1-56980-078-2
    1. College sports—Scholarships, fellowships, etc.—United States.
2. Universities and colleges—United States—Admission.
3. Universities and colleges—United States—Directories
4. Coaches (Athletics)—United States—Directories. I. Title.
GV351.T4   1996
378.3'0973—dc20   95–50950
                                                                CIP

First Trade Paperback Printing

Acknowledgments

To my wife Susan—
For your unconditional love and support of me and my dreams

To my parents Jacqueline and Barry—
because the two of you are truly the greatest teachers of life
and nurturing parents a son could ask for

To my newly acquired parents Bonnie and Robert—
I thank you for your unwavering support

To all those involved in helping to make this dream become a reality—
Thank you

Table of Contents

Introduction

WELCOME TO THE exciting college recruiting process. What you are about to read should prove invaluable in helping you, the student-athlete, attract and choose a college. By following this step-by-step method, you will give yourself a fighting chance at attaining some type of athletic scholarship package. While my personal experience was in football, this book was designed for the use of all high school student-athletes in all high school sports.

Getting an athletic scholarship is a contest, a competition, just like running a 1,500 meter race or playing a basketball game. There is, however, more than one winner. Each year colleges and universities award thousands of athletic scholarships in more than thirty sports. Seniors graduate, freshmen come in. There is always a chance for a competent, dedicated athlete, whether you play football or field hockey, run track or swim.

Of course, every program is looking for the top players. But every program has many roster spots to fill, and there are always places, coaches say, for hardworking, accomplished student-athletes.

But, just as every high school athlete isn't a number one recruit, not every school is in the running for the top prospects. Athletic scholarships can be won from colleges that are ranked in divisions 1A, 1AA, and 2. Division 3 schools do not offer athletic scholarships.

When Kerstin Kimel coached the women's lacrosse team at Davidson University, she says, "there was no way I could draw the top players...I'd go to high school games and look at the number three and four players on teams." Davidson—a small, liberal arts college in North Carolina—is ranked as "highly competitive" in college admission catalogs. Ninety percent of the incoming freshmen are in the top fifth of their graduating high school class, and tuition is about $12,000. Davidson has been one of the most successful small schools in the nation in sending its graduates onto prestigious Rhodes and Marshall Fellowships. So, a Davidson scholarship would be nothing to sneeze at.

"What we always tell kids is that if you want to play in college, there is a place for you somewhere," Kimel said. In 1995, she took over Duke University's new women's lacrosse program. "Now I've got a realistic shot at going after those top players."

And even if the effort doesn't yield a scholarship, a coach may go to bat for an athlete with the school's admissions committee. The makeup of any school's freshman class is a mixed bag, and a word from a coach sometimes gives a student-athlete a chance he or she may not have had otherwise.

So, if you are good—but not great—how do you go about making contact with coaches, putting your best foot forward—in a word "competing"? That's what this book is all about. It is a game plan for winning an athletic scholarship.

Collegiate athletics and its athletes are often the lifeblood of a university's growth. Some students are attracted to schools with topnotch athletic programs for the pure joy of being affiliated with that school. Athletics is a vital link in keeping alumni active and enthusiastic. Sometimes, athletics contribute to a school's financial growth through the revenue they generate. When one sees all the ways athletics and finances are intertwined in the development of colleges and universities, is there any wonder why collegiate athletics have such a following?

Why do colleges and universities put so much stock in athletics? In the first instance, it goes back to that Greek idea of a strong mind in a strong body. Colleges see their role as providing their students with a well-rounded experience that includes athletic competition as well as classroom work.

There is, of course, more to it than that. A university is a special kind of community. It includes not only the students and teachers, but the town in which it is located and the thousands of alumni that may be spread across the country and even the world. Collegiate athletics is one of the unifying elements for this community. The field of competition is also like a "town common," where the various elements of the community gather, interact, and share an experience. Sometimes the identity of a college or university is integrally tied to its sports teams.

And while Notre Dame may be football and Duke basketball, it isn't only these marquee sports that matter. At the University of Iowa, they gather at Carver Arena to watch wrestling. At Johns Hopkins University, homecoming is held in the spring at a lacrosse game.

Nor is it only men's sports. Consider that during the 1995 season, the University of Connecticut women's basketball team played before sold-out crowds in Gampel Pavilion at almost every home game before going on to win the National Championship.

College athletics provide this opportunity for the community and an identity for the institution. So, as long as everybody is going to get together and share this experience, it might as well be a winning one. That's where the college athlete comes in, and that is why they are valued members of the community. And that's why colleges vie for the best athletes they can get.

Unfortunately, the exercise isn't all sweetness and light. Alumni donations tend to go up in winning years and down in losing ones. Successful seasons bring in greater gate receipts and the prospect of broadcast revenues in some sports. Pressures on coaches, their programs, and their athletes can build. But if you remember you are a student—and not a professional athlete—and take care of business in the classroom as well as work hard at practice, everything else will sort itself out.

Even the recruiting process can be cutthroat, so before heading down this road, it is important to get organized and focused on what you are doing, what your goals are, and how you want to go about doing it.

One word of warning right up-front. No one should be playing a sport solely for the purpose of getting a scholarship. Life is too short, practices too long, and the chance of injury and disappointment too great to go through this exercise cynically. If you love your sport, love it enough to put in the hours that make you good enough to think you have a serious shot at a scholarship, then you ought to give it a try. But the ultimate reward for playing has to be on the field, the court, or wherever you compete.

Once you have decided to Go For It, you must do so with the same kind of effort you put into your sport. Take a chance and Live the American Dream. You will never know unless you try. There is no shame in trying and not succeeding. The only shame would be from not giving yourself the chance to succeed. So, let's give it a try.

Can I guarantee you a scholarship? No. All I can say is that I tried and succeeded and I hope to help you do the same.

MY STORY

The summer before seventh grade, I had a real urge to play football in the town recreation league. I had been playing backyard football with my friends, and I wanted to put on the pads. The real thing. My parents were hesitant at first because of my age, but after they thought it over, they signed the release forms. They figured that they would rather see me play with the protection of a football uniform than wearing shorts and a T-shirt in the backyard.

I can remember my mom dropping me off at football practice for the very first time. The date was August 15, 1981. The sky was brilliant, and it was about ninety degrees. Once I found my coach and the team that I would be playing with, we went over to the trailer to be issued our equipment for the season. As the coach opened the doors, I was struck by the horrible smell of all of the football equipment. Nothing seemed to have been washed in years.

As we waited in line, each athlete was issued all of his equipment, one by one. Then we tried on the pads and pants and the rest of it just to make sure they fit. Since this was my first year playing, and I was the only seventh grader on an eighth-grade team, I didn't have a clue as to what piece of equipment went on what part of my body!

I picked up a set of rib pads that were in the form of a vest but looked to me like something that I was supposed to put my legs through and tie around my waist. One eighth grader called out, "Hey, take a look at Tenkin. He's trying to wear his rib pads like a girdle!" Embarrassed doesn't cover how I felt. But as each practice passed, I began to learn more and more about the game of football.

The season came and went, and I was able to earn a starting job as a fullback and linebacker for my (no wins and nine losses) football team. All I can remember is getting knocked down more than I was knocking other people down. Basically, I wasn't very good, and I decided to retire from the game of football at the young age of twelve. I figured that I could concentrate my efforts elsewhere.

I don't know how or why it happened, but when the next season came around, I was back. But this year there was something different. I don't think that I realized it at the time, but I had a greater sense of self-confidence, and I didn't relish the memory of being beaten up the year before. This would be a new year, a new beginning. For starters, I put my rib pads on the correct way.

On the first day of practice, I was really looking forward to making my first tackle during drills. The year before I had been scared to death, and I never had wanted my coach to call my name for any of the drills.

Despite playing a whole year, I still didn't have much of a clue as to what I was doing except that when I was on offense, I knew to block the person in front of me. And when I was on defense, I killed the person with the ball. I also knew I was gaining the respect of my teammates and finding some success on the field. Forgetting the wins and losses, playing this type of sport was a very gratifying experience for me.

At that time my dad was in the process of starting a new business. Little did I know but this business was going to be a great help in my physical development as an athlete. That business was a health club. I spent a great deal of time there which marked the beginning of my formal weight training.

I entered high school as a freshman in the fall of 1983, strong but small and slow. Not exactly a great combination. I attribute part of my slowness to the fact that I was at that awkward stage for boys. Of course, another reason was that I was slow. But being around the club, I met a lot of the local high school athletes. They would always talk about going to play some sport at this college or that. I had heard many stories and started dreaming about doing the same thing.

I would watch the pro and college football games on television and be mesmerized by some of the athletes. In fact, I loved the whole athletic atmosphere so much that my bedroom was literally covered wall to wall with pictures and posters of college and pro football players. Soon it became a dream and a goal for me to receive a full athletic scholarship to a major university to play football.

As a freshman I was five feet six inches tall and weighed about 145 pounds. I played the positions of offensive guard and inside linebacker on defense. I was OK as a freshman, but I was, as I mentioned, small and slow. My only salvation was that I was aggressive with good instincts and had decent balance. Not much, but something to build on. After the season, I went back to the gym.

I also played baseball my freshman year, but as the season ended, I found that I had lost interest in the sport. That was the last year that I played baseball. From that moment on, I decided to commit myself twelve months a year to the sport of football. I was determined to achieve my goal of a full athletic scholarship from a major university.

Between my freshman and sophomore year, I gained in both size and strength. I stood at about five feet nine inches tall, and weighed about 175 pounds. As a sophomore football player, I improved my skills and was able to earn a starting job on the varsity level playing special teams.

After weeks of practice, it was finally opening day. My team was out in the huddle getting ready to kick off to mark the start of our season. This was the first time that I would be playing against varsity competition. The memory of standing in the huddle with the kicker calling the play is as vivid to me as if it happened ten minutes ago. Then we broke for our positions. Once I reached mine, I looked down the field and saw the opposing team.

They were huge! It seemed as if I only came up to everybody's waistline. My whole body was shaking with nervousness and anticipation. The referee finally blew his whistle to signal the start of the game. Our kicker stood there with his arm up and then began his approach to the ball. As he kicked the ball, I can still remember the feeling in my body as I sprinted down the field for the very first time as a varsity high school player. It seemed as if I was outside of my body looking down at the entire field and just floating.

As I was sprinting, I saw the man on the other team receive the ball and begin to run with it. He ran up the middle and then broke to his right. As he did, I quickly saw the huge blocker on the first line turn and face me. I was running full speed and aiming right at him. As I approached, I knew that there was going to be a giant collision, much like a car running into a brick wall. As I collided with him my helmet met his forearm and chest—SMACK! The next thing I knew, I bounced off of his body and began closing in on the runner. Meanwhile, the strangest colors were slam-dancing before my eyes, brilliant reds, blues, and oranges. I think that was what they call "having your bell rung." I didn't care. It was the greatest feeling just knowing that I was out there contributing as a player on the varsity level.

As a sophomore, I was just getting my feet wet as a varsity player. I played well on all the special teams and improved as the year progressed. I was even fortunate enough to play some linebacker on defense and make a few tackles that year.

Upon the conclusion of my sophomore year, I sat down with my father and explained to him that I wanted to play football in college for a major university. As we discussed the idea, we came to the realization that as a sophomore I was not ready to think about playing for any college. We decided to wait and see how well I would perform as a junior and whether I developed the right stuff.

So, it was back to the gym in the off-season. My size and strength increased as the year progressed, but I knew that I still had to really concentrate on my running and agility skills.

At the gym, I continued to meet new members and picked up more tips to enhance my workouts. One member in particular ended up being one of the key reasons I was able to reach my potential in the areas of running and agility. His name was Mike Beach.

Mike was a great guy. He spent countless hours working with me. His knowledge and personality inspired me as an athlete to strive for all of my goals. I owed a lot of my success to his coaching, and I will always have a great deal of respect for him. Mike worked with me throughout my sophomore and junior summers in preparation for the upcoming football seasons.

By my junior year, I had reached about five feet eleven inches and weighed 205 pounds. My confidence grew, and my athletic skills improved. I had a good season playing primarily inside linebacker on defense and guard on offense.

Again, throughout my junior season, my dad and I talked about the idea of playing major college football. When the season was over, dad and I contacted my Uncle Tom. Tom played college football for a Division 1 school and was currently the head football coach at the high school where he taught. We discussed the idea of me winning a full athletic scholarship. Tom asked to see some of my game film so that he could evaluate my play. After viewing the film, he felt I had a legitimate shot at attaining my goal.

I knew that if I wanted to play college football, my size would most likely limit me to the position of inside linebacker. By doing a little projection, I began to focus my attention and training toward mastering the skills of playing linebacker. Thus, my father, uncle, and I began the college-recruiting process.

We decided to draft a junior-year introductory letter and send it out to about forty Division 1A and ten Division 1AA universities. The letters were sent to the college coaches or recruiters of each university. The letters contained all of the vital information needed to capture the recruiters' attention and to make them aware of who I was as a student-athlete so that they could follow my progress throughout my senior athletic season and hold me in regard as a prospective scholarship athlete.

This was a very exciting time for me. Once the letters were mailed, the only thing that I could do was wait for a response. As the days, weeks, and months passed, I began to get nervous and discouraged because I was not receiving any responses.

Finally, about four months from the completion of my junior athletic season, I received my first response. The letter came from the Clemson Tigers! You can only imagine how excited I was. Then slowly but surely, I received more and more letters from universities that I had contacted through the introductory letters. The responses stated that they now knew who I was and that they would be following my progress as a student-athlete throughout my senior athletic season. I received a response from 98 percent of the schools.

As a senior I was up to six feet one inches tall and weighed 225 pounds. Again, I played the positions of inside linebacker on defense and offensive guard. This year I was able to see how the combination of physical maturity and proper training paid off. I had a very good senior football season.

I continued to receive letters. Then came the personal phone calls from the college coaches. All of this attention was mind-boggling and exhilarating. By the time football season was over, I had accumulated about one hundred pounds of responses. And best of all they came primarily in the form of personalized letters.

Then came the day. The date was December 1, 1986. That was when the NCAA allowed qualified universities to start offering athletic scholarships in the sport of football to all qualified senior high school recruits. (The rules have changed since 1986.) Some of the universities that were interested in me faded away, but out of the combined twenty division 1A and 1AA universities that physically came and evaluated my game films and me as a person, I was awarded my choice of four full athletic scholarships. All were from division 1AA universities. They were to the University of Massachusetts, the University of Maine, the University of Rhode Island, and the University of New Hampshire. Needless to say, I was very happy. I ended up accepting the offer of a free ride from the University of Massachusetts. The steps and methods that I used throughout the recruiting process proved to be extremely successful.

I have gone through the full recruiting process. I have experienced the ups and the downs. I set my goals, and I reached them. This book is about helping you do the same. You don't have to be a Bo Jackson or a Rebecca Lobo. You do have to be dedicated to your sport for the sake of your sport. Once you are, by using *Winning a Sports Scholarship* as your guide, you can develop your own game plan for your own free ride. You can increase the odds of going to college by playing the sport you love.

I hope this book will inform, educate, and assist each and every one of you with the recruiting process. Don't be discouraged. As the advertisement says, Just Do It.

Good luck.

ATHLETIC SCHOLARSHIPS—WHAT THEY ENTAIL

Earning an athletic scholarship carries a number of great benefits. The biggest and best is that you earned it solely on the merits of your own athletic and academic performances. That in itself is a great accomplishment.

The second benefit is that it saved you and your family a tremendous financial strain. A scholarship is not a loan. It does not have to be repaid to the university or any other financial institution. It is free, clear, and the result of your sweat and effort.

In many cases, it is also makes it a bit easier to gain admission. For example, if you were a student applying to a university, you would have to meet certain SAT and academic course requirements without exception. If you were a student-athlete, you might have the luxury of having to meet the minimum requirements set by the NCAA which are much less stringent than those of a pure student. (More on NCAA minimum academic eligibility for freshmen in chapter 4).

Another advantage to going in on a sports scholarship is the university will want to protect its investment. If you have trouble with your courses, the college will often arrange free tutoring. In addition, you are usually assigned a personal academic coordinator who will guide you throughout your academic college career. My academic coordinator helped me tremendously.

Here is a description of what to expect with a full or partial athletic scholarship.

A full athletic scholarship covers room, board, tuition, books, and insurance. These scholarships are awarded on a yearly basis and are renewed at the beginning of each year. The athletic department is allowed to renew the full or partial scholarship for each athlete for a maximum of five years within a six-year period. Partial scholarships, on the other hand, could contain one or more of the above-mentioned items with varying degrees of financial reward.

For example, my full football scholarship at UMASS for the spring semester of 1990 covered:

Tuition—nonresident	3,394.00
Authority fee	135.50
Activities fee	55.25
Health Fee	182.50
Athletic fee	74.00
Arts fee	23.50
Meal Plan	760.00
Rent	907.00
Telecommunications	87.00
Curriculum Support	690.00
George Barber Scholarship	2970.75
TOTAL	$9,279.50

A partial scholarship could be a percentage of each, some, or one of the items mentioned above. Or the college might offer full payment of tuition and nothing else. The partial scholarship is divided up and can contain whatever the coach wants to offer you in whatever areas he wants.

There are a lot of things that determine whether a school will offer an athlete a full or partial scholarship. Foremost is how badly the program wants an athlete and how much he or she is in demand. But this is tempered by how much money the program has to work with and how many athletes it is trying to recruit.

Jim Rudy, the coach of the UMASS's women's soccer team, explains, "This year [1995] I will have a total of eleven scholarships that I will be able to carry at one time. Those scholarships can be broken up any way that I choose."

Coaches expect athletes on scholarships to produce results in the classroom as well as on the field. The students are expected to stay on top of their studies at all times giving their best efforts. When they are having problems in the classroom, they are expected to see the coaches immediately for academic assistance. They must follow all academic rules and regulations of the university and should conduct themselves at all times in a fashion that reflects well on themselves as student-athletes and the team they represent. Coaches require the student-athletes to give their best efforts all the time be it in practice, meetings, or game situations.

It is possible to lose an athletic scholarship. A student-athlete may decide to stop playing the sport. He or she may become involved in illegal activities—in which case the student-athlete may be disciplined under NCAA rules or those of the university. Also, if a student-athlete can't cut it in the classroom, poor grades may result in the loss of eligibility.

In addition to athletic scholarships, a student may receive "financial aid." This financial assistance may include help with tuition and fees, room and board, and books. Financial aid is based on the student-athlete's family financial situation. How much aid awarded depends on the individual situation.

A financial aid package can cover some or all of a student-athlete's educational costs. Because there are many different types of aid packages, you should check with you high school guidance counselor and the financial aid offices of the colleges that you are interested in attending.

CHAPTER

2

What is Recruiting?

RECRUITING IS THE process of identifying talented athletes, contacting them, evaluating them, and getting them to play for a school's program. Collegiate coaches are your primary recruiters, but other recruiting sources include alumni, high school coaches, opposing high school coaches, and parents. Yes, parents can play an effective role in this process. The athlete that has been successfully recruited is rewarded by some type of an athletic scholarship package.

(For more information concerning the rules and regulations of recruiting, contact the NCAA regarding the booklet entitled "NCAA Guide for the College-Bound Student Athlete (913) 339-1906.")

The recruitment of athletes by any university is a business devoid of emotion and based on the laws of supply and demand. Each university is allotted a certain number of scholarships depending upon the sport and division of play. Scholarships become available much in the same way any business has job openings—through attrition, graduation, or resignation.

For major sports, recruiting is a long and calculated exercise. "We are watching student-athletes very closely when they are sophomores and juniors," says Doug Graber, the former head football coach at Rutgers University. "We also see a lot of athletes through our summer camps. During the winter, we mail out questionnaires to the high school coaches regarding possible upcoming recruits. Once we receive the questionnaires back from the high school coaches, we divide the responses up among our coaching staff. Then, in the spring, as a coaching staff, we go out into the high schools for one month and watch prospective athletes in game situations on videotape, collect and evaluate high school transcripts, and talk to high school coaches.

"After we have evaluated all of the information that we have accumulated on the prospective student-athletes, we then decide who is a definite recruit, who is a possible recruit that has to be reevaluated, and who is a rejection. The process is long and never ending because it is done year after year."

Scholarships go to fill open positions or when coaches feel they need added depth at a particular position. With this information, an athlete or parent needs only to ask the recruiter where the athlete fits in based on the scale of supply and demand.

But, both the supply and demand can change, complicating the recruiting exercise for athletes and coaches. For example, you're a six-foot-ten-inch basketball center. If you are the only big player in the crop, then your chances of getting recruited are excellent. But let's say that there are ten other big players coming out of high school the same year. Well, your chances have been diminished if they are being recruited by the same schools. This is not to say that scholarship opportunities don't exist because athletic scholarships are offered by schools in divisions 1, 1AA, and 2.

Similarly, if all the programs you are interested in already have big players, and they are looking for small, ball-handling guards, you probably aren't going to get a scholarship there, no matter how good you are.

Mike Hodges, the head football coach at the University of Massachusetts, explains the process this way:

"Each team recruits student-athletes based upon their specific team needs for each year. Therefore, just because a school does not recruit your son or daughter does not mean that they cannot play college athletics or earn an athletic scholarship package from other schools at the same level or any other level for that matter.

"What student-athletes and parents must understand is that there are only a limited number of scholarships each year, and each team must fill those scholarships in terms of team need, graduation, or the team's weaknesses or strengths at particular positions.

"For instance, if I see that I have a great number of offensive lineman that can play for the next few years, I will not go out and recruit offensive linemen. If I see that I am going to be losing three tailbacks through graduation, then you better believe that we are going out to recruit tailbacks.

"Parents and athletes must remember to look at recruiting from the recruiter's standpoint and not feel that their son or daughter is being rejected. At that point, recruiting becomes strictly a numbers game."

Kerstin Kimel, the coach of Duke's women's lacrosse program, adds, "This is one of the most difficult things we have to deal with. You can have a candidate who is a good student and a good player but just doesn't fit into your plans. Parents find it hard to accept, but it isn't a judgment about their daughter.

"For example, this year I am looking for attack [players] and speed. I've got a ton of defensive players." The edge that can help in some sports is versatility—the ability to play a number of roles. "The first thing I look for is overall athletic ability and versatility. Could this player play any place on the field?" Kimel says.

And not being a high school star doesn't necessarily mean you can't land a scholarship. "We do not always recruit the best high school players," Rutger's Graber says. "We recruit the best players that have the greatest potential to become good college players."

HOW ATHLETES FIND RECRUITERS / HOW RECRUITERS FIND ATHLETES / WHAT RECRUITERS ARE LOOKING FOR FROM STUDENT-ATHLETES

So, how do college programs find new talent? Every coach has his or her own technique, but because the recruiting game is so competitive, they are always looking for a little help, and they are always ready to look at an athlete who contacts them.

Consider the schedule of Julie LaFreniere, the coach of the women's track and field/cross country team at the University of Massachusetts. "Our program is in season from the start of September through June, so it becomes very difficult for us to get out and physically recruit these athletes because we are busy with our own meets just about every weekend throughout the school year.

"A few ways that we do find out about our athletes is from the high school: state, regional, and national meet results. Other ways that we find out about our athletes is from high school coaches directly, alumni, word of mouth, and the student-athletes themselves who are interested in our program and come up to the university."

University of Connecticut Associate Head Women's Basketball Coach Chris Dailey says there are a number of ways that she finds out about prospective recruits. "Probably one of the biggest recruiting tools that we use is the AAU [the Amateur Athletic Union]. For most sports in the U.S., there are AAU teams and programs in every state. These are developmental programs that give kids the opportunity to play throughout the year which are usually against higher levels of competition outside of their high school leagues, and it gives them the exposure to college coaches that they might not have received.

"Here we can see and evaluate hundreds of athletes at the same site. The current trend is that prospective student-athletes are going to these events at earlier ages. Recently, I went to a thirteen-years-and-younger AAU out in Amarillo, Texas. There I could identify some of the best kids in the country even at the earliest of ages. Once I find what I would consider to be a prospective recruit, I will follow them and evaluate them throughout each future season. Although these programs are helpful to us as college recruiters, they can become quite expensive for the student-athlete's family. Fear not because this is only one helpful avenue that we use to find recruits.

"Other sources of our recruitment come from high school coaches, parents, and student-athletes themselves through phone calls and letters, friends, research, reading the newspapers, etc.

"Some of the characteristics that we look for in our student-athletes are as follows: The first...is their high school grades and SAT scores. Remember, if they don't have the grades, they cannot be eligible to play in college. The next thing that we look for is the overall athletic talent of the recruit. We want to see how each recruit will fit into our needs for that particular year. Once we have targeted our recruits, we will look to evaluate their intangible qualities. For example, I will look to see how the athlete handles herself with her high school coach and her peers. How she handles adversity during a game situation. How she carries herself on the court. After, we have determined that we are interested in the athlete, we will take the process to the next step.

"I will then find out as much information as I can about who the athlete is as a total person. I will research and ask as many people as I can who know the athlete. Does she work hard in school? Does she come to school every day? Does she give her best effort all of the time? What are her goals? Is she a leader in the school? Does she have a good relationship with her teachers? Does she have a good relationship with her family? By asking these questions, I get a feeling of what kind of overall person she is and whether or not I want to continue to pursue her. As a result, we can evaluate the overall person to see how her qualities match up to both our needs as well as hers."

RECRUITING SERVICES

These are for-profit businesses that attempt to help student-athletes get into college. While these recruiting services are helpful in mass mailing the student-athlete's information to many colleges that they might not have had the chance to reach, they can be very expensive. You can do much the same thing yourself with time, a little research, and quite a few stamps, thereby saving a great deal of money.

THE PARENT'S ROLE:
UNREALISTIC GOALS AND DREAMS VS. REALITY

Many a parent, who has thrown a ball, sunk a basket, or hit a home run, firmly believes that their own son or daughter will someday be the very best in their chosen sport. These feelings are often implanted in the student-athletes when they are very young. The kids then dream of being the heroes they watch on television, see in commercials, and read about in the paper—with the ultimate reward of fame, adulation, and unbelievable salaries. But for the most part these dreams—whether nurtured by a parent of a young athlete or the athlete him or herself—are unattainable and pursuing them blindly may lead to disappointment and anger.

How many times do we see well-meaning parents with unrealistic goals and expectations trying to coach their children, or parents who are trying to live their unfulfilled athletic career through their children. This often does more harm than good because it puts a tremendous amount of unwanted tension on the parental-child relationship. Parents and athletes must be realistic when evaluating the dreams and goals of the athlete.

To John Ryan, head coach of the boys' soccer and track and field teams at Vernon Township High School, Vernon, New Jersey, "It is probably one of the most common issues that high school coaches deal with. Most parents have an inflated view of their child's athletic ability. One reason for this is both the student-athlete and the parents have not been exposed to the topnotch ability of players in colleges regardless of the college's division. Even though an athlete may start on his or her high school team does not mean that they are equal to the caliber of play at a college. Look at how many high schools there are in the United States; college coaches are out recruiting the top athletes in the country, not on one high school team.

"For example, even though a player may be the top high school player on his team, he may not compare equally when you spread it out over an entire state. The student-athlete might not even be in the top fifty players in the state. Therefore, athletes themselves, parents, and I must be realistic when evaluating the athlete to see what division of play would be most suitable for the athlete. This helps to narrow the list of schools and points the student-athlete in the correct direction."

Coach Ryan urges parents to first look at a school academically. Only then should they look at a school's athletic program. Parents should be realistic as to where the athlete can play and be both successful and happy.

"One thing that parents should understand," Coach Ryan says, "is that in the sport of soccer, full athletic scholarships are extremely hard to come by. Even the topnotch soccer universities in the United States usually only have one or two full scholarship athletes on a team at one time. The soccer programs do not have the funding to supply everyone with full athletic scholarships. That is why college coaches take their money and divide it among a greater number of athletes and give them partial scholarships. This way the college coaches can bring in a greater number of athletes to the team."

The situation is the same in sport after sport. Julie LaFreniere of UMASS says of unrealistic goals, "I think that it is real important for both the student-athlete and the parents to know that especially when speaking about scholarship opportunities in the sport of track and field–cross country at the division 1 level, even though scholarship opportunities are available, the scholarships are going to go to the top student-athlete in the state, region, or nation! Parents must remember that sports such as this are not always as fully funded for scholarships as compared with some of the other sports. Yes, this is unfair, but it is a fact. It is not easy to earn a scholarship to any university in this sport. The student-athlete may be able to help that particular division 1 school, but that does not mean that they are scholarship material.

"I think that it is unhealthy for any parent to put that kind of pressure on a student-athlete to get a scholarship for this sport or any other sport for that matter. I have had instances where a student-athlete was a state champion in high school with great race times, but that doesn't mean that they are scholarship material. They would need to have times that were competitive to the top levels in college in order to be considered as scholarship material. But, 'scholarship material' is considered differently ranging from division 1 through 1AA to division 2. The parents and student-athlete must understand where the college coaches are coming from when talking about what the college coaches feel is, 'scholarship material.'"

The parent's role in the recruiting process is a complex and tricky one. Recruiting is a tough-nosed business. Recruiters are first and foremost trying to fill rosters and second, trying to be fair and evenhanded with applicants.

So, a mature monitor of the process, who can ask the right questions and keep on top of the elusive and effusive coaches and recruiters who make promises but don't seem to deliver, is essential. And that is an important role for the parent. But the parent should not insinuate him or herself and become *too* involved. This has got to be between the coach and the athlete. For the coach is recruiting the young man or woman and not the parent. It is the coach and player that have to develop a working relationship. Indeed, when your son or daughter goes off to college, the coach will be seeing a lot more of them than you will.

"We are happy to answer parents' questions and respond to their concerns," says Duke's Kerstin Kimel, "but the person we want to hear from is the player. That's the person who should make first contact and if she has a question or a problem, she's the one we want to hear from."

Similarly, the final decision also has to rest with the athlete. "The student-athlete should be the person making the final decision of where they are going to be going to school," said UMASS's Hodges. "My experience has been that everybody who knows the student knows what's best for him: the mother, the father, the uncle, the coach, the teammates, the guy down the street. They are all very well meaning, but the only one who knows exactly what the recruit wants, needs, and is looking for is the recruit. What may be important for one person may be of absolutely no importance to the next guy. For example, one player may want to go to a school in a city-type atmosphere, and another may not care at all what type of atmosphere the school has. This is only one example and there are thousands of factors that go into making an important decision such as this."

Coach Dailey of UCONN feels that anyone who really wants to play in college can fulfill their dreams and make them happy and lasting ones, as long as they are realistic. She says that "I am a firm believer that there is a place for every person who wants to play at the college level if they can be realistic and objective about what they are looking for in a school and who they are as an athlete. That part in itself is very difficult for a student-athlete to do. They need the help of their high school coach. They need to get out and see the different levels of competition in actual game situations. They should try to get a feeling of where they might fit into the total package by getting some objective opinions. Unrealistic goals are probably thrust upon student-athletes more by parents than by high school coaches. As a result, the student-athlete is searching for a situation that she is not going to be successful in to begin with, and the student-athlete becomes confused and gets frustrated.

"The student-athlete must be honest with themselves and ask the questions: am I a division 1, 2, or 3 player? Do I want to play at a high division 2 school and have the possibility of playing for the shot of a national title, or do I want to play for a small school and be the big fish in the small pond, or do I just want to be a part of the team? These are just a few examples of questions that student-athletes must ask themselves. With these answers, they can begin to make realistic judgments of what type of situation would be best for them. You don't have to be a division 1 player to have a successful career as a student-athlete in college. You must match yourself to the school that best fits you as a person both academically and athletically. Basically, recruiting just becomes a realistic matching process."

Personally, I feel the parents' role throughout the recruiting process is to continually offer common sense and rational thought. The parents must first help the student-athlete to always think clearly and rationally without making any rash decisions based upon emotional highs. Any and all decisions that are made should be done after a careful and mature evaluation of each situation that they may encounter.

The parents' second role in assisting throughout this process is to make sure that they are staying on top of the student-athlete in order to keep him or her organized. For example, parents should see that the student-athlete is precise and prompt when writing and sending introductory letters, filling out questionnaires and college applications.

Parents also need to be thorough and follow through when asking for and receiving facts from college recruiters. Lastly, once all of the facts are gathered and evaluated, parents need to assist the student-athlete with advice on all the necessary decisions. But it should be just that—advice. All final decisions should be made by the student-athlete.

Once you realize that you are a part of the recruiting numbers game, it is important to get a clear sense where the student-athlete fits into the plans of the school you are interested in.

For example, let's assume that your son is a quarterback, and the university recruiting him knows that there are two quarterback positions coming available. You should ask the recruiter where your son fits in on the demand list, and they will give you a number. If two quarterback positions are coming available, they will go out and recruit ten quarterbacks. They do this knowing full well that if they are interested in an athlete, so are many other universities.

Assuming that your son is number five on the demand list at the beginning of the recruiting process, this does not necessarily mean that he will stay there. Suppose that number one has poor grades and cannot be accepted into the school, and numbers two and three commit to other schools, then your son moves up the ladder from number five to number two and number four moves to number one. Because this is the beginning of the recruiting process, your son can climb the ladder quickly and have a good chance of being offered that scholarship. Keeping track of the numbers in the game is something parents can do and athletes should not worry about.

Here's another example in the sport of women's swimming. Let's assume that the student-athlete is a very strong freestyle distance swimmer, but her shorter sprint race times are only average as compared to other recruits of that particular university. If the university is looking to fill in spots with either an overall versatile athlete who can play a variety of different roles or specifically with short sprint athletes because their current roster is stocked with long-distance swimmers, then the chances of being offered any type of an athletic scholarship become slim.

But, you never know. Another university may be stocked with sprinters, and it may need to recruit a bunch of long-distance swimmers. In this case, the student-athlete falls right into their recruiting plans.

Keep in mind that while the recruiting process is a business devoid of emotion, it is not necessarily meanspirited. Understanding this process is always a plus.

It is also important to remember that programs are recruiting, as Rutgers' Graber points out, not only the athlete they "see now," but the athlete they hope "to see in the future." In other words, the college recruiter tries to project the future of each prospect.

The term "projection" means to begin at a starting point and make an educated guess as to where something will be in the future. A college recruiter will look at each athlete he or she recruits first by position and second by physical attributes such as size, strength, speed, coordination, technique, agility, etc. Through extensive evaluations of highschool game films or personal observation, the recruiter will attempt to project how each athlete will mature physically over the years and where he or she will best be placed by position for the sake of the college team.

For individual sports such as freestyle wrestling, projection does not mean as much because the athlete is usually confined to a weight class, and their techniques will not change all that much. The recruiter will be looking primarily at attitude and technique. However, for a team sport such as football, projection means everything. Let us remember that we are dealing with a seventeen- or eighteen-year-old athlete. They are still maturing physically and how they mature can determine which position they might play in college.

Just because an athlete plays one position in high school does not mean that he or she will play that same position in college. The recruiters will make that decision based upon physical maturity, athletic talent, and team needs. Therefore, it is important to note that projection plays an important role depending upon your sport when recruiting time comes. You might be afraid of working a new place on the field or court, but have faith in the judgment of the recruiters who are excellent evaluators of talent.

It is, however, important for parents and the student-athlete alike to be realistic about prospects. The student-athlete needs to find the right school and the right team. "It is very difficult to tell anyone that they cannot do something, especially if they feel passionate about achieving their goals," says UMASS women's soccer coach Jim Rudy. "What I do is ask the student-athlete how they feel about playing time. On this level, it is not so easy to just come in and play for four years. If playing time is a big issue for them, then I may suggest playing for another college that plays at lower levels of competition. There, they might play and be very successful right out of high school. The high school student-athletes should ask the college coach where they fit into the scheme of that particular university and ask approximately how much playing time they will get. On the other hand, college coaches need to be honest with the student-athletes and tell them exactly how they feel the student-athlete will be projected as a player."

Coach Mike Hodges says, "I think this is a very difficult question to answer because it is very difficult to pinpoint how far a student-athlete can go with their college careers both academically and athletically. I am very hesitant to tell any student-athlete what their limitations are. The best way to get a realistic view of the entire situation is to go to the university and watch a practice or a game....This way they get a hands-on experience. They must remember to judge themselves up to the caliber of play that they are going to play against, not what they have played against in high school."

Obviously, a student-athlete can't attend practices and games for every school he or she is interested in, but after seeing a division 1A practice and comparing it to division 1AA or 2, you'll get a feel for the differences.

Matching the School to the Personality

WHEN YOU REALIZE that recruiting is a shifting numbers game, it becomes clear that if you are seeking a scholarship, it is difficult to peg your hopes on any one school. You might be one of the best middleweight wrestlers or softball catchers in the country, but if these positions are held by top collegiate athletes at the school you wish to attend, the chances of getting a scholarship is probably slim to none.

So, the best you can do is select a group of schools, any one of which you would be happy at. Your first instinct might be to apply to as many schools as possible and see what happens. Then go to whichever school seemed interested in you. That could be a mistake.

Many times parents and students choose a college that does not match up to the student's personality, wants, and needs. This is why you see so many students either drop out or transfer to other colleges after their first or second semester. Remember, it is the student who will be attending college, not the parents. And that while we are talking about athletic scholarships, the first objective is to get a good education in a nurturing setting.

If you want to make sure that your choice is a happy and lasting one, you must first be honest with yourself and ask yourself three simple questions.

"DOES THE COLLEGE OFFER ME AT LEAST TWO AREAS OF ACADEMIC INTEREST?" Remember, at the age of seventeen or eighteen, a lot of things will change in life—including career goals. It isn't unusual for a student to change his or her mind several times on the major and career they would like to pursue. It is very common for a student to switch majors once or twice while attending college. If you have at least two major areas of academic interest to choose from, you are playing it safe.

"WILL I FIT IN SOCIALLY WITH THE TYPE OF PEOPLE THAT I WILL BE AROUND FOR THE NEXT FOUR OR FIVE YEARS?" When you are picking your schools, be sure to give some thought to geographical location, school reputation, student and faculty attitudes, beliefs, religion, and ethnic diversity. Everyone is an individual with different priorities. These are just a few examples of the factors that must be carefully evaluated before committing to a college.

"AT WHAT SIZE COLLEGE WOULD I FEEL MOST COMFORTABLE?" The size of the school is key. Some people feel overwhelmed and alienated by large schools. Others find themselves chafing at the social and academic constraints of a small school. Generally, large universities tend to have large lecture-hall classes ranging from 100 to 1000 students per class. In this setting, personalized instruction can be a problem. The upside of the big university is a broader range of both academic and social opportunities. But an individual has to be able to seize the initiative on his or her own. Some students feel more comfortable in smaller schools that focus more intently on their undergraduates.

This is not to say that individualized instruction can't be found at large universities. Tutoring and study group programs, for example, are always available. The point is that the atmosphere of a large university versus a small college is very different.

In my case, after I had given careful consideration to all of the factors listed above as a recruit going through the process, I found that one of the best measures was to evaluate the people that I had met on each campus. Once I had visited a campus, I would digest all of the information and feelings that I had experienced. From there I was able to make realistic comparisons between what I liked and disliked about each place.

For example, one of the campuses that I had visited was perfect in all of the areas listed above, save one. I liked the fact that the school was large. The university offered me at least two areas of academic interest. The professors that I had met were very nice and seemed to really care for their students. But, and this was a big but, I really didn't like the players and their attitudes when I talked to them. As I reflected on the visit, I knew that deep in my heart this was not the place for me even though there were so many positives. If I didn't like the players and their attitudes after one short meeting, I could only imagine what my experience would have been like if I had decided to attend for four years.

On the other hand, when I toured Massachusetts, I fell in love with the entire university right from the start. The place was magnificent! From the student body to the professors, from the coaches to the players—this was it! This school had everything that I was looking for. I knew that this was the school that I wanted to attend without any equivocation. I just used my gut feeling and let that make my decision for me. Fortunately, it was something I have never regretted. In fact, if I had it to do all over, it would still be UMASS.

Vernon Township Coach John Ryan agrees that student-athletes should visit the schools they are deeply interested in. "The best way for a student-athlete to make sure that their choice of college will be a happy and lasting one would be for the student to visit the university when school is in session," he advises. Coach Ryan has helped hundreds of young athletes achieve some type of full or partial athletic scholarship package for college. He says, "The very first thing that I tell my athletes and their parents when their son comes into my program as a freshman is that every student-athlete has an individual personality that is natural to themselves, and every college has a personality that is natural to itself. Each college has its own type of look and atmosphere. This is why you have to make sure that you match the student's personality to the college. If the student-athlete does not fit into the type of personality at that school, then you can probably expect that student will not be at that particular school for very long.

"I do not recommend an athlete to attend a college where I feel that he is not going to be successful whether it is on a division 1, 2, or 3 level. By the time the athlete is ready for college, I usually know his strengths, weaknesses, likes, dislikes, etc. I do the research and try to get a feeling for the colleges. Once I have done the research, I will recommend where I feel that the student-athlete will best fit.

"Some of the things to look for are geographical location, the types of people at the campus—professors, students, and coaches—rural as opposed to urban setting, size of the college—enrollment, size of the classes, etc.

"Again, I try to look at all of these items when matching up the student-athlete to the college. If a student-athlete and his parents do not look at these items, they may see their son coming home very unhappy."

Coach Ryan goes on to advise the student-athlete to sit in on classes, talk to students, and professors. They should talk to other athletes in a relaxed setting and ask them if they like the athletic program, training, coaching staff, and university as a whole. They should check out the Student Union, and just sit down and watch the people walk by to get a feel for the atmosphere. They should walk the campus, all in an attempt to get the most realistic picture of what the college is all about.

The schools and coaches are just as anxious to get a good match because they are making an investment in the student-athlete. "Yes, matching up the school is definitely a factor and probably the most difficult factor to control," according to UMASS Coach Hodges. "The reason why it is so difficult is because we have such a limited amount of time to spend with each athlete. The NCAA limits the amount of contact that we can spend with these student-athletes. One of the things that we do is get feedback from our current athletes that are already part of the university, specifically, after the recruits come up for official visits. We have kids from every socioeconomic background, but what ties our team together is finding the kids whose personality matches up with our belief system to become successful. Our system is based on understanding the work ethic and discipline that is needed to become successful not only on the field but also off the field in the classroom, and in everyday life at the university."

As a college recruiter for women's track and field–cross country at UMASS, Coach Julie LaFreniere says, "What I do with recruiting is before the student-athlete even comes up for a visit, I tell them the truth of exactly what the University of Massachusetts is like. I do not try to paint a picture that is different from what they are going to experience or one that may sway the student-athlete to come and play for me. It would not do any good if the student-athlete came here and then did not like it. Then she is not happy and then I am not happy, so nobody wins by hiding the truth regardless if we are talking about UMASS or any other university. I explain to them that we are basically out in the country and are a small New England college town. The university, which is bigger than the town itself, gives the town a citylike atmosphere, but it is still in the country."

With all that said, teenage athletes are often fixed on certain schools because of their reputations (either academic, athletic, or social), the school's athletic program, the school's coach or, yes, even its mascot. When that school pays attention to that student, he or she is in seventh heaven. But that still may not be the right school for that individual.

"I always tell high school players, don't go to a school because of its program or coach or school colors," says Duke's Kimel. "Maybe those things figure in…. But the reason you are going is to go to school. Coaches leave. Programs change or even get shut down. Players get career-ending injuries. What you are left with is the school."

Kimel suggests that students make a list on paper of pros and cons for each school. "Then even if they won't admit that a particular university may not be right for them, at least it's on paper," she said.

As I stated earlier, you must first find a school that suits your academic needs. Then the school must suit your social needs. Lastly, the school must suit your athletic needs. Here you must be realistic.

Your athletic ability must match up with the caliber of play at that particular university. Athletic teams of all intercollegiate sports are ranked by division.

DIVISION 1A
Extremely competitive
Scholarships/Financial Aid are available.

DIVISION 1AA
Extremely competitive
Scholarships/Financial Aid are available.

DIVISION 2
Very competitive
Scholarships/Financial Aid are available.

DIVISION 3
Competitive
Financial Aid is available.

The athlete, parents, and high school coach must make a realistic evaluation of the athlete's ability as a junior and make a realistic projection of the athlete's improvement as a senior and then through college.

UMASS's Mike Hodges recommends that a high school athlete take a close look at the programs and level of play he or she is interested in. "The best way to get a realistic view of the entire situation is to go to the university and watch practice or a game," he said.

Obviously, you can't go to practices and games at every program where you might wish to apply. But make sure to see some representative games and practices, and ask yourself honestly if you can play at that level. You may decide that you would fare better in division 2 than division 1AA. This is not an admission of inadequacy. The goal here is to find a school you'd like, a team you can play on, and a program that will give you a scholarship. You have to decide if you'd be happy with a scholarship to a topflight smaller school where you'd get a chance to play or pay thousands of dollars in tuition to sit on the bench at a big school with a big-time program.

Once you have decided on the level or levels of play that would be suitable, you should begin to compile a list of target schools —at least fifty in no less than two divisions—that blend the right athletic and academic setting. You should send your introductory letters to these schools. Be sure they are places you would truly like to attend. NOTE: Obviously the more schools you contact, the more acknowledgments you will receive and the better your chances will be for receiving that scholarship or financial aid package.

Lastly, you should remember not only to be realistic when choosing your schools but also not to sell yourself short. If there is a school you are really interested in, let the recruiters turn *you* down. Don't take yourself out of the game before it begins. Aim as high as you feel comfortable.

ERIC MEIXNER, AN ATHLETE, ON MATCHING THE SCHOOL TO THE PERSONALITY

As a senior in high school, I had great aspirations to play soccer in college for the largest university that I could go to. I knew that I wanted to go to college and get a degree, but I did not know what I wanted to choose as a major. The main reason for me wanting to go to college at that time was strictly to play soccer.

I entered my senior athletic season with only the highest of hopes. I wanted it all. The season came and went, and I played very well against all of the competition. While my play did not attract the attention of big-time division 1 colleges, it did attract a few division 2 and 3 schools.

After the season, recruiting time came around, and I began to visit some of the schools that were interested in me as a prospective recruit. Two of the schools that I visited just did not appeal to me. I did not like the surroundings and the look of each campus. The coaches were very nice, and so were the players that I had met, but I just had this gut feeling that those schools were not for me.

The next school I visited, I took along my mom and brother. It had a topnotch division 2 soccer program. Once we arrived on campus, we walked around. I really liked the campus and the way that it was laid out. It was a small school of about thirty-five hundred students.

After our walk, we met with the coaching staff and some of the players on the team. They took us to eat at the dining hall where I had the opportunity to meet some of the students. The head coach seemed to have a very good rapport with most of the students on campus. He would stop and introduce me to them. He was just a very personable kind of guy.

On my return home, I began to reflect on the day's events. I came to the conclusion that I really liked the school, soccer program, coaches, and players.

During our conversation, the topic of scholarship money was discussed. He was very honest with me. He said he couldn't offer me anything as a freshman, but, depending upon how well I improved as a player over time, would probably give me the opportunity to earn some type of athletic scholarship.

As I said, I knew that I really wanted to play for the most competitive college soccer program that would accept me into their school as a student-athlete. I also knew that I wanted to get out of the small town that I came from and make a fresh new start. As a result, I chose to attend. I called the coach and gave him my commitment.

I finished up my high school career and graduated in June. Soon, it was August and time for preseason camp. As a high school player, I had always led the pack in any kind of running activity. For the start of preseason camp, we would begin with a two-mile run for time. I figured that this would be a great chance for me to show my stuff. But I only managed to beat four or five players out of approximately twenty-five. Needless to say, this was a real eyeopener. As the preseason led to the season, I was in awe of a lot of the players on my team. Coming from a small town, I did not have the exposure of playing with athletes of this caliber.

As the preseason neared the end, I knew that it was getting close to when the head coach would be picking the traveling team lineup. Out of the twenty-five players on the team, only eighteen of us would be traveling. Being a part of the traveling team meant that I would be getting some playing time. If I did not make the traveling team, it would be only practice for me that year. Honestly, I did not feel very confident that I was going to make the traveling team.

Finally the head coach posted the traveling roster for that year. As I approached the list, I became very apprehensive. I looked at it expecting the worst, and to my surprise, I found that I had made the team. I was elated and filled with joy. I guess that all the hard work that I had put in finally paid off for me. That year we had a very strong varsity team. In fact, we trounced most of our opponents. As a result of our team's performances, I was able to gain valuable playing time as a true freshman.

The next season I entered training camp with great expectations. I came into camp in the best shape of my life, and I ran a great two-mile test time. But, there was something that stopped me from that point on. My consistency and concentration in practice was not up to par with the rest of the team, and as a result, my play really dropped off. The end of training camp was coming near, and the traveling list was about to be posted. I knew that I was going to be vying for the eighteenth spot along with three other players.

After one of the last preseason practice sessions, the head coach called the four of us into his office to explain the situation. He told us what we already knew, that we were on the borderline for taking the eighteenth spot. He told me that he could either red-shirt me, which would mean that I would not lose a year of athletic eligibility, or we could take turns rotating us into the games. This would mean that I would be on the traveling team for one out of every four games.

After I had evaluated the situation, and talked it over with my parents, I decided to red-shirt for that year. I looked down the road at my chances for playing and came to the conclusion that I was not going to be getting as much playing time as I had originally thought at the time of my commitment out of high school. The caliber of play was getting much better at the college year after year, and I did not see myself improving my skills enough to keep up with the competition. I knew that I didn't want to sit the bench because I still really wanted to play.

Being that my athletic situation was not looking too bright at the time, and I still did not know which major I wanted to pursue for a career, the college had lost all of its appeal. I never really gave the college much thought on how my personality matched up to it except for the sole purpose of athletics. The situation was very upsetting so I decided to transfer.

This time I would think ahead and be rational about all of the aspects that go into making an important decision such as choosing a college, a college that would match my personal needs. I now realized that the reason that I was going to school was for the education and the entire college experience, not just to play sports.

The college I transferred to was a solid division 3 school back in my home state. I felt more comfortable being closer to home for a number of reasons. My parents were closer, so they were able to come down and watch me play more games. They were not able to do that as easily at my former school because of the distance.

The cost of school was also an issue. Being that I was going to school in my home state, the cost of the education was much less. I also felt that I would have a much better chance of earning a lot of playing time as an athlete. This was a much more realistic and self-satisfying situation for me to be in rather than the one that I picked before.

Looking back now in hindsight, I feel that I did not evaluate my situation and opportunities thoroughly enough upon the completion of my high school career. The only aspect that I was looking at was the athletic side of college. That proved to be a big mistake. For example, I did not look at the cost issue of paying back student loans if I was not able to earn some type of an athletic scholarship. I did not take into account the distance from home and that my parents would be limited in the number of times that they would be able to visit. I also became homesick, and that was a thought that had never even entered my mind.

In closing, my advice to every athlete who is going to eventually go through this type of similar experience would be to really look at your situation realistically and thoroughly before making any final decisions. It is not worth the hassle or the heartache to go through the situation of transferring. Make sure that the college matches up to your personality and needs regarding all expectations, because you want your first decision to be one that is satisfying and lasts.

High School Grades College SAT/ACT Exams

NCAA Eligibility Requirements

YOUR POINTS PER game and your speed in the forty-yard dash are important, but so are your grade point average and scores on college exams such as the ACT and the SAT. Grades and test scores will determine which schools can be in your pool. Obviously, the better your grades, the larger your pool.

"We see all kinds of athletes that are certainly capable of playing," says UMASS Football Coach Hodges, "but we cannot get involved with them because they are not academically sound. The NCAA makes changes to these academic requirements almost every year, making the criteria more and more difficult.

"The student-athlete must be solid in their academic achievements from their freshmen year in high school, all the way through the end of their senior year," according to Hodges. "If the student-athlete has a strong academic background, it will undoubtedly open up many doors...specifically in the area of being offered some kind of scholarship package."

There are two reasons that good grades and test scores are valued. First, every college is looking for good students and getting one that can block, jump, or dive is a bonus. Second, and most importantly, good grades show a coach that you will be able to cut it in college and that giving you a scholarship will not be a wasted exercise.

"If student-athletes do not take their grades and exams seriously in high school, then they are going to have a very difficult time in being successful in the classroom in college," said Julie LaFreniere, the women's track coach at UMASS. "The first two semesters are the most crucial and difficult in a student-athlete's college career because of the course load and just the fact of adjusting to college life."

Good grades are a sign to a coach that you can do the academic work, be there for practice, and be ready on game day. Another player may be faster and stronger, but the way this game works, it doesn't matter if they are not eligible to play because of poor grades.

"I would encourage all student-athletes to prepare themselves from the ninth grade all the way through their senior year, both in the classroom and regarding the SAT tests. They must fulfill all of their core requirements. They cannot wait until their junior or senior year because it is too late. High school student-athletes must take their grades very seriously right from the start," says Doug Graber of Rutgers.

Coach Jim Rudy says, "I would obviously like to see all of my student-athletes have both excellent high school grades and SAT scores. That scenario is not always the case. Personally, I do not put much stock in the SAT as an indicator as to how well a student-athlete will progress in the classroom. There are too many variables that are involved when taking the SAT that can alter the student-athlete's score. Unfortunately, the NCAA and the college admission offices do look at SAT scores and set minimum scores for student-athletes to achieve in order to be accepted into school.

"I put much greater stock into a student-athlete's high school grades. I think that their grades are a much better indicator of how the student-athlete will fair in the college classroom. The reason I feel this way is because high school grades are accumulated over four years. I am looking for a solid track record because that will tell me if the student-athlete is serious and disciplined enough to handle the college curriculum load."

In my own case, I always had a difficult time taking tests like the SAT and as a result, my scores were never as high as I would have liked. But I didn't believe that they properly showed my standing as a student or my potential to do well in college. I had a solid B average throughout high school, and I graduated from college with a 3.00 grade point. I think that consistent performance in the classroom helped persuade coaches that I was scholarship material. I have seen a lot of very academically talented kids who had scored over 1200 on the SAT, and they flunked out of college because they lacked the discipline to go to class and keep up on their studies.

The first thing that high school coach John Ryan says to his student-athletes is that everything begins in their freshman year. "They cannot and should not slack off at all at any time regarding their high school grades. College coaches want to see improvement and consistency in their grades from their freshman year on. They should also carry a strong academic load leading them toward the area of academic interest that they would like to pursue in college."

Coach Ryan goes on to say, "I feel that student-athletes should begin preparing for the SAT test in their freshman year of high school. They should take courses that teach students how to approach the test, and they should take courses that help to enhance their knowledge enrichment.

"Unfortunately, the SAT test is an important key to entering any college today. Student-athletes may take the SAT as many times as they like, so why not take advantage of the practice? At the very least, a student taking the SAT test will feel more and more comfortable by practicing the test. There are many students who bomb the test merely because they panic. If they wait until their junior year, they have missed out on valuable practice time. Then the pressure to do well on the test becomes insurmountable, leading to poor scores. Why take a chance like that if you have the materials available to you?"

The term "student-athlete" means just that. First and foremost, you are a student, and your obligation is to perform in the classroom. Only then are you an athlete who aims to produce results on the athletic field.

Because athletes are judged on this dual standard of classroom and field performance, their test scores and grades are often weighted differently than other applicants. If a person was to apply to a college solely as a student, the entrance criteria might be much more stringent. The grades and entrance exam scores would have to be much higher than a person who was applying as a student-athlete. This is why when you are sending your letters of introduction to colleges or universities, you should always go directly to the head coach or recruiting coordinator of that particular athletic team. I will go into greater detail regarding this point in the introductory letter section.

COLLEGE ATHLETIC ASSOCIATIONS

Colleges and universities are all members of athletic associations that compete on four levels or divisions—1, 1AA, 2, and 3. While the most widely known association is the NCAA (National Collegiate Athletic Association) which comprises most of the larger colleges and universities, there are also many other smaller associations, such as the NIAA.

Athletic associations have different criteria, so be sure to find out which colleges belong to which association. The differences are many and are found in the areas of recruitment, athletic-academic eligibility, rules, and regulations. This information is available to you by simply asking the coach of the college that you are interested in.

NCAA ACADEMIC ELIGIBILITY REQUIREMENTS
1995–FUTURE

NOTE: The current NCAA student-athlete eligibility requirements from the 1995 school year to the future are constantly being updated by the NCAA. These are just the basic requirements for academic eligibility and are by no means all of them. Always double-check theses requirements with your high school guidance counselor, the NCAA, the university where you will be attending, and the conference office prior to making any important decisions or commitments.

For more information, contact the NCAA regarding the booklet "NCAA Guide for the college-bound student-athlete." (913) 339-1906.

INITIAL ELIGIBILITY CLEARINGHOUSE

Check with your guidance counselor for all information regarding your mandatory registration with the clearinghouse. Your guidance counselor can obtain registration materials for the clearinghouse at no cost by calling (319) 337-1492.

- This is a central clearinghouse that certifies an athlete's eligibility in divisions 1 and 2.
- All athletes must register with the clearinghouse.

1995-1996: NCAA GENERAL ELIGIBILITY REQUIREMENTS FOR DIVISION 1 & 2 ATHLETES

In order for a student-athlete to be considered a "qualifier," which means that they are eligible to practice and play in their freshman year of college, they must meet the requirements of the NCAA bylaw 14.3.

REQUIREMENTS:
- Graduate from high school
- Have a 2.00 grade point average on a 4.00 scale
- Successfully completed 13 core curriculum courses
  English 3 years
  Math 2 years
  Social science 2 years
  Natural or physical science 2 years

(at least 1 laboratory class if offered)

2 additional courses in English, math, or natural/physical science

2 additional courses taken from existing categories:

(for example, foreign language, computer science, etc.)

- Have a 700 combined SAT score (verbal/math) if taken before April 1, 1995
- Have an 820 combined SAT score (verbal/math) if taken after April 1, 1995
- Or have a 17 composite score on the ACT if taken on or after October 28, 1989

AFTER AUGUST 1, 1996: NCAA GENERAL ELIGIBILITY REQUIREMENTS FOR DIVISION 1 QUALIFYING ATHLETES

In order for a student-athlete to be considered a "qualifier"—eligible to practice and play in their freshman year of college—after August 1, 1996, they must meet the requirements of the NCAA.

REQUIREMENTS:

- Graduate from high school
- Successfully complete 13 core curriculum courses

English 4 years

Math 2 years

One year of algebra/one year of geometry, or a higher level course where geometry is prerequisite

Social science 2 years

Natural or physical science 2 years

(including at least one laboratory if offered by school)

One additional course—

in English, math or natural/physical science

Two additional academic courses

(for example in foreign language, computer science, etc.)

- Using the 1996-1997 Qualifier Index (see page 45)

Have a grade point average based on a 4.000 scale

Have a combined score on the SAT- (verbal/math) or a composite score on the ACT

DIVISION I PARTIAL QUALIFIER—TO BE ELIGIBLE TO RECEIVE AN ATH-LETIC SCHOLARSHIP AT A DIVISION 1 SCHOOL AND PRACTICE WITH THEIR TEAM AT THEIR HOME FACILITY

REQUIREMENTS:

- Graduate from high school
- Using the 1996-1997 Qualifier Index

Have a grade point average based on a 4.000 scale
Have a combined score on the SAT- (verbal/math) or a composite
score on the ACT

NONQUALIFIER

- The student-athlete cannot practice or compete during their
  freshman year
- Still has four years of athletic eligibility during their college career
- Cannot receive athletic scholarship in freshman year
- Can receive need-based financial aid unrelated to athletics

NOTE: A nonqualifier is someone who has not graduated from high school
or did not achieve the core-curriculum grade point average and SAT/ACT
score required for a qualifier or a partial qualifier.

**AFTER AUGUST 1, 1996: NCAA GENERAL ELIGIBILITY REQUIREMENTS FOR
DIVISION 2 QUALIFYING ATHLETES**

REQUIREMENTS:
- Graduate from high school
- Have a minimum 2.000 grade point average based on a 4.000
  scale
- Have complete at least 13 core curriculum courses
  English 3 years
  Math 2 years
  Social science 2 years
  Physical science 2 years (including at least one laboratory class if
      offered)
  2 additional courses in English, math, or natural or physical science
  2 additional academic courses (for example, foreign language,
      computer science, etc.)
- Have a minimum combined score of 700 on the SAT or a minimum
  composite score of 17 on the ACT

FINANCIAL AID

Here are some of the general rules that must be followed from the NCAA
regarding financial aid.

If the requirements for bylaw 14.3 have been met, you may receive
financial aid if you are enrolled in a division 1 or 2 school. If the requirements for bylaw 14.3 have not been met, then financial aid may be received
under certain conditions.

In division 1, if you are someone who has not met the requirement of bylaw 14.3 but you have graduated with a minimum of a 2.000 grade point average—"Partial Qualifier"—then you may receive financial aid based on need for the 1995-1996 academic year.

In division 1, if you are someone who has not met the requirement of being either a qualifier or a partial qualifier—"Nonqualifier"—you can receive financial aid, but it cannot be related to athletics.

In division 2, a partial qualifier may receive institutional financial aid including athletically related financial aid. A nonqualifier may receive institutional financial aid unrelated to athletic ability.

If you are planning to attend a division 3 college, then you can receive financial aid that is based on need but not on athletic ability.

1996-1997 FRESHMAN-ELIGIBILITY STANDARDS
COLLEGE ENTRANTS 1996-97 AND THEREAFTER

Core GPA	Minimum Required SAT	Minimum Required ACT
2.500 & above	820	68
2.475	830	69
2.450	840-850	70
2.425	860	70
2.400	860	71
2.375	870	72
2.350	880	73
2.325	890	74
2.300	900	75
2.275	910	76
2.250	920	77
2.225	930	78
2.200	940	79
2.175	950	80
2.150	960	80
2.125	960	81
2.100	970	82
2.075	980	83
2.050	990	84
2.025	1000	85
2.000	1010	86
Below 2.000	xxx	xx
Not eligible	xxx	xx

1996-1997 PARTIAL QUALIFIER—
DOES NOT MEET STANDARDS FOR QUALIFIER

Core GPA	SAT	ACT
2.750 & above	720	59
2.725	730	59
2.700	730	60
2.675	740-750	61
2.650	760	62
2.625	770	63
2.600	780	64
2.575	790	65
2.550	800	66
2.525	810	67

Recruiting Aids for Student-Athletes and College Recruiters

RECRUITING CALENDAR: A recruiting calendar is exactly what it sounds like. This is when the college coaches/recruiters go out on the road and seek out new and promising high school student-athletes. The recruiting calendar is different for each sport. The recruiting season for a sport usually begins the minute after the last game or meet of the season.

Since various sports take place at different times of the year, it becomes imperative that you understand when the best time is for sending letters and receiving acknowledgments. Becoming familiar with the recruiting calendar for your particular sport will save you a lot of time and discouragement. Recruiting is the lifeblood of all athletic programs, but you must make your contacts with the recruiters through introductory letters at the proper time of the year.

For women's track and field–cross country, Coach Julie LaFreniere states, "There is no other sport that is on the road like we are. We are on the road from the beginning of September until June. The best time for contacting us with junior year introductory letters is any time."

Coach Jim Rudy of UMASS says, "The best time for athletes to contact college coaches in the sport of women's soccer is any time outside of the actual season. I would suggest that letters be sent in the student-athlete's sophomore and junior year. I would also suggest that the student-athlete and parents do not wait for anyone to do this for them. Start the process early and become aware of all of the rules that are governed by the NCAA regarding recruiting high school athletes. The rules are many, and they are often changed from year to year."

UMASS Football Coach Mike Hodges says, "During the season we are busy seven days per week. That means from August 1 to the end of the season. Once the season has been completed, we are always in search for recruits for the next year and also for years to come. The best time for contacting a division 1 football program is from the time the college's season ends which is around November or December, all the way through the winter, spring, and summer months."

UCONN's Coach Dailey remarks, "Let me start by saying that we try to respond to all high school student-athlete introductions whether they come from letters or phone calls. During our season, these initial contacts are good, but the student-athlete should also make follow-up contacts to be sure that contact was made with the college coaches. Student-athletes, parents, and high school coaches need to understand the constraints that we are under during our actual season because we are working with our own teams. The best time for making contact with us is usually any time outside of our actual season."

Without exception, you will get a response from the recruiters using patience and proper timing. Below are some sample recruiting calendars for various sports.

SAMPLE RECRUITING CALENDAR 1

FOOTBALL

August 1–November 30:
> The team is in season and very busy with no time for recruiting.
> This is *not* a good time to send letters of introduction and resumes.

December 1–February 28:
> Coaches are busy recruiting athletes for the upcoming season. This
> *is* a good time to send letters of introduction and resumes.

March 1–May 1:
> Coaches are preparing the team for spring practice sessions. This
> is an excellent time to send letters of introduction and resumes.

May 2–July 31:
> Break period for coaches and team members. July marks the start

of preparations for the upcoming season. This is also a good time for sending letters of introduction and resumes.

SAMPLE RECRUITING CALENDAR 2

BASKETBALL

November 1–March 1:

Coaches and team are very busy in their season both practicing and playing. This is not a good time for sending letters of introduction and resumes.

March 2–October 31:

Coaches are on the road recruiting and are involved in various other activities. This is a great time for sending letters of introduction and resumes.

SAMPLE RECRUITING CALENDAR 3

TRACK AND FIELD–CROSS COUNTRY

January 1–December 31:

This sport is in season twelve months per year. Any time is a good time for sending letters of introduction and resumes.

NOTE: With the exception of sports that compete twelve months per year, the only bad time for sending letters of introduction and resumes is during the college team's actual season. All other time periods are good for contacting these recruiters. When I say bad, I mean that the college coaches are so busy that they will not have the time to correspond with you as soon as you might like. They will file the information away for the months that they are in season, but once the season has concluded, they will respond. There will just be a waiting period on your part.

SOPHOMORE AND JUNIOR YEAR INTRODUCTORY LETTERS AND RESUMES

Now that you have a basic understanding of the recruiting process and schedule, it's time to go to work and aggressively seek that scholarship package. If you have received no inquiries from a university prior to your junior athletic season in high school, this is the time when you should alert the recruiters as to what they have been missing. There is no hard and fast rule about when to send these letters. In general, introductory letters should be sent upon completion of your sophomore or junior year athletic season.

John Ryan, the coach of the men's soccer team at Vernon Township High School, has his players send out letters in their sophomore year. "Once the letters are sent out," he explains, "then the ball gets rolling because now the college recruiters know who and where this prospective student-athlete is, and they can follow their progress through their junior and senior year."

Ryan contends that "all of the legwork and research must be completed by the end of their junior year because the window of opportunity comes to a close very quickly. Recruiters are recruiting the best athletes that they can find, and they are not waiting around for you. The athlete and parents must take the initiative to start the recruiting process in the athlete's sophomore year. This does not guarantee a scholarship package, but it does guarantee that the student-athlete will not be overlooked because of improper representation." Ryan's approach has certainly been successful. In fifteen years of coaching soccer and track, 126 of his athletes have won full or partial athletic scholarships.

When Ryan was asked the question "Do you feel that many student-athletes get overlooked each year because they were not properly guided through the recruiting process?" his response was "Yes, probably hundreds or thousands of student-athletes get overlooked each year because of improper representation in the recruiting process. A lot of that has to do with the high school coaches themselves who need to get the ball rolling for their student-athletes. I feel that it is the responsibility of the high school coach to help their athletes and to inform parents of how the recruiting process works.

"This is not to say that they will definitely receive some type of scholarship package from a college, but at least the athlete is getting a fair shot and proper representation. Remember, high school coaches do not offer athletic scholarships. College coaches offer athletic scholarships. The job of the high school coach is to introduce the college coaches to their athletes and to begin the recruiting process with all of the steps that are described in this book."

Mike Hodges of UMASS elaborates. "Most good players are seen by college recruiters on the division 1 level, but some student-athletes do get overlooked each year for a variety of reasons, such as high school coaches do not send in our requests for prospects; the student-athlete plays in an area that does not get a lot of publicity; the student-athlete did not play on a very successful high school team; the student-athlete played a position that did not receive very much recognition—for example a quarterback versus an offensive lineman—and lastly, nobody helped the student-athlete to become noticed."

When you are an athlete in one or more of these situations, you must market yourself to become noticed. Don't sit back and let someone else do it at their leisure or not do it at all. You must be the one to make it happen for you!

When Coach LaFreniere was asked "Do you feel that receiving a junior year introductory letter from the student-athlete would be beneficial to both you as a coach and to the student-athlete?" her response was, "Yes, I do feel that it would be beneficial to both the student-athlete and the college coaches because it identifies who the student-athlete is and gets the ball rolling to begin the recruiting process. Oftentimes, I find that we send out letters to the prospective student-athletes that we are interested in to the high school or high school coach, but we never receive any response to the letters. For whatever reason, the letters never get to the student-athlete, and this slows the recruiting process. So yes, if they send us letters, it speeds up the entire recruiting process."

Coach Chris Dailey of UCONN feels that introductory letters and resumes are very useful as long as they contain certain elements. "Sophomore and junior year introductory letters and resumes are helpful provided that they contain the correct information. For example, we are looking for information that will be helpful to us throughout the recruiting process.

"The vital information that we are looking for is: the student-athlete's height, weight, position, speed, SAT scores, what kind of student they are, their athletic schedule, address, phone numbers, etc. I can then make some evaluations of how that particular student-athlete might fit into our plans.

"I also feel that coaches and parents need to do their homework before calling or writing to the college coaches. They need to research the caliber of play that is offered at each university and make the realistic comparisons throughout the different divisions.

"Another important point is to address the letter and/or resume to the coach by name. Make the phone call to find out who the coach is that you are sending letters to. Do not address the information by saying 'Dear sir/madam.' That is very impersonal. Even if the information is incorrect, make the attempt to address the information to the person in charge."

Taking the list of prospective schools that you have compiled, you need to write a letter to the head coach of each with regard to your particular sport. The letter should contain vital information such as:

1. Head coach's full name and address at the school
2. Date
3. Your grade point average
4. Your PSAT/SAT/ACT scores
5. Your age, height, and weight

6. Position(s) you play
7. Honors and awards/physical capabilities, if applicable
8. Your full name, address, area code, and phone number
9. Name and address of your high school
10. Your high school coach's name and home and school phone number
11. That videotapes are available upon request

Although you can sign the letter, it is always more credible if your high school coach signs the letter for you.

Some college coaches also like to have resumes on file, which lay out the academics, extracurricular activities, athletic background, and any other details (community service, etc.) that may be helpful with the admissions committee. The resume should represent the student-athlete in a way that would give the college recruiter a better understanding of what he or she is all about, what they have accomplished, and what types of activities they are involved in.

Be sure to include references and their phone numbers. Another item that really helps college recruiters is for the student-athlete to send a schedule of their athletic contests. If time permits, college recruiters may want to come and see the student-athlete in action.

After you have mailed out your introductory letters and resumes to the college coaches, it is a good idea to either write a follow-up note thanking them for any attention they might give your introductory letter or call them directly to make sure the letter got to them, or both. Following up is one more way to make the coaches aware you exist and get them interested in following your progress for seasons to come.

Here are some representative introductory letters and resumes that you can use as is or alter for your own purposes. The italicized and underlined areas are where you are to fill in the correct information about you.

C/o Mr./Ms. *coach's full name*   Date _____
Head *sport* coach
Sport office
Address of school

Dear Coach *last name*:

My name is *full name*, and I have just completed my junior *name of sport* season for *name of high school/state*. I am writing to you as a student-athlete because I would very much like to become a part of your *sport* recruiting process.

As a student I currently hold a _____ grade point average on a 4.0 scale. I have also taken my PSAT test and scored a _____ . I will be taking the actual SAT this *month/day/year*.

As an athlete I played the positions of _____ . Currently I am _____ years old, _____ tall, and weigh _____ pounds. I run the forty-yard dash in _____ seconds. In the weight room, I can bench press _____ pounds and squat _____ pounds. As a junior I received the award of _____ .

Again, I hope that you will consider me as a recruit when you begin your recruiting process.

I look forward to hearing from you soon.

Sincerely,

Signature
Your full name
Address
Area code and telephone number

High school coach's name
High school coach's address
Coach's home/school phone number

SAMPLE LETTER 2

C/o Mr./Ms. *coach's full name*   Date _____

Head *sport* coach

Sport office

Address of university

Dear Coach *last name*:

My name is *student-athlete full name*, and I have just completed my junior *sport* season for *name of high school/state*. I am writing to you because I would very much like to become a part of your *sport* recruiting process.

As a student I currently hold a _____ grade point average on a 4.0 scale. I have also taken my PSAT test and scored a _____. I will be taking the SAT this *month/day/year*.

As an athlete I feel that I am very versatile because of the results that I have achieved in the following events: 1) 100m dash—10.00 sec. 2) High Jump—6' 1" 3) Shot Put—49' 8" 4) Discus—175' 6" With these results, I was fortunate enough to receive the honor of _____. Again, I hope that you would consider me as a potential recruit when you begin your recruiting process.

I look forward to hearing from you soon.

Sincerely,

Signature

Your full name

Address

Area code and telephone number

High school coach's name and address

High school coach's home and school phone number

Videotape available upon request

College coach full name
Address at university
Area code and telephone number

Student-athlete's name
Address
Area code and phone number

Interest in *university*—For as long as I can remember, I have always been the number one fan of *university*. As a child growing up, I would always watch your teams play the most formidable of opponents on national television. In fact, I have a section of my wardrobe dedicated to your school. It always has been a dream of mine to one day become a part of the great tradition and excellence that your university upholds to so many of the admiring such as myself. With the dedication and sacrifice that I have made to become a fine *sport* player, I only wish for the opportunity to become a part of your school.

ACADEMICS 1)*Current GPA* after junior athletic season— *3.5* on a 4.0 scale 2) PSAT score—*1000* 3) SAT—will be taken *month/day/year* 4) Advanced level courses _____ 5) Honors ____

ATHLETICS 1) *Texas State Diving Champion—0M: 1994/1995, 1995/1996* 2) *Texas State Diving Runner-up—3M: 1995/1996*

HONORS *All-Southwest Region: 1996; All-State First Team: 1996; All-State First Team: 1995; All-State Honorable Mention: 1994*

EXTRACURRICULAR ACTIVITIES 1) *Horseback riding* 2) *Rattlesnake hunting* 3) *Bridge jumping* 4) *Lifeguard at a public swimming pool*

CHARITY WORK *I helped to raise money for the Annual Food Drive to help the needy of southwest Texas: Money raised = More than $10,000*

REFERENCES Coach *John Doe—area code and phone number;* Coach John Jay—*area code and phone number;* Mr. *John Davis,* Principal of *high school—area code and phone number*

Date: _____
Student-athletes's full name
Address
Area Code and Telephone Number

Academics: Current Grade Point Average—
3.00 taking all Honors Courses
PSAT Score—*980*
SAT Score—*990*
Junior Class President

Athletics: Position—*Pitcher*
Left-handed
Pitching Speed—clocked at 85 mph.
Batting Average—.500
Teams playing on
Current high school team
Regional club team
Height _____ Weight _____

Honors/Awards: *19xx All-State First Team*
19xx All-County First Team
"Best Pitcher Award Recipient"
(Best in County) 19xx
Team Captain

Dreams/Goals: Earn a full athletic scholarship
Play in the NCAA World Series

Hobbies/
Special Interests: *Listening to music from all backgrounds*
Drama Club

Charity Work: *Recently helped to raise money to help*
physically disabled children

References: *Mr. A—Head Baseball Coach, High School,*
Telephone Number
Mr. B—High School Athletic Director
Mr. C—Head Club Team Baseball Coach

VIDEOTAPE

Videotapes and film duplications are used by recruiters. When college recruiters go out to recruit high school athletes, they want to see videotape of the athlete in a game situation whenever possible. The college coaches are looking at how you did against the competition. They want to see your skills and techniques, as well as you, the entire athlete. They want to evaluate you in areas ranging from size and strength to agility and concentration.

The most important point to remember is that you always want to make a strong first impression. You can assure this by showing the recruiter your best performances. I would pick the two best films showing you not only as a player in your particular position but ones that will also demonstrate all your athletic capabilities. Showing all your athletic capabilities to the recruiter makes you more marketable and valuable to the university.

Once you have chosen your two best videotapes, you should make copies of them for viewing purposes at your high school and for mailing purposes. Be sure to identify yourself in the videotape—jersey number, jersey color, and positions on offense and/or defense, if applicable.

In many places, high schools videotapes their own games regardless of the sport. If copies can be made of those tapes, they will be sufficient for the recruiter's purposes. Some people choose to have their parents videotape each athletic event. This, too, is all right, as long as the videotape is clear. I'm not going to tell you to go out and hire a professional. I think that would be a waste of money. But I would make sure that you are easily seen on the tape and seen often. Another important point to remember is there should be a clear view of the action. Avoid obstructions such as lighting poles, umbrellas of other fans, etc. You don't want anything that might distract the recruiter's attention away from you.

How much is enough? I cannot tell you that because each recruiter is different in the amount of film that they might like to see. Some may only want one contest, others may want to see two or more. Again, pick at least two of your best films that confirm all of your athletic capabilities.

Coach Dailey of UCONN confirms this, adding, "Always make sure that you make copies of the video because college coaches are notorious for not getting video back to the student-athletes. Make sure that the quality of the copy is good. Personally, I like to see the student-athlete in a normal game situation. Some people are beginning to make highlight tapes. I don't think that highlight tapes give the observer a realistic picture of the total athlete. I like to see how athletes react in a variety of different circumstances under normal game conditions.

"For us, we use videotape as a tool to help in the aid of the recruiting process. I will never make any decisions based solely on what I see from videotape. I will always want to see the athlete play in person."

SPORTS CAMPS AND SUMMER LEAGUES

Sports camps and summer leagues also serve as a great place for college scouts to become better acquainted and recognize student-athletes for their recruiting in upcoming years.

"For the sport of soccer regardless of gender," says Jim Rudy of UMASS, "a student-athlete must become exposed to college coaches. Playing for their high school alone is usually not enough. The athletes must get themselves involved in what is known as 'Club Leagues.' The club leagues go around and play other teams that cover a much broader geographical region. Club leagues are usually known for offering higher levels of competition, and they can also serve as scouting grounds for college coaches."

Coach Doug Graber also points out that the summer football camp held at Rutgers University is one of the primary places he sees new talent for upcoming years.

Chris Dailey of UCONN adds, "I think that if parents and student-athletes understand what type of camp the student-athlete is going to attend, it will make their experience at the camp much better. For example, some camps are solely designed for exposure while others concentrate on skill work. Exposure camps in general attract college coaches from around the country so that they will be able to evaluate these players. Parents and student-athletes should do their homework and research what type of camp would be best for their situation."

When I was a sophomore and junior in high school, I attended the Penn State Football Camp both summers. I got the idea from one of the athlete members of my dad's health club. In a conversation with my dad, this young athlete mentioned that he had just gotten back from the Penn State Football Camp. He raved about how much he had learned and what a great experience he had there. He gave us the information that we needed to make contact with Penn State camp's department, and they in turn sent us all the necessary forms for the upcoming year.

While the camp only exposed me to Penn State coaches, it was very beneficial, introducing me to athletes from all around the country. There were kids there from California to Florida. It was amazing. And these guys were very serious about playing football. Coming from a small town in northern New Jersey, I didn't have much experience with high levels of competition and ability until I got to this camp. I was playing with and against athletes with far more prowess than I and some with less. It was a good reality check for me.

This particular camp was open to all high school athletes, and it was a noncontact camp. It offered three (one-week) sessions from which an athlete could choose the time that best suited him. Parents would drop off their child at the beginning of the week and pick him up at the end. The student-athletes slept in dorms on the main campus, two to a room.

The camp schedule looked like this:

7:00 a.m.	wake up
7:30 a.m.	breakfast at the dining hall **NOTE:** The best CHOCOLATE MILK I've ever had!
8:30-10:30 a.m.	first practice session
11:30 a.m.	lunch
1:00-3:00 p.m.	second practice session
5:00 p.m.	dinner
6:30-8:00 p.m.	guest speaker/movie/free time/etc.
10:00 p.m.	lights out

The practice sessions were a lot of fun. We would start out with our stretching and calisthenics directed by the Penn State strength and conditioning coach. From there we would break up into our individual positions and go through various drills and techniques that were taught by either the Penn State coaches or various highly regarded high school coaches from around the country. The sessions were noncontact which meant we did not put on a football uniform and hit. The intent was to learn the proper skills and techniques for our particular positions. Each session would conclude with a member of the Penn State coaching staff giving his personal observations or a pep talk.

I recommend that any athlete, regardless of his or her sport, check into this type of summer camps. The experience is priceless. You have the opportunity to be seen by college recruiters, improve your skill work, compare yourself to other athletes from around the region or country, build your confidence, and meet nice people.

INTERVIEW WITH MIKE FLYNN—
OWNER AND HEAD OF BLUE STAR CAMPS,
PHILADELPHIA, PENNSYLVANIA

Blue Star is a women's basketball camp established to provide a "competitive camp experience," similar to that of the Five Star Camp for boys. The camp was organized in 1981 to give high school women basketball players the same exposure and college scholarship opportunities that high school boys were receiving.

I started Blue Star with three main goals. I wanted it to provide first, exposure; second, high levels of competition; and third, a first-class setting.

Presently, Blue Star consists of seven regional camps which are considered exposure/competition camps. We also have what is called "Blue Star Skills Camps." Here the athletes work on the athletic skills prior to entering the exposure/competition camps.

We also run "Blue Star Elite Camps." Here we will bring in thirty-six to fifty of the top players in the nation and run a skills camp. In addition there are the "Blue Star Shoot-Outs." This is a fall exposure/competition camp which lasts for either one or two days.

Because we are known as a major scouting ground for college coaches, we offer what is known as the "Blue Star Report." This is a newsletter on all of our athletes that goes out to the media, all of the colleges, and other selected people. We plan on providing subscriptions to this newsletter in the near future.

We also created what is known as the "Blue Star Index." This lists the top players, top one-hundred seniors, top recruiting classes, etc. This is a service to the college coaches which they sign up for.

So, "Blue Star" is the name of the camp itself which carries out a number of different functions for the student-athlete and college coaches in regard to exposure and recruiting over the entire year. Currently, we are the only major camp (girls/non-college basketball coaches organization) in America that is running camps for the student-athlete. The camp has been extremely effective in providing college athletic scholarship opportunities to many of our athletes. The bottom line is, "If you want to earn a scholarship, you must be seen by the college coaches regardless of the sport you play. Unless you are an athlete of great ability—and you are an athlete that fits into the category of average to above average—then you must be exposed to these coaches in as many ways possible." Blue Star provides this experience for the student-athlete.

As a student-athlete, the camp becomes a great investment because they are being exposed to hundreds of college coaches from various divisions at one time. It is also an investment for the college coaches because they can save time and money by viewing 300 to 400 athletes at one time, rather than making a trip somewhere to see only one athlete.

Throughout the year, we at Blue Star are scouting out who the top players are in the nation. As we do, we will take note of these individuals and invite them to the camp. After doing this over many different regions in the country, we will compile quite a long list and therefore have a very good attendance at each one of our various sessions.

Again, as I said, we are scouting the top players from each region. Now, when you combine these players and actually evaluate their play compared to each other, you can easily see that ability levels vary from region to region. An athlete may be the top player in her hometown, but when they come to the camp, one of three things will happen. One, they will remain at the top; two, they will just be average compared to the other competition; or three, they will get their "doors blown off!"

As a result, the players know exactly where they stand against the competition, and so do the college coaches who are out there recruiting. The camp is a very realistic situation where college coaches can make judgments, evaluations, and comparisons of all of the prospective student-athletes. The student-athlete should understand that by coming to Blue Star, they will be competing against the same type of competition in college.

Is this camp great for everyone? The answer is no. Some kids come into the camp thinking that they are great, only to find out they are not. This can be heartbreaking. But, if you come into the camp with a positive attitude and an attitude that wants to compete and learn, then the camp can be very positive for all those involved.

Some of the general criteria that we ask for when a student wants to come to our camp is: One, they should be a varsity starter on their high school team; or two, they are over five feet ten inches tall; or three, your high school coach has a background in women's basketball at the college level and he or she can realistically project you as a promising young athlete in the future. Although the criteria seems very steep, we will not restrict any one person from attending the camp.

Our exposure/competition/evaluation camps usually run for three or four days at a time. These camps run through the period of July 8 to July 31. The skills camps also run through July. The fall shoot-out camps run for three weeks. They usually start in the last two weeks in September and run through the first week in October. Because of the schedules of tournaments and other factors, our window of opportunity runs from July 8 through the first week in October. The rest of the year, we are out scouting and compiling various information on upcoming student-athletes.

The cost of the camp varies depending upon the session that the student-athlete attends. In general the cost is anywhere between $250 to $395. The costs become expensive because of our overhead. For example, if I want to rent out the Dean Smith Center at the University of North Carolina, it will cost us $2,500 each day, and that doesn't include the air conditioning!

The percentage of student-athletes signing to scholarship packages out of high school is extremely high. When we first started the camp, our percentage was up in the eighties. Now, we sign almost 90 percent of our athletes who attend Blue Star Camps to scholarship packages. As you can see, the camp is a vital tool that is used for both the student-athlete and the college coaches who are out searching for scholarship opportunities and prospective scholarship student-athletes.

In closing, when you go out to buy a car, are you going to buy one that is not safe and made cheaply because you want to cut corners and save money? The answer is no. It is the same situation when you are in the hunt for an athletic scholarship. You are talking about receiving a $100,000-plus education! Are you going to try and cut corners, or are you going to look for the best environment for helping your daughter to achieve her dreams? That is what we do here at Blue Star. We try to help these athletes make their dreams become realities.

After Your Sophomore/ Junior Season

AFTER YOU HAVE completed your sophomore/junior athletic season and you have mailed out all of your introductory letters, you should begin to receive responses within three to six months. Patience is key, and you must keep in mind the recruiting calendar for your particular sport.

Usually, the first response will be in the form of a letter stating that they now know who you are and that they will be following your progress throughout your upcoming athletic seasons. After the first response, you can expect much more contact if you have attracted their attention as an athlete. You will receive more letters and phone calls at home. (Check NCAA recruiting rules with regard to when colleges can contact recruits for specific sports.)

The following are some of the actual response letters I received after sending my junior year introductory letters:

OSU
September 9, 1986

Dear Chris,

Your name has recently been recommended as a possible student-athlete here at the Ohio State University. I have enclosed a football questionnaire for you to fill out and return as soon as possible so that we may learn more about you. We also ask that you send us tape or film of your first good game this coming season.

The Ohio State University is one of the finest universities in the country. The experience that students receive here will prepare them for the rapidly changing world ahead.

Our football program here at OSU stresses academics as well as athletics. OSU's athletic tradition and academic excellence combine to provide an athlete with the highest caliber education possible.

Your performance on the athletic field as well as your academic achievements will be important in considering you for a scholarship. I wish you the best of luck in both areas, and we are looking forward to hearing from you soon.

Sincerely,

xxx xxxxx
Recruiting coordinator

IOWA FOOTBALL
June 12, 1986

Dear Chris,

You have been strongly recommended to our staff here at the University of Iowa. Congratulations on a fine junior season at xxx high school.

During the next several months, Coach xxx and our entire staff hope to learn more about you and your athletic and educational goals. We will pay special attention to the upcoming season. At the same time, we want you to become fully acquainted with the excellence of both the university and our Hawkeye Football Program.

Enclosed is a questionnaire which will begin that important process. We ask that you complete and return it as your earliest convenience.

If you have any questions at all, please don't hesitate to write or call me. You can be sure that we will stay in touch.

Sincerely,

xxx xxxxx
Recruiting Coordinator/Assistant football coach

UNIVERSITY OF TENNESSEE FOOTBALL
March 7, 1986

Dear Chris,

You have been recommended to us as an outstanding college football prospect, and we would like to have more information concerning your ability.

Enclosed is a questionnaire which we would appreciate your completing and returning to us at your earliest convenience so that we may learn more concerning your qualifications and interest in the University of Tennessee, in both athletics and academics.

Please try to take the ACT or SAT test as soon as you can. It will help you.

Looking forward to hearing from you soon, and best wishes to you.

Sincerely,

xxx xxxx

Recruiting Coordinator

PENN STATE
March 10, 1986

Hello Chris,

There are many student-athletes that are recommended to us each year. You have been referred as one of the outstanding prospects in the class of 1987.

Over the years we have seen Penn State achieve great heights as a major college football power. We have achieved that goal without compromising our commitment to academic achievement and building character. In order to continue this excellent tradition, we need outstanding young men like yourself—great athletes with an interest in a quality education.

If you desire to be a part of our successful football program, we would like you to contact your guidance office and grant permission for us to receive a college board test ACT/SAT sent to Penn State. Also, please fill out the enclosed questionnaire and return it in the envelope provided.

Rest assured that we will be following your progress this season, and on behalf of Coach Paterno and the football staff, we would like to wish you continued success this year. Best of luck.

Sincerely,

xxx xxxx

Administrative Assistant and Recruiting Coordinator

Remember all of this contact is nice, but it does not mean a thing until the coach offers you some kind of athletic scholarship package to come and play for that university. It is the parents' job to keep this part of the recruiting process in perspective. A seventeen- or eighteen-year-old athlete can be swept off their feet rather quickly with all this attention and then have their dreams shattered if they are not offered that scholarship package.

When a program has some genuine interest in an athlete, he or she may be invited to the university for a recruiting weekend visit.

"We have our student-athletes come up to the university and pair up with an upper classman," Julie LaFreniere of UMASS explains. "The upper classman takes the recruit to class to actually see what it is like to be in a college class. They also take the recruits with them on their normal daily course of events to give the recruit the most realistic picture of what college life is like."

This is a great opportunity for you to see how you would fit in with the program, the school, and its students. But remember, while you are evaluating all these things, you are being evaluated by the coach, the team members, and students you are meeting.

The NCAA allows each student-athlete a total of five "official recruiting weekend visits" to universities on the division 1A, 1AA, and 2 levels. Official visits are those that are fully paid for by the university. The visit may last a maximum of forty-eight hours. The rules that control official visits are very specific. Make sure that you check with the NCAA or coaches that are recruiting you so that the rules are followed for your specific situation. Unofficial visits, on the other hand, are visits that are not paid for by the university. Here the student-athlete can come to the university as many times as they would like, for as long as they like.

Generally, it is on the official visit that the coaching staff gets the opportunity to see the student-athlete in a more relaxed setting. The student-athlete also takes the opportunity to tour the entire college campus including academics, athletics, and the social atmosphere.

Here is the schedule for a typical recruiting weekend visit.

SATURDAY

Noon	The recruit is greeted upon arrival to the university by a member of the coaching staff.
1:00 PM	Luncheon with other recruits and the entire coaching staff.
2:00 PM	The recruits take a campus tour seeing the sights both academically and athletically.

| 3:00 PM | The recruit has a meeting with a faculty member regarding their major area of academic interest with a question-and-answer period at the end. |
| 5:00 PM | The recruit is paired up with a varsity athlete for dinner and a night on the town in a social setting. |

SUNDAY

10:00 AM	Brunch with all other recruits, varsity athletes, and coaching staff.
Noon	The recruit has an individual meeting with the head coach.
1:00 PM	Depart for home.

MY "OFFICIAL WEEKEND RECRUITING VISIT" AT UMASS

Once I was invited to come up and take my weekend recruiting visit to UMASS, I knew that this was going to be my window of opportunity to really get a chance to evaluate everything that the university had to offer me.

It was a late Friday afternoon, and I had just come home from school. As the day turned to night, I began to get nervous and anxious about my recruiting visit that I was to go on the very next day. I sat down with my parents and reviewed all of the important points that we were going to evaluate and ask questions about during the visit. Going through the list that we had made calmed my nerves a bit. By the end of our conversation, I was feeling more focused.

My parents and I then packed our bags and organized all the small details so that we were able to leave at the crack of dawn. I went to bed that night anticipating the weekend's events.

Before I knew it, my alarm clock was piercing throughout the house. It was six o'clock in the morning and time for us to make the trip to UMASS. We didn't shove off until seven-thirty a.m. I was awake in the car for about the first fifteen minutes before I fell asleep from having expended so much nervous energy. Anyway, I slept for most of the trip. The itinerary that was sent to us called for us to meet one of the coaches at the main floor of the campus center upon our arrival.

It was about noon when we turned onto the campus from the highway, and I saw UMASS for the very first time. It looked like a city that was transplanted into a rural area. It was beautiful, and I liked it right from the start! I could not believe how big and how nice the campus looked. I could see the football stadium, the professional buildings, and the low-rise and high-rise (twenty-five-story) dormitories. This was the first good sign of the trip.

When we pulled into the parking lot of the campus center, one of the coaches was standing there waiting for us. After cordially greeting us and inquiring about our trip, he led me and my parents to the top of the campus center for a first-class luncheon.

There we dined with all of the other recruits and their parents, along with the UMASS football coaching staff and other important people affiliated with the university.

We were joined at our table by one of the assistant football coaches and had a very nice conversation. This was the time to get to know each other. During the luncheon, there were a few people who addressed all of the recruits and their parents including the head coach, other deans, and professors.

After the luncheon, we were taken on a campus tour with an assistant coach. We started at the northeast side of campus and were shown the dormitories, laboratories, and class buildings. Then it was on to the south side of the campus, site of Mullins Arena, and then through the southwest portion of campus where most of the on-campus students lived.

From there, he drove us down to the football stadium. We went inside to see where the Minutemen played their home games. As we exited the stadium, the assistant coach took us to the adjacent locker room where the football team prepared for practice as well as games. This would be my new home!

After that we toured the university's other athletic and academic facilities. The last stop was the football offices which were located in a large building in the center of campus. There we saw the weight room and training facilities. As the tour came to a close, we were ready to start the next item on the agenda.

Before I came up to the university, I was asked what area of academic study interested me. A formal meeting was arranged with some advisors and professors to explain what the university had to offer in those specialized academic areas. That meeting lasted for about two hours and was very informative.

The next item on the agenda was a return trip to the football office to be paired up with one of the varsity players. They tried to assign each recruit to someone who played their particular position. From there, my parents went out to dinner and stayed at the Campus Center Hotel. I left with my varsity player for a night on the town with a bunch of the other players on the team.

We started out by stopping in at the apartment of one player. There I met some of the other guys on the team. I thought that I was a pretty big coming out of high school, but some of the players that I had met were huge and made me look tiny. There was one who stood six feet six inches tall and weighed 300 pounds!

After introductions, we went out as a group to one of the local restaurants for dinner. The rest of the night was spent just socializing with the guys on the team, other recruits, and some of the local people. I really had the chance to relax and be myself and get to know the people that I might be around for the next four or five years. I have to say, the people that I met that night were great. Everyone was nice, and I had a good feeling in my gut. I really fit in with these guys.

As the night concluded, I was driven back to my room at the Campus Hotel. After I washed up and got under the covers, I kept rehashing the day's events. I knew that I was having a great time, and it was a great feeling.

The next morning a wake-up call got me moving again. I washed up and packed my bags. I then met my parents in the lobby to start on the next item of the agenda. We were scheduled to go to a local family restaurant for brunch at 10 o'clock. All the recruits came accompanied by their parents. Again, it was a first-class showing. The food was fabulous, and I certainly ate my share.

After the brunch, it was off to the football office for a one-on-one meeting with the head coach. He was very nice and hospitable. At the end of our meeting, he thanked us for attending the weekend recruiting visit, and we left for home.

In the car with my parents, I actually yelled and screamed out of joy. The weekend had been that great. On the drive home, we discussed everything that happened and compared notes. We all came to the same conclusion. This was the place for me!

The recruiting visit isn't a casual thing for the schools offering them. They are taking what in many cases will be the last, long hard look at the athlete. Often they will press top recruits for commitments and delaying to visit more schools may come with risks.

"I am seeing more and more colleges handling that situation the same way that we do," says UMASS's Hodges. "Let's assume that we are going to look to sign one quarterback for the upcoming season. We will go out and offer as many quarterbacks that we see that we feel can play for us .... Assuming that we offered ten student-athletes, we will tell all of them that we have offered ten student-athletes full scholarships to come and play the position of quarterback, and we will take the first one that will give us a verbal commitment. The verbal commitment demonstrates a verbal agreement to come and play for the university.

"So, we do not want to tell student-athletes they should not take their visits, but if they wait too long, they may lose out. It may not be a problem if the college team is looking to fill only one or two positions with one or two people."

"Now, if you are a person who has offers from ten or fifteen schools, then taking all your visitations does not mean a whole lot," Hodges added, "because you can pick your opportunities. But if you are one of those people who only has one or two offers, then you must choose your steps wisely and probably not wait too long."

The student-athlete must ask these recruiters how many people they are looking at to fill in those positions that are specific to him, how many the college has offered, and how many student-athletes have verbally committed to them.

To minimize confusion, Coach Hodges will "truthfully communicate all facts to the following people: 1) the student-athlete; 2) the parents; and 3) the high school coach. By communicating to all three groups, we ensure that the entire process runs smoothly."

If and when a recruiter offers you that treasured scholarship package, you can usually expect it to happen by telephone, in person at your high school, or in person at your home. This will be one of the happiest and most fulfilling moments in both the athlete's and parents' lives. Enjoy your success.

MY EXPERIENCE OF BEING OFFERED A FULL ATHLETIC SCHOLARSHIP TO THE UNIVERSITY OF MASSACHUSETTS—IT SEEMS LIKE IT WAS YESTERDAY!

I had just come home from a hard day at school. It was the last day before the winter break in December. As soon as I walked through the door, my parents were rushing me to pack my suitcase so that we could get started on our way to visit relatives for the holidays. Everyone was running around like crazy because we wanted to get going as soon as possible to beat the traffic. As you could guess, the tension was pretty high!

As I was packing my bags, the telephone rang. It rang once. It rang twice. I didn't feel like getting it. My mom yelled, "Chris, please answer that." So off I went. It rang three times. On the fourth ring, I picked up the receiver and said, "Hello!"

The voice on the other end of the phone politely asked, "May I please speak with Chris?"

"This is he," I replied.

The voice then said, "Chris, this is your coach from the University of Massachusetts. After I brought back your game film to the head coach for his evaluation, he instructed me to offer you a full four-year athletic scholarship. What do you think of that?"

Think of that? I nearly fell on the floor!

"Coach, could you please repeat that?!"

As he did, my whole body started to tingle with joy and exhilaration.

The tension of packing for the holidays quickly left as my parents and I celebrated the scholarship offer.

WALK-ONS

In the event that you have gone through the entire recruiting process and no colleges have offered you any type of athletic scholarship package, or you had your heart set on attending a particular university and playing for their athletic team and no athletic scholarships were available, then there is always the option of "walking on."

A student-athlete can enter a university without any commitment from the athletic department and still try out for a team. Such a student is referred to as a "walk-on." The rules and procedures for becoming a walk-on vary from college to college. You should check with the individual coach of the particular team that you are interested in playing for.

Even though as a walk-on you are not receiving any type of athletic scholarship at the beginning of your athletic career, there is still a chance that someday you will be able to earn a scholarship package after you have proved yourself a worthy prospect. Again, check with the coach of the team to discuss this avenue as a possibility

Preparatory School/ Junior College

PREP SCHOOL/JUNIOR college is another option that should be considered after high school graduation. Depending upon the individual student-athlete and his or her situation, prep school/junior college may also be a route for continuing athletics after high school while searching for a scholarship package.

There are many advantages and few disadvantages for students who choose to attend these schools. Prep school/junior college give the individual time to mature academically, socially, and athletically.

With increased academic and social maturity, the student-athlete will learn how to handle the heavier load of academics and social interaction more effectively before entering college. In preps/junior colleges, the transition to academic and social maturity is made easier. All aspects of prep school are harder than high school, yet easier than college. Students learn how to improve their study habits and time-management skills which leads to success in the classroom once attending college.

With the additional one or two years, the student-athlete can mature physically and mentally on the athletic field. The student gains athletic experience without cutting into their collegiate years of eligibility. With this maturity, the athlete who was not offered a scholarship/financial aid package may improve his or her chances of receiving such a package.

Again, the option of prep school/junior college may be the direction the student-athlete wants to take depending upon their own personal situation. This situation should be carefully considered and investigated before any final decision is made. A disadvantage to attending prep school is the risk of injury. The decision to go to such a school is one that should be made with the student, parents, and high school coach.

Coach Hodges feels that both prep school and/or junior college can be beneficial to certain student-athletes. "For example, we have a lineman who played for an unsuccessful high school team that did not receive much publicity. He was not offered any scholarships by anyone. He decided to go to prep school to increase his chances of being seen by college recruiters. After one year, we found him and offered him a full athletic scholarship as did two or three other schools. That just happened to be the right situation for that specific student-athlete.

"Some kids use prep school to help them with their academics before entering college. One point that most student-athletes and parents do not know about prep school regarding division 1 and 1AA colleges is that a student must first fulfill their high school academic core requirements if they are to be considered qualified for any college or university. Once a student-athlete graduates from high school, if the core requirements are not met, then there is nothing that the student-athlete can do to become qualified. If the student-athlete has not graduated from high school, then the core requirements can be fulfilled.

"The key to making sure that they do qualify is to be on top of their academics starting when they are freshmen in high school and not waiting until their junior or senior year to do something about it. By that time it is to late. Probably the biggest reason why student-athletes go to prep school today is because they do not qualify for university standards on their SAT tests. You can go to prep school and qualify for the NCAA SAT requirements once you have graduated from high school because the SAT does not involve the core requirements that are needed in high school to qualify for college.

"Another reason why student-athletes go to prep school is because they want an extra year of athletic maturity. Some kids try to give themselves an extra year because of a senior-year injury, which can help their evaluation by college coaches. As for junior colleges, or any college for that matter, once a student-athlete begins college, he or she has five years to play four years of athletic eligibility. If a student is a nonqualifier out of high school either because of core requirements or SAT scores and earns an associate degree, then the student-athlete becomes eligible for a scholarship and athletics as far as NCAA standards. But each university may have certain standards and criteria that must be met. So, he or she may or may not be accepted by the school depending upon the college's individual standards."

There are so many different rules and regulations that you should investigate all the facts pertinent to your particular situation.

Success Story:
Lansing Holman

INTERVIEW WITH MR. Lansing Holman, father of division 1A full athletic scholarship recipient to the University of Iowa, Tarig Holman.

Q. Mr. Holman, would you please tell all student-athletes, parents, and high school coaches how you went about guiding your son, Tarig, through the entire high school recruiting process which ultimately put Tarig in the exciting position of choosing between five full scholarship offers to division 1A universities?

A. The recruiting process itself is not an exact science. Each college or university may go about the process differently from one another, but there are still basic parts of the process that are the same. Being a former coach myself, I had some general insight as to how college recruiters go about their recruiting. For football, the recruiting process should start right after the student-athlete's junior high school athletic season.

Tarig had expressed to me early on that he had a strong desire to play football for a major university. As a sophomore, I began to evaluate his athletic ability. When I watched him play, I could see that his running and catching ability was well-above average for a sophomore. At that point I felt that he might have a shot at attaining his goal by the time he was a senior.

Tarig played well as a sophomore and on through his junior season. I watched him mature mentally and physically as a football player, and it appeared that his dream was coming closer and closer.

After Tarig's junior football season, he and I wrote introductory letters to the coaches of the universities where Tarig wanted to attend to tell them about Tarig as a prospective recruit.

Please note, anyone can do this. All you have to do is write the letters and mail them. You do not have to be anyone special to get through to the coach/recruiting coordinator that is in charge of the recruiting for that particular sport. You can do this for any sport. In fact, you can also call the coaches and talk to them directly. Every college in America has a "1-800" number, and your call will be transferred to the sport team of your interest at no charge to you.

The introductory letters introduced Tarig to each staff as a prospective recruit for the upcoming year. The contents of the letters included vital information such as: Tarig's strong desire to attend and play football for that particular university; Tarig's name and address, physical size, strength, speed, positions played, high school grades, PSAT and SAT scores, awards and honors; the high school's name and address; and that videotape was available upon request.

Now each of these colleges knew who Tarig was, and they could follow his progress as a student-athlete throughout his senior year. Please note, college coaches are usually very receptive to learning about new recruits. Don't be bashful!

As I said, after Tarig's junior football season, we sent these letters to the coaches. They then began to contact him through letters of their own and then follow-up questionnaires. It is very important that the student-athlete fills out each and every questionnaire because they are put on file at the university by the coaching staff.

During the summer between Tarig's junior and senior year, I took him to visit some of the schools that he had shown interest in attending. These visits are known as "unofficial visits." Here, Tarig was able to meet some of the coaches and talk to people about each university. Usually the coaching staff had a "get acquainted" informal-type meeting with the student-athletes and parents who were interested in that particular university.

Personally, I recommend this type of visit because it really helps to inform both the student-athlete and parents firsthand as to exactly what to expect throughout the recruiting process. Another reason why unofficial visits are important is because it helps to teach both the student-athlete and the parents the important aspects to look for in a university. Some of these aspects include academic areas of interest, academic facilities, athletic facilities, dormitory rooms, the campus itself, types of people, attitudes of people, etc. Try and get the most realistic picture that you can, but you can only do this by physically going out to visit these universities.

Starting August 1, coaches can contact recruits by telephone once per week. It is very important for the student-athlete to know how to talk to these coaches especially if they have not met them face to face. As the coach is talking to the student-athlete, he or she is getting a feel for the student-athlete's personality and interests.

The student-athlete should conduct themselves very professionally over the telephone. That does not mean that they should not be themselves, but the student-athlete should carry themselves with a few thoughts in mind. They should show the coach that they have confidence in themselves, not cockiness. They should always be polite, and they should always be themselves.

From October through January of the student-athlete's senior athletic season, the universities can invite certain student-athletes to come out for an "official visit." Note, each student-athlete is allowed a total of five official visits to universities on the division 1, 1AA, and 2 levels, but student-athletes do not have to take all of these visitations if they choose not to. Tarig took his official visits to the University of Iowa, Wake Forest University, and the University of Illinois.

Prior to Tarig making any official visits to any of the universities, I had each head coach commit a full athletic scholarship to Tarig, to me, and to Tarig's high school coach. The coaches did this over the telephone.

In order for Tarig to make a rational decision and not an emotional one about where he would like to attend college, I created some lists and assigned numerical values to each item (1 to 5). For example, the score of 5 would mean that that particular item on the list was very important to Tarig. The score of 3 represented some degree of importance, and a 1 meant very little or no degree of importance. The scores of 2 and 4 fell somewhere in between.

The items on the lists were ones that were of importance to Tarig. They included: size of the university, academics and choice of major, athletic facilities, types of people at each campus, the coaches and athletes, surrounding towns, social life. When Tarig came home from each university, we sat down and filled in the numbers. Once the numbers were assigned to each item, we were then able to tally up the points to come up with a grand total for each university.

The date was December 19 at about 2:00 a.m. Tarig and I had completed totaling the numbers for all of the schools that had offered him scholarships and that he had visited. The scores were very close. They were so close that it was still difficult to make a decision. I told Tarig to sleep on it and make his final decision in the morning.

When he awoke, he came out of his room and announced, "Dad, I'm gonna be a Hawkeye!!" Tarig ended up attending the University of Iowa on a full athletic scholarship for the sport of football

MR. LANSING HOLMAN'S RATING SHEET
FOR COLLEGE EVALUATIONS

NAME OF COLLEGE: _____

ITEM OF IMPORTANCE: RATING SCORE (1-5)

ITEM OF IMPORTANCE:	RATING SCORE (1-5)
1.	1.
2.	2.
3.	3.
4.	4.
5.	5.
6.	6.
7.	7.
8.	8.
9.	9.
10.	10.
	TOTAL _____

Some Last Thoughts

DOUG GRABER
Rutger's University—head football coach

THE KEY IS not whether the student-athlete is recruited or not, it is the preparation that goes into it. I think that it is very unfair for parents to have unrealistic dreams and goals for their student-athletes to receive full athletic scholarships because they are not easy to attain. High school coaches and college coaches need to be honest when evaluating these kids as prospective student-athletes. The student-athlete needs to know at what level they can realistically play at, whether it be division 1A, 1AA, 2, or 3. Another way to make a judgment is to physically go and watch some games at their desired level of competition. That can give the student-athlete a good idea of where they might be best placed.

The first thing that student-athletes and parents must realize is just how good a student-athlete must be in order to receive any scholarship package for their particular sport. I am also a parent that has kids involved in athletics, and I think that as a parent you can become blinded because you always feel that your child is the best; and you always want the best for your child. There are also some people who are mislead by outside influences and sources that judge whether or not an athlete is of scholarship material.

Student-athletes and parents should know that we as college coaches are the only ones who make the decision as to whether a student-athlete will be offered any type of athletic scholarship package. High school coaches, athletic directors, and guidance counselors do not make those decisions.

Student-athletes also need to prepare themselves academically first and athletically second. Sometimes as parents and student-athletes, we lose sight that the student-athlete is just that. They are a student first and an athlete second.

JULIE LAFRENIERE
University of Massachusetts—head coach
women's track and field–cross country

In summary, I think that the student-athlete, parents, and high school coaches should look at the recruiting process realistically. Just because your son or daughter was one of the top athletes in their geographical area does not necessarily mean that they will receive any type of scholarship package. In order to earn any type of athletic scholarship package in the sport of track and field–cross country at the division 1 level, the student–athlete must be in the top rankings in either a region or nation. Parents should also be a lot more sensitive to their son or daughter and not put pressure on them to receive an athletic scholarship. If it were that easy, then everyone would have one. This does not mean that scholarships are not achievable or that they cannot participate and contribute to an athletic team at that level. But receiving an athletic scholarship in this sport usually means that you are in an elite group that covers a vast area of competition.

JIM RUDY
University of Massachusetts—head coach women's soccer

When student-athletes send their introductory letters/resumes to college coaches, make sure that they have a list of coaches who the college coach can talk to with—NAMES, ADDRESSES, AND TELEPHONE NUMBERS! If I have an athlete that I am interested in, and I do not have this VITAL information, it makes it extremely difficult to make the proper contacts.

Another plus for a student-athlete involved in the sport of soccer would be to have a personal trainer specifically in soccer skill work. Skill work is the most important aspect in this sport. Not everyone can afford a personal trainer because they are expensive, but they do help.

JOHN RYAN
Vernon Township High School—head coach
men's soccer–track and field

You must make a realistic evaluation of both your academic and athletic capabilities beginning in your sophomore year of high school and project where you are going to be as a senior so that you are properly looking at colleges that match you as an overall person.

There are too many people in the world who either have no knowledge of the college athletic recruiting process or are greatly misinformed in most aspects of it. Unless you have had direct and previous experience in dealing with the process, you cannot have the knowledge and the tools to make it work for you. The process is a one-shot deal. Nobody is expected to be born knowing what to do. You need to become properly informed and to make the proper contacts in the proper fashion.

MIKE HODGES
University of Massachusetts—head coach football

I think that the one thing that makes the process run smoothly is for the coaches and recruiters to tell the truth. If they are not interested in a player, then the player should be told. We will not string a player along hoping to get him or someone else just in case we don't get the players we want so that we have backups. It is not fair to the student-athlete.

In some cases we lose those student-athletes, but at least we are being honest with them and are not leading them on. We will either tell the student-athlete we want you or we do not want you. Yes, there are some coaches and recruiters that do abuse the system by leading the student-athlete on and then dropping them in the end if they get who they want. But for the most part, college recruiters will tell the truth and be honest with the student-athlete.

The student-athlete must start this process early by going to the college and watching practices, spring games, in-season games, investigating their academic opportunities and all of the factors that will help to make the decision of attending certain colleges of the student-athlete's choice. But, the process should be started as early as the student-athlete's sophomore or junior year!

CHRIS DAILEY
University of Connecticut—associate head coach
women's basketball

Student-athletes need to put themselves into a situation where they can make informed decisions. The student-athlete must first be honest with themselves and find out what they are interested in academically and athletically. Parents and adults cannot make these decisions for the student-athletes. They can guide and assist them, but all final decisions must be made by the student-athlete.

Remember, the entire theme here is to find the right school for your student-athlete. Be active in that role. Do not sit back and let things pass you by. You must aggressively research all the factors that go into making an important decision such as this. Also, there is not just one place where student-athletes can be successful and happy; there are many places. The key is to try and find the closest match for your student-athlete.

MIKE FLYNN
Blue Star Women's Basketball Camps,
Philadelphia, Pennsylvania—director

For the athlete who really desires earning a scholarship package, the bottom line is that regardless of a person's ability, student-athletes must get themselves seen by as many college coaches, in as many ways possible. Playing for club teams, legions, and summer leagues are all OK as long as you are understanding what type of exposure you are actually getting in those situations.

When you play in those situations, you are not guaranteed that the level of play will be high enough. You are also not guaranteed getting sufficient playing time, and whether or not college recruiters will be at those events. Even if they do come down to those events, if you're not playing at the time that they are evaluating, then you have probably missed out on your chance of being seen at that point in time.

In camps such as Blue Star, you are guaranteed playing time through the way that we design the camp. You are also guaranteed that college coaches will come to our camp to see you, and you will get the proper exposure. These are questions that must be asked before making any final decisions about what types of camps/summer leagues, club teams, etc., your son or daughter will be attending. Your expectations of these venues may not actually be what you were looking for, therefore, make sure that you thoroughly research all of your options.

KERSTIN KIMEL
Duke University—head coach women's lacrosse

When talking about scholarships for the sport of women's lacrosse, student-athletes and parents must understand that there is not an abundant amount of them out there as compared to high-revenue sports such as football and basketball.

Therefore, if a coach only offers the student-athlete a partial scholarship or no scholarship at all, the decision might not have been made as a direct indication of the student-athlete's ability. Sometimes these scholarships are given to student-athletes who are in a situation that dictates more financial need than others, or there might not have been any scholarship availability for that year. By the same token, this does not mean that the very same student-athlete cannot find scholarship opportunities elsewhere.

Tips to Remember

THIS BOOK WAS designed for the use of ALL high school student-athletes for all sports.

■ You don't have to be the best athlete in the world to receive some type of athletic scholarship package. Most of the scholarship athletes that the world sees are the ones who play at the top levels and receive national recognition by playing on TV. Remember, athletic scholarships are offered from schools at division 1, 1AA, and 2 levels.

■ Be sure to give this process your best effort. You will never know if you could have earned an athletic scholarship unless you try. There is no shame in not attaining your goal. The only shame is in not trying to give it your best shot.

■ Being a student-athlete that has an athletic scholarship offers some great benefits.

■ College coaches are looking for student-athletes that can achieve success in the classroom, on the athletic field, and in everyday life.

■ College coaches recruit student-athletes from year to year on the basis of team need. Just because a college does not recruit you, doesn't necessarily mean that you can't earn an athletic scholarship to another school at that level or any other level. The rejection part of the recruiting process is not always a reflection of your athletic talent. Remember, recruiting should not be taken personally.

■ The parents role in the recruiting process is to assist their child by giving them the advice they need in making all important decisions, not to make the decisions for the student-athlete.

■ All decisions throughout the recruiting process should be made after thorough investigation and from an objective standpoint.

■ Student-athletes must be honest in evaluating all of their expectations of a college. They must also match their personality to the colleges personality in order to ensure a happy and lasting college career.

■ Student-athletes must be honest when matching up their athletic talent to the different colleges within different divisions. Be sure to get objective and realistic opinions from others.

■ Student-athletes should keep up their grades throughout their entire high school career.

■ Be sure to practice the SAT/ACT as many times as you can so that you feel comfortable with the test.

■ Good grades and test scores can open up many doors for all prospective student-athletes.

■ Be sure to register the student-athlete in the Initial Eligibility Clearinghouse.

■ Stay on top of all current and future recruiting rules/regulations and academic eligibility requirements that pertain to the student-athlete.

■ Get to know the recruiting calendar for your sport.

■ Be sure to include ALL VITAL INFORMATION in your introductory letters/resumes.

■ Always address the information in the letters/resumes to a specific person not "Dear Sir/Madam."

■ Follow up all mailings with either a thank-you note or a phone call or both to check that contact was made with the college coaches.

■ BE PERSISTENT.

- Be sure to have videotapes of your best athletic contests for viewing at the high school and for mailing purposes. Also, be sure to make numerous copies of the tapes and identify yourself in them.

- Be sure that the video is free of obstructions and of good quality.

- Investigate sports camps and leagues as an option for gaining exposure and skill work depending upon your individual situation.

- Be patient, responses will soon be on the way.

- During official and unofficial visits, be sure to keep a level head and evaluate the entire college—not just the athletic side.

- Use the college rating sheet to help you make objective decisions. Never make spontaneous and irrational decisions that are based purely on emotional highs.

- Review the options of prep school/junior college.

- MAKE SURE THAT YOU START THE PROCESS EARLY. DON'T WAIT FOR SOMEONE ELSE TO DO IT FOR YOU. TAKE IT UPON YOURSELF TO CONTROL YOUR OWN DESTINY.

CHAPTER

11

The Step-by-Step Method

1. Get an understanding of what full/partial athletic scholarships are.

2. Get an understanding of recruiting and how the recruiting process works.

3. Make sure that the student-athlete's high school grades and college SAT/ACT exams qualify for college, and register the athlete with the Initial Eligibility Clearinghouse.

4. Be honest in matching up the schools to the personality.

5. Make sure that your dreams and goals are realistic. Try to attend summer camps/leagues.

6. Project the athlete as best you can.

7. Get to know the recruiting calendar for you sport.

8. Review the option of prep school.

THE STEP-BY-STEP METHOD 91

9. Choose your schools by division and compile a long list.

10. Mail out all introductory letters/resumes to schools upon completion of your sophomore/junior year athletic season—the process has begun.

11. Be patient, keep the recruiting process in perspective. Acknowledgments will soon be on the way.

12. ENJOY YOUR SUCCESS!

In Conclusion

IF YOU ARE a student-athlete that thinks you have what it takes to participate in athletics on the collegiate level, then you must follow this step-by-step method and make the most of your special opportunity.

Do not procrastinate. Life is too short. Once this opportunity has passed you by, it will be gone forever. So don't hesitate. Get yourself started right away. These are the types of dreams that can and do come true. It happened to me, and I hope that you to can reap the same rewards of success.

Remember, you do not have to be the ultimate athlete to receive an athletic scholarship package. You need to be the most persistent person you can be in following these simple steps. Don't rely on anyone else to get yourself noticed by college recruiters. You must lead this "personal marketing campaign" just as if you were running for the presidency of the United States! With a great work ethic, desire, and persistence, you too can live the American dream!

You should take the introductory letters/resumes and then surround that information with all of the other information given in the chapters. The letters are the most crucial tools that you will use to make contact with all recruiters.

I wish all of you the best of luck when beginning your recruiting process. I know that the methods are extremely effective because I used them myself during my recruiting process.

And please, once you have successfully completed the process and have been awarded a scholarship package, write me a letter and share your success with me.

SEND TO:
Chris Tenkin
c/o Barricade Books
150 Fifth Avenue—Suite 700
New York, New York 10011

Glossary

ACADEMIC MATURITY: Learning to improve the student's study habits in the areas of time management and effective studying which helps the student to handle the heavier load of all academic subjects.

ATHLETIC MATURITY: When the athlete physically matures and improves upon attributes such as size, strength, coordination, agility, and balance.

ATHLETIC CAPABILITIES: What the athlete can do on the field. *See* athletic maturity.

COLLEGE TESTS: Tests that are needed as prerequisites to entering college; ACT/SAT.

DEPTH CHART: A listing of all players on the team by position and what team they are. First team, second team.

FINANCIAL AID: Funds set aside to help pay for the student-athlete's monetary costs for college.

INITIAL ELIGIBILITY CLEARINGHOUSE: The mandatory service that is provided by the NCAA that confirms that all incoming freshman student-athletes on the division 1 and 2 levels are academically eligible to compete. Be sure to register. For more information see your high school guidance counselor.

LETTERS OF INTRODUCTION: The letters that the student-athlete will send to the head coach of their particular sport introducing themselves with all of the vital information to begin the recruiting process.

MAJOR: The prime area of academic interest that the student-athlete will be studying to prepare them for a career after college.

MARKETABILITY: Making yourself attractive for all recruiters, showing all of your athletic talents and capabilities.

EMOTIONAL MATURITY: Being able to handle all academic, athletic, and social rigors acquainted with college.

NCAA: National Collegiate Athletic Association—body ruling over most collegiate athletics.

OFFICIAL VISIT: A fully paid visit to a university by the university for a student-athlete. The student-athlete is allowed five visits to schools that belong to either division 1 or 2, and they must not exceed a forty-eight-hour period at each campus. Check with the NCAA regarding the specifics to your situation.

PREP SCHOOL: Preparatory School—a school before college, usually one to two years which allows the athlete to mature academically, emotionally, and athletically.

PROJECTION: The process of evaluating an athlete and placing them properly for their own good as well as for team needs.

RECRUITER: The person/coach that does the recruiting.

RECRUITING: The process of attracting athletes to come and play for a university.

RECRUITING CALENDAR: A schedule for each individual sport that shows exactly at what time of the year recruiting occurs and when introductory letters should be mailed out.

RECRUITING COORDINATOR: The top person in charge of recruiting for each individual school—is usually a staff member from the team.

RECRUITING PROCESS: Recruiting in its entirety, everything from choosing your schools to signing your scholarship.

SCALE OF SUPPLY AND DEMAND: The process of evaluating and balancing a team's stock. Who they have at what position, and who they have to recruit.

SCHOLARSHIP—FULL: A package that pays entirely for the student-athlete's room, board, tuition, books, and insurance.

STUDENT-ATHLETE: The high school student who is being recruited by the college.

UNOFFICIAL VISIT: A visit to a university by a student-athlete where none of the cost is covered by the university. All expenses were endured by the student-athlete. The visit can be as long as the student-athlete wants, and they can visit as many times as they want.

WEEKEND VISITS: The student-athlete visits the college for the weekend touring the campus, academic and athletic facilities, social life, and meeting with the coaching staff and team members.

College with NCAA-Sponsored Sports

BY SPORT, GENDER, DIVISION

WRESTLING

DIVISION I

District 1

BOSTON COLLEGE
Chestnut Hill, MA 02167-3934

BOSTON UNIVERSITY
Boston, MA 02215

BROWN UNIVERSITY
Providence, RI 02912

CENTRAL CONN. STATE UNIV.
New Britain, CT 06050-4010

HARVARD UNIVERSITY
Cambridge, MA 02138-3800

District 2

AMERICAN UNIVERSITY
Washington, DC 20016

BLOOMSBURG UNIVERSITY
Bloomsburg, PA 17815

BUCKNELL UNIVERSITY
Lewisburg, PA 17837

STATE UNIV. OF N.Y. at BUFFALO
Buffalo, NY 14260

CALIFORNIA UNIVERSITY
California, PA 15419

CLARION UNIVERSITY
Clarion, PA 16214

COLUMBIA UNIV.-BARNARD
COLLEGE
New York, NY 10027

CORNELL UNIVERSITY
Ithaca, NY 14853

DELAWARE STATE UNIVERSITY
Dover, DE 19901

DREXEL UNIVERSITY
Philadelphia, PA 19104

DUQUESNE UNIVERSITY
Pittsburgh, PA 15282

EAST STROUDSBURG UNIVERSITY
East Stroudsburg, PA 18301

EDINBORO UNIVERSITY
Edinboro, PA 16444-0001

FRANKLIN & MARSHALL COLLEGE
Lancaster, PA 17604-3003

GEORGE MASON UNIVERSITY
Fairfax, VA 22030

HOFSTRA UNIVERSITY
Hempstead, NY 11550

HOWARD UNIVERSITY
Washington, DC 20059

JAMES MADISON UNIVERSITY
Harrisonburg, VA 22807

LA SALLE UNIVERSITY
Philadelphia, PA 19141-1199

LEHIGH UNIVERSITY
Bethlehem, PA 18015-3089

LOCK HAVEN UNIVERSITY
Lock Haven, PA 17745

MILLERSVILLE UNIVERSITY
Millersville, PA 17551-0302

MORGAN STATE UNIVERSITY
Baltimore, MD 21239

PENNSYLVANIA STATE UNIV.
University Park, PA 16802

UNIVERSITY OF PENNSYLVANIA
Philadelphia, PA 19104-6380

UNIVERSITY OF PITTSBURGH
Pittsburgh, PA 15260

PRINCETON UNIVERSITY
Princeton, NJ 08544

RIDER UNIVERSITY
Lawrenceville, NJ 08648-3099

RUTGERS UNIVERSITY
New Brunswick, NJ 08903

SETON HALL UNIVERSITY
South Orange, NJ 07079

SLIPPERY ROCK UNIVERSITY
Slippery Rock, PA 16057

SYRACUSE UNIVERSITY
Syracuse, NY 13244

U.S. MILITARY ACADEMY
West Point, NY 10996

U.S. NAVAL ACADEMY
Annapolis, MD 21402

WAGNER COLLEGE
Staten Island, NY 10301-4495

WEST VIRGINIA UNIVERSITY
Morgantown, WV 26506-6201

WILKES UNIVERSITY
Wilkes-Barre, PA 18766

District 3

APPALACHIAN STATE UNIVERSITY
Boone, NC 28608

CAMPBELL UNIVERSITY
Buies Creek, NC 27506

THE CITADEL
Charleston, SC 29409

COPPIN STATE COLLEGE
Baltimore, MD 21216

DAVIDSON COLLEGE
Davidson, NC 28036

DUKE UNIVERSITY
Durham, NC 27708-0555

GEORGIA STATE UNIVERSITY
Atlanta, GA 30303-3083

UNIVERSITY OF MARYLAND
College Park, MD 20740

UNIVERSITY OF NORTH
CAROLINA
Chapel Hill, NC 27514

UNIVERSITY OF NORTH
CAROLINA
Greensboro, NC 27412-5001

NORTH CAROLINA STATE UNIV.
Raleigh, NC 27695-7001

OLD DOMINION UNIVERSITY
Norfolk, VA 23529

UNIVERSITY OF TENNESSEE
Chattanooga, TN 37403-2598

VIRGINIA MILITARY INSTITUTE
Lexington, VA 24450-0304

VIRGINIA POLYTECHNIC
INSTITUTE
Blacksburg, VA 24061

UNIVERSITY OF VIRGINIA
Charlottesville, VA 22903

District 4

CENTRAL MICHIGAN UNIVERSITY
Mount Pleasant, MI 48859

CHICAGO STATE UNIVERSITY
Chicago, IL 60628-1598

CLEVELAND STATE UNIVERSITY
Cleveland, OH 44115

EASTERN ILLINOIS UNIVERSITY
Charleston, IL 61920-3099

EASTERN MICHIGAN UNIVERSITY
Ypsilanti, MI 48197

UNIVERSITY OF ILLINOIS
Champaign, IL 61820

INDIANA UNIVERSITY
Bloomington, IN 47405

UNIVERSITY OF IOWA
Iowa City, IA 52242

KENT STATE UNIVERSITY
Kent, OH 44242

MARQUETTE UNIVERSITY
Milwaukee, WI 53201-1881

MIAMI UNIVERSITY
Oxford, OH 45056

MICHIGAN STATE UNIVERSITY
East Lansing, MI 48824

UNIVERSITY OF MICHIGAN
Ann Arbor, MI 48109-2201

UNIV. OF MINNESOTA-TWIN
CITIES
Minneapolis, MN 55455

NORTHERN ILLINOIS UNIVERSITY
De Kalb, IL 60115-2854

NORTHWESTERN UNIVERSITY
Evanston, IL 60208

OHIO STATE UNIVERSITY
Columbus, OH 43210

OHIO UNIVERSITY
Athens, OH 45701

PURDUE UNIVERSITY
West Lafayette, IN 47907

UNIVERSITY OF WISCONSIN
Madison, WI 53711

District 5

IOWA STATE UNIVERSITY
Ames, IA 50011

UNIV. OF MISSOURI-COLUMBIA
Columbia, MO 65211

UNIVERSITY OF NEBRASKA
Lincoln, NE 68588

UNIVERSITY OF NORTHERN IOWA
Cedar Falls, IA 50614

OKLAHOMA STATE UNIVERSITY
Stillwater, OK 74078

UNIVERSITY OF OKLAHOMA
Norman, OK 73019

District 7

BOISE STATE UNIVERSITY
Boise, ID 83725

BRIGHAM YOUNG UNIVERSITY
Provo, UT 84602

CALIF. STATE UNIV.-FRESNO
Fresno, CA 93740-0048

UNIVERSITY OF NEW MEXICO
Albuquerque, NM 87131

U.S. AIR FORCE ACADEMY
USAF Academy, CO 80840-5461

UNIVERSITY OF WYOMING
Laramie, WY 82071

District 8

ARIZONA STATE UNIVERSITY
Tempe, AZ 85287-2505

UNIV. OF CALIFORNIA-DAVIS
Davis, CA 95616

CALIF. POLYTECHNIC STATE UNIV.
San Luis Obispo, CA 93407

CALIF. STATE UNIV.-BAKERSFIELD
Bakersfield, CA 93311-1099

CALIF. STATE UNIV.-FULLERTON
Fullerton, CA 92634-9480

OREGON STATE UNIVERSITY
Corvallis, OR 97331

UNIVERSITY OF OREGON
Eugene, OR 97403-1226

STANFORD UNIVERSITY
Stanford, CA 94305

DIVISION II
District 1
AMERICAN INTERNATIONAL
COLLEGE
Springfield, MA 01109-3189

UNIV. OF MASSACHUSETTS-
LOWELL
Lowell, MA 01854

SOUTHERN CONNECTICUT ST.
UNIV.
New Haven, CT 06515

District 2
STATE UNIV. OF N.Y. at ALBANY
Albany, NY 12222

CHEYNEY UNIVERSITY
Cheyney, PA 19319

GANNON UNIVERSITY
Erie, PA 16541

KUTZTOWN UNIVERSITY
Kutztown, PA 19530-0721

MANSFIELD UNIVERSITY
Mansfield, PA 16933

UNIVERSITY OF PITTSBURGH
Johnstown, PA 15904-2990

SHIPPENSBURG UNIVERSITY
Shippensburg, PA 17257

WEST LIBERTY STATE COLLEGE
West Liberty, WV 26074

District 3
CARSON-NEWMAN COLLEGE
Jefferson City, TN 37760

GARDNER-WEBB UNIVERSITY
Boiling Springs, NC 28017

LONGWOOD COLLEGE
Farmville, VA 23909-1899

NORFOLK STATE UNIVERSITY
Norfolk, VA 23504

PEMBROKE STATE UNIVERSITY
Pembroke, NC 28372-1510

District 4
ASHLAND UNIVERSITY
Ashland, OH 44805

UNIVERSITY OF INDIANAPOLIS
Indianapolis, IN 46227

UNIVERSITY OF MINNESOTA-
DULUTH
Duluth, MN 55812

UNIVERSITY OF MINNESOTA-
MORRIS
Morris, MN 56267

MOORHEAD STATE UNIVERSITY
Moorhead, MN 56563-2996

SOUTHERN ILLINOIS UNIVERSITY
Edwardsville, IL 62026

SOUTHWEST STATE UNIVERSITY
Marshall, MN 56258

UNIV. OF WISCONSIN-PARKSIDE
Kenosha, WI 53141-2000

District 5
AUGUSTANA COLLEGE
Sioux Falls, SD 57197

CENTRAL MISSOURI STATE UNIV.
Warrensburg, MO 64093

CHADRON STATE COLLEGE
Chadron, NE 69337

MANKATO STATE UNIVERSITY
Mankato, MN 56002-8400

UNIV. OF NEBRASKA at KEARNEY
Kearney, NE 68849

UNIVERSITY OF NEBRASKA at
OMAHA
Omaha, NE 68182

NORTH DAKOTA STATE
UNIVERSITY
Fargo, ND 58105

UNIVERSITY OF NORTH DAKOTA
Grand Forks, ND 58202

NORTHEAST MISSOURI STATE
UNIV.
Kirksville, MO 63501

UNIV. OF NORTHERN COLORADO
Greeley, CO 80639

NORTHERN STATE UNIVERSITY
Aberdeen, SD 57401

SOUTH DAKOTA STATE
UNIVERSITY
Brookings, SD 57007

ST. CLOUD STATE UNIVERSITY
St. Cloud, MN 56301-4498

District 6
UNIVERSITY OF CENTRAL OKLAHOMA
Edmond, OK 73034

District 7
ADAMS STATE COLLEGE
Alamosa, CO 81102

COLORADO SCHOOL OF MINES
Golden, CO 80401

FORT HAYS STATE UNIVERSITY
Hays, KS 67601

UNIV. OF SOUTHERN COLORADO
Pueblo, CO 81001-4901

WESTERN STATE COLLEGE
Gunnison, CO 81231

District 8
PORTLAND STATE UNIVERSITY
Portland, OR 97207-0751

SAN FRANCISCO STATE UNIVERSITY
San Francisco, CA 94132

NCAA PROVISIONAL MEMBERS
District 2
UNIV. OF PUERTO RICO-MAYAGUEZ
Mayaguez, PR 00709

UNIV. OF PUERTO RICO-BAYAMON
Bayamon, PR 00619-1919

District 3
ANDERSON COLLEGE
Anderson, SC 29621

District 8
CENTRAL WASHINGTON UNIV.
Ellensburg, WA 98926

MEN'S WATERPOLO

DIVISION I
District 1
BOSTON COLLEGE
Chestnut Hill, MA 02167-3934

BROWN UNIVERSITY
Providence, RI 02912

HARVARD UNIVERSITY
Cambridge, MA 02138-3800

UNIV. OF MASSACHUSETTS-AMHERST
Amherst, MA 01003

District 2
BUCKNELL UNIVERSITY
Lewisburg, PA 17837

FORDHAM UNIVERSITY
Bronx, NY 10458-5155

GEORGE WASHINGTON UNIVERSITY
Washington, DC 20052

IONA COLLEGE
New Rochelle, NY 10801

PRINCETON UNIVERSITY
Princeton, NJ 08544

ST. FRANCIS COLLEGE
Brooklyn Heights, NY 11201

U.S. NAVAL ACADEMY
Annapolis, MD 21402

VILLANOVA UNIVERSITY
Villanova, PA 19085

District 3
UNIVERSITY OF RICHMOND
Richmond, VA 23173-1903

District 7
U.S. AIR FORCE ACADEMY
USAF Academy, CO 80840-5461

District 8
UNIV. OF CALIFORNIA-BERKELEY
Berkeley, CA 94720

UNIV. OF CALIF.-LOS ANGELES
Los Angeles, CA 90095-1405

UNIV. OF CALIF.-SANTA BARBARA
Santa Barbara, CA 93106

UNIV. OF CALIFORNIA-IRVINE
Irvine, CA 92717

LONG BEACH STATE UNIVERSITY
Long Beach, CA 90840-0118

LOYOLA MARYMOUNT UNIVERSITY
Los Angeles, CA 90045-2699

UNIVERSITY OF THE PACIFIC
Stockton, CA 95211

PEPPERDINE UNIVERSITY
Malibu, CA 90263

SANTA CLARA UNIVERSITY
Santa Clara, CA 95053

UNIV. OF SOUTHERN CALIFORNIA
Los Angeles, CA 90089-0012

STANFORD UNIVERSITY
Stanford, CA 94305

DIVISION II
District 2
QUEENS COLLEGE (NY)
Flushing, NY 11367

SLIPPERY ROCK UNIVERSITY
Slippery Rock, PA 16057
District 8
UNIV. OF CALIFORNIA-DAVIS
Davis, CA 95616
CHAMINADE UNIVERSITY
Honolulu, HI 96816

MEN'S BASKETBALL

DIVISION I
District 1
BOSTON COLLEGE
Chestnut Hill, MA 02167-3934
BOSTON UNIVERSITY
Boston, MA 02215
BROWN UNIVERSITY
Providence, RI 02912
CENTRAL CONN. STATE UNIV.
New Britain, CT 06050-4010
UNIVERSITY OF CONNECTICUT
Storrs, CT 06269
DARTMOUTH COLLEGE
Hanover, NH 03755
FAIRFIELD UNIVERSITY
Fairfield, CT 06430-5195
UNIVERSITY OF HARTFORD
West Hartford, CT 06117-1599
HARVARD UNIVERSITY
Cambridge, MA 02138-3800
COLLEGE OF THE HOLY CROSS
Worcester, MA 01610-2395
UNIVERSITY OF MAINE
Orono, ME 04469
UNIV. OF MASSACHUSETTS-
AMHERST
Amherst, MA 01003
UNIVERSITY OF NEW HAMPSHIRE
Durham, NH 03824
NORTHEASTERN UNIVERSITY
Boston, MA 02115-5096
PROVIDENCE COLLEGE
Providence, RI 02918
UNIVERSITY OF RHODE ISLAND
Kingston, RI 02881
UNIVERSITY OF VERMONT
Burlington, VT 05405
YALE UNIVERSITY
New Haven, CT 06520-7398

District 2
AMERICAN UNIVERSITY
Washington, DC 20016
BUCKNELL UNIVERSITY
Lewisburg, PA 17837
STATE UNIV. OF N.Y. at BUFFALO
Buffalo, NY 14260
CANISIUS COLLEGE
Buffalo, NY 14208-1098
COLGATE UNIVERSITY
Hamilton, NY 13346-1304
COLUMBIA UNIV.-BARNARD
COLLEGE
New York, NY 10027
CORNELL UNIVERSITY
Ithaca, NY 14853
DELAWARE STATE UNIVERSITY
Dover, DE 19901
UNIVERSITY OF DELAWARE
Newark, DE 19716
DREXEL UNIVERSITY
Philadelphia, PA 19104
DUQUESNE UNIVERSITY
Pittsburgh, PA 15282
FAIRLEIGH DICKINSON-TEANECK
Teaneck, NJ 07666
FORDHAM UNIVERSITY
Bronx, NY 10458-5155
GEORGE MASON UNIVERSITY
Fairfax, VA 22030
GEORGE WASHINGTON
UNIVERSITY
Washington, DC 20052
GEORGETOWN UNIVERSITY
Washington, DC 20057
HAMPTON UNIVERSITY
Hampton, VA 23668
HOFSTRA UNIVERSITY
Hempstead, NY 11550

HOWARD UNIVERSITY
Washington, DC 20059

IONA COLLEGE
New Rochelle, NY 10801

JAMES MADISON UNIVERSITY
Harrisonburg, VA 22807

LA SALLE UNIVERSITY
Philadelphia, PA 19141-1199

LAFAYETTE COLLEGE
Easton, PA 18042

LEHIGH UNIVERSITY
Bethlehem, PA 18015-3089

LONG ISLAND UNIV.-BROOKLYN
Brooklyn, NY 11201

LOYOLA COLLEGE
Baltimore, MD 21210

MANHATTAN COLLEGE
Riverdale, NY 10471

MARIST COLLEGE
Poughkeepsie, NY 12601-1387

UNIV. OF MARYLAND-BALT. CO.
Baltimore, MD 21228-5398

U. OF MARYLAND-EASTERN
SHORE
Princess Anne, MD 21853-1299

MONMOUTH UNIVERSITY
West Long Branch, NJ 07764

MORGAN STATE UNIVERSITY
Baltimore, MD 21239

MOUNT ST. MARY'S COLLEGE
Emmitsburg, MD 21727-7799

NIAGARA UNIVERSITY
Niagara University, NY 14109

PENNSYLVANIA STATE UNIV.
University Park, PA 16802

UNIVERSITY OF PENNSYLVANIA
Philadelphia, PA 19104-6380

UNIVERSITY OF PITTSBURGH
Pittsburgh, PA 15260

PRINCETON UNIVERSITY
Princeton, NJ 08544

RIDER UNIVERSITY
Lawrenceville, NJ 08648-3099

ROBERT MORRIS COLLEGE
Coraopolis, PA 15108-1189

RUTGERS UNIVERSITY
New Brunswick, NJ 08903

SETON HALL UNIVERSITY
South Orange, NJ 07079

SIENA COLLEGE
Loudonville, NY 12211-1462

ST. BONAVENTURE UNIVERSITY
St. Bonaventure, NY 14778

ST. FRANCIS COLLEGE
Brooklyn Heights, NY 11201

ST. FRANCIS COLLEGE
Loretto, PA 15940-0600

ST. JOHN'S UNIVERSITY
Jamaica, NY 11439

ST. JOSEPH'S UNIVERSITY
Philadelphia, PA 19131-1395

ST. PETER'S COLLEGE
Jersey City, NJ 07306

SYRACUSE UNIVERSITY
Syracuse, NY 13244

TEMPLE UNIVERSITY
Philadelphia, PA 19122

TOWSON STATE UNIVERSITY
Towson, MD 21204

U.S. MILITARY ACADEMY
West Point, NY 10996

U.S. NAVAL ACADEMY
Annapolis, MD 21402

VILLANOVA UNIVERSITY
Villanova, PA 19085

WAGNER COLLEGE
Staten Island, NY 10301-4495

WEST VIRGINIA UNIVERSITY
Morgantown, WV 26506-6201

COLLEGE OF WILLIAM & MARY
Williamsburg, VA 23187

District 3

ALABAMA STATE UNIVERSITY
Montgomery, AL 36101-0271

UNIV. OF ALABAMA at
TUSCALOOSA
Tuscaloosa, AL 35487

UNIV. OF ALABAMA at
BIRMINGHAM
Birmingham, AL 35294-0110

APPALACHIAN STATE UNIVERSITY
Boone, NC 28608

AUBURN UNIVERSITY
Auburn University, AL 36849-5113

AUSTIN PEAY STATE UNIVERSITY
Clarksville, TN 37044-4576

BETHUNE-COOKMAN COLLEGE
Daytona Beach, FL 32114-3099

CAMPBELL UNIVERSITY
Buies Creek, NC 27506

UNIVERSITY OF CENTRAL
FLORIDA
Orlando, FL 32816-0002

CHARLESTON SOUTHERN UNIV.
Charleston, SC 29423-8087

COLLEGE OF CHARLESTON
Charleston, SC 29424

THE CITADEL
Charleston, SC 29409

CLEMSON UNIVERSITY
Clemson, SC 29632

COASTAL CAROLINA UNIVERSITY
Conway, SC 29526

COPPIN STATE COLLEGE
Baltimore, MD 21216

DAVIDSON COLLEGE
Davidson, NC 28036

DUKE UNIVERSITY
Durham, NC 27708-0555

EAST CAROLINA UNIVERSITY
Greenville, NC 27858-4353

EAST TENNESSEE STATE UNIV.
Johnson City, TN 37614

EASTERN KENTUCKY UNIVERSITY
Richmond, KY 40475-3101

FLORIDA A&M UNIVERSITY
Tallahassee, FL 32307

FLORIDA ATLANTIC UNIVERSITY
Boca Raton, FL 33431-0991

FLORIDA INTERNATIONAL UNIV.
Miami, FL 33199

FLORIDA STATE UNIVERSITY
Tallahassee, FL 32306

UNIVERSITY OF FLORIDA
Gainesville, FL 32604

FURMAN UNIVERSITY
Greenville, SC 29613

GEORGIA INSTITUTE OF TECH.
Atlanta, GA 30332

GEORGIA SOUTHERN UNIVERSITY
Statesboro, GA 30460-8033

GEORGIA STATE UNIVERSITY
Atlanta, GA 30303-3083

UNIVERSITY OF GEORGIA
Athens, GA 30613

JACKSONVILLE STATE
UNIVERSITY
Jacksonville, AL 36265-9982

JACKSONVILLE UNIVERSITY
Jacksonville, FL 32211-3394

UNIVERSITY OF KENTUCKY
Lexington, KY 40506-0032

LIBERTY UNIVERSITY
Lynchburg, VA 24506

LOUISIANA STATE UNIVERSITY
Baton Rouge, LA 70803

UNIVERSITY OF LOUISVILLE
Louisville, KY 40292

MARSHALL UNIVERSITY
Huntington, WV 25755

UNIVERSITY OF MARYLAND
College Park, MD 20740

UNIVERSITY OF MEMPHIS
Memphis, TN 38152

MERCER UNIVERSITY
Macon, GA 31207

UNIVERSITY OF MIAMI
Coral Gables, FL 33124-6710

MIDDLE TENNESSEE STATE UNIV.
Murfreesboro, TN 37132

MISSISSIPPI STATE UNIVERSITY
Mississippi State, MS 39762-5509

UNIVERSITY OF MISSISSIPPI
University, MS 38677

MOREHEAD STATE UNIVERSITY
Morehead, KY 40351-1689

MURRAY STATE UNIVERSITY
Murray, KY 42071-0009

UNIVERSITY OF NEW ORLEANS
New Orleans, LA 70148

UNIVERSITY OF NORTH
CAROLINA
Asheville, NC 28804-3299

UNIVERSITY OF NORTH
CAROLINA
Chapel Hill, NC 27514

UNIVERSITY OF NORTH
CAROLINA
Charlotte, NC 28223

UNIVERSITY OF NORTH
CAROLINA
Greensboro, NC 27412-5001

UNIVERSITY OF NORTH
CAROLINA
Wilmington, NC 28403-3297

NORTH CAROLINA A&T ST. UNIV.
Greensboro, NC 27411

NORTH CAROLINA STATE UNIV.
Raleigh, NC 27695-7001

OLD DOMINION UNIVERSITY
Norfolk, VA 23529

RADFORD UNIVERSITY
Radford, VA 24142

UNIVERSITY OF RICHMOND
Richmond, VA 23173-1903

SAMFORD UNIVERSITY
Birmingham, AL 35229

UNIVERSITY OF SOUTH ALABAMA
Mobile, AL 36688

SOUTH CAROLINA STATE UNIV.
Orangeburg, SC 29117-0001

UNIVERSITY OF SOUTH CAROLINA
Columbia, SC 29208

UNIVERSITY OF SOUTH FLORIDA
Tampa, FL 33620

SOUTHEASTERN LOUISIANA UNIV.
Hammond, LA 70402

UNIV. OF SOUTHERN MISSISSIPPI
Hattiesburg, MS 39406-5001

STETSON UNIVERSITY
De Land, FL 32720

TENNESSEE STATE UNIVERSITY
Nashville, TN 37209-1561

TENNESSEE TECHNOLOGICAL
UNIV.
Cookeville, TN 38505-0001

UNIVERSITY OF TENNESSEE
Chattanooga, TN 37403-2598

THE UNIVERSITY OF TENNESSEE
Knoxville, TN 37996

UNIV. OF TENNESSEE at MARTIN
Martin, TN 38238-5021

TROY STATE UNIVERSITY
Troy, AL 36082

TULANE UNIVERSITY
New Orleans, LA 70118

VANDERBILT UNIVERSITY
Nashville, TN 37212

VIRGINIA COMMONWEALTH UNIV.
Richmond, VA 23284-2003

VIRGINIA MILITARY INSTITUTE
Lexington, VA 24450-0304

VIRGINIA POLYTECHNIC
INSTITUTE
Blacksburg, VA 24061

UNIVERSITY OF VIRGINIA
Charlottesville, VA 22903

WAKE FOREST UNIVERSITY
Winston-Salem, NC 27109

WESTERN CAROLINA UNIVERSITY
Cullowhee, NC 28723

WESTERN KENTUCKY
UNIVERSITY
Bowling Green, KY 42101-3576

WINTHROP UNIVERSITY
Rock Hill, SC 29733

WOFFORD COLLEGE
Spartanburg, SC 29303-3663

District 4

UNIVERSITY OF AKRON
Akron, OH 44325

BALL STATE UNIVERSITY
Muncie, IN 47306

BOWLING GREEN STATE UNIV.
Bowling Green, OH 43403

BUTLER UNIVERSITY
Indianapolis, IN 46208

CENTRAL MICHIGAN UNIVERSITY
Mount Pleasant, MI 48859

CHICAGO STATE UNIVERSITY
Chicago, IL 60628-1598

UNIVERSITY OF CINCINNATI
Cincinnati, OH 45221

CLEVELAND STATE UNIVERSITY
Cleveland, OH 44115

UNIVERSITY OF DAYTON
Dayton, OH 45469

DE PAUL UNIVERSITY
Chicago, IL 60604-2287

UNIVERSITY OF DETROIT-MERCY
Detroit, MI 48219-0900

EASTERN ILLINOIS UNIVERSITY
Charleston, IL 61920-3099

EASTERN MICHIGAN UNIVERSITY
Ypsilanti, MI 48197

UNIVERSITY OF EVANSVILLE
Evansville, IN 47722

ILLINOIS STATE UNIVERSITY
Normal, IL 61761

UNIVERSITY OF ILLINOIS
Champaign, IL 61820

UNIVERSITY OF ILLINOIS
Chicago, IL 60607

INDIANA UNIVERSITY
Bloomington, IN 47405

UNIVERSITY OF IOWA
Iowa City, IA 52242

KENT STATE UNIVERSITY
Kent, OH 44242

LOYOLA UNIVERSITY
Chicago, IL 60626

MARQUETTE UNIVERSITY
Milwaukee, WI 53201-1881

MIAMI UNIVERSITY
Oxford, OH 45056

MICHIGAN STATE UNIVERSITY
East Lansing, MI 48824

UNIVERSITY OF MICHIGAN
Ann Arbor, MI 48109-2201

UNIV. OF MINNESOTA-TWIN CITIES
Minneapolis, MN 55455

NORTHEASTERN ILLINOIS UNIV.
Chicago, IL 60625-4699

NORTHERN ILLINOIS UNIVERSITY
De Kalb, IL 60115-2854

NORTHWESTERN UNIVERSITY
Evanston, IL 60208

UNIVERSITY OF NOTRE DAME
Notre Dame, IN 46556

OHIO STATE UNIVERSITY
Columbus, OH 43210

OHIO UNIVERSITY
Athens, OH 45701

PURDUE UNIVERSITY
West Lafayette, IN 47907

UNIVERSITY OF TOLEDO
Toledo, OH 43606

VALPARAISO UNIVERSITY
Valparaiso, IN 46383-6493

WESTERN ILLINOIS UNIVERSITY
Macomb, IL 61455

WESTERN MICHIGAN UNIVERSITY
Kalamazoo, MI 49008-5134

UNIVERSITY OF WISCONSIN
Green Bay, WI 54311-7001

UNIVERSITY OF WISCONSIN
Madison, WI 53711

UNIVERSITY OF WISCONSIN
Milwaukee, WI 53201

WRIGHT STATE UNIVERSITY
Dayton, OH 45435-0001

XAVIER UNIVERSITY
Cincinnati, OH 45207-6114

YOUNGSTOWN STATE UNIVERSITY
Youngstown, OH 44555-0001

District 5

BRADLEY UNIVERSITY
Peoria, IL 61625

UNIVERSITY OF COLORADO
Boulder, CO 80309

CREIGHTON UNIVERSITY
Omaha, NE 68178-0001

DRAKE UNIVERSITY
Des Moines, IA 50311-4505

INDIANA STATE UNIVERSITY
Terre Haute, IN 47809

IOWA STATE UNIVERSITY
Ames, IA 50011

KANSAS STATE UNIVERSITY
Manhattan, KS 66506

UNIVERSITY OF KANSAS
Lawrence, KS 66045

UNIV. OF MISSOURI-COLUMBIA
Columbia, MO 65211

UNIV. OF MISSOURI-KANSAS CITY
Kansas City, MO 64110

UNIVERSITY OF NEBRASKA
Lincoln, NE 68588

UNIVERSITY OF NORTHERN IOWA
Cedar Falls, IA 50614

OKLAHOMA STATE UNIVERSITY
Stillwater, OK 74078

UNIVERSITY OF OKLAHOMA
Norman, OK 73019

ORAL ROBERTS UNIVERSITY
Tulsa, OK 74171

SOUTHEAST MISSOURI STATE UNIV.
Cape Girardeau, MO 63701-4799

SOUTHERN ILLINOIS UNIVERSITY
Carbondale, IL 62901

SOUTHWEST MISSOURI STATE UNIV.
Springfield, MO 65804

ST. LOUIS UNIVERSITY
St. Louis, MO 63108

UNIVERSITY OF TULSA
Tulsa, OK 74104

WICHITA STATE UNIVERSITY
Wichita, KS 67260

District 6

ALCORN STATE UNIVERSITY
Lorman, MS 39096-9402

ARKANSAS STATE UNIVERSITY
State University, AR 72467

UNIVERSITY OF ARKANSAS
Fayetteville, AR 72701

UNIVERSITY OF ARKANSAS
Little Rock, AR 72204-1099

BAYLOR UNIVERSITY
Waco, TX 76798

CENTENARY COLLEGE
Shreveport, LA 71134-1188

GRAMBLING STATE UNIVERSITY
Grambling, LA 71245

UNIVERSITY OF HOUSTON
Houston, TX 77204

JACKSON STATE UNIVERSITY
Jackson, MS 39217

LAMAR UNIVERSITY
Beaumont, TX 77710

LOUISIANA TECH UNIVERSITY
Ruston, LA 71272

MCNEESE STATE UNIVERSITY
Lake Charles, LA 70609

MISSISSIPPI VALLEY ST. UNIV.
Itta Bena, MS 38941-1400

NICHOLLS STATE UNIVERSITY
Thibodaux, LA 70310

UNIVERSITY OF NORTH TEXAS
Denton, TX 76203-6737

NORTHEAST LOUISIANA
UNIVERSITY
Monroe, LA 71209-3000

NORTHWESTERN STATE
UNIVERSITY
Natchitoches, LA 71497-0003

PRAIRIE VIEW A&M UNIVERSITY
Prairie View, TX 77446

RICE UNIVERSITY
Houston, TX 77251

SAM HOUSTON STATE
UNIVERSITY
Huntsville, TX 77341

SOUTHERN METHODIST
UNIVERSITY
Dallas, TX 75275

SOUTHERN UNIVERSITY
Baton Rouge, LA 70813

SOUTHWEST TEXAS STATE UNIV.
San Marcos, TX 78666-4615

UNIV. OF SOUTHWESTERN LA.
Lafayette, LA 70504-1008

STEPHEN F. AUSTIN STATE UNIV.
Nacogdoches, TX 75962

UNIVERSITY OF TEXAS
Arlington, TX 76019

UNIVERSITY OF TEXAS
Austin, TX 78712

UNIVERSITY OF TEXAS
San Antonio, TX 78249

TEXAS A&M UNIVERSITY
College Station, TX 77843-1228

TEXAS CHRISTIAN UNIVERSITY
Fort Worth, TX 76129-0001

UNIV. OF TEXAS-PAN AMERICAN
Edinburg, TX 78539-2999

TEXAS SOUTHERN UNIVERSITY
Houston, TX 77004

TEXAS TECH UNIVERSITY
Lubbock, TX 79409

District 7

BOISE STATE UNIVERSITY
Boise, ID 83725

BRIGHAM YOUNG UNIVERSITY
Provo, UT 84602

CALIF. STATE UNIV.-FRESNO
Fresno, CA 93740-0048

COLORADO STATE UNIVERSITY
Fort Collins, CO 80523-0100

GONZAGA UNIVERSITY
Spokane, WA 99258

UNIVERSITY OF HAWAII-MANOA
Honolulu, HI 96822-2370

IDAHO STATE UNIVERSITY
Pocatello, ID 83209

UNIVERSITY OF IDAHO
Moscow, ID 83843

MONTANA STATE UNIV-BOZEMAN
Bozeman, MT 59717-0338

THE UNIVERSITY OF MONTANA
Missoula, MT 59812-1291

UNIVERSITY OF NEVADA
Reno, NV 89557

UNIVERSITY OF NEW MEXICO
Albuquerque, NM 87131

NORTHERN ARIZONA UNIVERSITY
Flagstaff, AZ 86011

SAN DIEGO STATE UNIVERSITY
San Diego, CA 92182

SOUTHERN UTAH UNIVERSITY
Cedar City, UT 84720

UNIVERSITY OF TEXAS-EL PASO
El Paso, TX 79968

U.S. AIR FORCE ACADEMY
USAF Academy, CO 80840-5461

UNIVERSITY OF UTAH
Salt Lake City, UT 84112

WEBER STATE UNIVERSITY
Ogden, UT 84408-2701

UNIVERSITY OF WYOMING
Laramie, WY 82071

District 8

ARIZONA STATE UNIVERSITY
Tempe, AZ 85287-2505

UNIVERSITY OF ARIZONA
Tucson, AZ 85721

UNIV. OF CALIFORNIA-BERKELEY
Berkeley, CA 94720

UNIV. OF CALIF.-LOS ANGELES
Los Angeles, CA 90095-1405

UNIV. OF CALIF-SANTA BARBARA
Santa Barbara, CA 93106

UNIV. OF CALIFORNIA-IRVINE
Irvine, CA 92717

CALIF. POLYTECHNIC STATE UNIV.
San Luis Obispo, CA 93407

CALIF. STATE UNIV.-FULLERTON
Fullerton, CA 92634-9480

CALIF. STATE UNIV.-NORTHRIDGE
Northridge, CA 91330

CALIF. STATE UNIV.-SACRAMENTO
Sacramento, CA 95819

EASTERN WASHINGTON
UNIVERSITY
Cheney, WA 99004

LONG BEACH STATE UNIVERSITY
Long Beach, CA 90840-0118

LOYOLA MARYMOUNT
UNIVERSITY
Los Angeles, CA 90045-2699

UNIVERSITY OF NEVADA
Las Vegas, NV 89154

NEW MEXICO STATE UNIVERSITY
Las Cruces, NM 88003

OREGON STATE UNIVERSITY
Corvallis, OR 97331

UNIVERSITY OF OREGON
Eugene, OR 97403-1226

UNIVERSITY OF THE PACIFIC
Stockton, CA 95211

PEPPERDINE UNIVERSITY
Malibu, CA 90263

UNIVERSITY OF PORTLAND
Portland, OR 97203-5798

UNIVERSITY OF SAN DIEGO
San Diego, CA 92110-2492

UNIVERSITY OF SAN FRANCISCO
San Francisco, CA 94117-1080

SAN JOSE STATE UNIVERSITY
San Jose, CA 95192

SANTA CLARA UNIVERSITY
Santa Clara, CA 95053

UNIV. OF SOUTHERN CALIFORNIA
Los Angeles, CA 90089-0012

ST. MARY'S COLLEGE
Moraga, CA 94556

STANFORD UNIVERSITY
Stanford, CA 94305

UTAH STATE UNIVERSITY
Logan, UT 84322-7400

WASHINGTON STATE UNIVERSITY
Pullman, WA 99164

UNIVERSITY OF WASHINGTON
Seattle, WA 98195

NCAA PROVISIONAL MEMBERS
DIVISION I
District 6

UNIVERSITY OF ARKANSAS-PINE
BLUFF
Pine Bluff, AR 71601

DIVISION II
District 1

AMERICAN INTERNATIONAL
COLLEGE
Springfield, MA 01109-3189

ASSUMPTION COLLEGE
Worcester, MA 01615-0005

BENTLEY COLLEGE
Waltham, MA 02154-4705

UNIVERSITY OF BRIDGEPORT
Bridgeport, CT 06601

BRYANT COLLEGE
Smithfield, RI 02917-1284

FRANKLIN PIERCE COLLEGE
Rindge, NH 03461

KEENE STATE COLLEGE
Keene, NH 03431-4183

UNIV. OF MASSACHUSETTS-
LOWELL
Lowell, MA 01854

MERRIMACK COLLEGE
North Andover, MA 01845

NEW HAMPSHIRE COLLEGE
Hooksett, NH 03106-1045

UNIVERSITY OF NEW HAVEN
West Haven, CT 06516-1999

QUINNIPIAC COLLEGE
Hamden, CT 06518-1940

SACRED HEART UNIVERSITY
Fairfield, CT 06432-1000

SOUTHERN CONNECTICUT ST.
UNIV.
New Haven, CT 06515

ST. ANSELM COLLEGE
Manchester, NH 03102-1310

ST. MICHAEL'S COLLEGE
Colchester, VT 05439

STONEHILL COLLEGE
North Easton, MA 02357

District 2

ADELPHI UNIVERSITY
Garden City, NY 11530

STATE UNIV. OF N.Y. at ALBANY
Albany, NY 12222

ALDERSON-BROADDUS COLLEGE
Philippi, WV 26416

AMERICAN UNIV. OF PUERTO RICO
Bayamon, PR 00960-2037

BLOOMSBURG UNIVERSITY
Bloomsburg, PA 17815

BLUEFIELD STATE COLLEGE
Bluefield, WV 24701-2198

CALIFORNIA UNIVERSITY
California, PA 15419

THE UNIVERSITY OF
CHARLESTON
Charleston, WV 25304

CHEYNEY UNIVERSITY
Cheyney, PA 19319

CLARION UNIVERSITY
Clarion, PA 16214

CONCORD COLLEGE
Athens, WV 24712

CONCORDIA COLLEGE
Bronxville, NY 10708

DAVIS AND ELKINS COLLEGE
Elkins, WV 26241

UNIV. OF DISTRICT OF COLUMBIA
Washington, DC 20008

DOWLING COLLEGE
Oakdale, NY 11769-1999

EAST STROUDSBURG UNIVERSITY
East Stroudsburg, PA 18301

EDINBORO UNIVERSITY
Edinboro, PA 16444-0001

FAIRMONT STATE COLLEGE
Fairmont, WV 26554

GANNON UNIVERSITY
Erie, PA 16541

GLENVILLE STATE COLLEGE
Glenville, WV 26351

INDIANA UNIV. OF PENNSYLVANIA
Indiana, PA 15705

KUTZTOWN UNIVERSITY
Kutztown, PA 19530-0721

LE MOYNE COLLEGE
Syracuse, NY 13214-1399

LOCK HAVEN UNIVERSITY
Lock Haven, PA 17745

LONG ISLAND U./C.W. POST
CAMPUS
Brookville, NY 11548

MANSFIELD UNIVERSITY
Mansfield, PA 16933

MERCY COLLEGE
Dobbs Ferry, NY 10522

MERCYHURST COLLEGE
Erie, PA 16546

MILLERSVILLE UNIVERSITY
Millersville, PA 17551-0302

MOLLOY COLLEGE
Rockville Centre, NY 11570

NEW YORK INSTITUTE OF TECH.
Old Westbury, NY 11568-8000

PACE UNIVERSITY
New York, NY 10038-1502

PHILA. COLLEGE OF TEXT. & SCI.
Philadelphia, PA 19144-5497

UNIVERSITY OF PITTSBURGH
Johnstown, PA 15904-2990

QUEENS COLLEGE (NY)
Flushing, NY 11367

SALEM-TEIKYO UNIVERSITY
Salem, WV 26426

SHEPHERD COLLEGE
Shepherdstown, WV 25443

SHIPPENSBURG UNIVERSITY
Shippensburg, PA 17257

SLIPPERY ROCK UNIVERSITY
Slippery Rock, PA 16057

SOUTHAMPTON CAMPUS OF L.I.U.
Southampton, NY 11968

THE COLLEGE OF ST. ROSE
Albany, NY 12203

STATE UNIV. OF N.Y. at STONY
BROOK
Stony Brook, NY 11794

WEST CHESTER UNIVERSITY
West Chester, PA 19383

WEST LIBERTY STATE COLLEGE
West Liberty, WV 26074

WEST VIRGINIA INST. OF TECH
Montgomery, WV 25136

WEST VIRGINIA WESLEYAN
COLLEGE
Buckhannon, WV 26201

WHEELING JESUIT COLLEGE
Wheeling, WV 26003-6295

District 3

ALABAMA A&M UNIVERSITY
Normal, AL 35762

UNIV. OF ALABAMA-HUNTSVILLE
Huntsville, AL 35899

ALBANY STATE COLLEGE
Albany, GA 31705

ARMSTRONG STATE COLLEGE
Savannah, GA 31419-1997

AUGUSTA COLLEGE
Augusta, GA 30910

BARRY UNIVERSITY
Miami Shores, FL 33161

BARTON COLLEGE
Wilson, NC 27893

BELLARMINE COLLEGE
Louisville, KY 40205-0671

BELMONT ABBEY COLLEGE
Belmont, NC 28012-2795

BOWIE STATE UNIVERSITY
Bowie, MD 20715-9465

CARSON-NEWMAN COLLEGE
Jefferson City, TN 37760

CATAWBA COLLEGE
Salisbury, NC 28144-2488

CLARK ATLANTA UNIVERSITY
Atlanta, GA 30314

COKER COLLEGE
Hartsville, SC 29550

COLUMBUS COLLEGE
Columbus, GA 31907-2079

DELTA STATE UNIVERSITY
Cleveland, MS 38733

ECKERD COLLEGE
St. Petersburg, FL 33733

ELIZABETH CITY STATE UNIV.
Elizabeth City, NC 27909

ELON COLLEGE
Elon College, NC 27244

ERSKINE COLLEGE
Due West, SC 29639

FAYETTEVILLE STATE
UNIVERSITY
Fayetteville, NC 28301-4298

FLORIDA INSTITUTE OF TECH.
Melbourne, FL 32901

FLORIDA SOUTHERN COLLEGE
Lakeland, FL 33801-5698

FORT VALLEY STATE COLLEGE
Fort Valley, GA 31030

FRANCIS MARION UNIVERSITY
Florence, SC 29501-0547

GARDNER-WEBB UNIVERSITY
Boiling Springs, NC 28017

GEORGIA COLLEGE
Milledgeville, GA 31061

HIGH POINT UNIVERSITY
High Point, NC 27262-3598

JOHNSON C. SMITH UNIVERSITY
Charlotte, NC 28216

KENNESAW STATE COLLEGE
Marietta, GA 30061

KENTUCKY STATE UNIVERSITY
Frankfort, KY 40601

KENTUCKY WESLEYAN COLLEGE
Owensboro, KY 42302-1039

LANDER UNIVERSITY
Greenwood, SC 29649-2099

LANE COLLEGE
Jackson, TN 38301

LE MOYNE-OWEN COLLEGE
Memphis, TN 38126

LEES-MCRAE COLLEGE
Banner Elk, NC 28604-0128

LENOIR-RHYNE COLLEGE
Hickory, NC 28603

LIMESTONE COLLEGE
Gaffney, SC 29340-3799

LINCOLN MEMORIAL UNIVERSITY
Harrogate, TN 37752

LIVINGSTONE COLLEGE
Salisbury, NC 28144

LONGWOOD COLLEGE
Farmville, VA 23909-1899

LYNN UNIVERSITY
Boca Raton, FL 33431

MARS HILL COLLEGE
Mars Hill, NC 28754

MILES COLLEGE
Birmingham, AL 35208

MISSISSIPPI COLLEGE
Clinton, MS 39058

MOREHOUSE COLLEGE
Atlanta, GA 30314

MORRIS BROWN COLLEGE
Atlanta, GA 30314

MOUNT OLIVE COLLEGE
Mount Olive, NC 28365

NEWBERRY COLLEGE
Newberry, SC 29108

NORFOLK STATE UNIVERSITY
Norfolk, VA 23504

UNIVERSITY OF NORTH ALABAMA
Florence, AL 35632

NORTH CAROLINA CENTRAL
UNIV.
Durham, NC 27707

UNIVERSITY OF NORTH FLORIDA
Jacksonville, FL 32224-2645

NORTHERN KENTUCKY
UNIVERSITY
Highland Heights, KY 41099

PAINE COLLEGE
Augusta, GA 30901-3182

PEMBROKE STATE UNIVERSITY
Pembroke, NC 28372-1510

PFEIFFER COLLEGE
Misenheimer, NC 28109-0960

PRESBYTERIAN COLLEGE
Clinton, SC 29325-2998

QUEENS COLLEGE (NC)
Charlotte, NC 28274

ROLLINS COLLEGE
Winter Park, FL 32789

SAVANNAH STATE COLLEGE
Savannah, GA 31404

SHAW UNIVERSITY
Raleigh, NC 27611

UNIV. OF SOUTH CAROLINA-
AIKEN
Aiken, SC 29801

U. OF SO. CAROLINA-
SPARTANBURG
Spartanburg, SC 29303

ST. ANDREWS PRESBYTERIAN
COLL.
Laurinburg, NC 28352-5598

ST. AUGUSTINE'S COLLEGE
Raleigh, NC 27610

ST. LEO COLLEGE
Saint Leo, FL 33574

ST. PAUL'S COLLEGE
Lawrenceville, VA 23868

UNIVERSITY OF TAMPA
Tampa, FL 33606-1490

TUSKEGEE UNIVERSITY
Tuskegee, AL 36088

VALDOSTA STATE UNIVERSITY
Valdosta, GA 31698

VIRGINIA STATE UNIVERSITY
Petersburg, VA 23806

VIRGINIA UNION UNIVERSITY
Richmond, VA 23220-1790

UNIVERSITY OF WEST ALABAMA
Livingston, AL 35470

UNIVERSITY OF WEST FLORIDA
Pensacola, FL 32514

WEST GEORGIA COLLEGE
Carrollton, GA 30118

WINGATE UNIVERSITY
Wingate, NC 28174

WINSTON-SALEM STATE UNIV.
Winston-Salem, NC 27110

District 4

ASHLAND UNIVERSITY
Ashland, OH 44805

BEMIDJI STATE UNIVERSITY
Bemidji, MN 56601-2699

FERRIS STATE UNIVERSITY
Big Rapids, MI 49307-2295

GRAND VALLEY STATE
UNIVERSITY
Allendale, MI 49401

HILLSDALE COLLEGE
Hillsdale, MI 49242-1298

INDIANA UNIV.-PURDUE UNIV.
Indianapolis, IN 46202

INDIANA UNIV.-PURDUE UNIV.
Fort Wayne, IN 46805-1499

UNIVERSITY OF INDIANAPOLIS
Indianapolis, IN 46227

LAKE SUPERIOR STATE UNIV.
Sault Sainte Marie, MI 49783

LEWIS UNIVERSITY
Romeoville, IL 60441

MICHIGAN TECHNOLOGICAL
UNIV.
Houghton, MI 49931-1295

UNIV. OF MINNESOTA-DULUTH
Duluth, MN 55812

UNIV. OF MINNESOTA-MORRIS
Morris, MN 56267

MOORHEAD STATE UNIVERSITY
Moorhead, MN 56563-2996

NORTHERN MICHIGAN
UNIVERSITY
Marquette, MI 49855-5391

NORTHWOOD UNIVERSITY
Midland, MI 48640

OAKLAND CITY COLLEGE
Oakland City, IN 47660-1099

OAKLAND UNIVERSITY
Rochestser, MI 48309-4401

QUINCY UNIVERSITY
Quincy, IL 62301-2699

SAGINAW VALLEY STATE UNIV.
University Center, MI 48710

SOUTHERN ILLINOIS UNIVERSITY
Edwardsville, IL 62026

UNIV. OF SOUTHERN INDIANA
Evansville, IN 47712

SOUTHWEST STATE UNIVERSITY
Marshall, MN 56258

COLLEGE OF ST. FRANCIS
Joliet, IL 60435

SAINT JOSEPH'S COLLEGE
Rensselaer, IN 47978

WAYNE STATE UNIVERSITY
Detroit, MI 48202

WINONA STATE UNIVERSITY
Winona, MN 55987-5838

UNIV. OF WISCONSIN-PARKSIDE
Kenosha, WI 53141-2000

District 5

AUGUSTANA COLLEGE
Sioux Falls, SD 57197

CENTRAL MISSOURI STATE UNIV.
Warrensburg, MO 64093

CHADRON STATE COLLEGE
Chadron, NE 69337

DRURY COLLEGE
Springfield, MO 65802

EMPORIA STATE UNIVERSITY
Emporia, KS 66801-5087

LINCOLN UNIVERSITY
Jefferson City, MO 65102-0029

MANKATO STATE UNIVERSITY
Mankato, MN 56002-8400

MISSOURI SOUTHERN ST.
COLLEGE
Joplin, MO 64801-1595

MISSOURI WESTERN ST. COLLEGE
St. Joseph, MO 64507

UNIVERSITY OF MISSOURI
Rolla, MO 65401

UNIVERSITY OF MISSOURI
St. Louis, MO 63121-4499

MORNINGSIDE COLLEGE
Sioux City, IA 51106-1751

UNIV. OF NEBRASKA at KEARNEY
Kearney, NE 68849

UNIV. OF NEBRASKA at OMAHA
Omaha, NE 68182

NORTH DAKOTA STATE
UNIVERSITY
Fargo, ND 58105

UNIVERSITY OF NORTH DAKOTA
Grand Forks, ND 58202

NORTHEAST MISSOURI STATE
UNIV.
Kirksville, MO 63501

UNIV. OF NORTHERN COLORADO
Greeley, CO 80639

NORTHERN STATE UNIVERSITY
Aberdeen, SD 57401

NORTHWEST MISSOURI STATE
UNIV.
Maryville, MO 64468-6001

PITTSBURG STATE UNIVERSITY
Pittsburg, KS 66762

SOUTH DAKOTA STATE
UNIVERSITY
Brookings, SD 57007

UNIVERSITY OF SOUTH DAKOTA
Vermillion, SD 57069-2390

SOUTHWEST BAPTIST
UNIVERSITY
Bolivar, MO 65613

ST. CLOUD STATE UNIVERSITY
St. Cloud, MN 56301-4498

WASHBURN UNIVERSITY
Topeka, KS 66621

WAYNE STATE COLLEGE
Wayne, NE 68787-1172

District 6

ABILENE CHRISTIAN UNIVERSITY
Abilene, TX 79699

ANGELO STATE UNIVERSITY
San Angelo, TX 76909

CAMERON UNIVERSITY
Lawton, OK 73505-6377

UNIV. OF CENTRAL ARKANSAS
Conway, AR 72035-0001

UNIVERSITY OF CENTRAL
OKLAHOMA
Edmond, OK 73034

EAST TEXAS STATE UNIVERSITY
Commerce, TX 75429-3011

EASTERN NEW MEXICO
UNIVERSITY
Portales, NM 88130

HENDERSON STATE UNIVERSITY
Arkadelphia, AR 71999-0001

TARLETON STATE UNIVERSITY
Stephenville, TX 76402

TEXAS A&M UNIV.-KINGSVILLE
Kingsville, TX 78363

WEST TEXAS A&M UNIVERSITY
Canyon, TX 79016-0999

WESTERN NEW MEXICO
UNIVERSITY
Silver City, NM 88061

District 7

ADAMS STATE COLLEGE
Alamosa, CO 81102

COLORADO CHRISTIAN
UNIVERSITY
Lakewood, CO 80226

COLORADO SCHOOL OF MINES
Golden, CO 80401

UNIV. OF COLORADO-COLO.
SPRINGS
Colorado Springs, CO 80933-7150

UNIVERSITY OF DENVER
Denver, CO 80208

FORT HAYS STATE UNIVERSITY
Hays, KS 67601

FORT LEWIS COLLEGE
Durango, CO 81301-3999

GRAND CANYON UNIVERSITY
Phoenix, AZ 85017

MESA STATE COLLEGE
Grand Junction, CO 81501

METROPOLITAN STATE COLLEGE
Denver, CO 80217-3362

MONTANA STATE UNIVERSITY
Billings, MT 59101-0298

NEW MEXICO HIGHLANDS UNIV.
Las Vegas, NM 87701

REGIS UNIVERSITY
Denver, CO 80221-1099

UNIV. OF SOUTHERN COLORADO
Pueblo, CO 81001-4901

WESTERN STATE COLLEGE
Gunnison, CO 81231

District 8

UNIVERSITY OF ALASKA-
ANCHORAGE
Anchorage, AK 99508

UNIVERSITY OF ALASKA-
FAIRBANKS
Fairbanks, AK 99775-7500

UNIV. OF CALIFORNIA-DAVIS
Davis, CA 95616

UNIV. OF CALIFORNIA-RIVERSIDE
Riverside, CA 92521

CALIF. STATE POLYTECHNIC UNIV.
Pomona, CA 91768

CALIF. STATE UNIV.-BAKERSFIELD
Bakersfield, CA 93311-1099

CALIF. STATE UNIV.-CHICO
Chico, CA 95929-0300

CALIF. STATE U-DOMINGUEZ
HILLS
Carson, CA 90747

CALIF. STATE UNIV.-HAYWARD
Hayward, CA 94542

CALIF. STATE UNIV.-LOS ANGELES
Los Angeles, CA 90032-8240

CALIF. STATE U.-SAN BERNARDINO
San Bernardino, CA 92407-2397

CALIF. STATE UNIV.-STANISLAUS
Turlock, CA 95382

CHAMINADE UNIVERSITY
Honolulu, HI 96816

UNIVERSITY OF HAWAII-HILO
Hilo, HI 96720-4091

HUMBOLDT STATE UNIVERSITY
Arcata, CA 95521

COLLEGE OF NOTRE DAME
Belmont, CA 94002-9974

SAN FRANCISCO STATE
UNIVERSITY
San Francisco, CA 94132

SEATTLE PACIFIC UNIVERSITY
Seattle, WA 98119

SONOMA STATE UNIVERSITY
Rohnert Park, CA 94928

**NCAA PROVISIONAL MEMBERS
DIVISION II**

District 2

UNIV. OF PUERTO RICO-
MAYAGUEZ
Mayaguez, PR 00709

UNIV. OF PUERTO RICO-BAYAMON
Bayamon, PR 00619-1919

UNIVERSITY OF VIRGIN ISLANDS
St. Thomas, VI 00802

WEST VIRGINIA STATE COLLEGE
Institute, WV 25112-1000

WESTMINSTER COLLEGE
New Wilmington, PA 16172

District 3

ANDERSON COLLEGE
Anderson, SC 29621

CHRISTIAN BROTHERS
UNIVERSITY
Memphis, TN 38104

CLAYTON STATE COLLEGE
Morrow, GA 30260

COLUMBIA UNION COLLEGE
Takoma Park, MD 20912

GEORGIA SOUTHWESTERN
COLLEGE
Americus, GA 31709-4693

LAMBUTH UNIVERSITY
Jackson, TN 38301

UNIVERSITY OF MONTEVALLO
Montevallo, AL 35115-6001

TUSCULUM COLLEGE
Greeneville, TN 37743

District 5

EAST CENTRAL UNIVERSITY
Ada, OK 74820

LANGSTON UNIVERSITY
Langston, OK 73050

NORTHWESTERN OKLAHOMA ST.
U.
Alva, OK 73717

OKLAHOMA PANHANDLE ST. UNIV.
Goodwell, OK 73939

ROCKHURST COLLEGE
Kansas City, MO 64110

UNIV. OF SCIENCE & ARTS
Chickasha, OK 73018

SOUTHEASTERN OKLA. ST. UNIV.
Durant, OK 74701

SOUTHWESTERN OKLAHOMA ST.
UNIV.
Weatherford, OK 73096

District 6

ARKANSAS TECH UNIVERSITY
Russellville, AR 72801-2222

UNIV. OF ARKANSAS-MONTICELLO
Monticello, AR 71656-3596

CONCORDIA UNIVERSITY at
AUSTIN
Austin, TX 78705-2799

EAST TEXAS BAPTIST UNIVERSITY
Marshall, TX 75670-1498

HARDING UNIVERSITY
Searcy, AR 72149-0001

HOUSTON BAPTIST UNIVERSITY
Houston, TX 77074-3298

INCARNATE WORD COLLEGE
San Antonio, TX 78209

LYON COLLEGE
Batesville, AR 72503-2317

UNIV. OF MARY HARDIN-BAYLOR
Belton, TX 76513

MIDWESTERN STATE UNIVERSITY
Wichita Falls, TX 76308

OUACHITA BAPTIST UNIVERSITY
Arkadelphia, AR 71998-0001

SCHREINER COLLEGE
Keerville, TX 78028

SOUTHERN ARKANSAS
UNIVERSITY
Magnolia, AR 71753-5000

ST. EDWARD'S UNIVERSITY
Austin, TX 78704

ST. MARY'S UNIVERSITY
San Antonio, TX 78228-8572

TEXAS LUTHERAN COLLEGE
Seguin, TX 78155

TEXAS WESLEYAN UNIVERSITY
Fort Worth, TX 76105

District 7

LEWIS-CLARK STATE COLLEGE
Lewiston, ID 83501

District 8

BRIGHAM YOUNG UNIVERSITY
Laie, HI 96762-1294

CENTRAL WASHINGTON UNIV
Ellensburg, WA 98926

HAWAII PACIFIC UNIVERSITY
Honolulu, HI 96813

ST. MARTIN'S COLLEGE
Lacey, WA 98503

WESTERN WASHINGTON UNIV
Bellingham, WA 98225

WOMEN'S BASKETBALL

DIVISION I
District 1
BOSTON COLLEGE
Chestnut Hill, MA 02167-3934

BOSTON UNIVERSITY
Boston, MA 02215

BROWN UNIVERSITY
Providence, RI 02912

CENTRAL CONN. STATE UNIV.
New Britain, CT 06050-4010

UNIVERSITY OF CONNECTICUT
Storrs, CT 06269

DARTMOUTH COLLEGE
Hanover, NH 03755

FAIRFIELD UNIVERSITY
Fairfield, CT 06430-5195

UNIVERSITY OF HARTFORD
West Hartford, CT 06117-1599

HARVARD UNIVERSITY
Cambridge, MA 02138-3800

COLLEGE OF THE HOLY CROSS
Worcester, MA 01610-2395

UNIVERSITY OF MAINE
Orono, ME 04469

UNIV. OF MASSACHUSETTS-
AMHERST
Amherst, MA 01003

UNIVERSITY OF NEW HAMPSHIRE
Durham, NH 03824

NORTHEASTERN UNIVERSITY
Boston, MA 02115-5096

PROVIDENCE COLLEGE
Providence, RI 02918

UNIVERSITY OF RHODE ISLAND
Kingston, RI 02881

UNIVERSITY OF VERMONT
Burlington, VT 05405

YALE UNIVERSITY
New Haven, CT 06520-7398

District 2

AMERICAN UNIVERSITY
Washington, DC 20016

BUCKNELL UNIVERSITY
Lewisburg, PA 17837

STATE UNIV. OF N.Y. at BUFFALO
Buffalo, NY 14260

CANISIUS COLLEGE
Buffalo, NY 14208-1098

COLGATE UNIVERSITY
Hamilton, NY 13346-1304

COLUMBIA UNIV.-BARNARD
COLLEGE
New York, NY 10027

CORNELL UNIVERSITY
Ithaca, NY 14853

DELAWARE STATE UNIVERSITY
Dover, DE 19901

UNIVERSITY OF DELAWARE
Newark, DE 19716

DREXEL UNIVERSITY
Philadelphia, PA 19104

DUQUESNE UNIVERSITY
Pittsburgh, PA 15282

FAIRLEIGH DICKINSON-TEANECK
Teaneck, NJ 07666

FORDHAM UNIVERSITY
Bronx, NY 10458-5155

GEORGE MASON UNIVERSITY
Fairfax, VA 22030

GEORGE WASHINGTON
UNIVERSITY
Washington, DC 20052

GEORGETOWN UNIVERSITY
Washington, DC 20057

HAMPTON UNIVERSITY
Hampton, VA 23668

HOFSTRA UNIVERSITY
Hempstead, NY 11550

HOWARD UNIVERSITY
Washington, DC 20059

IONA COLLEGE
New Rochelle, NY 10801

JAMES MADISON UNIVERSITY
Harrisonburg, VA 22807

LA SALLE UNIVERSITY
Philadelphia, PA 19141-1199

LAFAYETTE COLLEGE
Easton, PA 18042

LEHIGH UNIVERSITY
Bethlehem, PA 18015-3089

LONG ISLAND UNIV-BROOKLYN
Brooklyn, NY 11201

LOYOLA COLLEGE
Baltimore, MD 21210

MANHATTAN COLLEGE
Riverdale, NY 10471

MARIST COLLEGE
Poughkeepsie, NY 12601-1387

UNIV. OF MARYLAND-BALT. CO.
Baltimore, MD 21228-5398

U. OF MARYLAND-EASTERN
SHORE
Princess Anne, MD 21853-1299

MONMOUTH UNIVERSITY
West Long Branch, NJ 07764

MORGAN STATE UNIVERSITY
Baltimore, MD 21239

MOUNT ST. MARY'S COLLEGE
Emmitsburg, MD 21727-7799

NIAGARA UNIVERSITY
Niagara University, NY 14109

PENNSYLVANIA STATE UNIV.
University Park, PA 16802

UNIVERSITY OF PENNSYLVANIA
Philadelphia, PA 19104-6380

UNIVERSITY OF PITTSBURGH
Pittsburgh, PA 15260

PRINCETON UNIVERSITY
Princeton, NJ 08544

RIDER UNIVERSITY
Lawrenceville, NJ 08648-3099

ROBERT MORRIS COLLEGE
Coraopolis, PA 15108-1189

RUTGERS UNIVERSITY
New Brunswick, NJ 08903

SETON HALL UNIVERSITY
South Orange, NJ 07079

SIENA COLLEGE
Loudonville, NY 12211-1462

ST. BONAVENTURE UNIVERSITY
St. Bonaventure, NY 14778

ST. FRANCIS COLLEGE
Brooklyn Heights, NY 11201

ST. FRANCIS COLLEGE
Loretto, PA 15940-0600

ST. JOHN'S UNIVERSITY
Jamaica, NY 11439

ST. JOSEPH'S UNIVERSITY
Philadelphia, PA 19131-1395

ST. PETER'S COLLEGE
Jersey City, NJ 07306

SYRACUSE UNIVERSITY
Syracuse, NY 13244

TEMPLE UNIVERSITY
Philadelphia, PA 19122

TOWSON STATE UNIVERSITY
Towson, MD 21204

U.S. MILITARY ACADEMY
West Point, NY 10996

U.S. NAVAL ACADEMY
Annapolis, MD 21402

VILLANOVA UNIVERSITY
Villanova, PA 19085

WAGNER COLLEGE
Staten Island, NY 10301-4495

WEST VIRGINIA UNIVERSITY
Morgantown, WV 26506-6201

COLLEGE OF WILLIAM & MARY
Williamsburg, VA 23187

District 3

ALABAMA STATE UNIVERSITY
Montgomery, AL 36101-0271

UNIV. OF ALABAMA at
TUSCALOOSA
Tuscaloosa, AL 35487

UNIV. OF ALABAMA at
BIRMINGHAM
Birmingham, AL 35294-0110

APPALACHIAN STATE UNIVERSITY
Boone, NC 28608

AUBURN UNIVERSITY
Auburn University, AL 36849-5113

AUSTIN PEAY STATE UNIVERSITY
Clarksville, TN 37044-4576

BETHUNE-COOKMAN COLLEGE
Daytona Beach, FL 32114-3099

CAMPBELL UNIVERSITY
Buies Creek, NC 27506

UNIVERSITY OF CENTRAL
FLORIDA
Orlando, FL 32816-0002

CHARLESTON SOUTHERN UNIV.
Charleston, SC 29423-8087

COLLEGE OF CHARLESTON
Charleston, SC 29424

CLEMSON UNIVERSITY
Clemson, SC 29632

COASTAL CAROLINA UNIVERSITY
Conway, SC 29526

COPPIN STATE COLLEGE
Baltimore, MD 21216

DAVIDSON COLLEGE
Davidson, NC 28036

DUKE UNIVERSITY
Durham, NC 27708-0555

EAST CAROLINA UNIVERSITY
Greenville, NC 27858-4353

EAST TENNESSEE STATE UNIV.
Johnson City, TN 37614

EASTERN KENTUCKY UNIVERSITY
Richmond, KY 40475-3101

FLORIDA A&M UNIVERSITY
Tallahassee, FL 32307

FLORIDA ATLANTIC UNIVERSITY
Boca Raton, FL 33431-0991

FLORIDA INTERNATIONAL UNIV.
Miami, FL 33199

FLORIDA STATE UNIVERSITY
Tallahassee, FL 32306

UNIVERSITY OF FLORIDA
Gainesville, FL 32604

FURMAN UNIVERSITY
Greenville, SC 29613

GEORGIA INSTITUTE OF TECH.
Atlanta, GA 30332

GEORGIA SOUTHERN UNIVERSITY
Statesboro, GA 30460-8033

GEORGIA STATE UNIVERSITY
Atlanta, GA 30303-3083

UNIVERSITY OF GEORGIA
Athens, GA 30613

JACKSONVILLE STATE
UNIVERSITY
Jacksonville, AL 36265-9982

JUNIVERSITY OF KENTUCKY
Lexington, KY 40506-0032

LIBERTY UNIVERSITY
Lynchburg, VA 24506

LOUISIANA STATE UNIVERSITY
Baton Rouge, LA 70803

UNIVERSITY OF LOUISVILLE
Louisville, KY 40292

MARSHALL UNIVERSITY
Huntington, WV 25755

UNIVERSITY OF MARYLAND
College Park, MD 20740

UNIVERSITY OF MEMPHIS
Memphis, TN 38152

MERCER UNIVERSITY
Macon, GA 31207

UNIVERSITY OF MIAMI
Coral Gables, FL 33124-6710

MIDDLE TENNESSEE STATE UNIV.
Murfreesboro, TN 37132

MISSISSIPPI STATE UNIVERSITY
Mississippi State, MS 39762-5509

UNIVERSITY OF MISSISSIPPI
University, MS 38677

MOREHEAD STATE UNIVERSITY
Morehead, KY 40351-1689

MURRAY STATE UNIVERSITY
Murray, KY 42071-0009

UNIVERSITY OF NEW ORLEANS
New Orleans, LA 70148

UNIVERSITY OF NORTH
CAROLINA
Asheville, NC 28804-3299

UNIVERSITY OF NORTH
CAROLINA
Chapel Hill, NC 27514

UNIVERSITY OF NORTH
CAROLINA
Charlotte, NC 28223

UNIVERSITY OF NORTH
CAROLINA
Greensboro, NC 27412-5001

UNIVERSITY OF NORTH
CAROLINA
Wilmington, NC 28403-3297

NORTH CAROLINA A&T ST. UNIV.
Greensboro, NC 27411

NORTH CAROLINA STATE UNIV.
Raleigh, NC 27695-7001

OLD DOMINION UNIVERSITY
Norfolk, VA 23529

RADFORD UNIVERSITY
Radford, VA 24142

UNIVERSITY OF RICHMOND
Richmond, VA 23173-1903

UNIVERSITY OF SOUTH ALABAMA
Mobile, AL 36688

SOUTH CAROLINA STATE UNIV.
Orangeburg, SC 29117-0001

UNIVERSITY OF SOUTH CAROLINA
Columbia, SC 29208

UNIVERSITY OF SOUTH FLORIDA
Tampa, FL 33620

SOUTHEASTERN LOUISIANA UNIV.
Hammond, LA 70402

UNIV. OF SOUTHERN MISSISSIPPI
Hattiesburg, MS 39406-5001

STETSON UNIVERSITY
De Land, FL 32720

TENNESSEE STATE UNIVERSITY
Nashville, TN 37209-1561

TENNESSEE TECHNOLOGICAL
UNIV.
Cookeville, TN 38505-0001

UNIVERSITY OF TENNESSEE
Chattanooga, TN 37403-2598

THE UNIVERSITY OF TENNESSEE
Knoxville, TN 37996

UNIV. OF TENNESSEE at MARTIN
Martin, TN 38238-5021

TROY STATE UNIVERSITY
Troy, AL 36082

TULANE UNIVERSITY
New Orleans, LA 70118

VANDERBILT UNIVERSITY
Nashville, TN 37212

VIRGINIA COMMONWEALTH UNIV.
Richmond, VA 23284-2003

VIRGINIA POLYTECHNIC
INSTITUTE
Blacksburg, VA 24061

UNIVERSITY OF VIRGINIA
Charlottesville, VA 22903

WAKE FOREST UNIVERSITY
Winston-Salem, NC 27109

WESTERN CAROLINA UNIVERSITY
Cullowhee, NC 28723

WESTERN KENTUCKY
UNIVERSITY
Bowling Green, KY 42101-3576

WINTHROP UNIVERSITY
Rock Hill, SC 29733

WOFFORD COLLEGE
Spartanburg, SC 29303-3663

District 4

UNIVERSITY OF AKRON
Akron, OH 44325

BALL STATE UNIVERSITY
Muncie, IN 47306

BOWLING GREEN STATE UNIV.
Bowling Green, OH 43403

BUTLER UNIVERSITY
Indianapolis, IN 46208

CENTRAL MICHIGAN UNIVERSITY
Mount Pleasant, MI 48859

CHICAGO STATE UNIVERSITY
Chicago, IL 60628-1598

UNIVERSITY OF CINCINNATI
Cincinnati, OH 45221

CLEVELAND STATE UNIVERSITY
Cleveland, OH 44115

UNIVERSITY OF DAYTON
Dayton, OH 45469

DE PAUL UNIVERSITY
Chicago, IL 60604-2287

UNIVERSITY OF DETROIT-MERCY
Detroit, MI 48219-0900

EASTERN ILLINOIS UNIVERSITY
Charleston, IL 61920-3099

EASTERN MICHIGAN UNIVERSITY
Ypsilanti, MI 48197

UNIVERSITY OF EVANSVILLE
Evansville, IN 47722

ILLINOIS STATE UNIVERSITY
Normal, IL 61761

UNIVERSITY OF ILLINOIS
Champaign, IL 61820

UNIVERSITY OF ILLINOIS
Chicago, IL 60607

INDIANA UNIVERSITY
Bloomington, IN 47405

UNIVERSITY OF IOWA
Iowa City, IA 52242

KENT STATE UNIVERSITY
Kent, OH 44242

LOYOLA UNIVERSITY
Chicago, IL 60626

MARQUETTE UNIVERSITY
Milwaukee, WI 53201-1881

MIAMI UNIVERSITY
Oxford, OH 45056

MICHIGAN STATE UNIVERSITY
East Lansing, MI 48824

UNIVERSITY OF MICHIGAN
Ann Arbor, MI 48109-2201

UNIV. OF MINNESOTA-TWIN
CITIES
Minneapolis, MN 55455

NORTHEASTERN ILLINOIS UNIV.
Chicago, IL 60625-4699

NORTHERN ILLINOIS UNIVERSITY
De Kalb, IL 60115-2854

NORTHWESTERN UNIVERSITY
Evanston, IL 60208

UNIVERSITY OF NOTRE DAME
Notre Dame, IN 46556

OHIO STATE UNIVERSITY
Columbus, OH 43210

OHIO UNIVERSITY
Athens, OH 45701

PURDUE UNIVERSITY
West Lafayette, IN 47907

UNIVERSITY OF TOLEDO
Toledo, OH 43606

VALPARAISO UNIVERSITY
Valparaiso, IN 46383-6493

WESTERN ILLINOIS UNIVERSITY
Macomb, IL 61455

WESTERN MICHIGAN UNIVERSITY
Kalamazoo, MI 49008-5134

UNIVERSITY OF WISCONSIN
Green Bay, WI 54311-7001

UNIVERSITY OF WISCONSIN
Madison, WI 53711

UNIVERSITY OF WISCONSIN
Milwaukee, WI 53201

WRIGHT STATE UNIVERSITY
Dayton, OH 45435-0001

XAVIER UNIVERSITY
Cincinnati, OH 45207-6114

YOUNGSTOWN STATE
UNIVERSITY
Youngstown, OH 44555-0001

District 5

BRADLEY UNIVERSITY
Peoria, IL 61625

UNIVERSITY OF COLORADO
Boulder, CO 80309

CREIGHTON UNIVERSITY
Omaha, NE 68178-0001

DRAKE UNIVERSITY
Des Moines, IA 50311-4505

INDIANA STATE UNIVERSITY
Terre Haute, IN 47809

IOWA STATE UNIVERSITY
Ames, IA 50011

KANSAS STATE UNIVERSITY
Manhattan, KS 66506

UNIVERSITY OF KANSAS
Lawrence, KS 66045

UNIV. OF MISSOURI-COLUMBIA
Columbia, MO 65211

UNIV. OF MISSOURI-KANSAS CITY
Kansas City, MO 64110

UNIVERSITY OF NEBRASKA
Lincoln, NE 68588

UNIVERSITY OF NORTHERN IOWA
Cedar Falls, IA 50614

OKLAHOMA STATE UNIVERSITY
Stillwater, OK 74078

UNIVERSITY OF OKLAHOMA
Norman, OK 73019

ORAL ROBERTS UNIVERSITY
Tulsa, OK 74171

SOUTHEAST MISSOURI STATE
UNIV.
Cape Girardeau, MO 63701-4799

SOUTHERN ILLINOIS UNIVERSITY
Carbondale, IL 62901

SOUTHWEST MISSOURI STATE
UNIV.
Springfield, MO 65804

ST. LOUIS UNIVERSITY
St. Louis, MO 63108

WICHITA STATE UNIVERSITY
Wichita, KS 67260

District 6

ALCORN STATE UNIVERSITY
Lorman, MS 39096-9402

ARKANSAS STATE UNIVERSITY
State University, AR 72467

UNIVERSITY OF ARKANSAS
Fayetteville, AR 72701

UNIVERSITY OF ARKANSAS
Little Rock, AR 72204-1099

BAYLOR UNIVERSITY
Waco, TX 76798

GRAMBLING STATE UNIVERSITY
Grambling, LA 71245

UNIVERSITY OF HOUSTON
Houston, TX 77204

JACKSON STATE UNIVERSITY
Jackson, MS 39217

LAMAR UNIVERSITY
Beaumont, TX 77710

LOUISIANA TECH UNIVERSITY
Ruston, LA 71272

MCNESSE STATE UNIVERSITY
Lake Charles, LA 70609

MISSISSIPPI VALLEY ST. UNIV.
Itta Bena, MS 38941-1400

NICHOLLS STATE UNIVERSITY
Thibodaux, LA 70310

UNIVERSITY OF NORTH TEXAS
Denton, TX 76203-6737

NORTHEAST LOUISIANA
UNIVERSITY
Monroe, LA 71209-3000

NORTHWESTERN STATE
UNIVERSITY
Natchitoches, LA 71497-0003

PRAIRIE VIEW A&M UNIVERSITY
Prairie View, TX 77446

RICE UNIVERSITY
Houston, TX 77251

SAM HOUSTON STATE
UNIVERSITY
Huntsville, TX 77341

SOUTHERN METHODIST
UNIVERSITY
Dallas, TX 75275

SOUTHERN UNIVERSITY
Baton Rouge, LA 70813

SOUTHWEST TEXAS STATE UNIV.
San Marcos, TX 78666 4615

UNIV. OF SOUTHWESTERN LA.
Lafayette, LA 70504-1008

STEPHEN F. AUSTIN STATE UNIV.
Nacogdoches, TX 75962

UNIVERSITY OF TEXAS
Arlington, TX 76019

UNIVERSITY OF TEXAS
Austin, TX 78712

UNIVERSITY OF TEXAS
San Antonio, TX 78249

TEXAS A&M UNIVERSITY
College Station, TX 77843-1228

TEXAS CHRISTIAN UNIVERSITY
Fort Worth, TX 76129-0001

UNIV. OF TEXAS-PAN AMERICAN
Edinburg, TX 78539-2999

TEXAS SOUTHERN UNIVERSITY
Houston, TX 77004

TEXAS TECH UNIVERSITY
Lubbock, TX 79409

District 7

BOISE STATE UNIVERSITY
Boise, ID 83725

BRIGHAM YOUNG UNIVERSITY
Provo, UT 84602

CALIF. STATE UNIV.-FRESNO
Fresno, CA 93740-0048

COLORADO STATE UNIVERSITY
Fort Collins, CO 80523-0100

GONZAGA UNIVERSITY
Spokane, WA 99258

UNIVERSITY OF HAWAII-MANOA
Honolulu, HI 96822-2370

IDAHO STATE UNIVERSITY
Pocatello, ID 83209

UNIVERSITY OF IDAHO
Moscow, ID 83843

MONTANA STATE UNIV-BOZEMAN
Bozeman, MT 59717-0338

THE UNIVERSITY OF MONTANA
Missoula, MT 59812-1291

UNIVERSITY OF NEVADA
Reno, NV 89557

UNIVERSITY OF NEW MEXICO
Albuquerque, NM 87131

NORTHERN ARIZONA UNIVERSITY
Flagstaff, AZ 86011

SAN DIEGO STATE UNIVERSITY
San Diego, CA 92182

SOUTHERN UTAH UNIVERSITY
Cedar City, UT 84720

UNIVERSITY OF TEXAS-EL PASO
El Paso, TX 79968

UNIVERSITY OF UTAH
Salt Lake City, UT 84112

WEBER STATE UNIVERSITY
Ogden, UT 84408-2701

UNIVERSITY OF WYOMING
Laramie, WY 82071

District 8

ARIZONA STATE UNIVERSITY
Tempe, AZ 85287-2505

UNIVERSITY OF ARIZONA
Tucson, AZ 85721

UNIV. OF CALIFORNIA-BERKELEY
Berkeley, CA 94720

UNIV. OF CALIF.-LOS ANGELES
Los Angeles, CA 90095-1405

UNIV. OF CALIF-SANTA BARBARA
Santa Barbara, CA 93106

UNIV. OF CALIFORNIA-IRVINE
Irvine, CA 92717

CALIF. POLYTECHNIC STATE UNIV.
San Luis Obispo, CA 93407

CALIF. STATE UNIV.-FULLERTON
Fullerton, CA 92634-9480

CALIF. STATE UNIV.-NORTHRIDGE
Northridge, CA 91330

CALIF. STATE UNIV.-SACRAMENTO
Sacramento, CA 95819

EASTERN WASHINGTON
UNIVERSITY
Cheney, WA 99004

LONG BEACH STATE UNIVERSITY
Long Beach, CA 90840-0118

LOYOLA MARYMOUNT
UNIVERSITY
Los Angeles, CA 90045-2699

UNIVERSITY OF NEVADA
Las Vegas, NV 89154

NEW MEXICO STATE UNIVERSITY
Las Cruces, NM 88003

OREGON STATE UNIVERSITY
Corvallis, OR 97331

UNIVERSITY OF OREGON
Eugene, OR 97403-1226

UNIVERSITY OF THE PACIFIC
Stockton, CA 95211

PEPPERDINE UNIVERSITY
Malibu, CA 90263

UNIVERSITY OF PORTLAND
Portland, OR 97203-5798

UNIVERSITY OF SAN DIEGO
San Diego, CA 92110-2492

UNIVERSITY OF SAN FRANCISCO
San Francisco, CA 94117-1080

SAN JOSE STATE UNIVERSITY
San Jose, CA 95192

SANTA CLARA UNIVERSITY
Santa Clara, CA 95053

UNIV. OF SOUTHERN CALIFORNIA
Los Angeles, CA 90089-0012

ST. MARY'S COLLEGE
Moraga, CA 94556

STANFORD UNIVERSITY
Stanford, CA 94305

WASHINGTON STATE UNIVERSITY
Pullman, WA 99164

UNIVERSITY OF WASHINGTON
Seattle, WA 98195

NCAA PROVISIONAL MEMBERS

DIVISION I

District 6

UNIVERSITY OF ARKANSAS-PINE
BLUFF
Pine Bluff, AR 71601

DIVISION II

District 1

AMERICAN INTERNATIONAL
COLLEGE
Springfield, MA 01109-3189

ASSUMPTION COLLEGE
Worcester, MA 01615-0005

BENTLEY COLLEGE
Waltham, MA 02154-4705

UNIVERSITY OF BRIDGEPORT
Bridgeport, CT 06601

BRYANT COLLEGE
Smithfield, RI 02917-1284

FRANKLIN PIERCE COLLEGE
Rindge, NH 03461

KEENE STATE COLLEGE
Keene, NH 03431-4183

UNIV. OF MASSACHUSETTS-
LOWELL
Lowell, MA 01854

MERRIMACK COLLEGE
North Andover, MA 01845

NEW HAMPSHIRE COLLEGE
Hooksett, NH 03106-1045

UNIVERSITY OF NEW HAVEN
West Haven, CT 06516-1999

QUINNIPIAC COLLEGE
Hamden, CT 06518-1940

SACRED HEART UNIVERSITY
Fairfield, CT 06432-1000

SOUTHERN CONNECTICUT ST.
UNIV.
New Haven, CT 06515

ST. ANSELM COLLEGE
Manchester, NH 03102-1310

ST. MICHAEL'S COLLEGE
Colchester, VT 05439

STONEHILL COLLEGE
North Easton, MA 02357

District 2

ADELPHI UNIVERSITY
Garden City, NY 11530

STATE UNIV. OF N.Y. at ALBANY
Albany, NY 12222

ALDERSON-BROADDUS COLLEGE
Philippi, WV 26416

AMERICAN UNIV. OF PUERTO RICO
Bayamon, PR 00960-2037

BLOOMSBURG UNIVERSITY
Bloomsburg, PA 17815

BLUEFIELD STATE COLLEGE
Bluefield, WV 24701-2198

CALIFORNIA UNIVERSITY
California, PA 15419

THE UNIVERSITY OF
CHARLESTON
Charleston, WV 25304

CHEYNEY UNIVERSITY
Cheyney, PA 19319

CLARION UNIVERSITY
Clarion, PA 16214

CONCORD COLLEGE
Athens, WV 24712

CONCORDIA COLLEGE
Bronxville, NY 10708

DAVIS AND ELKINS COLLEGE
Elkins, WV 26241

UNIV. OF DISTRICT OF COLUMBIA
Washington, DC 20008

DOWLING COLLEGE
Oakdale, NY 11769-1999

EAST STROUDSBURG UNIVERSITY
East Stroudsburg, PA 18301

EDINBORO UNIVERSITY
Edinboro, PA 16444-0001

FAIRMONT STATE COLLEGE
Fairmont, WV 26554

GANNON UNIVERSITY
Erie, PA 16541

GLENVILLE STATE COLLEGE
Glenville, WV 26351

INDIANA UNIV. OF PENNSYLVANIA
Indiana, PA 15705

KUTZTOWN UNIVERSITY
Kutztown, PA 19530-0721

LE MOYNE COLLEGE
Syracuse, NY 13214-1399

LOCK HAVEN UNIVERSITY
Lock Haven, PA 17745

LONG ISLAND U./C.W. POST
CAMPUS
Brookville, NY 11548

MANSFIELD UNIVERSITY
Mansfield, PA 16933

MERCY COLLEGE
Dobbs Ferry, NY 10522

MERCYHURST COLLEGE
Erie, PA 16546

MILLERSVILLE UNIVERSITY
Millersville, PA 17551-0302

MOLLOY COLLEGE
Rockville Centre, NY 11570

PACE UNIVERSITY
New York, NY 10038-1502

PHILA. COLLEGE OF TEXT. & SCI.
Philadelphia, PA 19144-5497

UNIVERSITY OF PITTSBURGH
Johnstown, PA 15904-2990

QUEENS COLLEGE (NY)
Flushing, NY 11367

SALEM-TEIKYO UNIVERSITY
Salem, WV 26426

SHEPHERD COLLEGE
Shepherdstown, WV 25443

SHIPPENSBURG UNIVERSITY
Shippensburg, PA 17257

SLIPPERY ROCK UNIVERSITY
Slippery Rock, PA 16057

SOUTHAMPTON CAMPUS OF L.I.U.
Southampton, NY 11968

THE COLLEGE OF ST. ROSE
Albany, NY 12203

STATE UNIV. OF N.Y. at STONY
BROOK
Stony Brook, NY 11794

WEST CHESTER UNIVERSITY
West Chester, PA 19383

WEST LIBERTY STATE COLLEGE
West Liberty, WV 26074

WEST VIRGINIA INST. OF TECH
Montgomery, WV 25136

WEST VIRGINIA WESLEYAN
COLLEGE
Buckhannon, WV 26201

WHEELING JESUIT COLLEGE
Wheeling, WV 26003-6295

District 3

ALABAMA A&M UNIVERSITY
Normal, AL 35762

UNIV. OF ALABAMA-HUNTSVILLE
Huntsville, AL 35899

ALBANY STATE COLLEGE
Albany, GA 31705

ARMSTRONG STATE COLLEGE
Savannah, GA 31419-1997

AUGUSTA COLLEGE
Augusta, GA 30910

BARRY UNIVERSITY
Miami Shores, FL 33161

BARTON COLLEGE
Wilson, NC 27893

BELLARMINE COLLEGE
Louisville, KY 40205-0671

BELMONT ABBEY COLLEGE
Belmont, NC 28012-2795

BOWIE STATE UNIVERSITY
Bowie, MD 20715-9465

CARSON-NEWMAN COLLEGE
Jefferson City, TN 37760

CATAWBA COLLEGE
Salisbury, NC 28144-2488

CLARK ATLANTA UNIVERSITY
Atlanta, GA 30314

COKER COLLEGE
Hartsville, SC 29550

COLUMBUS COLLEGE
Columbus, GA 31907-2079

DELTA STATE UNIVERSITY
Cleveland, MS 38733

ECKERD COLLEGE
St. Petersburg, FL 33733

ELIZABETH CITY STATE UNIV.
Elizabeth City, NC 27909

ELON COLLEGE
Elon College, NC 27244

ERSKINE COLLEGE
Due West, SC 29639

FAYETTEVILLE STATE
UNIVERSITY
Fayetteville, NC 28301-4298

FLORIDA INSTITUTE OF TECH.
Melbourne, FL 32901

FLORIDA SOUTHERN COLLEGE
Lakeland, FL 33801-5698

FORT VALLEY STATE COLLEGE
Fort Valley, GA 31030

FRANCIS MARION UNIVERSITY
Florence, SC 29501-0547

GARDNER-WEBB UNIVERSITY
Boiling Springs, NC 28017

GEORGIA COLLEGE
Milledgeville, GA 31061

HIGH POINT UNIVERSITY
High Point, NC 27262-3598

JOHNSON C. SMITH UNIVERSITY
Charlotte, NC 28216

KENNESAW STATE COLLEGE
Marietta, GA 30061

KENTUCKY STATE UNIVERSITY
Frankfort, KY 40601

KENTUCKY WESLEYAN COLLEGE
Owensboro, KY 42302-1039

LANDER UNIVERSITY
Greenwood, SC 29649-2099

LANE COLLEGE
Jackson, TN 38301

LE MOYNE-OWEN COLLEGE
Memphis, TN 38126

LEES-MCRAE COLLEGE
Banner Elk, NC 28604-0128

LENOIR-RHYNE COLLEGE
Hickory, NC 28603

LIMESTONE COLLEGE
Gaffney, SC 29340-3799

LINCOLN MEMORIAL UNIVERSITY
Harrogate, TN 37752

LIVINGSTONE COLLEGE
Salisbury, NC 28144

LONGWOOD COLLEGE
Farmville, VA 23909-1899

LYNN UNIVERSITY
Boca Raton, FL 33431

MARS HILL COLLEGE
Mars Hill, NC 28754

MILES COLLEGE
Birmingham, AL 35208

MISSISSIPPI COLLEGE
Clinton, MS 39058

MISSISSIPPI UNIV. FOR WOMEN
Columbua, MS 39701

MORRIS BROWN COLLEGE
Atlanta, GA 30314

MOUNT OLIVE COLLEGE
Mount Olive, NC 28365

NEWBERRY COLLEGE
Newberry, SC 29108

NORFOLK STATE UNIVERSITY
Norfolk, VA 23504

UNIVERSITY OF NORTH ALABAMA
Florence, AL 35632

NORTH CAROLINA CENTRAL
UNIV.
Durham, NC 27707

UNIVERSITY OF NORTH FLORIDA
Jacksonville, FL 32224-2645

NORTHERN KENTUCKY
UNIVERSITY
Highland Heights, KY 41099

PAINE COLLEGE
Augusta, GA 30901-3182

PEMBROKE STATE UNIVERSITY
Pembroke, NC 28372-1510

PFEIFFER COLLEGE
Misenheimer, NC 28109-0960

PRESBYTERIAN COLLEGE
Clinton, SC 29325-2998

QUEENS COLLEGE (NC)
Charlotte, NC 28274

ROLLINS COLLEGE
Winter Park, FL 32789

SAVANNAH STATE COLLEGE
Savannah, GA 31404

SHAW UNIVERSITY
Raleigh, NC 27611

UNIV. OF SOUTH CAROLINA-
AIKEN
Aiken, SC 29801

U. OF SO. CAROLINA-
SPARTANBURG
Spartanburg, SC 29303

ST. ANDREWS PRESBYTERIAN
COLL.
Laurinburg, NC 28352-5598

ST. AUGUSTINE'S COLLEGE
Raleigh, NC 27610

ST. LEO COLLEGE
Saint Leo, FL 33574

ST. PAUL'S COLLEGE
Lawrenceville, VA 23868

UNIVERSITY OF TAMPA
Tampa, FL 33606-1490

TUSKEGEE UNIVERSITY
Tuskegee, AL 36088

VALDOSTA STATE UNIVERSITY
Valdosta, GA 31698

VIRGINIA STATE UNIVERSITY
Petersburg, VA 23806

VIRGINIA UNION UNIVERSITY
Richmond, VA 23220-1790

UNIVERSITY OF WEST ALABAMA
Livingston, AL 35470

UNIVERSITY OF WEST FLORIDA
Pensacola, FL 32514

WEST GEORGIA COLLEGE
Carrollton, GA 30118

WINGATE UNIVERSITY
Wingate, NC 28174

WINSTON-SALEM STATE UNIV.
Winston-Salem, NC 27110

District 4

ASHLAND UNIVERSITY
Ashland, OH 44805

BEMIDJI STATE UNIVERSITY
Bemidji, MN 56601-2699

FERRIS STATE UNIVERSITY
Big Rapids, MI 49307-2295

GRAND VALLEY STATE
UNIVERSITY
Allendale, MI 49401

HILLSDALE COLLEGE
Hillsdale, MI 49242-1298

INDIANA UNIV.-PURDUE UNIV.
Indianapolis, IN 46202

INDIANA UNIV.-PURDUE UNIV.
Fort Wayne, IN 46805-1499

UNIVERSITY OF INDIANAPOLIS
Indianapolis, IN 46227

LAKE SUPERIOR STATE UNIV.
Sault Sainte Marie, MI 49783

LEWIS UNIVERSITY
Romeoville, IL 60441

MICHIGAN TECHNOLOGICAL
UNIV.
Houghton, MI 49931-1295

UNIV. OF MINNESOTA-DULUTH
Duluth, MN 55812

UNIV. OF MINNESOTA-MORRIS
Morris, MN 56267

MOORHEAD STATE UNIVERSITY
Moorhead, MN 56563-2996

NORTHERN MICHIGAN
UNIVERSITY
Marquette, MI 49855-5391

NORTHWOOD UNIVERSITY
Midland, MI 48640

OAKLAND CITY COLLEGE
Oakland City, IN 47660-1099

OAKLAND UNIVERSITY
Rochestser, MI 48309-4401

QUINCY UNIVERSITY
Quincy, IL 62301-2699

SAGINAW VALLEY STATE UNIV.
University Center, MI 48710

SOUTHERN ILLINOIS UNIVERSITY
Edwardsville, IL 62026

UNIV. OF SOUTHERN INDIANA
Evansville, IN 47712

SOUTHWEST STATE UNIVERSITY
Marshall, MN 56258

COLLEGE OF ST. FRANCIS
Joliet, IL 60435

SAINT JOSEPH'S COLLEGE
Rensselaer, IN 47978

WAYNE STATE UNIVERSITY
Detroit, MI 48202

WINONA STATE UNIVERSITY
Winona, MN 55987-5838

UNIV. OF WISCONSIN-PARKSIDE
Kenosha, WI 53141-2000

District 5

AUGUSTANA COLLEGE
Sioux Falls, SD 57197

CENTRAL MISSOURI STATE UNIV.
Warrensburg, MO 64093

CHADRON STATE COLLEGE
Chadron, NE 69337

EMPORIA STATE UNIVERSITY
Emporia, KS 66801-5087

LINCOLN UNIVERSITY
Jefferson City, MO 65102-0029

MANKATO STATE UNIVERSITY
Mankato, MN 56002-8400

MISSOURI SOUTHERN ST.
COLLEGE
Joplin, MO 64801-1595

MISSOURI WESTERN ST. COLLEGE
St. Joseph, MO 64507

UNIVERSITY OF MISSOURI
Rolla, MO 65401

UNIVERSITY OF MISSOURI
St. Louis, MO 63121-4499

MORNINGSIDE COLLEGE
Sioux City, IA 51106-1751

UNIV. OF NEBRASKA at KEARNEY
Kearney, NE 68849

UNIV. OF NEBRASKA at OMAHA
Omaha, NE 68182

NORTH DAKOTA STATE UNIVERSITY
Fargo, ND 58105

UNIVERSITY OF NORTH DAKOTA
Grand Forks, ND 58202

NORTHEAST MISSOURI STATE UNIV.
Kirksville, MO 63501

UNIV. OF NORTHERN COLORADO
Greeley, CO 80639

NORTHERN STATE UNIVERSITY
Aberdeen, SD 57401

NORTHWEST MISSOURI STATE UNIV.
Maryville, MO 64468-6001

PITTSBURG STATE UNIVERSITY
Pittsburg, KS 66762

SOUTH DAKOTA STATE UNIVERSITY
Brookings, SD 57007

UNIVERSITY OF SOUTH DAKOTA
Vermillion, SD 57069-2390

SOUTHWEST BAPTIST UNIVERSITY
Bolivar, MO 65613

ST. CLOUD STATE UNIVERSITY
St. Cloud, MN 56301-4498

WASHBURN UNIVERSITY
Topeka, KS 66621

WAYNE STATE COLLEGE
Wayne, NE 68787-1172

District 6

ABILENE CHRISTIAN UNIVERSITY
Abilene, TX 79699

ANGELO STATE UNIVERSITY
San Angelo, TX 76909

CAMERON UNIVERSITY
Lawton, OK 73505-6377

UNIV. OF CENTRAL ARKANSAS
Conway, AR 72035-0001

UNIVERSITY OF CENTRAL OKLAHOMA
Edmond, OK 73034

EAST TEXAS STATE UNIVERSITY
Commerce, TX 75429-3011

EASTERN NEW MEXICO UNIVERSITY
Portales, NM 88130

HENDERSON STATE UNIVERSITY
Arkadelphia, AR 71999-0001

TARLETON STATE UNIVERSITY
Stephenville, TX 76402

TEXAS A&M UNIV.-KINGSVILLE
Kingsville, TX 78363

TEXAS WOMEN'S UNIVERSITY
Denton, TX 76204

WEST TEXAS A&M UNIVERSITY
Canyon, TX 79016-0999

WESTERN NEW MEXICO UNIVERSITY
Silver City, NM 88061

District 7

ADAMS STATE COLLEGE
Alamosa, CO 81102

COLORADO CHRISTIAN UNIVERSITY
Lakewood, CO 80226

COLORADO SCHOOL OF MINES
Golden, CO 80401

UNIV. OF COLORADO-COLO. SPRINGS
Colorado Springs, CO 80933-7150

UNIVERSITY OF DENVER
Denver, CO 80208

FORT HAYS STATE UNIVERSITY
Hays, KS 67601

FORT LEWIS COLLEGE
Durango, CO 81301-3999

GRAND CANYON UNIVERSITY
Phoenix, AZ 85017

MESA STATE COLLEGE
Grand Junction, CO 81501

METROPOLITAN STATE COLLEGE
Denver, CO 80217-3362

MONTANA STATE UNIVERSITY
Billings, MT 59101-0298

NEW MEXICO HIGHLANDS UNIV.
Las Vegas, NM 87701

REGIS UNIVERSITY
Denver, CO 80221-1099

UNIV. OF SOUTHERN COLORADO
Pueblo, CO 81001-4901

U.S. AIR FORCE ACADEMY
USAF Academy, CO 80840-5461

WESTERN STATE COLLEGE
Gunnison, CO 81231

District 8

UNIV. OF ALASKA-ANCHORAGE
Anchorage, AK 99508

UNIV. OF ALASKA-FAIRBANKS
Fairbanks, AK 99775-7500

UNIV. OF CALIFORNIA-DAVIS
Davis, CA 95616

UNIV. OF CALIFORNIA-RIVERSIDE
Riverside, CA 92521

CALIF. STATE POLYTECHNIC UNIV.
Pomona, CA 91768

CALIF. STATE UNIV.-CHICO
Chico, CA 95929-0300

CALIF. STATE U-DOMINGUEZ
HILLS
Carson, CA 90747

CALIF. STATE UNIV.-HAYWARD
Hayward, CA 94542

CALIF. STATE UNIV.-LOS ANGELES
Los Angeles, CA 90032-8240

CALIF. STATE U.-SAN BERNARDINO
San Bernardino, CA 92407-2397

CALIF. STATE UNIV.-STANISLAUS
Turlock, CA 95382

HUMBOLDT STATE UNIVERSITY
Arcata, CA 95521

COLLEGE OF NOTRE DAME
Belmont, CA 94002-9974

PORTLAND STATE UNIVERSITY
Portland, OR 97207-0751

SAN FRANCISCO STATE
UNIVERSITY
San Francisco, CA 94132

SEATTLE PACIFIC UNIVERSITY
Seattle, WA 98119

SONOMA STATE UNIVERSITY
Rohnert Park, CA 94928

NCAA PROVISIONSAL MEMBERS

DIVISION II

District 2

UNIV. OF PUERTO RICO-
MAYAGUEZ
Mayaguez, PR 00709

UNIV. OF PUERTO RICO-BAYAMON
Bayamon, PR 00619-1919

WEST VIRGINIA STATE COLLEGE
Institute, WV 25112-1000

WESTMINSTER COLLEGE
New Wilmington, PA 16172

District 3

ANDERSON COLLEGE
Anderson, SC 29621

CHRISTIAN BROTHERS
UNIVERSITY
Memphis, TN 38104

CLAYTON STATE COLLEGE
Morrow, GA 30260

COLUMBIA UNION COLLEGE
Takoma Park, MD 20912

GEORGIA SOUTHWESTERN
COLLEGE
Americus, GA 31709-4693

LAMBUTH UNIVERSITY
Jackson, TN 38301

UNIVERSITY OF MONTEVALLO
Montevallo, AL 35115-6001

TUSCULUM COLLEGE
Greeneville, TN 37743

District 5

EAST CENTRAL UNIVERSITY
Ada, OK 74820

LANGSTON UNIVERSITY
Langston, OK 73050

NORTHWESTERN OKLAHOMA ST. U.
Alva, OK 73717

OKLAHOMA PANHANDLE ST. UNIV.
Goodwell, OK 73939

ROCKHURST COLLEGE
Kansas City, MO 64110

UNIV. OF SCIENCE & ARTS
Chickasha, OK 73018

SOUTHEASTERN OKLA. ST. UNIV.
Durant, OK 74701

SOUTHWESTERN OKLAHOMA ST.
UNIV.
Weatherford, OK 73096

District 6

ARKANSAS TECH UNIVERSITY
Russellville, AR 72801-2222

UNIV. OF ARKANSAS-MONTICELLO
Monticello, AR 71656-3596

CONCORDIA UNIVERSITY at
AUSTIN
Austin, TX 78705-2799

EAST TEXAS BAPTIST UNIVERSITY
Marshall, TX 75670-1498

HARDING UNIVERSITY
Searcy, AR 72149-0001

INCARNATE WORD COLLEGE
San Antonio, TX 78209

LYON COLLEGE
Batesville, AR 72503-2317

UNIV. OF MARY HARDIN-BAYLOR
Belton, TX 76513

MIDWESTERN STATE UNIVERSITY
Wichita Falls, TX 76308

OUACHITA BAPTIST UNIVERSITY
Arkadelphia, AR 71998-0001

SCHREINER COLLEGE
Keerville, TX 78028

SOUTHERN ARKANSAS
UNIVERSITY
Magnolia, AR 71753-5000

ST. EDWARD'S UNIVERSITY
Austin, TX 78704

ST. MARY'S UNIVERSITY
San Antonio, TX 78228-8572

TEXAS LUTHERAN COLLEGE
Seguin, TX 78155

TEXAS WESLEYAN UNIVERSITY
Fort Worth, TX 76105 .

District 7
LEWIS-CLARK STATE COLLEGE
Lewiston, ID 83501

District 8
CENTRAL WASHINGTON UNIV.
Ellensburg, WA 98926

ST. MARTIN'S COLLEGE
Lacey, WA 98503

WESTERN WASHINGTON UNIV.
Bellingham, WA 98225

MEN'S CROSS COUNTRY

DIVISION I

District 1

BOSTON COLLEGE
Chestnut Hill, MA 02167-3934

BOSTON UNIVERSITY
Boston, MA 02215

BROWN UNIVERSITY
Providence, RI 02912

CENTRAL CONN. STATE UNIV.
New Britain, CT 06050-4010

UNIVERSITY OF CONNECTICUT
Storrs, CT 06269

DARTMOUTH COLLEGE
Hanover, NH 03755

FAIRFIELD UNIVERSITY
Fairfield, CT 06430-5195

UNIVERSITY OF HARTFORD
West Hartford, CT 06117-1599

HARVARD UNIVERSITY
Cambridge, MA 02138-3800

COLLEGE OF THE HOLY CROSS
Worcester, MA 01610-2395

UNIVERSITY OF MAINE
Orono, ME 04469

UNIV. OF MASSACHUSETTS-
AMHERST
Amherst, MA 01003

UNIVERSITY OF NEW HAMPSHIRE
Durham, NH 03824

NORTHEASTERN UNIVERSITY
Boston, MA 02115-5096

PROVIDENCE COLLEGE
Providence, RI 02918

UNIVERSITY OF RHODE ISLAND
Kingston, RI 02881

UNIVERSITY OF VERMONT
Burlington, VT 05405

YALE UNIVERSITY
New Haven, CT 06520-7398

District 2

AMERICAN UNIVERSITY
Washington, DC 20016

BUCKNELL UNIVERSITY
Lewisburg, PA 17837

STATE UNIV. OF N.Y. at BUFFALO
Buffalo, NY 14260

CANISIUS COLLEGE
Buffalo, NY 14208-1098

COLGATE UNIVERSITY
Hamilton, NY 13346-1304

COLUMBIA UNIV.-BARNARD
COLLEGE
New York, NY 10027

CORNELL UNIVERSITY
Ithaca, NY 14853

DELAWARE STATE UNIVERSITY
Dover, DE 19901

UNIVERSITY OF DELAWARE
Newark, DE 19716

DREXEL UNIVERSITY
Philadelphia, PA 19104

DUQUESNE UNIVERSITY
Pittsburgh, PA 15282

FAIRLEIGH DICKINSON-TEANECK
Teaneck, NJ 07666

FORDHAM UNIVERSITY
Bronx, NY 10458-5155

GEORGE MASON UNIVERSITY
Fairfax, VA 22030

GEORGE WASHINGTON
UNIVERSITY
Washington, DC 20052

GEORGETOWN UNIVERSITY
Washington, DC 20057

HAMPTON UNIVERSITY
Hampton, VA 23668

HOFSTRA UNIVERSITY
Hempstead, NY 11550

HOWARD UNIVERSITY
Washington, DC 20059

IONA COLLEGE
New Rochelle, NY 10801

JAMES MADISON UNIVERSITY
Harrisonburg, VA 22807

LA SALLE UNIVERSITY
Philadelphia, PA 19141-1199

LAFAYETTE COLLEGE
Easton, PA 18042

LEHIGH UNIVERSITY
Bethlehem, PA 18015-3089

LONG ISLAND UNIV.-BROOKLYN
Brooklyn, NY 11201

LOYOLA COLLEGE
Baltimore, MD 21210

MANHATTAN COLLEGE
Riverdale, NY 10471

MARIST COLLEGE
Poughkeepsie, NY 12601-1387

UNIV. OF MARYLAND-BALT. CO.
Baltimore, MD 21228-5398

U. OF MARYLAND-EASTERN
SHORE
Princess Anne, MD 21853-1299

MONMOUTH UNIVERSITY
West Long Branch, NJ 07764

MORGAN STATE UNIVERSITY
Baltimore, MD 21239

MOUNT ST. MARY'S COLLEGE
Emmitsburg, MD 21727-7799

NIAGARA UNIVERSITY
Niagara University, NY 14109

PENNSYLVANIA STATE UNIV.
University Park, PA 16802

UNIVERSITY OF PENNSYLVANIA
Philadelphia, PA 19104-6380

UNIVERSITY OF PITTSBURGH
Pittsburgh, PA 15260

PRINCETON UNIVERSITY
Princeton, NJ 08544

RIDER UNIVERSITY
Lawrenceville, NJ 08648-3099

ROBERT MORRIS COLLEGE
Coraopolis, PA 15108-1189

RUTGERS UNIVERSITY
New Brunswick, NJ 08903

SETON HALL UNIVERSITY
South Orange, NJ 07079

SIENA COLLEGE
Loudonville, NY 12211-1462

ST. BONAVENTURE UNIVERSITY
St. Bonaventure, NY 14778

ST. FRANCIS COLLEGE
Brooklyn Heights, NY 11201

ST. FRANCIS COLLEGE
Loretto, PA 15940-0600

ST. JOHN'S UNIVERSITY
Jamaica, NY 11439

ST. JOSEPH'S UNIVERSITY
Philadelphia, PA 19131-1395

ST. PETER'S COLLEGE
Jersey City, NJ 07306

SYRACUSE UNIVERSITY
Syracuse, NY 13244

TOWSON STATE UNIVERSITY
Towson, MD 21204

U.S. MILITARY ACADEMY
West Point, NY 10996

U.S. NAVAL ACADEMY
Annapolis, MD 21402

VILLANOVA UNIVERSITY
Villanova, PA 19085

WAGNER COLLEGE
Staten Island, NY 10301-4495

WEST VIRGINIA UNIVERSITY
Morgantown, WV 26506-6201

COLLEGE OF WILLIAM & MARY
Williamsburg, VA 23187

District 3

ALABAMA STATE UNIVERSITY
Montgomery, AL 36101-0271

UNIV. OF ALABAMA at
TUSCALOOSA
Tuscaloosa, AL 35487

UNIV. OF ALABAMA at
BIRMINGHAM
Birmingham, AL 35294-0110

APPALACHIAN STATE UNIVERSITY
Boone, NC 28608

AUBURN UNIVERSITY
Auburn University, AL 36849-5113

AUSTIN PEAY STATE UNIVERSITY
Clarksville, TN 37044-4576

BETHUNE-COOKMAN COLLEGE
Daytona Beach, FL 32114-3099

CAMPBELL UNIVERSITY
Buies Creek, NC 27506

UNIVERSITY OF CENTRAL
FLORIDA
Orlando, FL 32816-0002

CHARLESTON SOUTHERN UNIV.
Charleston, SC 29423-8087

COLLEGE OF CHARLESTON
Charleston, SC 29424

THE CITADEL
Charleston, SC 29409

CLEMSON UNIVERSITY
Clemson, SC 29632

COASTAL CAROLINA UNIVERSITY
Conway, SC 29526

COPPIN STATE COLLEGE
Baltimore, MD 21216

DAVIDSON COLLEGE
Davidson, NC 28036

DUKE UNIVERSITY
Durham, NC 27708-0555

EAST CAROLINA UNIVERSITY
Greenville, NC 27858-4353

EAST TENNESSEE STATE UNIV.
Johnson City, TN 37614

EASTERN KENTUCKY UNIVERSITY
Richmond, KY 40475-3101

FLORIDA A&M UNIVERSITY
Tallahassee, FL 32307

FLORIDA ATLANTIC UNIVERSITY
Boca Raton, FL 33431-0991

FLORIDA INTERNATIONAL UNIV.
Miami, FL 33199

FLORIDA STATE UNIVERSITY
Tallahassee, FL 32306

UNIVERSITY OF FLORIDA
Gainesville, FL 32604

FURMAN UNIVERSITY
Greenville, SC 29613

GEORGIA INSTITUTE OF TECH.
Atlanta, GA 30332

GEORGIA SOUTHERN UNIVERSITY
Statesboro, GA 30460-8033

GEORGIA STATE UNIVERSITY
Atlanta, GA 30303-3083

UNIVERSITY OF GEORGIA
Athens, GA 30613

JACKSONVILLE STATE
UNIVERSITY
Jacksonville, AL 36265-9982

JACKSONVILLE UNIVERSITY
Jacksonville, FL 32211-3394

UNIVERSITY OF KENTUCKY
Lexington, KY 40506-0032

LIBERTY UNIVERSITY
Lynchburg, VA 24506

LOUISIANA STATE UNIVERSITY
Baton Rouge, LA 70803

UNIVERSITY OF LOUISVILLE
Louisville, KY 40292

MARSHALL UNIVERSITY
Huntington, WV 25755

UNIVERSITY OF MARYLAND
College Park, MD 20740

UNIVERSITY OF MEMPHIS
Memphis, TN 38152

MERCER UNIVERSITY
Macon, GA 31207

UNIVERSITY OF MIAMI
Coral Gables, FL 33124-6710

MIDDLE TENNESSEE STATE UNIV.
Murfreesboro, TN 37132

MISSISSIPPI STATE UNIVERSITY
Mississippi State, MS 39762-5509

UNIVERSITY OF MISSISSIPPI
University, MS 38677

MOREHEAD STATE UNIVERSITY
Morehead, KY 40351-1689

MURRAY STATE UNIVERSITY
Murray, KY 42071-0009

UNIVERSITY OF NEW ORLEANS
New Orleans, LA 70148

UNIVERSITY OF NORTH
CAROLINA
Asheville, NC 28804-3299

UNIVERSITY OF NORTH
CAROLINA
Chapel Hill, NC 27514

UNIVERSITY OF NORTH
CAROLINA
Charlotte, NC 28223

UNIVERSITY OF NORTH
CAROLINA
Greensboro, NC 27412-5001

UNIVERSITY OF NORTH
CAROLINA
Wilmington, NC 28403-3297

NORTH CAROLINA A&T ST. UNIV.
Greensboro, NC 27411

NORTH CAROLINA STATE UNIV.
Raleigh, NC 27695-7001

RADFORD UNIVERSITY
Radford, VA 24142

UNIVERSITY OF RICHMOND
Richmond, VA 23173-1903

SAMFORD UNIVERSITY
Birmingham, AL 35229

UNIVERSITY OF SOUTH ALABAMA
Mobile, AL 36688

SOUTH CAROLINA STATE UNIV.
Orangeburg, SC 29117-0001

UNIVERSITY OF SOUTH CAROLINA
Columbia, SC 29208

UNIVERSITY OF SOUTH FLORIDA
Tampa, FL 33620

SOUTHEASTERN LOUISIANA UNIV.
Hammond, LA 70402

UNIV. OF SOUTHERN MISSISSIPPI
Hattiesburg, MS 39406-5001

STETSON UNIVERSITY
De Land, FL 32720

TENNESSEE STATE UNIVERSITY
Nashville, TN 37209-1561

TENNESSEE TECHNOLOGICAL
UNIV.
Cookeville, TN 38505-0001

UNIVERSITY OF TENNESSEE
Chattanooga, TN 37403-2598

THE UNIVERSITY OF TENNESSEE
Knoxville, TN 37996

UNIV. OF TENNESSEE at MARTIN
Martin, TN 38238-5021

TROY STATE UNIVERSITY
Troy, AL 36082

TULANE UNIVERSITY
New Orleans, LA 70118

VANDERBILT UNIVERSITY
Nashville, TN 37212

VIRGINIA COMMONWEALTH UNIV.
Richmond, VA 23284-2003

VIRGINIA MILITARY INSTITUTE
Lexington, VA 24450-0304

VIRGINIA POLYTECHNIC
INSTITUTE
Blacksburg, VA 24061

UNIVERSITY OF VIRGINIA
Charlottesville, VA 22903

WAKE FOREST UNIVERSITY
Winston-Salem, NC 27109

WESTERN CAROLINA UNIVERSITY
Cullowhee, NC 28723

WESTERN KENTUCKY
UNIVERSITY
Bowling Green, KY 42101-3576

WINTHROP UNIVERSITY
Rock Hill, SC 29733

WOFFORD COLLEGE
Spartanburg, SC 29303-3663

District 4

UNIVERSITY OF AKRON
Akron, OH 44325

BALL STATE UNIVERSITY
Muncie, IN 47306

BOWLING GREEN STATE UNIV.
Bowling Green, OH 43403

BUTLER UNIVERSITY
Indianapolis, IN 46208

CENTRAL MICHIGAN UNIVERSITY
Mount Pleasant, MI 48859

CHICAGO STATE UNIVERSITY
Chicago, IL 60628-1598

UNIVERSITY OF CINCINNATI
Cincinnati, OH 45221

UNIVERSITY OF DAYTON
Dayton, OH 45469

DE PAUL UNIVERSITY
Chicago, IL 60604-2287

UNIVERSITY OF DETROIT-MERCY
Detroit, MI 48219-0900

EASTERN ILLINOIS UNIVERSITY
Charleston, IL 61920-3099

EASTERN MICHIGAN UNIVERSITY
Ypsilanti, MI 48197

UNIVERSITY OF EVANSVILLE
Evansville, IN 47722

ILLINOIS STATE UNIVERSITY
Normal, IL 61761

UNIVERSITY OF ILLINOIS
Champaign, IL 61820

UNIVERSITY OF ILLINOIS
Chicago, IL 60607

INDIANA UNIVERSITY
Bloomington, IN 47405

UNIVERSITY OF IOWA
Iowa City, IA 52242

KENT STATE UNIVERSITY
Kent, OH 44242

LOYOLA UNIVERSITY
Chicago, IL 60626

MARQUETTE UNIVERSITY
Milwaukee, WI 53201-1881

MIAMI UNIVERSITY
Oxford, OH 45056

MICHIGAN STATE UNIVERSITY
East Lansing, MI 48824

UNIVERSITY OF MICHIGAN
Ann Arbor, MI 48109-2201

UNIV. OF MINNESOTA-TWIN
CITIES
Minneapolis, MN 55455

NORTHEASTERN ILLINOIS UNIV.
Chicago, IL 60625-4699

UNIVERSITY OF NOTRE DAME
Notre Dame, IN 46556

OHIO STATE UNIVERSITY
Columbus, OH 43210

OHIO UNIVERSITY
Athens, OH 45701

PURDUE UNIVERSITY
West Lafayette, IN 47907

UNIVERSITY OF TOLEDO
Toledo, OH 43606

VALPARAISO UNIVERSITY
Valparaiso, IN 46383-6493

WESTERN ILLINOIS UNIVERSITY
Macomb, IL 61455

WESTERN MICHIGAN UNIVERSITY
Kalamazoo, MI 49008-5134

UNIVERSITY OF WISCONSIN
Green Bay, WI 54311-7001

UNIVERSITY OF WISCONSIN
Madison, WI 53711

UNIVERSITY OF WISCONSIN
Milwaukee, WI 53201

WRIGHT STATE UNIVERSITY
Dayton, OH 45435-0001

XAVIER UNIVERSITY
Cincinnati, OH 45207-6114

YOUNGSTOWN STATE
UNIVERSITY
Youngstown, OH 44555-0001

District 5

BRADLEY UNIVERSITY
Peoria, IL 61625

UNIVERSITY OF COLORADO
Boulder, CO 80309

CREIGHTON UNIVERSITY
Omaha, NE 68178-0001

DRAKE UNIVERSITY
Des Moines, IA 50311-4505

INDIANA STATE UNIVERSITY
Terre Haute, IN 47809

IOWA STATE UNIVERSITY
Ames, IA 50011

KANSAS STATE UNIVERSITY
Manhattan, KS 66506

UNIVERSITY OF KANSAS
Lawrence, KS 66045

UNIV. OF MISSOURI-COLUMBIA
Columbia, MO 65211

UNIV. OF MISSOURI-KANSAS CITY
Kansas City, MO 64110

UNIVERSITY OF NEBRASKA
Lincoln, NE 68588

UNIVERSITY OF NORTHERN IOWA
Cedar Falls, IA 50614

OKLAHOMA STATE UNIVERSITY
Stillwater, OK 74078

UNIVERSITY OF OKLAHOMA
Norman, OK 73019

ORAL ROBERTS UNIVERSITY
Tulsa, OK 74171

SOUTHEAST MISSOURI STATE
UNIV.
Cape Girardeau, MO 63701-4799

SOUTHERN ILLINOIS UNIVERSITY
Carbondale, IL 62901

SOUTHWEST MISSOURI STATE
UNIV.
Springfield, MO 65804

ST. LOUIS UNIVERSITY
St. Louis, MO 63108

UNIVERSITY OF TULSA
Tulsa, OK 74104

WICHITA STATE UNIVERSITY
Wichita, KS 67260

District 6 .

ALCORN STATE UNIVERSITY
Lorman, MS 39096-9402

ARKANSAS STATE UNIVERSITY
State University, AR 72467

UNIVERSITY OF ARKANSAS
Fayetteville, AR 72701

UNIVERSITY OF ARKANSAS
Little Rock, AR 72204-1099

BAYLOR UNIVERSITY
Waco, TX 76798

CENTENARY COLLEGE
Shreveport, LA 71134-1188

GRAMBLING STATE UNIVERSITY
Grambling, LA 71245

UNIVERSITY OF HOUSTON
Houston, TX 77204

JACKSON STATE UNIVERSITY
Jackson, MS 39217

LAMAR UNIVERSITY
Beaumont, TX 77710

LOUISIANA TECH UNIVERSITY
Ruston, LA 71272

MCNESSE STATE UNIVERSITY
Lake Charles, LA 70609

MISSISSIPPI VALLEY ST. UNIV.
Itta Bena, MS 38941-1400

NICHOLLS STATE UNIVERSITY
Thibodaux, LA 70310

UNIVERSITY OF NORTH TEXAS
Denton, TX 76203-6737

NORTHEAST LOUISIANA
UNIVERSITY
Monroe, LA 71209-3000

NORTHWESTERN STATE
UNIVERSITY
Natchitoches, LA 71497-0003

PRAIRIE VIEW A&M UNIVERSITY
Prairie View, TX 77446

RICE UNIVERSITY
Houston, TX 77251

SAM HOUSTON STATE
UNIVERSITY
Huntsville, TX 77341

SOUTHERN METHODIST
UNIVERSITY
Dallas, TX 75275

SOUTHERN UNIVERSITY
Baton Rouge, LA 70813

SOUTHWEST TEXAS STATE UNIV.
San Marcos, TX 78666-4615

UNIV. OF SOUTHWESTERN LA.
Lafayette, LA 70504-1008

STEPHEN F. AUSTIN STATE UNIV.
Nacogdoches, TX 75962

UNIVERSITY OF TEXAS
Arlington, TX 76019

UNIVERSITY OF TEXAS
Austin, TX 78712

UNIVERSITY OF TEXAS
San Antonio, TX 78249

TEXAS A&M UNIVERSITY
College Station, TX 77843-1228

TEXAS CHRISTIAN UNIVERSITY
Fort Worth, TX 76129-0001

UNIV. OF TEXAS-PAN AMERICAN
Edinburg, TX 78539-2999

TEXAS SOUTHERN UNIVERSITY
Houston, TX 77004

TEXAS TECH UNIVERSITY
Lubbock, TX 79409

District 7

BOISE STATE UNIVERSITY
Boise, ID 83725

BRIGHAM YOUNG UNIVERSITY
Provo, UT 84602

CALIF. STATE UNIV.-FRESNO
Fresno, CA 93740-0048

COLORADO STATE UNIVERSITY
Fort Collins, CO 80523-0100

GONZAGA UNIVERSITY
Spokane, WA 99258

IDAHO STATE UNIVERSITY
Pocatello, ID 83209

UNIVERSITY OF IDAHO
Moscow, ID 83843

MONTANA STATE UNIV-BOZEMAN
Bozeman, MT 59717-0338

THE UNIVERSITY OF MONTANA
Missoula, MT 59812-1291

UNIVERSITY OF NEW MEXICO
Albuquerque, NM 87131

NORTHERN ARIZONA UNIVERSITY
Flagstaff, AZ 86011

SOUTHERN UTAH UNIVERSITY
Cedar City, UT 84720

UNIVERSITY OF TEXAS-EL PASO
El Paso, TX 79968

U.S. AIR FORCE ACADEMY
USAF Academy, CO 80840-5461

UNIVERSITY OF UTAH
Salt Lake City, UT 84112

WEBER STATE UNIVERSITY
Ogden, UT 84408-2701

UNIVERSITY OF WYOMING
Laramie, WY 82071

District 8

ARIZONA STATE UNIVERSITY
Tempe, AZ 85287-2505

UNIVERSITY OF ARIZONA
Tucson, AZ 85721

UNIV. OF CALIFORNIA-BERKELEY
Berkeley, CA 94720

UNIV. OF CALIF.-LOS ANGELES
Los Angeles, CA 90095-1405

UNIV. OF CALIF-SANTA BARBARA
Santa Barbara, CA 93106

UNIV. OF CALIFORNIA-IRVINE
Irvine, CA 92717

CALIF. POLYTECHNIC STATE UNIV.
San Luis Obispo, CA 93407

CALIF. STATE UNIV.-FULLERTON
Fullerton, CA 92634-9480

CALIF. STATE UNIV.-NORTHRIDGE
Northridge, CA 91330

CALIF. STATE UNIV.-SACRAMENTO
Sacramento, CA 95819

EASTERN WASHINGTON
UNIVERSITY
Cheney, WA 99004

LONG BEACH STATE UNIVERSITY
Long Beach, CA 90840-0118

LOYOLA MARYMOUNT
UNIVERSITY
Los Angeles, CA 90045-2699

NEW MEXICO STATE UNIVERSITY
Las Cruces, NM 88003

UNIVERSITY OF OREGON
Eugene, OR 97403-1226

PEPPERDINE UNIVERSITY
Malibu, CA 90263

UNIVERSITY OF PORTLAND
Portland, OR 97203-5798

UNIVERSITY OF SAN DIEGO
San Diego, CA 92110-2492

UNIVERSITY OF SAN FRANCISCO
San Francisco, CA 94117-1080

SANTA CLARA UNIVERSITY
Santa Clara, CA 95053

ST. MARY'S COLLEGE
Moraga, CA 94556

STANFORD UNIVERSITY
Stanford, CA 94305

UTAH STATE UNIVERSITY
Logan, UT 84322-7400

WASHINGTON STATE UNIVERSITY
Pullman, WA 99164

UNIVERSITY OF WASHINGTON
Seattle, WA 98195

DIVISION II
District 1
ASSUMPTION COLLEGE
Worcester, MA 01615-0005

BENTLEY COLLEGE
Waltham, MA 02154-4705

UNIVERSITY OF BRIDGEPORT
Bridgeport, CT 06601

BRYANT COLLEGE
Smithfield, RI 02917-1284

KEENE STATE COLLEGE
Keene, NH 03431-4183

UNIV. OF MASSACHUSETTS-
LOWELL
Lowell, MA 01854

MERRIMACK COLLEGE
North Andover, MA 01845

UNIVERSITY OF NEW HAVEN
West Haven, CT 06516-1999

QUINNIPIAC COLLEGE
Hamden, CT 06518-1940

SACRED HEART UNIVERSITY
Fairfield, CT 06432-1000

SOUTHERN CONNECTICUT ST.
UNIV.
New Haven, CT 06515

ST. ANSELM COLLEGE
Manchester, NH 03102-1310

ST. MICHAEL'S COLLEGE
Colchester, VT 05439

STONEHILL COLLEGE
North Easton, MA 02357

District 2
STATE UNIV. OF N.Y. at ALBANY
Albany, NY 12222

ALDERSON-BROADDUS COLLEGE
Philippi, WV 26416

AMERICAN UNIV. OF PUERTO RICO
Bayamon, PR 00960-2037

BLOOMSBURG UNIVERSITY
Bloomsburg, PA 17815

BLUEFIELD STATE COLLEGE
Bluefield, WV 24701-2198

CALIFORNIA UNIVERSITY
California, PA 15419

CHEYNEY UNIVERSITY
Cheyney, PA 19319

CLARION UNIVERSITY
Clarion, PA 16214

CONCORD COLLEGE
Athens, WV 24712

CONCORDIA COLLEGE
Bronxville, NY 10708

DAVIS AND ELKINS COLLEGE
Elkins, WV 26241

UNIV. OF DISTRICT OF COLUMBIA
Washington, DC 20008

EAST STROUDSBURG UNIVERSITY
East Stroudsburg, PA 18301

EDINBORO UNIVERSITY
Edinboro, PA 16444-0001

FAIRMONT STATE COLLEGE
Fairmont, WV 26554

GANNON UNIVERSITY
Erie, PA 16541

GLENVILLE STATE COLLEGE
Glenville, WV 26351

INDIANA UNIV. OF PENNSYLVANIA
Indiana, PA 15705

KUTZTOWN UNIVERSITY
Kutztown, PA 19530-0721

LE MOYNE COLLEGE
Syracuse, NY 13214-1399

LOCK HAVEN UNIVERSITY
Lock Haven, PA 17745

LONG ISLAND U./C.W. POST
CAMPUS
Brookville, NY 11548

MANSFIELD UNIVERSITY
Mansfield, PA 16933

MERCY COLLEGE
Dobbs Ferry, NY 10522

MERCYHURST COLLEGE
Erie, PA 16546

MILLERSVILLE UNIVERSITY
Millersville, PA 17551-0302

MOLLOY COLLEGE
Rockville Centre, NY 11570

NEW YORK INSTITUTE OF TECH.
Old Westbury, NY 11568-8000

PACE UNIVERSITY
New York, NY 10038-1502

QUEENS COLLEGE (NY)
Flushing, NY 11367

SHEPHERD COLLEGE
Shepherdstown, WV 25443

SHIPPENSBURG UNIVERSITY
Shippensburg, PA 17257

SLIPPERY ROCK UNIVERSITY
Slippery Rock, PA 16057

THE COLLEGE OF ST. ROSE
Albany, NY 12203

STATE UNIV. OF N.Y. at STONY
BROOK
Stony Brook, NY 11794

WEST CHESTER UNIVERSITY
West Chester, PA 19383

WEST LIBERTY STATE COLLEGE
West Liberty, WV 26074

WEST VIRGINIA WESLEYAN
COLLEGE
Buckhannon, WV 26201

WHEELING JESUIT COLLEGE
Wheeling, WV 26003-6295

District 3

ALABAMA A&M UNIVERSITY
Normal, AL 35762

UNIV. OF ALABAMA-HUNTSVILLE
Huntsville, AL 35899

ALBANY STATE COLLEGE
Albany, GA 31705

ARMSTRONG STATE COLLEGE
Savannah, GA 31419-1997

AUGUSTA COLLEGE
Augusta, GA 30910

BELLARMINE COLLEGE
Louisville, KY 40205-0671

BELMONT ABBEY COLLEGE
Belmont, NC 28012-2795

BOWIE STATE UNIVERSITY
Bowie, MD 20715-9465

CARSON-NEWMAN COLLEGE
Jefferson City, TN 37760

CATAWBA COLLEGE
Salisbury, NC 28144-2488

COLUMBUS COLLEGE
Columbus, GA 31907-2079

ELIZABETH CITY STATE UNIV.
Elizabeth City, NC 27909

ELON COLLEGE
Elon College, NC 27244

ERSKINE COLLEGE
Due West, SC 29639

FAYETTEVILLE STATE
UNIVERSITY
Fayetteville, NC 28301-4298

FLORIDA INSTITUTE OF TECH.
Melbourne, FL 32901

FLORIDA SOUTHERN COLLEGE
Lakeland, FL 33801-5698

FRANCIS MARION UNIVERSITY
Florence, SC 29501-0547

GARDNER-WEBB UNIVERSITY
Boiling Springs, NC 28017

GEORGIA COLLEGE
Milledgeville, GA 31061

HIGH POINT UNIVERSITY
High Point, NC 27262-3598

JOHNSON C. SMITH UNIVERSITY
Charlotte, NC 28216

KENNESAW STATE COLLEGE
Marietta, GA 30061

KENTUCKY STATE UNIVERSITY
Frankfort, KY 40601

LANDER UNIVERSITY
Greenwood, SC 29649-2099

LANE COLLEGE
Jackson, TN 38301

LE MOYNE-OWEN COLLEGE
Memphis, TN 38126

LEES-MCRAE COLLEGE
Banner Elk, NC 28604-0128

LENOIR-RHYNE COLLEGE
Hickory, NC 28603

LINCOLN MEMORIAL UNIVERSITY
Harrogate, TN 37752

LIVINGSTONE COLLEGE
Salisbury, NC 28144

MARS HILL COLLEGE
Mars Hill, NC 28754

MILES COLLEGE
Birmingham, AL 35208

MISSISSIPPI COLLEGE
Clinton, MS 39058

MOREHOUSE COLLEGE
Atlanta, GA 30314

MORRIS BROWN COLLEGE
Atlanta, GA 30314

MOUNT OLIVE COLLEGE
Mount Olive, NC 28365

NORFOLK STATE UNIVERSITY
Norfolk, VA 23504

UNIVERSITY OF NORTH ALABAMA
Florence, AL 35632

NORTH CAROLINA CENTRAL
UNIV.
Durham, NC 27707

UNIVERSITY OF NORTH FLORIDA
Jacksonville, FL 32224-2645

NORTHERN KENTUCKY
UNIVERSITY
Highland Heights, KY 41099

PAINE COLLEGE
Augusta, GA 30901-3182

PEMBROKE STATE UNIVERSITY
Pembroke, NC 28372-1510

PFEIFFER COLLEGE
Misenheimer, NC 28109-0960

ROLLINS COLLEGE
Winter Park, FL 32789

SHAW UNIVERSITY
Raleigh, NC 27611

UNIV. OF SOUTH CAROLINA-
AIKEN
Aiken, SC 29801

U. OF SO. CAROLINA-
SPARTANBURG
Spartanburg, SC 29303

ST. ANDREWS PRESBYTERIAN
COLL.
Laurinburg, NC 28352-5598

ST. AUGUSTINE'S COLLEGE
Raleigh, NC 27610

ST. PAUL'S COLLEGE
Lawrenceville, VA 23868

UNIVERSITY OF TAMPA
Tampa, FL 33606-1490

VALDOSTA STATE UNIVERSITY
Valdosta, GA 31698

VIRGINIA STATE UNIVERSITY
Petersburg, VA 23806

VIRGINIA UNION UNIVERSITY
Richmond, VA 23220-1790

UNIVERSITY OF WEST FLORIDA
Pensacola, FL 32514

WEST GEORGIA COLLEGE
Carrollton, GA 30118

WINGATE UNIVERSITY
Wingate, NC 28174

WINSTON-SALEM STATE UNIV.
Winston-Salem, NC 27110

District 4

ASHLAND UNIVERSITY
Ashland, OH 44805

GRAND VALLEY STATE
UNIVERSITY
Allendale, MI 49401

HILLSDALE COLLEGE
Hillsdale, MI 49242-1298

INDIANA UNIV.-PURDUE UNIV.
Fort Wayne, IN 46805-1499

UNIVERSITY OF INDIANAPOLIS
Indianapolis, IN 46227

LAKE SUPERIOR STATE UNIV.
Sault Sainte Marie, MI 49783

LEWIS UNIVERSITY
Romeoville, IL 60441

MICHIGAN TECHNOLOGICAL
UNIV.
Houghton, MI 49931-1295

UNIV. OF MINNESOTA-DULUTH
Duluth, MN 55812

MOORHEAD STATE UNIVERSITY
Moorhead, MN 56563-2996

NORTHERN MICHIGAN UNIVERSITY
Marquette, MI 49855-5391

NORTHWOOD UNIVERSITY
Midland, MI 48640

OAKLAND CITY COLLEGE
Oakland City, IN 47660-1099

OAKLAND UNIVERSITY
Rochestser, MI 48309-4401

QUINCY UNIVERSITY
Quincy, IL 62301-2699

SAGINAW VALLEY STATE UNIV.
University Center, MI 48710

SOUTHERN ILLINOIS UNIVERSITY
Edwardsville, IL 62026

UNIV. OF SOUTHERN INDIANA
Evansville, IN 47712

SAINT JOSEPH'S COLLEGE
Rensselaer, IN 47978

WAYNE STATE UNIVERSITY
Detroit, MI 48202

UNIV. OF WISCONSIN-PARKSIDE
Kenosha, WI 53141-2000

District 5

AUGUSTANA COLLEGE
Sioux Falls, SD 57197

CENTRAL MISSOURI STATE UNIV.
Warrensburg, MO 64093

EMPORIA STATE UNIVERSITY
Emporia, KS 66801-5087

MANKATO STATE UNIVERSITY
Mankato, MN 56002-8400

MISSOURI SOUTHERN ST. COLLEGE
Joplin, MO 64801-1595

UNIVERSITY OF MISSOURI
Rolla, MO 65401

MORNINGSIDE COLLEGE
Sioux City, IA 51106-1751

UNIV. OF NEBRASKA at KEARNEY
Kearney, NE 68849

NORTH DAKOTA STATE UNIVERSITY
Fargo, ND 58105

UNIVERSITY OF NORTH DAKOTA
Grand Forks, ND 58202

NORTHEAST MISSOURI STATE UNIV.
Kirksville, MO 63501

NORTHERN STATE UNIVERSITY
Aberdeen, SD 57401

NORTHWEST MISSOURI STATE UNIV.
Maryville, MO 64468-6001

PITTSBURG STATE UNIVERSITY
Pittsburg, KS 66762

SOUTH DAKOTA STATE UNIVERSITY
Brookings, SD 57007

UNIVERSITY OF SOUTH DAKOTA
Vermillion, SD 57069-2390

SOUTHWEST BAPTIST UNIVERSITY
Bolivar, MO 65613

ST. CLOUD STATE UNIVERSITY
St. Cloud, MN 56301-4498

WAYNE STATE COLLEGE
Wayne, NE 68787-1172

District 6

ABILENE CHRISTIAN UNIVERSITY
Abilene, TX 79699

ANGELO STATE UNIVERSITY
San Angelo, TX 76909

UNIVERSITY OF CENTRAL OKLAHOMA
Edmond, OK 73034

EAST TEXAS STATE UNIVERSITY
Commerce, TX 75429-3011

TARLETON STATE UNIVERSITY
Stephenville, TX 76402

TEXAS A&M UNIV.-KINGSVILLE
Kingsville, TX 78363

WEST TEXAS A&M UNIVERSITY
Canyon, TX 79016-0999

District 7

ADAMS STATE COLLEGE
Alamosa, CO 81102

COLORADO CHRISTIAN UNIVERSITY
Lakewood, CO 80226

COLORADO SCHOOL OF MINES
Golden, CO 80401

FORT HAYS STATE UNIVERSITY
Hays, KS 67601

FORT LEWIS COLLEGE
Durango, CO 81301-3999

GRAND CANYON UNIVERSITY
Phoenix, AZ 85017

MONTANA STATE UNIVERSITY
Billings, MT 59101-0298

NEW MEXICO HIGHLANDS UNIV.
Las Vegas, NM 87701

WESTERN STATE COLLEGE
Gunnison, CO 81231

District 8

UNIVERSITY OF ALASKA-ANCHORAGE
Anchorage, AK 99508

UNIVERSITY OF ALASKA-FAIRBANKS
Fairbanks, AK 99775-7500

UNIV. OF CALIFORNIA-DAVIS
Davis, CA 95616

UNIV. OF CALIFORNIA-RIVERSIDE
Riverside, CA 92521

CALIF. STATE POLYTECHNIC UNIV.
Pomona, CA 91768

CALIF. STATE UNIV.-CHICO
Chico, CA 95929-0300

CALIF. STATE UNIV.-HAYWARD
Hayward, CA 94542

CALIF. STATE UNIV.-LOS ANGELES
Los Angeles, CA 90032-8240

CALIF. STATE UNIV.-STANISLAUS
Turlock, CA 95382

CHAMINADE UNIVERSITY
Honolulu, HI 96816

UNIVERSITY OF HAWAII-HILO
Hilo, HI 96720-4091

HUMBOLDT STATE UNIVERSITY
Arcata, CA 95521

COLLEGE OF NOTRE DAME
Belmont, CA 94002-9974

PORTLAND STATE UNIVERSITY
Portland, OR 97207-0751

SAN FRANCISCO STATE UNIVERSITY
San Francisco, CA 94132

SEATTLE PACIFIC UNIVERSITY
Seattle, WA 98119

**NCAA PROVISIONAL MEMBERS
DIVISON II**

District 2

UNIV. OF PUERTO RICO-MAYAGUEZ
Mayaguez, PR 00709

UNIV. OF PUERTO RICO-BAYAMON
Bayamon, PR 00619-1919

WESTMINSTER COLLEGE
New Wilmington, PA 16172

District 3

CHRISTIAN BROTHERS UNIVERSITY
Memphis, TN 38104

COLUMBIA UNION COLLEGE
Takoma Park, MD 20912

GEORGIA SOUTHWESTERN COLLEGE
Americus, GA 31709-4693

LAMBUTH UNIVERSITY
Jackson, TN 38301

TUSCULUM COLLEGE
Greeneville, TN 37743

District 5

OKLAHOMA PANHANDLE ST. UNIV.
Goodwell, OK 73939

UNIV. OF SCIENCE & ARTS
Chickasha, OK 73018

District 6

HARDING UNIVERSITY
Searcy, AR 72149-0001

INCARNATE WORD COLLEGE
San Antonio, TX 78209

LYON COLLEGE
Batesville, AR 72503-2317

UNIV. OF MARY HARDIN-BAYLOR
Belton, TX 76513

OUACHITA BAPTIST UNIVERSITY
Arkadelphia, AR 71998-0001

SOUTHERN ARKANSAS UNIVERSITY
Magnolia, AR 71753-5000

District 8

CENTRAL WASHINGTON UNIV.
Ellensburg, WA 98926

HAWAII PACIFIC UNIVERSITY
Honolulu, HI 96813

WESTERN WASHINGTON UNIV.
Bellingham, WA 98225

WOMEN'S CROSS COUNTRY

DIVISION I

District 1

BOSTON COLLEGE
Chestnut Hill, MA 02167-3934

BOSTON UNIVERSITY
Boston, MA 02215

BROWN UNIVERSITY
Providence, RI 02912

CENTRAL CONN. STATE UNIV.
New Britain, CT 06050-4010

UNIVERSITY OF CONNECTICUT
Storrs, CT 06269

DARTMOUTH COLLEGE
Hanover, NH 03755

FAIRFIELD UNIVERSITY
Fairfield, CT 06430-5195

UNIVERSITY OF HARTFORD
West Hartford, CT 06117-1599

HARVARD UNIVERSITY
Cambridge, MA 02138-3800

COLLEGE OF THE HOLY CROSS
Worcester, MA 01610-2395

UNIVERSITY OF MAINE
Orono, ME 04469

UNIV. OF MASSACHUSETTS-
AMHERST
Amherst, MA 01003

UNIVERSITY OF NEW HAMPSHIRE
Durham, NH 03824

NORTHEASTERN UNIVERSITY
Boston, MA 02115-5096

PROVIDENCE COLLEGE
Providence, RI 02918

UNIVERSITY OF RHODE ISLAND
Kingston, RI 02881

UNIVERSITY OF VERMONT
Burlington, VT 05405

YALE UNIVERSITY
New Haven, CT 06520-7398

District 2

AMERICAN UNIVERSITY
Washington, DC 20016

BUCKNELL UNIVERSITY
Lewisburg, PA 17837

STATE UNIV. OF N.Y. at BUFFALO
Buffalo, NY 14260

CANISIUS COLLEGE
Buffalo, NY 14208-1098

COLGATE UNIVERSITY
Hamilton, NY 13346-1304

COLUMBIA UNIV.-BARNARD
COLLEGE
New York, NY 10027

CORNELL UNIVERSITY
Ithaca, NY 14853

DELAWARE STATE UNIVERSITY
Dover, DE 19901

UNIVERSITY OF DELAWARE
Newark, DE 19716

DREXEL UNIVERSITY
Philadelphia, PA 19104

DUQUESNE UNIVERSITY
Pittsburgh, PA 15282

FAIRLEIGH DICKINSON-TEANECK
Teaneck, NJ 07666

FORDHAM UNIVERSITY
Bronx, NY 10458-5155

GEORGE MASON UNIVERSITY
Fairfax, VA 22030

GEORGE WASHINGTON
UNIVERSITY
Washington, DC 20052

GEORGETOWN UNIVERSITY
Washington, DC 20057

HAMPTON UNIVERSITY
Hampton, VA 23668

HOFSTRA UNIVERSITY
Hempstead, NY 11550

HOWARD UNIVERSITY
Washington, DC 20059

IONA COLLEGE
New Rochelle, NY 10801

JAMES MADISON UNIVERSITY
Harrisonburg, VA 22807

LA SALLE UNIVERSITY
Philadelphia, PA 19141-1199

LAFAYETTE COLLEGE
Easton, PA 18042

LEHIGH UNIVERSITY
Bethlehem, PA 18015-3089

LONG ISLAND UNIV.-BROOKLYN
Brooklyn, NY 11201

LOYOLA COLLEGE
Baltimore, MD 21210

MANHATTAN COLLEGE
Riverdale, NY 10471

MARIST COLLEGE
Poughkeepsie, NY 12601-1387

UNIV. OF MARYLAND-BALT. CO.
Baltimore, MD 21228-5398

U. OF MARYLAND-EASTERN
SHORE
Princess Anne, MD 21853-1299

MONMOUTH UNIVERSITY
West Long Branch, NJ 07764

MORGAN STATE UNIVERSITY
Baltimore, MD 21239

MOUNT ST. MARY'S COLLEGE
Emmitsburg, MD 21727-7799

NIAGARA UNIVERSITY
Niagara University, NY 14109

PENNSYLVANIA STATE UNIV.
University Park, PA 16802

UNIVERSITY OF PENNSYLVANIA
Philadelphia, PA 19104-6380

UNIVERSITY OF PITTSBURGH
Pittsburgh, PA 15260

PRINCETON UNIVERSITY
Princeton, NJ 08544

RIDER UNIVERSITY
Lawrenceville, NJ 08648-3099

ROBERT MORRIS COLLEGE
Coraopolis, PA 15108-1189

RUTGERS UNIVERSITY
New Brunswick, NJ 08903

SETON HALL UNIVERSITY
South Orange, NJ 07079

SIENA COLLEGE
Loudonville, NY 12211-1462

ST. BONAVENTURE UNIVERSITY
St. Bonaventure, NY 14778

ST. FRANCIS COLLEGE
Brooklyn Heights, NY 11201

ST. FRANCIS COLLEGE
Loretto, PA 15940-0600

ST. JOHN'S UNIVERSITY
Jamaica, NY 11439

ST. JOSEPH'S UNIVERSITY
Philadelphia, PA 19131-1395

ST. PETER'S COLLEGE
Jersey City, NJ 07306

SYRACUSE UNIVERSITY
Syracuse, NY 13244

TOWSON STATE UNIVERSITY
Towson, MD 21204

U.S. MILITARY ACADEMY
West Point, NY 10996

U.S. NAVAL ACADEMY
Annapolis, MD 21402

VILLANOVA UNIVERSITY
Villanova, PA 19085

WAGNER COLLEGE
Staten Island, NY 10301-4495

WEST VIRGINIA UNIVERSITY
Morgantown, WV 26506-6201

COLLEGE OF WILLIAM & MARY
Williamsburg, VA 23187

District 3

ALABAMA STATE UNIVERSITY
Montgomery, AL 36101-0271

UNIV. OF ALABAMA at
TUSCALOOSA
Tuscaloosa, AL 35487

UNIV. OF ALABAMA at
BIRMINGHAM
Birmingham, AL 35294-0110

APPALACHIAN STATE UNIVERSITY
Boone, NC 28608

AUBURN UNIVERSITY
Auburn University, AL 36849-5113

AUSTIN PEAY STATE UNIVERSITY
Clarksville, TN 37044-4576

BETHUNE-COOKMAN COLLEGE
Daytona Beach, FL 32114-3099

CAMPBELL UNIVERSITY
Buies Creek, NC 27506

UNIVERSITY OF CENTRAL
FLORIDA
Orlando, FL 32816-0002

CHARLESTON SOUTHERN UNIV.
Charleston, SC 29423-8087

COLLEGE OF CHARLESTON
Charleston, SC 29424

CLEMSON UNIVERSITY
Clemson, SC 29632

COASTAL CAROLINA UNIVERSITY
Conway, SC 29526

COPPIN STATE COLLEGE
Baltimore, MD 21216

DAVIDSON COLLEGE
Davidson, NC 28036

DUKE UNIVERSITY
Durham, NC 27708-0555

EAST CAROLINA UNIVERSITY
Greenville, NC 27858-4353

EAST TENNESSEE STATE UNIV.
Johnson City, TN 37614

EASTERN KENTUCKY UNIVERSITY
Richmond, KY 40475-3101

FLORIDA A&M UNIVERSITY
Tallahassee, FL 32307

FLORIDA ATLANTIC UNIVERSITY
Boca Raton, FL 33431-0991

FLORIDA INTERNATIONAL UNIV.
Miami, FL 33199

FLORIDA STATE UNIVERSITY
Tallahassee, FL 32306

UNIVERSITY OF FLORIDA
Gainesville, FL 32604

FURMAN UNIVERSITY
Greenville, SC 29613

GEORGIA INSTITUTE OF TECH.
Atlanta, GA 30332

GEORGIA SOUTHERN UNIVERSITY
Statesboro, GA 30460-8033

GEORGIA STATE UNIVERSITY
Atlanta, GA 30303-3083

UNIVERSITY OF GEORGIA
Athens, GA 30613

JACKSONVILLE STATE
UNIVERSITY
Jacksonville, AL 36265-9982

JACKSONVILLE UNIVERSITY
Jacksonville, FL 32211-3394

UNIVERSITY OF KENTUCKY
Lexington, KY 40506-0032

LIBERTY UNIVERSITY
Lynchburg, VA 24506

LOUISIANA STATE UNIVERSITY
Baton Rouge, LA 70803

UNIVERSITY OF LOUISVILLE
Louisville, KY 40292

MARSHALL UNIVERSITY
Huntington, WV 25755

UNIVERSITY OF MARYLAND
College Park, MD 20740

UNIVERSITY OF MEMPHIS
Memphis, TN 38152

MERCER UNIVERSITY
Macon, GA 31207

UNIVERSITY OF MIAMI
Coral Gables, FL 33124-6710

MIDDLE TENNESSEE STATE UNIV.
Murfreesboro, TN 37132

MISSISSIPPI STATE UNIVERSITY
Mississippi State, MS 39762-5509

UNIVERSITY OF MISSISSIPPI
University, MS 38677

MOREHEAD STATE UNIVERSITY
Morehead, KY 40351-1689

MURRAY STATE UNIVERSITY
Murray, KY 42071-0009

UNIVERSITY OF NEW ORLEANS
New Orleans, LA 70148

UNIVERSITY OF NORTH
CAROLINA
Asheville, NC 28804-3299

UNIVERSITY OF NORTH
CAROLINA
Chapel Hill, NC 27514

UNIVERSITY OF NORTH
CAROLINA
Charlotte, NC 28223

UNIVERSITY OF NORTH
CAROLINA
Greensboro, NC 27412-5001

UNIVERSITY OF NORTH
CAROLINA
Wilmington, NC 28403-3297

NORTH CAROLINA A&T ST. UNIV.
Greensboro, NC 27411

OLD DOMINION UNIVERSITY
Norfolk, VA 23529

RADFORD UNIVERSITY
Radford, VA 24142

UNIVERSITY OF RICHMOND
Richmond, VA 23173-1903

SAMFORD UNIVERSITY
Birmingham, AL 35229

UNIVERSITY OF SOUTH ALABAMA
Mobile, AL 36688

SOUTH CAROLINA STATE UNIV.
Orangeburg, SC 29117-0001

UNIVERSITY OF SOUTH CAROLINA
Columbia, SC 29208

UNIVERSITY OF SOUTH FLORIDA
Tampa, FL 33620

SOUTHEASTERN LOUISIANA UNIV.
Hammond, LA 70402

UNIV. OF SOUTHERN MISSISSIPPI
Hattiesburg, MS 39406-5001

STETSON UNIVERSITY
De Land, FL 32720

TENNESSEE STATE UNIVERSITY
Nashville, TN 37209-1561

TENNESSEE TECHNOLOGICAL
UNIV.
Cookeville, TN 38505-0001

UNIVERSITY OF TENNESSEE
Chattanooga, TN 37403-2598

THE UNIVERSITY OF TENNESSEE
Knoxville, TN 37996

UNIV. OF TENNESSEE at MARTIN
Martin, TN 38238-5021

TROY STATE UNIVERSITY
Troy, AL 36082

TULANE UNIVERSITY
New Orleans, LA 70118

VANDERBILT UNIVERSITY
Nashville, TN 37212

VIRGINIA COMMONWEALTH UNIV.
Richmond, VA 23284-2003

VIRGINIA POLYTECHNIC
INSTITUTE
Blacksburg, VA 24061

UNIVERSITY OF VIRGINIA
Charlottesville, VA 22903

WAKE FOREST UNIVERSITY
Winston-Salem, NC 27109

WESTERN CAROLINA UNIVERSITY
Cullowhee, NC 28723

WESTERN KENTUCKY
UNIVERSITY
Bowling Green, KY 42101-3576

WINTHROP UNIVERSITY
Rock Hill, SC 29733

WOFFORD COLLEGE
Spartanburg, SC 29303-3663

District 4

UNIVERSITY OF AKRON
Akron, OH 44325

BALL STATE UNIVERSITY
Muncie, IN 47306

BOWLING GREEN STATE UNIV.
Bowling Green, OH 43403

BUTLER UNIVERSITY
Indianapolis, IN 46208

CENTRAL MICHIGAN UNIVERSITY
Mount Pleasant, MI 48859

CHICAGO STATE UNIVERSITY
Chicago, IL 60628-1598

UNIVERSITY OF CINCINNATI
Cincinnati, OH 45221

CLEVELAND STATE UNIVERSITY
Cleveland, OH 44115

UNIVERSITY OF DAYTON
Dayton, OH 45469

DE PAUL UNIVERSITY
Chicago, IL 60604-2287

UNIVERSITY OF DETROIT-MERCY
Detroit, MI 48219-0900

EASTERN ILLINOIS UNIVERSITY
Charleston, IL 61920-3099

EASTERN MICHIGAN UNIVERSITY
Ypsilanti, MI 48197

UNIVERSITY OF EVANSVILLE
Evansville, IN 47722

ILLINOIS STATE UNIVERSITY
Normal, IL 61761

UNIVERSITY OF ILLINOIS
Champaign, IL 61820

UNIVERSITY OF ILLINOIS
Chicago, IL 60607

INDIANA UNIVERSITY
Bloomington, IN 47405

UNIVERSITY OF IOWA
Iowa City, IA 52242

KENT STATE UNIVERSITY
Kent, OH 44242

LOYOLA UNIVERSITY
Chicago, IL 60626

MARQUETTE UNIVERSITY
Milwaukee, WI 53201-1881

MIAMI UNIVERSITY
Oxford, OH 45056

MICHIGAN STATE UNIVERSITY
East Lansing, MI 48824

UNIVERSITY OF MICHIGAN
Ann Arbor, MI 48109-2201

UNIV. OF MINNESOTA-TWIN
CITIES
Minneapolis, MN 55455

NORTHEASTERN ILLINOIS UNIV.
Chicago, IL 60625-4699

NORTHERN ILLINOIS UNIVERSITY
De Kalb, IL 60115-2854

UNIVERSITY OF NOTRE DAME
Notre Dame, IN 46556

OHIO STATE UNIVERSITY
Columbus, OH 43210

OHIO UNIVERSITY
Athens, OH 45701

PURDUE UNIVERSITY
West Lafayette, IN 47907

UNIVERSITY OF TOLEDO
Toledo, OH 43606

VALPARAISO UNIVERSITY
Valparaiso, IN 46383-6493

WESTERN ILLINOIS UNIVERSITY
Macomb, IL 61455

WESTERN MICHIGAN UNIVERSITY
Kalamazoo, MI 49008-5134

UNIVERSITY OF WISCONSIN
Green Bay, WI 54311-7001

UNIVERSITY OF WISCONSIN
Madison, WI 53711

UNIVERSITY OF WISCONSIN
Milwaukee, WI 53201

WRIGHT STATE UNIVERSITY
Dayton, OH 45435-0001

XAVIER UNIVERSITY
Cincinnati, OH 45207-6114

YOUNGSTOWN STATE
UNIVERSITY
Youngstown, OH 44555-0001

District 5

BRADLEY UNIVERSITY
Peoria, IL 61625

UNIVERSITY OF COLORADO
Boulder, CO 80309

CREIGHTON UNIVERSITY
Omaha, NE 68178-0001

DRAKE UNIVERSITY
Des Moines, IA 50311-4505

INDIANA STATE UNIVERSITY
Terre Haute, IN 47809

IOWA STATE UNIVERSITY
Ames, IA 50011

KANSAS STATE UNIVERSITY
Manhattan, KS 66506

UNIVERSITY OF KANSAS
Lawrence, KS 66045

UNIV. OF MISSOURI-COLUMBIA
Columbia, MO 65211

UNIV. OF MISSOURI-KANSAS CITY
Kansas City, MO 64110

UNIVERSITY OF NEBRASKA
Lincoln, NE 68588

UNIVERSITY OF NORTHERN IOWA
Cedar Falls, IA 50614

OKLAHOMA STATE UNIVERSITY
Stillwater, OK 74078

UNIVERSITY OF OKLAHOMA
Norman, OK 73019

ORAL ROBERTS UNIVERSITY
Tulsa, OK 74171

SOUTHEAST MISSOURI STATE
UNIV.
Cape Girardeau, MO 63701-4799

SOUTHERN ILLINOIS UNIVERSITY
Carbondale, IL 62901

SOUTHWEST MISSOURI STATE
UNIV.
Springfield, MO 65804

ST. LOUIS UNIVERSITY
St. Louis, MO 63108

UNIVERSITY OF TULSA
Tulsa, OK 74104

WICHITA STATE UNIVERSITY
Wichita, KS 67260

District 6

ALCORN STATE UNIVERSITY
Lorman, MS 39096-9402

ARKANSAS STATE UNIVERSITY
State University, AR 72467

UNIVERSITY OF ARKANSAS
Fayetteville, AR 72701

UNIVERSITY OF ARKANSAS
Little Rock, AR 72204-1099

BAYLOR UNIVERSITY
Waco, TX 76798

CENTENARY COLLEGE
Shreveport, LA 71134-1188

GRAMBLING STATE UNIVERSITY
Grambling, LA 71245

UNIVERSITY OF HOUSTON
Houston, TX 77204

JACKSON STATE UNIVERSITY
Jackson, MS 39217

LAMAR UNIVERSITY
Beaumont, TX 77710

LOUISIANA TECH UNIVERSITY
Ruston, LA 71272

MCNESSE STATE UNIVERSITY
Lake Charles, LA 70609

MISSISSIPPI VALLEY ST. UNIV.
Itta Bena, MS 38941-1400

NICHOLLS STATE UNIVERSITY
Thibodaux, LA 70310

UNIVERSITY OF NORTH TEXAS
Denton, TX 76203-6737

NORTHEAST LOUISIANA
UNIVERSITY
Monroe, LA 71209-3000

NORTHWESTERN STATE
UNIVERSITY
Natchitoches, LA 71497-0003

PRAIRIE VIEW A&M UNIVERSITY
Prairie View, TX 77446

RICE UNIVERSITY
Houston, TX 77251

SAM HOUSTON STATE
UNIVERSITY
Huntsville, TX 77341

SOUTHERN METHODIST
UNIVERSITY
Dallas, TX 75275

SOUTHERN UNIVERSITY
Baton Rouge, LA 70813

SOUTHWEST TEXAS STATE UNIV.
San Marcos, TX 78666-4615

UNIV. OF SOUTHWESTERN LA.
Lafayette, LA 70504-1008

STEPHEN F. AUSTIN STATE UNIV.
Nacogdoches, TX 75962

UNIVERSITY OF TEXAS
Arlington, TX 76019

UNIVERSITY OF TEXAS
Austin, TX 78712

UNIVERSITY OF TEXAS
San Antonio, TX 78249

TEXAS A&M UNIVERSITY
College Station, TX 77843-1228

TEXAS CHRISTIAN UNIVERSITY
Fort Worth, TX 76129-0001

UNIV. OF TEXAS-PAN AMERICAN
Edinburg, TX 78539-2999

TEXAS SOUTHERN UNIVERSITY
Houston, TX 77004

TEXAS TECH UNIVERSITY
Lubbock, TX 79409

District 7

BOISE STATE UNIVERSITY
Boise, ID 83725

BRIGHAM YOUNG UNIVERSITY
Provo, UT 84602

CALIF. STATE UNIV.-FRESNO
Fresno, CA 93740-0048

COLORADO STATE UNIVERSITY
Fort Collins, CO 80523-0100

GONZAGA UNIVERSITY
Spokane, WA 99258

UNIVERSITY OF HAWAII-MANOA
Honolulu, HI 96822-2370

IDAHO STATE UNIVERSITY
Pocatello, ID 83209

UNIVERSITY OF IDAHO
Moscow, ID 83843

MONTANA STATE UNIV-BOZEMAN
Bozeman, MT 59717-0338

THE UNIVERSITY OF MONTANA
Missoula, MT 59812-1291

UNIVERSITY OF NEVADA
Reno, NV 89557

UNIVERSITY OF NEW MEXICO
Albuquerque, NM 87131

NORTHERN ARIZONA UNIVERSITY
Flagstaff, AZ 86011

SAN DIEGO STATE UNIVERSITY
San Diego, CA 92182

SOUTHERN UTAH UNIVERSITY
Cedar City, UT 84720

UNIVERSITY OF TEXAS-EL PASO
El Paso, TX 79968

UNIVERSITY OF UTAH
Salt Lake City, UT 84112

WEBER STATE UNIVERSITY
Ogden, UT 84408-2701

UNIVERSITY OF WYOMING
Laramie, WY 82071

District 8

ARIZONA STATE UNIVERSITY
Tempe, AZ 85287-2505

UNIVERSITY OF ARIZONA
Tucson, AZ 85721

UNIV. OF CALIFORNIA-BERKELEY
Berkeley, CA 94720

UNIV. OF CALIF.-LOS ANGELES
Los Angeles, CA 90095-1405

UNIV. OF CALIF-SANTA BARBARA
Santa Barbara, CA 93106

UNIV. OF CALIFORNIA-IRVINE
Irvine, CA 92717

CALIF. POLYTECHNIC STATE UNIV.
San Luis Obispo, CA 93407

CALIF. STATE UNIV.-FULLERTON
Fullerton, CA 92634-9480

CALIF. STATE UNIV.-NORTHRIDGE
Northridge, CA 91330

CALIF. STATE UNIV.-SACRAMENTO
Sacramento, CA 95819

EASTERN WASHINGTON
UNIVERSITY
Cheney, WA 99004

LONG BEACH STATE UNIVERSITY
Long Beach, CA 90840-0118

LOYOLA MARYMOUNT
UNIVERSITY
Los Angeles, CA 90045-2699

UNIVERSITY OF NEVADA
Las Vegas, NV 89154

NEW MEXICO STATE UNIVERSITY
Las Cruces, NM 88003

UNIVERSITY OF OREGON
Eugene, OR 97403-1226

UNIVERSITY OF THE PACIFIC
Stockton, CA 95211

PEPPERDINE UNIVERSITY
Malibu, CA 90263

UNIVERSITY OF PORTLAND
Portland, OR 97203-5798

UNIVERSITY OF SAN DIEGO
San Diego, CA 92110-2492

UNIVERSITY OF SAN FRANCISCO
San Francisco, CA 94117-1080

SAN JOSE STATE UNIVERSITY
San Jose, CA 95192

SANTA CLARA UNIVERSITY
Santa Clara, CA 95053

UNIV. OF SOUTHERN CALIFORNIA
Los Angeles, CA 90089-0012

ST. MARY'S COLLEGE
Moraga, CA 94556

STANFORD UNIVERSITY
Stanford, CA 94305

UTAH STATE UNIVERSITY
Logan, UT 84322-7400

WASHINGTON STATE UNIVERSITY
Pullman, WA 99164

UNIVERSITY OF WASHINGTON
Seattle, WA 98195

NCAA PROVISIONAL MEMBERS

DIVISION I

District 6

UNIVERSITY OF ARKANSAS-PINE
BLUFF
Pine Bluff, AR 71601

DIVISION II

District 1

ASSUMPTION COLLEGE
Worcester, MA 01615-0005

BENTLEY COLLEGE
Waltham, MA 02154-4705

UNIVERSITY OF BRIDGEPORT
Bridgeport, CT 06601

BRYANT COLLEGE
Smithfield, RI 02917-1284

KEENE STATE COLLEGE
Keene, NH 03431-4183

UNIV. OF MASSACHUSETTS-
LOWELL
Lowell, MA 01854

MERRIMACK COLLEGE
North Andover, MA 01845

NEW HAMPSHIRE COLLEGE
Hooksett, NH 03106-1045

QUINNIPIAC COLLEGE
Hamden, CT 06518-1940

SACRED HEART UNIVERSITY
Fairfield, CT 06432-1000

SOUTHERN CONNECTICUT ST.
UNIV.
New Haven, CT 06515

ST. ANSELM COLLEGE
Manchester, NH 03102-1310

ST. MICHAEL'S COLLEGE
Colchester, VT 05439

STONEHILL COLLEGE
North Easton, MA 02357

District 2

STATE UNIV. OF N.Y. at ALBANY
Albany, NY 12222

ALDERSON-BROADDUS COLLEGE
Philippi, WV 26416

AMERICAN UNIV. OF PUERTO RICO
Bayamon, PR 00960-2037

BLOOMSBURG UNIVERSITY
Bloomsburg, PA 17815

BLUEFIELD STATE COLLEGE
Bluefield, WV 24701-2198

CALIFORNIA UNIVERSITY
California, PA 15419

CHEYNEY UNIVERSITY
Cheyney, PA 19319

CLARION UNIVERSITY
Clarion, PA 16214

CONCORD COLLEGE
Athens, WV 24712

CONCORDIA COLLEGE
Bronxville, NY 10708

DAVIS AND ELKINS COLLEGE
Elkins, WV 26241

UNIV. OF DISTRICT OF COLUMBIA
Washington, DC 20008

EAST STROUDSBURG UNIVERSITY
East Stroudsburg, PA 18301

EDINBORO UNIVERSITY
Edinboro, PA 16444-0001

FAIRMONT STATE COLLEGE
Fairmont, WV 26554

GANNON UNIVERSITY
Erie, PA 16541

GLENVILLE STATE COLLEGE
Glenville, WV 26351

INDIANA UNIV. OF PENNSYLVANIA
Indiana, PA 15705

KUTZTOWN UNIVERSITY
Kutztown, PA 19530-0721

LE MOYNE COLLEGE
Syracuse, NY 13214-1399

LOCK HAVEN UNIVERSITY
Lock Haven, PA 17745

LONG ISLAND U./C.W. POST
CAMPUS
Brookville, NY 11548

MANSFIELD UNIVERSITY
Mansfield, PA 16933

MERCY COLLEGE
Dobbs Ferry, NY 10522

MERCYHURST COLLEGE
Erie, PA 16546

MILLERSVILLE UNIVERSITY
Millersville, PA 17551-0302

MOLLOY COLLEGE
Rockville Centre, NY 11570

NEW YORK INSTITUTE OF TECH.
Old Westbury, NY 11568-8000

PACE UNIVERSITY
New York, NY 10038-1502

UNIVERSITY OF PITTSBURGH
Johnstown, PA 15904-2990

QUEENS COLLEGE (NY)
Flushing, NY 11367

SHEPHERD COLLEGE
Shepherdstown, WV 25443

SHIPPENSBURG UNIVERSITY
Shippensburg, PA 17257

SLIPPERY ROCK UNIVERSITY
Slippery Rock, PA 16057

THE COLLEGE OF ST. ROSE
Albany, NY 12203

STATE UNIV. OF N.Y. at STONY
BROOK
Stony Brook, NY 11794

WEST CHESTER UNIVERSITY
West Chester, PA 19383

WEST LIBERTY STATE COLLEGE
West Liberty, WV 26074

WEST VIRGINIA WESLEYAN
COLLEGE
Buckhannon, WV 26201

WHEELING JESUIT COLLEGE
Wheeling, WV 26003-6295

District 3

ALABAMA A&M UNIVERSITY
Normal, AL 35762

UNIV. OF ALABAMA-HUNTSVILLE
Huntsville, AL 35899

ALBANY STATE COLLEGE
Albany, GA 31705

ARMSTRONG STATE COLLEGE
Savannah, GA 31419-1997

AUGUSTA COLLEGE
Augusta, GA 30910

BELLARMINE COLLEGE
Louisville, KY 40205-0671

BELMONT ABBEY COLLEGE
Belmont, NC 28012-2795

BOWIE STATE UNIVERSITY
Bowie, MD 20715-9465

CARSON-NEWMAN COLLEGE
Jefferson City, TN 37760

CATAWBA COLLEGE
Salisbury, NC 28144-2488

COLUMBUS COLLEGE
Columbus, GA 31907-2079

DELTA STATE UNIVERSITY
Cleveland, MS 38733

ECKERD COLLEGE
St. Petersburg, FL 33733

ELIZABETH CITY STATE UNIV.
Elizabeth City, NC 27909

ELON COLLEGE
Elon College, NC 27244

ERSKINE COLLEGE
Due West, SC 29639

FAYETTEVILLE STATE
UNIVERSITY
Fayetteville, NC 28301-4298

FLORIDA INSTITUTE OF TECH.
Melbourne, FL 32901

FLORIDA SOUTHERN COLLEGE
Lakeland, FL 33801-5698

FRANCIS MARION UNIVERSITY
Florence, SC 29501-0547

GARDNER-WEBB UNIVERSITY
Boiling Springs, NC 28017

GEORGIA COLLEGE
Milledgeville, GA 31061

HIGH POINT UNIVERSITY
High Point, NC 27262-3598

JOHNSON C. SMITH UNIVERSITY
Charlotte, NC 28216

KENNESAW STATE COLLEGE
Marietta, GA 30061

KENTUCKY STATE UNIVERSITY
Frankfort, KY 40601

LANDER UNIVERSITY
Greenwood, SC 29649-2099

LANE COLLEGE
Jackson, TN 38301

LE MOYNE-OWEN COLLEGE
Memphis, TN 38126

LENOIR-RHYNE COLLEGE
Hickory, NC 28603

LINCOLN MEMORIAL UNIVERSITY
Harrogate, TN 37752

LIVINGSTONE COLLEGE
Salisbury, NC 28144

MARS HILL COLLEGE
Mars Hill, NC 28754

MILES COLLEGE
Birmingham, AL 35208

MORRIS BROWN COLLEGE
Atlanta, GA 30314

MOUNT OLIVE COLLEGE
Mount Olive, NC 28365

NORFOLK STATE UNIVERSITY
Norfolk, VA 23504

UNIVERSITY OF NORTH ALABAMA
Florence, AL 35632

NORTH CAROLINA CENTRAL
UNIV.
Durham, NC 27707

UNIVERSITY OF NORTH FLORIDA
Jacksonville, FL 32224-2645

NORTHERN KENTUCKY
UNIVERSITY
Highland Heights, KY 41099

PAINE COLLEGE
Augusta, GA 30901-3182

PEMBROKE STATE UNIVERSITY
Pembroke, NC 28372-1510

PFEIFFER COLLEGE
Misenheimer, NC 28109-0960

ROLLINS COLLEGE
Winter Park, FL 32789

SAVANNAH STATE COLLEGE
Savannah, GA 31404

SHAW UNIVERSITY
Raleigh, NC 27611

UNIV. OF SOUTH CAROLINA-
AIKEN
Aiken, SC 29801

U. OF SO. CAROLINA-
SPARTANBURG
Spartanburg, SC 29303

ST. ANDREWS PRESBYTERIAN
COLL.
Laurinburg, NC 28352-5598

ST. AUGUSTINE'S COLLEGE
Raleigh, NC 27610

ST. PAUL'S COLLEGE
Lawrenceville, VA 23868

UNIVERSITY OF TAMPA
Tampa, FL 33606-1490

TUSKEGEE UNIVERSITY
Tuskegee, AL 36088

VALDOSTA STATE UNIVERSITY
Valdosta, GA 31698

VIRGINIA STATE UNIVERSITY
Petersburg, VA 23806

VIRGINIA UNION UNIVERSITY
Richmond, VA 23220-1790

UNIVERSITY OF WEST FLORIDA
Pensacola, FL 32514

WEST GEORGIA COLLEGE
Carrollton, GA 30118

WINGATE UNIVERSITY
Wingate, NC 28174

WINSTON-SALEM STATE UNIV.
Winston-Salem, NC 27110

District 4

ASHLAND UNIVERSITY
Ashland, OH 44805

FERRIS STATE UNIVERSITY
Big Rapids, MI 49307-2295

GRAND VALLEY STATE
UNIVERSITY
Allendale, MI 49401

HILLSDALE COLLEGE
Hillsdale, MI 49242-1298

INDIANA UNIV.-PURDUE UNIV.
Fort Wayne, IN 46805-1499

UNIVERSITY OF INDIANAPOLIS
Indianapolis, IN 46227

LAKE SUPERIOR STATE UNIV.
Sault Sainte Marie, MI 49783

LEWIS UNIVERSITY
Romeoville, IL 60441

MICHIGAN TECHNOLOGICAL
UNIV.
Houghton, MI 49931-1295

UNIV. OF MINNESOTA-DULUTH
Duluth, MN 55812

MOORHEAD STATE UNIVERSITY
Moorhead, MN 56563-2996

NORTHERN MICHIGAN
UNIVERSITY
Marquette, MI 49855-5391

NORTHWOOD UNIVERSITY
Midland, MI 48640

OAKLAND CITY COLLEGE
Oakland City, IN 47660-1099

OAKLAND UNIVERSITY
Rochestser, MI 48309-4401

QUINCY UNIVERSITY
Quincy, IL 62301-2699

SAGINAW VALLEY STATE UNIV.
University Center, MI 48710

SOUTHERN ILLINOIS UNIVERSITY
Edwardsville, IL 62026

UNIV. OF SOUTHERN INDIANA
Evansville, IN 47712

COLLEGE OF ST. FRANCIS
Joliet, IL 60435

SAINT JOSEPH'S COLLEGE
Rensselaer, IN 47978

WAYNE STATE UNIVERSITY
Detroit, MI 48202

WINONA STATE UNIVERSITY
Winona, MN 55987-5838

UNIV. OF WISCONSIN-PARKSIDE
Kenosha, WI 53141-2000

District 5

AUGUSTANA COLLEGE
Sioux Falls, SD 57197

CENTRAL MISSOURI STATE UNIV.
Warrensburg, MO 64093

EMPORIA STATE UNIVERSITY
Emporia, KS 66801-5087

LINCOLN UNIVERSITY
Jefferson City, MO 65102-0029

MANKATO STATE UNIVERSITY
Mankato, MN 56002-8400

MISSOURI SOUTHERN ST.
COLLEGE
Joplin, MO 64801-1595

UNIVERSITY OF MISSOURI
Rolla, MO 65401

MORNINGSIDE COLLEGE
Sioux City, IA 51106-1751

UNIV. OF NEBRASKA at KEARNEY
Kearney, NE 68849

UNIV. OF NEBRASKA at OMAHA
Omaha, NE 68182

NORTH DAKOTA STATE
UNIVERSITY
Fargo, ND 58105

UNIVERSITY OF NORTH DAKOTA
Grand Forks, ND 58202

NORTHEAST MISSOURI STATE
UNIV.
Kirksville, MO 63501

UNIVERSITY OF NORTHERN
COLORADO
Greeley, CO 80639

NORTHERN STATE UNIVERSITY
Aberdeen, SD 57401

NORTHWEST MISSOURI STATE
UNIV.
Maryville, MO 64468-6001

PITTSBURG STATE UNIVERSITY
Pittsburg, KS 66762

SOUTH DAKOTA STATE
UNIVERSITY
Brookings, SD 57007

UNIVERSITY OF SOUTH DAKOTA
Vermillion, SD 57069-2390

SOUTHWEST BAPTIST
UNIVERSITY
Bolivar, MO 65613

ST. CLOUD STATE UNIVERSITY
St. Cloud, MN 56301-4498

WAYNE STATE COLLEGE
Wayne, NE 68787-1172

District 6

ABILENE CHRISTIAN UNIVERSITY
Abilene, TX 79699

ANGELO STATE UNIVERSITY
San Angelo, TX 76909

UNIV. OF CENTRAL ARKANSAS
Conway, AR 72035-0001

UNIVERSITY OF CENTRAL
OKLAHOMA
Edmond, OK 73034

EAST TEXAS STATE UNIVERSITY
Commerce, TX 75429-3011

HENDERSON STATE UNIVERSITY
Arkadelphia, AR 71999-0001

TARLETON STATE UNIVERSITY
Stephenville, TX 76402

TEXAS A&M UNIV.-KINGSVILLE
Kingsville, TX 78363

WEST TEXAS A&M UNIVERSITY
Canyon, TX 79016-0999

District 7

ADAMS STATE COLLEGE
Alamosa, CO 81102

COLORADO CHRISTIAN
UNIVERSITY
Lakewood, CO 80226

COLORADO SCHOOL OF MINES
Golden, CO 80401

FORT HAYS STATE UNIVERSITY
Hays, KS 67601

FORT LEWIS COLLEGE
Durango, CO 81301-3999

GRAND CANYON UNIVERSITY
Phoenix, AZ 85017

MESA STATE COLLEGE
Grand Junction, CO 81501

MONTANA STATE UNIVERSITY
Billings, MT 59101-0298

NEW MEXICO HIGHLANDS UNIV.
Las Vegas, NM 87701

U.S. AIR FORCE ACADEMY
USAF Academy, CO 80840-5461

WESTERN STATE COLLEGE
Gunnison, CO 81231

District 8

UNIVERSITY OF ALASKA-
FAIRBANKS
Fairbanks, AK 99775-7500

UNIV. OF CALIFORNIA-DAVIS
Davis, CA 95616

UNIV. OF CALIFORNIA-RIVERSIDE
Riverside, CA 92521

CALIF. STATE POLYTECHNIC UNIV.
Pomona, CA 91768

CALIF. STATE UNIV.-CHICO
Chico, CA 95929-0300

CALIF. STATE UNIV.-HAYWARD
Hayward, CA 94542

CALIF. STATE UNIV.-LOS ANGELES
Los Angeles, CA 90032-8240

CALIF. STATE UNIV.-STANISLAUS
Turlock, CA 95382

CHAMINADE UNIVERSITY
Honolulu, HI 96816

UNIVERSITY OF HAWAII-HILO
Hilo, HI 96720-4091

HUMBOLDT STATE UNIVERSITY
Arcata, CA 95521

COLLEGE OF NOTRE DAME
Belmont, CA 94002-9974

PORTLAND STATE UNIVERSITY
Portland, OR 97207-0751

SAN FRANCISCO STATE
UNIVERSITY
San Francisco, CA 94132

SEATTLE PACIFIC UNIVERSITY
Seattle, WA 98119

**NCAA PROVISIONAL MEMBERS
DIVISION II**

District 2

UNIV. OF PUERTO RICO-MAYAGUEZ
Mayaguez, PR 00709

UNIV. OF PUERTO RICO-BAYAMON
Bayamon, PR 00619-1919

WESTMINSTER COLLEGE
New Wilmington, PA 16172

District 3

CHRISTIAN BROTHERS UNIVERSITY
Memphis, TN 38104

COLUMBIA UNION COLLEGE
Takoma Park, MD 20912

GEORGIA SOUTHWESTERN
COLLEGE
Americus, GA 31709-4693

LAMBUTH UNIVERSITY
Jackson, TN 38301

TUSCULUM COLLEGE
Greeneville, TN 37743

District 5

EAST CENTRAL UNIVERSITY
Ada, OK 74820

LANGSTON UNIVERSITY
Langston, OK 73050

NORTHWESTERN OKLAHOMA ST. U.
Alva, OK 73717

OKLAHOMA PANHANDLE ST. UNIV.
Goodwell, OK 73939

UNIV. OF SCIENCE & ARTS
Chickasha, OK 73018

SOUTHEASTERN OKLA. ST. UNIV.
Durant, OK 74701

SOUTHWESTERN OKLAHOMA ST.
UNIV.
Weatherford, OK 73096

District 6

ARKANSAS TECH UNIVERSITY
Russellville, AR 72801-2222

UNIV. OF ARKANSAS-MONTICELLO
Monticello, AR 71656-3596

EAST TEXAS BAPTIST UNIVERSITY
Marshall, TX 75670-1498

HARDING UNIVERSITY
Searcy, AR 72149-0001

INCARNATE WORD COLLEGE
San Antonio, TX 78209

LYON COLLEGE
Batesville, AR 72503-2317

UNIV. OF MARY HARDIN-BAYLOR
Belton, TX 76513

OUACHITA BAPTIST UNIVERSITY
Arkadelphia, AR 71998-0001

SOUTHERN ARKANSAS
UNIVERSITY
Magnolia, AR 71753-5000

District 8

CENTRAL WASHINGTON UNIV.
Ellensburg, WA 98926

HAWAII PACIFIC UNIVERSITY
Honolulu, HI 96813

WESTERN WASHINGTON UNIV.
Bellingham, WA 98225

MEN'S FENCING

DIVISION I

District 1

BOSTON COLLEGE
Chestnut Hill, MA 02167-3934

BROWN UNIVERSITY
Providence, RI 02912

HARVARD UNIVERSITY
Cambridge, MA 02138-3800

YALE UNIVERSITY
New Haven, CT 06520-7398

District 2

COLUMBIA UNIV.-BARNARD
COLLEGE
New York, NY 10027

PENNSYLVANIA STATE UNIV.
University Park, PA 16802

UNIVERSITY OF PENNSYLVANIA
Philadelphia, PA 19104-6380

PRINCETON UNIVERSITY
Princeton, NJ 08544

RUTGERS UNIVERSITY
New Brunswick, NJ 08903

ST. JOHN'S UNIVERSITY
Jamaica, NY 11439

COLLEGE OF WILLIAM & MARY
Williamsburg, VA 23187

District 3

DUKE UNIVERSITY
Durham, NC 27708-0555

UNIVERSITY OF NORTH
CAROLINA
Chapel Hill, NC 27514

District 4

CLEVELAND STATE UNIVERSITY
Cleveland, OH 44115

UNIVERSITY OF DETROIT-MERCY
Detroit, MI 48219-0900

MICHIGAN STATE UNIVERSITY
East Lansing, MI 48824

UNIVERSITY OF NOTRE DAME
Notre Dame, IN 46556

OHIO STATE UNIVERSITY
Columbus, OH 43210

District 7

U.S. AIR FORCE ACADEMY
USAF Academy, CO 80840-5461

District 8

CALIF. STATE UNIV.-FULLERTON
Fullerton, CA 92634-9480

LONG BEACH STATE UNIVERSITY
Long Beach, CA 90840-0118

STANFORD UNIVERSITY
Stanford, CA 94305

DIVISION II

District 4

WAYNE STATE UNIVERSITY
Detroit, MI 48202

WOMEN'S FENCING

DIVISION I

District 1

BOSTON COLLEGE
Chestnut Hill, MA 02167-3934

BROWN UNIVERSITY
Providence, RI 02912

HARVARD UNIVERSITY
Cambridge, MA 02138-3800

YALE UNIVERSITY
New Haven, CT 06520-7398

District 2

COLUMBIA UNIV.-BARNARD COLLEGE
New York, NY 10027

CORNELL UNIVERSITY
Ithaca, NY 14853

FAIRLEIGH DICKINSON-TEANECK
Teaneck, NJ 07666

JAMES MADISON UNIVERSITY
Harrisonburg, VA 22807

PENNSYLVANIA STATE UNIV.
University Park, PA 16802

UNIVERSITY OF PENNSYLVANIA
Philadelphia, PA 19104-6380

PRINCETON UNIVERSITY
Princeton, NJ 08544

RUTGERS UNIVERSITY
New Brunswick, NJ 08903

ST. JOHN'S UNIVERSITY
Jamaica, NY 11439

TEMPLE UNIVERSITY
Philadelphia, PA 19122

District 3

DUKE UNIVERSITY
Durham, NC 27708-0555

UNIVERSITY OF NORTH CAROLINA
Chapel Hill, NC 27514

District 4

CLEVELAND STATE UNIVERSITY
Cleveland, OH 44115

UNIVERSITY OF DETROIT-MERCY
Detroit, MI 48219-0900

NORTHWESTERN UNIVERSITY
Evanston, IL 60208

UNIVERSITY OF NOTRE DAME
Notre Dame, IN 46556

OHIO STATE UNIVERSITY
Columbus, OH 43210

District 8

CALIF. STATE UNIV.-FULLERTON
Fullerton, CA 92634-9480

LONG BEACH STATE UNIVERSITY
Long Beach, CA 90840-0118

STANFORD UNIVERSITY
Stanford, CA 94305

DIVISION II

District 4

WAYNE STATE UNIVERSITY
Detroit, MI 48202

District 7

U.S. AIR FORCE ACADEMY
USAF Academy, CO 80840-5461

FIELD HOCKEY

DIVISION I

District 1

BOSTON COLLEGE
Chestnut Hill, MA 02167-3934

BOSTON UNIVERSITY
Boston, MA 02215

BROWN UNIVERSITY
Providence, RI 02912

UNIVERSITY OF CONNECTICUT
Storrs, CT 06269

DARTMOUTH COLLEGE
Hanover, NH 03755

FAIRFIELD UNIVERSITY
Fairfield, CT 06430-5195

HARVARD UNIVERSITY
Cambridge, MA 02138-3800

COLLEGE OF THE HOLY CROSS
Worcester, MA 01610-2395

UNIVERSITY OF MAINE
Orono, ME 04469

UNIV. OF MASSACHUSETTS-AMHERST
Amherst, MA 01003

UNIVERSITY OF NEW HAMPSHIRE
Durham, NH 03824

NORTHEASTERN UNIVERSITY
Boston, MA 02115-5096

PROVIDENCE COLLEGE
Providence, RI 02918

UNIVERSITY OF RHODE ISLAND
Kingston, RI 02881

UNIVERSITY OF VERMONT
Burlington, VT 05405

YALE UNIVERSITY
New Haven, CT 06520-7398

District 2

AMERICAN UNIVERSITY
Washington, DC 20016

BUCKNELL UNIVERSITY
Lewisburg, PA 17837

COLGATE UNIVERSITY
Hamilton, NY 13346-1304

COLUMBIA UNIV.-BARNARD
COLLEGE
New York, NY 10027

CORNELL UNIVERSITY
Ithaca, NY 14853

DAVIS AND ELKINS COLLEGE
Elkins, WV 26241

UNIVERSITY OF DELAWARE
Newark, DE 19716

DREXEL UNIVERSITY
Philadelphia, PA 19104

GEORGETOWN UNIVERSITY
Washington, DC 20057

HOFSTRA UNIVERSITY
Hempstead, NY 11550

JAMES MADISON UNIVERSITY
Harrisonburg, VA 22807

LA SALLE UNIVERSITY
Philadelphia, PA 19141-1199

LAFAYETTE COLLEGE
Easton, PA 18042

LEHIGH UNIVERSITY
Bethlehem, PA 18015-3089

PENNSYLVANIA STATE UNIV.
University Park, PA 16802

UNIVERSITY OF PENNSYLVANIA
Philadelphia, PA 19104-6380

PRINCETON UNIVERSITY
Princeton, NJ 08544

RIDER UNIVERSITY
Lawrenceville, NJ 08648-3099

RUTGERS UNIVERSITY
New Brunswick, NJ 08903

SIENA COLLEGE
Loudonville, NY 12211-1462

ST. JOSEPH'S UNIVERSITY
Philadelphia, PA 19131-1395

SYRACUSE UNIVERSITY
Syracuse, NY 13244

TEMPLE UNIVERSITY
Philadelphia, PA 19122

TOWSON STATE UNIVERSITY
Towson, MD 21204

URSINUS COLLEGE
Collegeville, PA 19426

VILLANOVA UNIVERSITY
Villanova, PA 19085

WEST CHESTER UNIVERSITY
West Chester, PA 19383

COLLEGE OF WILLIAM & MARY
Williamsburg, VA 23187

District 3

APPALACHIAN STATE UNIVERSITY
Boone, NC 28608

DAVIDSON COLLEGE
Davidson, NC 28036

DUKE UNIVERSITY
Durham, NC 27708-0555

UNIVERSITY OF LOUISVILLE
Louisville, KY 40292

UNIVERSITY OF MARYLAND
College Park, MD 20740

UNIVERSITY OF NORTH
CAROLINA
Chapel Hill, NC 27514

OLD DOMINION UNIVERSITY
Norfolk, VA 23529

RADFORD UNIVERSITY
Radford, VA 24142

UNIVERSITY OF RICHMOND
Richmond, VA 23173-1903

VIRGINIA COMMONWEALTH UNIV.
Richmond, VA 23284-2003

UNIVERSITY OF VIRGINIA
Charlottesville, VA 22903

WAKE FOREST UNIVERSITY
Winston-Salem, NC 27109

District 4

BALL STATE UNIVERSITY
Muncie, IN 47306

CENTRAL MICHIGAN UNIVERSITY
Mount Pleasant, MI 48859

UNIVERSITY OF IOWA
Iowa City, IA 52242

KENT STATE UNIVERSITY
Kent, OH 44242

MIAMI UNIVERSITY
Oxford, OH 45056

MICHIGAN STATE UNIVERSITY
East Lansing, MI 48824

UNIVERSITY OF MICHIGAN
Ann Arbor, MI 48109-2201

NORTHWESTERN UNIVERSITY
Evanston, IL 60208

OHIO STATE UNIVERSITY
Columbus, OH 43210

OHIO UNIVERSITY
Athens, OH 45701

District 5

SOUTHWEST MISSOURI STATE UNIV.
Springfield, MO 65804

ST. LOUIS UNIVERSITY
St. Louis, MO 63108

District 8

UNIV. OF CALIFORNIA-BERKELEY
Berkeley, CA 94720

LONG BEACH STATE UNIVERSITY
Long Beach, CA 90840-0118

UNIVERSITY OF THE PACIFIC
Stockton, CA 95211

STANFORD UNIVERSITY
Stanford, CA 94305

DIVISION II

District 1

ASSUMPTION COLLEGE
Worcester, MA 01615-0005

BENTLEY COLLEGE
Waltham, MA 02154-4705

KEENE STATE COLLEGE
Keene, NH 03431-4183

UNIV. OF MASSACHUSETTS-LOWELL
Lowell, MA 01854

MERRIMACK COLLEGE
North Andover, MA 01845

QUINNIPIAC COLLEGE
Hamden, CT 06518-1940

SACRED HEART UNIVERSITY
Fairfield, CT 06432-1000

SOUTHERN CONNECTICUT ST. UNIV.
New Haven, CT 06515

ST. MICHAEL'S COLLEGE
Colchester, VT 05439

District 2

STATE UNIV. OF N.Y. at ALBANY
Albany, NY 12222

BLOOMSBURG UNIVERSITY
Bloomsburg, PA 17815

EAST STROUDSBURG UNIVERSITY
East Stroudsburg, PA 18301

INDIANA UNIV. OF PENNSYLVANIA
Indiana, PA 15705

KUTZTOWN UNIVERSITY
Kutztown, PA 19530-0721

LOCK HAVEN UNIVERSITY
Lock Haven, PA 17745

LONG ISLAND U./C.W. POST CAMPUS
Brookville, NY 11548

MANSFIELD UNIVERSITY
Mansfield, PA 16933

MILLERSVILLE UNIVERSITY
Millersville, PA 17551-0302

PHILA. COLLEGE OF TEXT. & SCI.
Philadelphia, PA 19144-5497

SHIPPENSBURG UNIVERSITY
Shippensburg, PA 17257

SLIPPERY ROCK UNIVERSITY
Slippery Rock, PA 16057

District 3

BELLARMINE COLLEGE
Louisville, KY 40205-0671

CATAWBA COLLEGE
Salisbury, NC 28144-2488

LONGWOOD COLLEGE
Farmville, VA 23909-1899

FOOTBALL

DIVISION IA

District 1

BOSTON COLLEGE
Chestnut Hill, MA 02167-3934

District 2

PENNSYLVANIA STATE UNIV.
University Park, PA 16802

UNIVERSITY OF PITTSBURGH
Pittsburgh, PA 15260

RUTGERS UNIVERSITY
New Brunswick, NJ 08903

SYRACUSE UNIVERSITY
Syracuse, NY 13244

TEMPLE UNIVERSITY
Philadelphia, PA 19122

U.S. MILITARY ACADEMY
West Point, NY 10996

U.S. NAVAL ACADEMY
Annapolis, MD 21402

WEST VIRGINIA UNIVERSITY
Morgantown, WV 26506-6201

District 3

UNIV. OF ALABAMA at
TUSCALOOSA
Tuscaloosa, AL 35487

AUBURN UNIVERSITY
Auburn University, AL 36849-5113

CLEMSON UNIVERSITY
Clemson, SC 29632

DUKE UNIVERSITY
Durham, NC 27708-0555

EAST CAROLINA UNIVERSITY
Greenville, NC 27858-4353

FLORIDA STATE UNIVERSITY
Tallahassee, FL 32306

UNIVERSITY OF FLORIDA
Gainesville, FL 32604

GEORGIA INSTITUTE OF TECH.
Atlanta, GA 30332

UNIVERSITY OF GEORGIA
Athens, GA 30613

UNIVERSITY OF KENTUCKY
Lexington, KY 40506-0032

LOUISIANA STATE UNIVERSITY
Baton Rouge, LA 70803

UNIVERSITY OF LOUISVILLE
Louisville, KY 40292

UNIVERSITY OF MARYLAND
College Park, MD 20740

UNIVERSITY OF MEMPHIS
Memphis, TN 38152

UNIVERSITY OF MIAMI
Coral Gables, FL 33124-6710

MISSISSIPPI STATE UNIVERSITY
Mississippi State, MS 39762-5509

UNIVERSITY OF MISSISSIPPI
University, MS 38677

UNIVERSITY OF NORTH
CAROLINA
Chapel Hill, NC 27514·

NORTH CAROLINA STATE UNIV.
Raleigh, NC 27695-7001

UNIVERSITY OF SOUTH CAROLINA
Columbia, SC 29208

UNIV. OF SOUTHERN MISSISSIPPI
Hattiesburg, MS 39406-5001

THE UNIVERSITY OF TENNESSEE
Knoxville, TN 37996

TULANE UNIVERSITY
New Orleans, LA 70118

VANDERBILT UNIVERSITY
Nashville, TN 37212

VIRGINIA POLYTECHNIC
INSTITUTE
Blacksburg, VA 24061

UNIVERSITY OF VIRGINIA
Charlottesville, VA 22903

WAKE FOREST UNIVERSITY
Winston-Salem, NC 27109

District 4

UNIVERSITY OF AKRON
Akron, OH 44325

BALL STATE UNIVERSITY
Muncie, IN 47306

BOWLING GREEN STATE UNIV.
Bowling Green, OH 43403

CENTRAL MICHIGAN UNIVERSITY
Mount Pleasant, MI 48859

UNIVERSITY OF CINCINNATI
Cincinnati, OH 45221

EASTERN MICHIGAN UNIVERSITY
Ypsilanti, MI 48197

UNIVERSITY OF ILLINOIS
Champaign, IL 61820

INDIANA UNIVERSITY
Bloomington, IN 47405

UNIVERSITY OF IOWA
Iowa City, IA 52242

KENT STATE UNIVERSITY
Kent, OH 44242

MIAMI UNIVERSITY
Oxford, OH 45056

MICHIGAN STATE UNIVERSITY
East Lansing, MI 48824

UNIVERSITY OF MICHIGAN
Ann Arbor, MI 48109-2201

UNIV. OF MINNESOTA-TWIN
CITIES
Minneapolis, MN 55455

NORTHEAST ILLINOIS
UNIVERSITY
Ed Kalb, IL 60115-2854

NORTHWESTERN UNIVERSITY
Evanston, IL 60208

UNIVERSITY OF NOTRE DAME
Notre Dame, IN 46556

OHIO STATE UNIVERSITY
Columbus, OH 43210

OHIO UNIVERSITY
Athens, OH 45701

PURDUE UNIVERSITY
West Lafayette, IN 47907

UNIVERSITY OF TOLEDO
Toledo, OH 43606

WESTERN MICHIGAN UNIVERSITY
Kalamazoo, MI 49008-5134

UNIVERSITY OF WISCONSIN
Madison, WI 53711

District 5

UNIVERSITY OF COLORADO
Boulder, CO 80309

IOWA STATE UNIVERSITY
Ames, IA 50011

KANSAS STATE UNIVERSITY
Manhattan, KS 66506

UNIVERSITY OF KANSAS
Lawrence, KS 66045

UNIV. OF MISSOURI-COLUMBIA
Columbia, MO 65211

UNIVERSITY OF NEBRASKA
Lincoln, NE 68588

OKLAHOMA STATE UNIVERSITY
Stillwater, OK 74078

UNIVERSITY OF OKLAHOMA
Norman, OK 73019

UNIVERSITY OF TULSA
Tulsa, OK 74104

District 6

ARKANSAS STATE UNIVERSITY
State University, AR 72467

UNIVERSITY OF ARKANSAS
Fayetteville, AR 72701

BAYLOR UNIVERSITY
Waco, TX 76798

UNIVERSITY OF HOUSTON
Houston, TX 77204

LOUISIANA TECH UNIVERSITY
Ruston, LA 71272

UNIVERSITY OF NORTH TEXAS
Denton, TX 76203-6737

NORTHEAST LOUISIANA
UNIVERSITY
Monroe, LA 71209-3000

RICE UNIVERSITY
Houston, TX 77251

SOUTHERN METHODIST
UNIVERSITY
Dallas, TX 75275

UNIV. OF SOUTHWESTERN LA.
Lafayette, LA 70504-1008

UNIVERSITY OF TEXAS
Austin, TX 78712

TEXAS A&M UNIVERSITY
College Station, TX 77843-1228

TEXAS CHRISTIAN UNIVERSITY
Fort Worth, TX 76129-0001

TEXAS TECH UNIVERSITY
Lubbock, TX 79409

District 7

BRIGHAM YOUNG UNIVERSITY
Provo, UT 84602

CALIF. STATE UNIV.-FRESNO
Fresno, CA 93740-0048

COLORADO STATE UNIVERSITY
Fort Collins, CO 80523-0100

UNIVERSITY OF HAWAII-MANOA
Honolulu, HI 96822-2370

UNIVERSITY OF NEVADA
Reno, NV 89557

UNIVERSITY OF NEW MEXICO
Albuquerque, NM 87131

SAN DIEGO STATE UNIVERSITY
San Diego, CA 92182

UNIVERSITY OF TEXAS-EL PASO
El Paso, TX 79968

U.S. AIR FORCE ACADEMY
USAF Academy, CO 80840-5461

UNIVERSITY OF UTAH
Salt Lake City, UT 84112

UNIVERSITY OF WYOMING
Laramie, WY 82071

District 8

ARIZONA STATE UNIVERSITY
Tempe, AZ 85287-2505

UNIVERSITY OF ARIZONA
Tucson, AZ 85721

UNIV. OF CALIFORNIA-BERKELEY
Berkeley, CA 94720

UNIV. OF CALIF.-LOS ANGELES
Los Angeles, CA 90095-1405

UNIVERSITY OF NEVADA
Las Vegas, NV 89154

NEW MEXICO STATE UNIVERSITY
Las Cruces, NM 88003

OREGON STATE UNIVERSITY
Corvallis, OR 97331

UNIVERSITY OF OREGON
Eugene, OR 97403-1226

UNIVERSITY OF THE PACIFIC
Stockton, CA 95211

SAN JOSE STATE UNIVERSITY
San Jose, CA 95192

UNIV. OF SOUTHERN CALIFORNIA
Los Angeles, CA 90089-0012

STANFORD UNIVERSITY
Stanford, CA 94305

UTAH STATE UNIVERSITY
Logan, UT 84322-7400

WASHINGTON STATE UNIVERSITY
Pullman, WA 99164

UNIVERSITY OF WASHINGTON
Seattle, WA 98195

DIVISION IAA

District 1

BOSTON UNIVERSITY
Boston, MA 02215

BROWN UNIVERSITY
Providence, RI 02912

CENTRAL CONN. STATE UNIV.
New Britain, CT 06050-4010

UNIVERSITY OF CONNECTICUT
Storrs, CT 06269

DARTMOUTH COLLEGE
Hanover, NH 03755

HARVARD UNIVERSITY
Cambridge, MA 02138-3800

COLLEGE OF THE HOLY CROSS
Worcester, MA 01610-2395

UNIVERSITY OF MAINE
Orono, ME 04469

UNIV. OF MASSACHUSETTS-
AMHERST
Amherst, MA 01003

UNIVERSITY OF NEW HAMPSHIRE
Durham, NH 03824

NORTHEASTERN UNIVERSITY
Boston, MA 02115-5096

UNIVERSITY OF RHODE ISLAND
Kingston, RI 02881

YALE UNIVERSITY
New Haven, CT 06520-7398

District 2

BUCKNELL UNIVERSITY
Lewisburg, PA 17837

STATE UNIV. OF N.Y. at BUFFALO
Buffalo, NY 14260

CANISIUS COLLEGE
Buffalo, NY 14208-1098

COLGATE UNIVERSITY
Hamilton, NY 13346-1304

COLUMBIA UNIV.-BARNARD
COLLEGE
New York, NY 10027

CORNELL UNIVERSITY
Ithaca, NY 14853

DELAWARE STATE UNIVERSITY
Dover, DE 19901

UNIVERSITY OF DELAWARE
Newark, DE 19716

DUQUESNE UNIVERSITY
Pittsburgh, PA 15282

FORDHAM UNIVERSITY
Bronx, NY 10458-5155

GEORGETOWN UNIVERSITY
Washington, DC 20057

HAMPTON UNIVERSITY
Hampton, VA 23668

HOFSTRA UNIVERSITY
Hempstead, NY 11550

HOWARD UNIVERSITY
Washington, DC 20059

IONA COLLEGE
New Rochelle, NY 10801

JAMES MADISON UNIVERSITY
Harrisonburg, VA 22807

LAFAYETTE COLLEGE
Easton, PA 18042

LEHIGH UNIVERSITY
Bethlehem, PA 18015-3089

MARIST COLLEGE
Poughkeepsie, NY 12601-1387

MONMOUTH UNIVERSITY
West Long Branch, NJ 07764

MORGAN STATE UNIVERSITY
Baltimore, MD 21239

UNIVERSITY OF PENNSYLVANIA
Philadelphia, PA 19104-6380

PRINCETON UNIVERSITY
Princeton, NJ 08544

ROBERT MORRIS COLLEGE
Coraopolis, PA 15108-1189

SIENA COLLEGE
Loudonville, NY 12211-1462

ST. FRANCIS COLLEGE
Loretto, PA 15940-0600

ST. JOHN'S UNIVERSITY
Jamaica, NY 11439

ST. PETER'S COLLEGE
Jersey City, NJ 07306

TOWSON STATE UNIVERSITY
Towson, MD 21204

VILLANOVA UNIVERSITY
Villanova, PA 19085

WAGNER COLLEGE
Staten Island, NY 10301-4495

COLLEGE OF WILLIAM & MARY
Williamsburg, VA 23187

District 3

ALABAMA STATE UNIVERSITY
Montgomery, AL 36101-0271

UNIV. OF ALABAMA at
BIRMINGHAM
Birmingham, AL 35294-0110

APPALACHIAN STATE UNIVERSITY
Boone, NC 28608

AUSTIN PEAY STATE UNIVERSITY
Clarksville, TN 37044-4576

BETHUNE-COOKMAN COLLEGE
Daytona Beach, FL 32114-3099

UNIVERSITY OF CENTRAL
FLORIDA
Orlando, FL 32816-0002

CHARLESTON SOUTHERN UNIV.
Charleston, SC 29423-8087

THE CITADEL
Charleston, SC 29409

DAVIDSON COLLEGE
Davidson, NC 28036

EAST TENNESSEE STATE UNIV.
Johnson City, TN 37614

EASTERN KENTUCKY UNIVERSITY
Richmond, KY 40475-3101

FLORIDA A&M UNIVERSITY
Tallahassee, FL 32307

FURMAN UNIVERSITY
Greenville, SC 29613

GEORGIA SOUTHERN UNIVERSITY
Statesboro, GA 30460-8033

JACKSONVILLE STATE
UNIVERSITY
Jacksonville, AL 36265-9982

LIBERTY UNIVERSITY
Lynchburg, VA 24506

MARSHALL UNIVERSITY
Huntington, WV 25755

MIDDLE TENNESSEE STATE UNIV.
Murfreesboro, TN 37132

MOREHEAD STATE UNIVERSITY
Morehead, KY 40351-1689

MURRAY STATE UNIVERSITY
Murray, KY 42071-0009

NORTH CAROLINA A&T ST. UNIV.
Greensboro, NC 27411

UNIVERSITY OF RICHMOND
Richmond, VA 23173-1903

SAMFORD UNIVERSITY
Birmingham, AL 35229

SOUTH CAROLINA STATE UNIV.
Orangeburg, SC 29117-0001

TENNESSEE STATE UNIVERSITY
Nashville, TN 37209-1561

TENNESSEE TECHNOLOGICAL
UNIV.
Cookeville, TN 38505-0001

UNIVERSITY OF TENNESSEE
Chattanooga, TN 37403-2598

UNIV. OF TENNESSEE at MARTIN
Martin, TN 38238-5021

TROY STATE UNIVERSITY
Troy, AL 36082

VIRGINIA MILITARY INSTITUTE
Lexington, VA 24450-0304

WESTERN CAROLINA UNIVERSITY
Cullowhee, NC 28723

WESTERN KENTUCKY
UNIVERSITY
Bowling Green, KY 42101-3576

WOFFORD COLLEGE
Spartanburg, SC 29303-3663

District 4

BUTLER UNIVERSITY
Indianapolis, IN 46208

UNIVERSITY OF DAYTON
Dayton, OH 45469

EASTERN ILLINOIS UNIVERSITY
Charleston, IL 61920-3099

UNIVERSITY OF EVANSVILLE
Evansville, IN 47722

ILLINOIS STATE UNIVERSITY
Normal, IL 61761

VALPARAISO UNIVERSITY
Valparaiso, IN 46383-6493

WESTERN ILLINOIS UNIVERSITY
Macomb, IL 61455

YOUNGSTOWN STATE
UNIVERSITY
Youngstown, OH 44555-0001

District 5

DRAKE UNIVERSITY
Des Moines, IA 50311-4505

INDIANA STATE UNIVERSITY
Terre Haute, IN 47809

UNIVERSITY OF NORTHERN IOWA
Cedar Falls, IA 50614

SOUTHEAST MISSOURI STATE
UNIV.
Cape Girardeau, MO 63701-4799

SOUTHERN ILLINOIS UNIVERSITY
Carbondale, IL 62901

SOUTHWEST MISSOURI STATE
UNIV.
Springfield, MO 65804

District 6

ALCORN STATE UNIVERSITY
Lorman, MS 39096-9402

GRAMBLING STATE UNIVERSITY
Grambling, LA 71245

JACKSON STATE UNIVERSITY
Jackson, MS 39217

MCNESSE STATE UNIVERSITY
Lake Charles, LA 70609

MISSISSIPPI VALLEY ST. UNIV.
Itta Bena, MS 38941-1400

NICHOLLS STATE UNIVERSITY
Thibodaux, LA 70310

NORTHWESTERN STATE
UNIVERSITY
Natchitoches, LA 71497-0003

PRAIRIE VIEW A&M UNIVERSITY
Prairie View, TX 77446

SAM HOUSTON STATE
UNIVERSITY
Huntsville, TX 77341

SOUTHERN UNIVERSITY
Baton Rouge, LA 70813

SOUTHWEST TEXAS STATE UNIV.
San Marcos, TX 78666-4615

STEPHEN F. AUSTIN STATE UNIV.
Nacogdoches, TX 75962

TEXAS SOUTHERN UNIVERSITY
Houston, TX 77004

District 7

BOISE STATE UNIVERSITY
Boise, ID 83725

IDAHO STATE UNIVERSITY
Pocatello, ID 83209

UNIVERSITY OF IDAHO
Moscow, ID 83843

MONTANA STATE UNIV-BOZEMAN
Bozeman, MT 59717-0338

THE UNIVERSITY OF MONTANA
Missoula, MT 59812-1291

NORTHERN ARIZONA UNIVERSITY
Flagstaff, AZ 86011

SOUTHERN UTAH UNIVERSITY
Cedar City, UT 84720

WEBER STATE UNIVERSITY
Ogden, UT 84408-2701

District 8

CALIF. POLYTECHNIC STATE UNIV.
San Luis Obispo, CA 93407

CALIF. STATE UNIV.-NORTHRIDGE
Northridge, CA 91330

CALIF. STATE UNIV.-SACRAMENTO
Sacramento, CA 95819

EASTERN WASHINGTON
UNIVERSITY
Cheney, WA 99004

UNIVERSITY OF SAN DIEGO
San Diego, CA 92110-2492

ST. MARY'S COLLEGE
Moraga, CA 94556

NCAA PROVISIONAL MEMBERS

District 6

UNIVERSITY OF ARKANSAS-PINE
BLUFF
Pine Bluff, AR 71601

DIVISION II

District 1

AMERICAN INTERNATIONAL
COLLEGE
Springfield, MA 01109-3189

ASSUMPTION COLLEGE
Worcester, MA 01615-0005

BENTLEY COLLEGE
Waltham, MA 02154-4705

UNIV. OF MASSACHUSETTS-
LOWELL
Lowell, MA 01854

UNIVERSITY OF NEW HAVEN
West Haven, CT 06516-1999

SACRED HEART UNIVERSITY
Fairfield, CT 06432-1000

SOUTHERN CONNECTICUT ST.
UNIV.
New Haven, CT 06515

STONEHILL COLLEGE
North Easton, MA 02357

District 2

STATE UNIV. OF N.Y. at ALBANY
Albany, NY 12222

BLOOMSBURG UNIVERSITY
Bloomsburg, PA 17815

CALIFORNIA UNIVERSITY
California, PA 15419

CHEYNEY UNIVERSITY
Cheyney, PA 19319

CLARION UNIVERSITY
Clarion, PA 16214

CONCORD COLLEGE
Athens, WV 24712

EAST STROUDSBURG UNIVERSITY
East Stroudsburg, PA 18301

EDINBORO UNIVERSITY
Edinboro, PA 16444-0001

FAIRMONT STATE COLLEGE
Fairmont, WV 26554

GANNON UNIVERSITY
Erie, PA 16541

GLENVILLE STATE COLLEGE
Glenville, WV 26351

INDIANA UNIV. OF PENNSYLVANIA
Indiana, PA 15705

KUTZTOWN UNIVERSITY
Kutztown, PA 19530-0721

LOCK HAVEN UNIVERSITY
Lock Haven, PA 17745

LONG ISLAND U./C.W. POST
CAMPUS
Brookville, NY 11548

MANSFIELD UNIVERSITY
Mansfield, PA 16933

MERCYHURST COLLEGE
Erie, PA 16546

MILLERSVILLE UNIVERSITY
Millersville, PA 17551-0302

PACE UNIVERSITY
New York, NY 10038-1502

SHEPHERD COLLEGE
Shepherdstown, WV 25443

SHIPPENSBURG UNIVERSITY
Shippensburg, PA 17257

SLIPPERY ROCK UNIVERSITY
Slippery Rock, PA 16057

STATE UNIV. OF N.Y. at STONY
BROOK
Stony Brook, NY 11794

WEST CHESTER UNIVERSITY
West Chester, PA 19383

WEST LIBERTY STATE COLLEGE
West Liberty, WV 26074

WEST VIRGINIA INST. OF TECH
Montgomery, WV 25136

WEST VIRGINIA WESLEYAN
COLLEGE
Buckhannon, WV 26201

District 3

ALABAMA A&M UNIVERSITY
Normal, AL 35762

ALBANY STATE COLLEGE
Albany, GA 31705

BOWIE STATE UNIVERSITY
Bowie, MD 20715-9465

CARSON-NEWMAN COLLEGE
Jefferson City, TN 37760

CATAWBA COLLEGE
Salisbury, NC 28144-2488

CLARK ATLANTA UNIVERSITY
Atlanta, GA 30314

DELTA STATE UNIVERSITY
Cleveland, MS 38733

ELIZABETH CITY STATE UNIV.
Elizabeth City, NC 27909

ELON COLLEGE
Elon College, NC 27244

FAYETTEVILLE STATE
UNIVERSITY
Fayetteville, NC 28301-4298

FORT VALLEY STATE COLLEGE
Fort Valley, GA 31030

GARDNER-WEBB UNIVERSITY
Boiling Springs, NC 28017

JOHNSON C. SMITH UNIVERSITY
Charlotte, NC 28216

KENTUCKY STATE UNIVERSITY
Frankfort, KY 40601

KENTUCKY WESLEYAN COLLEGE
Owensboro, KY 42302-1039

LANE COLLEGE
Jackson, TN 38301

LENOIR-RHYNE COLLEGE
Hickory, NC 28603

LIVINGSTONE COLLEGE
Salisbury, NC 28144

MARS HILL COLLEGE
Mars Hill, NC 28754

MILES COLLEGE
Birmingham, AL 35208

MISSISSIPPI COLLEGE
Clinton, MS 39058

MOREHOUSE COLLEGE
Atlanta, GA 30314

MORRIS BROWN COLLEGE
Atlanta, GA 30314

NEWBERRY COLLEGE
Newberry, SC 29108

NORFOLK STATE UNIVERSITY
Norfolk, VA 23504

UNIVERSITY OF NORTH ALABAMA
Florence, AL 35632

NORTH CAROLINA CENTRAL UNIV.
Durham, NC 27707

PRESBYTERIAN COLLEGE
Clinton, SC 29325-2998

SAVANNAH STATE COLLEGE
Savannah, GA 31404

TUSKEGEE UNIVERSITY
Tuskegee, AL 36088

VALDOSTA STATE UNIVERSITY
Valdosta, GA 31698

VIRGINIA STATE UNIVERSITY
Petersburg, VA 23806

VIRGINIA UNION UNIVERSITY
Richmond, VA 23220-1790

UNIVERSITY OF WEST ALABAMA
Livingston, AL 35470

WEST GEORGIA COLLEGE
Carrollton, GA 30118

WINGATE UNIVERSITY
Wingate, NC 28174

WINSTON-SALEM STATE UNIV.
Winston-Salem, NC 27110

District 4

ASHLAND UNIVERSITY
Ashland, OH 44805

BEMIDJI STATE UNIVERSITY
Bemidji, MN 56601-2699

FERRIS STATE UNIVERSITY
Big Rapids, MI 49307-2295

GRAND VALLEY STATE UNIVERSITY
Allendale, MI 49401

HILLSDALE COLLEGE
Hillsdale, MI 49242-1298

UNIVERSITY OF INDIANAPOLIS
Indianapolis, IN 46227

MICHIGAN TECHNOLOGICAL UNIV.
Houghton, MI 49931-1295

UNIV. OF MINNESOTA-DULUTH
Duluth, MN 55812

UNIVERSITY OF MINNESOTA-MORRIS
Morris, MN 56267

MOORHEAD STATE UNIVERSITY
Moorhead, MN 56563-2996

NORTHERN MICHIGAN UNIVERSITY
Marquette, MI 49855-5391

NORTHWOOD UNIVERSITY
Midland, MI 48640

SAGINAW VALLEY STATE UNIV.
University Center, MI 48710

SOUTHWEST STATE UNIVERSITY
Marshall, MN 56258

COLLEGE OF ST. FRANCIS
Joliet, IL 60435

SAINT JOSEPH'S COLLEGE
Rensselaer, IN 47978

WAYNE STATE UNIVERSITY
Detroit, MI 48202

WINONA STATE UNIVERSITY
Winona, MN 55987-5838

District 5

AUGUSTANA COLLEGE
Sioux Falls, SD 57197

CENTRAL MISSOURI STATE UNIV.
Warrensburg, MO 64093

CHADRON STATE COLLEGE
Chadron, NE 69337

EMPORIA STATE UNIVERSITY
Emporia, KS 66801-5087

MANKATO STATE UNIVERSITY
Mankato, MN 56002-8400

MISSOURI SOUTHERN ST. COLLEGE
Joplin, MO 64801-1595

MISSOURI WESTERN ST. COLLEGE
St. Joseph, MO 64507

UNIVERSITY OF MISSOURI
Rolla, MO 65401

MORNINGSIDE COLLEGE
Sioux City, IA 51106-1751

UNIV. OF NEBRASKA at KEARNEY
Kearney, NE 68849

UNIV. OF NEBRASKA at OMAHA
Omaha, NE 68182

NORTH DAKOTA STATE UNIVERSITY
Fargo, ND 58105

UNIVERSITY OF NORTH DAKOTA
Grand Forks, ND 58202

NORTHEAST MISSOURI STATE UNIV.
Kirksville, MO 63501

UNIV. OF NORTHERN COLORADO
Greeley, CO 80639

NORTHERN STATE UNIVERSITY
Aberdeen, SD 57401

NORTHWEST MISSOURI STATE UNIV.
Maryville, MO 64468-6001

PITTSBURG STATE UNIVERSITY
Pittsburg, KS 66762

SOUTH DAKOTA STATE
UNIVERSITY
Brookings, SD 57007

UNIVERSITY OF SOUTH DAKOTA
Vermillion, SD 57069-2390

SOUTHWEST BAPTIST
UNIVERSITY
Bolivar, MO 65613

ST. CLOUD STATE UNIVERSITY
St. Cloud, MN 56301-4498

WASHBURN UNIVERSITY
Topeka, KS 66621

WAYNE STATE COLLEGE
Wayne, NE 68787-1172

District 6

ABILENE CHRISTIAN UNIVERSITY
Abilene, TX 79699

ANGELO STATE UNIVERSITY
San Angelo, TX 76909

UNIV. OF CENTRAL ARKANSAS
Conway, AR 72035-0001

UNIVERSITY OF CENTRAL
OKLAHOMA
Edmond, OK 73034

EAST TEXAS STATE UNIVERSITY
Commerce, TX 75429-3011

EASTERN NEW MEXICO
UNIVERSITY
Portales, NM 88130

HENDERSON STSATE
UNIVERSISTY
Arkadelphia, AR 71999-0001

TARLETON STATE UNIVERSITY
Stephenville, TX 76402

TEXAS A&M UNIV.-KINGSVILLE
Kingsville, TX 78363

WEST TEXAS A&M UNIVERSITY
Canyon, TX 79016-0999

WESTERN NEW MEXICO
UNIVERSITY
Silver City, NM 88061

District 7

ADAMS STATE COLLEGE
Alamosa, CO 81102

COLORADO SCHOOL OF MINES
Golden, CO 80401

FORT HAYS STATE UNIVERSITY
Hays, KS 67601

FORT LEWIS COLLEGE
Durango, CO 81301-3999

MESA STATE COLLEGE
Grand Junction, CO 81501

NEW MEXICO HIGHLANDS UNIV.
Las Vegas, NM 87701

WESTERN STATE COLLEGE
Gunnison, CO 81231

District 8

UNIV. OF CALIFORNIA-DAVIS
Davis, CA 95616

CALIF. STATE UNIV.-CHICO
Chico, CA 95929-0300

HUMBOLDT STATE UNIVERSITY
Arcata, CA 95521

PORTLAND STATE UNIVERSITY
Portland, OR 97207-0751

SONOMA STATE UNIVERSITY
Rohnert Park, CA 94928

NCAA PROVISIONAL MEMBERS

District 2

WEST VIRGINIA STATE COLLEGE
Institute, WV 25112-1000

WESTMINSTER COLLEGE
New Wilmington, PA 16172

District 3

LAMBUTH UNIVERSITY
Jackson, TN 38301

TUSCULUM COLLEGE
Greeneville, TN 37743

District 5

EAST CENTRAL UNIVERSITY
Ada, OK 74820

LANGSTON UNIVERSITY
Langston, OK 73050

NORTHWESTERN OKLAHOMA ST. U.
Alva, OK 73717

OKLAHOMA PANHANDLE ST. UNIV.
Goodwell, OK 73939

SOUTHEASTERN OKLA. ST. UNIV.
Durant, OK 74701

SOUTHWESTERN OKLAHOMA ST.
UNIV.
Weatherford, OK 73096

District 6

ARKANSAS TECH UNIVERSITY
Russellville, AR 72801-2222

UNIV. OF ARKANSAS-MONTICELLO
Monticello, AR 71656-3596

HARDING UNIVERSITY
Searcy, AR 72149-0001

MIDWESTERN STATE UNIVERSITY
Wichita Falls, TX 76308

OUACHITA BAPTIST UNIVERSITY
Arkadelphia, AR 71998-0001

SOUTHERN ARKANSAS
UNIVERSITY
Magnolia, AR 71753-5000

District 8

CENTRAL WASHINGTON UNIV.
Ellensburg, WA 98926

WESTERN WASHINGTON UNIV.
Bellingham, WA 98225

MEN'S GOLF

DIVISION I

District 1

BOSTON COLLEGE
Chestnut Hill, MA 02167-3934

BOSTON UNIVERSITY
Boston, MA 02215

CENTRAL CONN. STATE UNIV.
New Britain, CT 06050-4010

UNIVERSITY OF CONNECTICUT
Storrs, CT 06269

DARTMOUTH COLLEGE
Hanover, NH 03755

FAIRFIELD UNIVERSITY
Fairfield, CT 06430-5195

UNIVERSITY OF HARTFORD
West Hartford, CT 06117-1599

HARVARD UNIVERSITY
Cambridge, MA 02138-3800

COLLEGE OF THE HOLY CROSS
Worcester, MA 01610-2395

UNIVERSITY OF MAINE
Orono, ME 04469

UNIVERSITY OF NEW HAMPSHIRE
Durham, NH 03824

NORTHEASTERN UNIVERSITY
Boston, MA 02115-5096

PROVIDENCE COLLEGE
Providence, RI 02918

UNIVERSITY OF RHODE ISLAND
Kingston, RI 02881

UNIVERSITY OF VERMONT
Burlington, VT 05405

YALE UNIVERSITY
New Haven, CT 06520-7398

District 2

AMERICAN UNIVERSITY
Washington, DC 20016

BUCKNELL UNIVERSITY
Lewisburg, PA 17837

CANISIUS COLLEGE
Buffalo, NY 14208-1098

COLGATE UNIVERSITY
Hamilton, NY 13346-1304

COLUMBIA UNIV.-BARNARD
COLLEGE
New York, NY 10027

CORNELL UNIVERSITY
Ithaca, NY 14853

UNIVERSITY OF DELAWARE
Newark, DE 19716

DREXEL UNIVERSITY
Philadelphia, PA 19104

DUQUESNE UNIVERSITY
Pittsburgh, PA 15282

FAIRLEIGH DICKINSON-TEANECK
Teaneck, NJ 07666

FORDHAM UNIVERSITY
Bronx, NY 10458-5155

GEORGE MASON UNIVERSITY
Fairfax, VA 22030

GEORGE WASHINGTON
UNIVERSITY
Washington, DC 20052

GEORGETOWN UNIVERSITY
Washington, DC 20057

HAMPTON UNIVERSITY
Hampton, VA 23668

HOFSTRA UNIVERSITY
Hempstead, NY 11550

IONA COLLEGE
New Rochelle, NY 10801

JAMES MADISON UNIVERSITY
Harrisonburg, VA 22807

LA SALLE UNIVERSITY
Philadelphia, PA 19141-1199

LAFAYETTE COLLEGE
Easton, PA 18042

LEHIGH UNIVERSITY
Bethlehem, PA 18015-3089

LONG ISLAND UNIV.-BROOKLYN
Brooklyn, NY 11201

LOYOLA COLLEGE
Baltimore, MD 21210

MANHATTAN COLLEGE
Riverdale, NY 10471

UNIV. OF MARYLAND-BALT. CO.
Baltimore, MD 21228-5398

MONMOUTH UNIVERSITY
West Long Branch, NJ 07764

MOUNT ST. MARY'S COLLEGE
Emmitsburg, MD 21727-7799

NIAGARA UNIVERSITY
Niagara University, NY 14109

PENNSYLVANIA STATE UNIV.
University Park, PA 16802

UNIVERSITY OF PENNSYLVANIA
Philadelphia, PA 19104-6380

PRINCETON UNIVERSITY
Princeton, NJ 08544

RIDER UNIVERSITY
Lawrenceville, NJ 08648-3099

ROBERT MORRIS COLLEGE
Coraopolis, PA 15108-1189

RUTGERS UNIVERSITY
New Brunswick, NJ 08903

SETON HALL UNIVERSITY
South Orange, NJ 07079

SIENA COLLEGE
Loudonville, NY 12211-1462

ST. BONAVENTURE UNIVERSITY
St. Bonaventure, NY 14778

ST. FRANCIS COLLEGE
Loretto, PA 15940-0600

ST. JOHN'S UNIVERSITY
Jamaica, NY 11439

ST. JOSEPH'S UNIVERSITY
Philadelphia, PA 19131-1395

ST. PETER'S COLLEGE
Jersey City, NJ 07306

TEMPLE UNIVERSITY
Philadelphia, PA 19122

TOWSON STATE UNIVERSITY
Towson, MD 21204

U.S. MILITARY ACADEMY
West Point, NY 10996

U.S. NAVAL ACADEMY
Annapolis, MD 21402

VILLANOVA UNIVERSITY
Villanova, PA 19085

WAGNER COLLEGE
Staten Island, NY 10301-4495

COLLEGE OF WILLIAM & MARY
Williamsburg, VA 23187

District 3

ALABAMA STATE UNIVERSITY
Montgomery, AL 36101-0271

UNIV. OF ALABAMA at
TUSCALOOSA
Tuscaloosa, AL 35487

UNIV. OF ALABAMA at
BIRMINGHAM
Birmingham, AL 35294-0110

APPALACHIAN STATE UNIVERSITY
Boone, NC 28608

AUBURN UNIVERSITY
Auburn University, AL 36849-5113

AUGUSTA COLLEGE
Augusta, GA 30910

AUSTIN PEAY STATE UNIVERSITY
Clarksville, TN 37044-4576

CAMPBELL UNIVERSITY
Buies Creek, NC 27506

UNIVERSITY OF CENTRAL
FLORIDA
Orlando, FL 32816-0002

CHARLESTON SOUTHERN UNIV.
Charleston, SC 29423-8087

COLLEGE OF CHARLESTON
Charleston, SC 29424

THE CITADEL
Charleston, SC 29409

CLEMSON UNIVERSITY
Clemson, SC 29632

COASTAL CAROLINA UNIVERSITY
Conway, SC 29526

DAVIDSON COLLEGE
Davidson, NC 28036

DUKE UNIVERSITY
Durham, NC 27708-0555

EAST CAROLINA UNIVERSITY
Greenville, NC 27858-4353

EAST TENNESSEE STATE UNIV.
Johnson City, TN 37614

EASTERN KENTUCKY UNIVERSITY
Richmond, KY 40475-3101

FLORIDA A&M UNIVERSITY
Tallahassee, FL 32307

FLORIDA ATLANTIC UNIVERSITY
Boca Raton, FL 33431-0991

FLORIDA INTERNATIONAL UNIV.
Miami, FL 33199

FLORIDA STATE UNIVERSITY
Tallahassee, FL 32306

UNIVERSITY OF FLORIDA
Gainesville, FL 32604

FURMAN UNIVERSITY
Greenville, SC 29613

GEORGIA INSTITUTE OF TECH.
Atlanta, GA 30332

GEORGIA SOUTHERN UNIVERSITY
Statesboro, GA 30460-8033

GEORGIA STATE UNIVERSITY
Atlanta, GA 30303-3083

UNIVERSITY OF GEORGIA
Athens, GA 30613

JACKSONVILLE STATE
UNIVERSITY
Jacksonville, AL 36265-9982

JACKSONVILLE UNIVERSITY
Jacksonville, FL 32211-3394

UNIVERSITY OF KENTUCKY
Lexington, KY 40506-0032

LIBERTY UNIVERSITY
Lynchburg, VA 24506

LOUISIANA STATE UNIVERSITY
Baton Rouge, LA 70803

UNIVERSITY OF LOUISVILLE
Louisville, KY 40292

MARSHALL UNIVERSITY
Huntington, WV 25755

UNIVERSITY OF MARYLAND
College Park, MD 20740

UNIVERSITY OF MEMPHIS
Memphis, TN 38152

MERCER UNIVERSITY
Macon, GA 31207

MIDDLE TENNESSEE STATE UNIV.
Murfreesboro, TN 37132

MISSISSIPPI STATE UNIVERSITY
Mississippi State, MS 39762-5509

UNIVERSITY OF MISSISSIPPI
University, MS 38677

MOREHEAD STATE UNIVERSITY
Morehead, KY 40351-1689

MURRAY STATE UNIVERSITY
Murray, KY 42071-0009

UNIVERSITY OF NEW ORLEANS
New Orleans, LA 70148

UNIVERSITY OF NORTH
CAROLINA
Chapel Hill, NC 27514

UNIVERSITY OF NORTH
CAROLINA
Charlotte, NC 28223

UNIVERSITY OF NORTH
CAROLINA
Greensboro, NC 27412-5001

UNIVERSITY OF NORTH
CAROLINA
Wilmington, NC 28403-3297

NORTH CAROLINA STATE UNIV.
Raleigh, NC 27695-7001

OLD DOMINION UNIVERSITY
Norfolk, VA 23529

RADFORD UNIVERSITY
Radford, VA 24142

UNIVERSITY OF RICHMOND
Richmond, VA 23173-1903

SAMFORD UNIVERSITY
Birmingham, AL 35229

UNIVERSITY OF SOUTH ALABAMA
Mobile, AL 36688

SOUTH CAROLINA STATE UNIV.
Orangeburg, SC 29117-0001

UNIVERSITY OF SOUTH CAROLINA
Columbia, SC 29208

UNIVERSITY OF SOUTH FLORIDA
Tampa, FL 33620

SOUTHEASTERN LOUISIANA UNIV.
Hammond, LA 70402

UNIV. OF SOUTHERN MISSISSIPPI
Hattiesburg, MS 39406-5001

STETSON UNIVERSITY
De Land, FL 32720

TENNESSEE STATE UNIVERSITY
Nashville, TN 37209-1561

TENNESSEE TECHNOLOGICAL
UNIV.
Cookeville, TN 38505-0001

UNIVERSITY OF TENNESSEE
Chattanooga, TN 37403-2598

THE UNIVERSITY OF TENNESSEE
Knoxville, TN 37996

UNIV. OF TENNESSEE at MARTIN
Martin, TN 38238-5021

TROY STATE UNIVERSITY
Troy, AL 36082

TULANE UNIVERSITY
New Orleans, LA 70118

VANDERBILT UNIVERSITY
Nashville, TN 37212

VIRGINIA COMMONWEALTH UNIV.
Richmond, VA 23284-2003

VIRGINIA MILITARY INSTITUTE
Lexington, VA 24450-0304

VIRGINIA POLYTECHNIC
INSTITUTE
Blacksburg, VA 24061

UNIVERSITY OF VIRGINIA
Charlottesville, VA 22903

WAKE FOREST UNIVERSITY
Winston-Salem, NC 27109

WESTERN CAROLINA UNIVERSITY
Cullowhee, NC 28723

WESTERN KENTUCKY
UNIVERSITY
Bowling Green, KY 42101-3576

WINTHROP UNIVERSITY
Rock Hill, SC 29733

WOFFORD COLLEGE
Spartanburg, SC 29303-3663

District 4

UNIVERSITY OF AKRON
Akron, OH 44325

BALL STATE UNIVERSITY
Muncie, IN 47306

BOWLING GREEN STATE UNIV.
Bowling Green, OH 43403

BUTLER UNIVERSITY
Indianapolis, IN 46208

UNIVERSITY OF CINCINNATI
Cincinnati, OH 45221

CLEVELAND STATE UNIVERSITY
Cleveland, OH 44115

UNIVERSITY OF DAYTON
Dayton, OH 45469

DE PAUL UNIVERSITY
Chicago, IL 60604-2287

UNIVERSITY OF DETROIT-MERCY
Detroit, MI 48219-0900

EASTERN ILLINOIS UNIVERSITY
Charleston, IL 61920-3099

EASTERN MICHIGAN UNIVERSITY
Ypsilanti, MI 48197

UNIVERSITY OF EVANSVILLE
Evansville, IN 47722

ILLINOIS STATE UNIVERSITY
Normal, IL 61761

UNIVERSITY OF ILLINOIS
Champaign, IL 61820

INDIANA UNIVERSITY
Bloomington, IN 47405

UNIVERSITY OF IOWA
Iowa City, IA 52242

KENT STATE UNIVERSITY
Kent, OH 44242

LOYOLA UNIVERSITY
Chicago, IL 60626

MARQUETTE UNIVERSITY
Milwaukee, WI 53201-1881

MIAMI UNIVERSITY
Oxford, OH 45056

MICHIGAN STATE UNIVERSITY
East Lansing, MI 48824

UNIVERSITY OF MICHIGAN
Ann Arbor, MI 48109-2201

UNIV. OF MINNESOTA-TWIN
CITIES
Minneapolis, MN 55455

NORTHEASTERN ILLINOIS UNIV.
Chicago, IL 60625-4699

NORTHERN ILLINOIS UNIVERSITY
De Kalb, IL 60115-2854

NORTHWESTERN UNIVERSITY
Evanston, IL 60208

UNIVERSITY OF NOTRE DAME
Notre Dame, IN 46556

OHIO STATE UNIVERSITY
Columbus, OH 43210

OHIO UNIVERSITY
Athens, OH 45701

PURDUE UNIVERSITY
West Lafayette, IN 47907

UNIVERSITY OF TOLEDO
Toledo, OH 43606

WESTERN ILLINOIS UNIVERSITY
Macomb, IL 61455

UNIVERSITY OF WISCONSIN
Green Bay, WI 54311-7001

UNIVERSITY OF WISCONSIN
Madison, WI 53711

WRIGHT STATE UNIVERSITY
Dayton, OH 45435-0001

XAVIER UNIVERSITY
Cincinnati, OH 45207-6114

YOUNGSTOWN STATE
UNIVERSITY
Youngstown, OH 44555-0001

District 5

BRADLEY UNIVERSITY
Peoria, IL 61625

UNIVERSITY OF COLORADO
Boulder, CO 80309

CREIGHTON UNIVERSITY
Omaha, NE 68178-0001

DRAKE UNIVERSITY
Des Moines, IA 50311-4505

IOWA STATE UNIVERSITY
Ames, IA 50011

KANSAS STATE UNIVERSITY
Manhattan, KS 66506

UNIVERSITY OF KANSAS
Lawrence, KS 66045

UNIV. OF MISSOURI-COLUMBIA
Columbia, MO 65211

UNIV. OF MISSOURI-KANSAS CITY
Kansas City, MO 64110

UNIVERSITY OF NEBRASKA
Lincoln, NE 68588

UNIVERSITY OF NORTHERN IOWA
Cedar Falls, IA 50614

OKLAHOMA STATE UNIVERSITY
Stillwater, OK 74078

UNIVERSITY OF OKLAHOMA
Norman, OK 73019

ORAL ROBERTS UNIVERSITY
Tulsa, OK 74171

SOUTHEAST MISSOURI STATE
UNIV.
Cape Girardeau, MO 63701-4799

SOUTHERN ILLINOIS UNIVERSITY
Carbondale, IL 62901

SOUTHWEST MISSOURI STATE
UNIV.
Springfield, MO 65804

ST. LOUIS UNIVERSITY
St. Louis, MO 63108

UNIVERSITY OF TULSA
Tulsa, OK 74104

WICHITA STATE UNIVERSITY
Wichita, KS 67260

District 6

ALCORN STATE UNIVERSITY
Lorman, MS 39096-9402

ARKANSAS STATE UNIVERSITY
State University, AR 72467

UNIVERSITY OF ARKANSAS
Fayetteville, AR 72701

UNIVERSITY OF ARKANSAS
Little Rock, AR 72204-1099

BAYLOR UNIVERSITY
Waco, TX 76798

CENTENARY COLLEGE
Shreveport, LA 71134-1188

GRAMBLING STATE UNIVERSITY
Grambling, LA 71245

UNIVERSITY OF HOUSTON
Houston, TX 77204

JACKSON STATE UNIVERSITY
Jackson, MS 39217

LAMAR UNIVERSITY
Beaumont, TX 77710

LOUISIANA TECH UNIVERSITY
Ruston, LA 71272

MCNESSE STATE UNIVERSITY
Lake Charles, LA 70609

MISSISSIPPI VALLEY ST. UNIV.
Itta Bena, MS 38941-1400

NICHOLLS STATE UNIVERSITY
Thibodaux, LA 70310

UNIVERSITY OF NORTH TEXAS
Denton, TX 76203-6737

NORTHEAST LOUISIANA
UNIVERSITY
Monroe, LA 71209-3000

NORTHWESTERN STATE
UNIVERSITY
Natchitoches, LA 71497-0003

PRAIRIE VIEW A&M UNIVERSITY
Prairie View, TX 77446

RICE UNIVERSITY
Houston, TX 77251

SAM HOUSTON STATE
UNIVERSITY
Huntsville, TX 77341

SOUTHERN METHODIST
UNIVERSITY
Dallas, TX 75275

SOUTHERN UNIVERSITY
Baton Rouge, LA 70813

SOUTHWEST TEXAS STATE UNIV.
San Marcos, TX 78666-4615

UNIV. OF SOUTHWESTERN LA.
Lafayette, LA 70504-1008

STEPHEN F. AUSTIN STATE UNIV.
Nacogdoches, TX 75962

UNIVERSITY OF TEXAS
Arlington, TX 76019

UNIVERSITY OF TEXAS
Austin, TX 78712

UNIVERSITY OF TEXAS
San Antonio, TX 78249

TEXAS A&M UNIVERSITY
College Station, TX 77843-1228

TEXAS CHRISTIAN UNIVERSITY
Fort Worth, TX 76129-0001

UNIV. OF TEXAS-PAN AMERICAN
Edinburg, TX 78539-2999

TEXAS SOUTHERN UNIVERSITY
Houston, TX 77004

TEXAS TECH UNIVERSITY
Lubbock, TX 79409

District 7

BOISE STATE UNIVERSITY
Boise, ID 83725

BRIGHAM YOUNG UNIVERSITY
Provo, UT 84602

CALIF. STATE UNIV.-FRESNO
Fresno, CA 93740-0048

COLORADO STATE UNIVERSITY
Fort Collins, CO 80523-0100

GONZAGA UNIVERSITY
Spokane, WA 99258

UNIVERSITY OF HAWAII-MANOA
Honolulu, HI 96822-2370

IDAHO STATE UNIVERSITY
Pocatello, ID 83209

UNIVERSITY OF IDAHO
Moscow, ID 83843

UNIVERSITY OF NEVADA
Reno, NV 89557

UNIVERSITY OF NEW MEXICO
Albuquerque, NM 87131

SAN DIEGO STATE UNIVERSITY
San Diego, CA 92182

SOUTHERN UTAH UNIVERSITY
Cedar City, UT 84720

UNIVERSITY OF TEXAS-EL PASO
El Paso, TX 79968

U.S. AIR FORCE ACADEMY
USAF Academy, CO 80840-5461

UNIVERSITY OF UTAH
Salt Lake City, UT 84112

WEBER STATE UNIVERSITY
Ogden, UT 84408-2701

UNIVERSITY OF WYOMING
Laramie, WY 82071

District 8

ARIZONA STATE UNIVERSITY
Tempe, AZ 85287-2505

UNIVERSITY OF ARIZONA
Tucson, AZ 85721

UNIV. OF CALIFORNIA-BERKELEY
Berkeley, CA 94720

UNIV. OF CALIF.-LOS ANGELES
Los Angeles, CA 90095-1405

UNIV. OF CALIF-SANTA BARBARA
Santa Barbara, CA 93106

UNIV. OF CALIFORNIA-IRVINE
Irvine, CA 92717

CALIF. STATE UNIV.-NORTHRIDGE
Northridge, CA 91330

CALIF. STATE UNIV.-SACRAMENTO
Sacramento, CA 95819

EASTERN WASHINGTON
UNIVERSITY
Cheney, WA 99004

LONG BEACH STATE UNIVERSITY
Long Beach, CA 90840-0118

LOYOLA MARYMOUNT
UNIVERSITY
Los Angeles, CA 90045-2699

UNIVERSITY OF NEVADA
Las Vegas, NV 89154

NEW MEXICO STATE UNIVERSITY
Las Cruces, NM 88003

OREGON STATE UNIVERSITY
Corvallis, OR 97331

UNIVERSITY OF OREGON
Eugene, OR 97403-1226

UNIVERSITY OF THE PACIFIC
Stockton, CA 95211

PEPPERDINE UNIVERSITY
Malibu, CA 90263

UNIVERSITY OF PORTLAND
Portland, OR 97203-5798

UNIVERSITY OF SAN DIEGO
San Diego, CA 92110-2492

UNIVERSITY OF SAN FRANCISCO
San Francisco, CA 94117-1080

SAN JOSE STATE UNIVERSITY
San Jose, CA 95192

SANTA CLARA UNIVERSITY
Santa Clara, CA 95053

UNIV. OF SOUTHERN CALIFORNIA
Los Angeles, CA 90089-0012

ST. MARY'S COLLEGE
Moraga, CA 94556

STANFORD UNIVERSITY
Stanford, CA 94305

UTAH STATE UNIVERSITY
Logan, UT 84322-7400

WASHINGTON STATE UNIVERSITY
Pullman, WA 99164

UNIVERSITY OF WASHINGTON
Seattle, WA 98195

DIVISION II

District 1

AMERICAN INTERNATIONAL COLLEGE
Springfield, MA 01109-3189

ASSUMPTION COLLEGE
Worcester, MA 01615-0005

BENTLEY COLLEGE
Waltham, MA 02154-4705

BRYANT COLLEGE
Smithfield, RI 02917-1284

FRANKLIN PIERCE COLLEGE
Rindge, NH 03461

UNIV. OF MASSACHUSETTS-LOWELL
Lowell, MA 01854

MERRIMACK COLLEGE
North Andover, MA 01845

QUINNIPIAC COLLEGE
Hamden, CT 06518-1940

SACRED HEART UNIVERSITY
Fairfield, CT 06432-1000

ST. MICHAEL'S COLLEGE
Colchester, VT 05439

District 2

ADELPHI UNIVERSITY
Garden City, NY 11530

BLUEFIELD STATE COLLEGE
Bluefield, WV 24701-2198

THE UNIVERSITY OF CHARLESTON
Charleston, WV 25304

CLARION UNIVERSITY
Clarion, PA 16214

CONCORD COLLEGE
Athens, WV 24712

DAVIS AND ELKINS COLLEGE
Elkins, WV 26241

DOWLING COLLEGE
Oakdale, NY 11769-1999

EDINBORO UNIVERSITY
Edinboro, PA 16444-0001

FAIRMONT STATE COLLEGE
Fairmont, WV 26554

GANNON UNIVERSITY
Erie, PA 16541

GLENVILLE STATE COLLEGE
Glenville, WV 26351

INDIANA UNIV. OF PENNSYLVANIA
Indiana, PA 15705

LE MOYNE COLLEGE
Syracuse, NY 13214-1399

MERCY COLLEGE
Dobbs Ferry, NY 10522

MERCYHURST COLLEGE
Erie, PA 16546

MILLERSVILLE UNIVERSITY
Millersville, PA 17551-0302

MOLLOY COLLEGE
Rockville Centre, NY 11570

PHILA. COLLEGE OF TEXT. & SCI.
Philadelphia, PA 19144-5497

SALEM-TEIKYO UNIVERSITY
Salem, WV 26426

SHEPHERD COLLEGE
Shepherdstown, WV 25443

SLIPPERY ROCK UNIVERSITY
Slippery Rock, PA 16057

WEST CHESTER UNIVERSITY
West Chester, PA 19383

WEST LIBERTY STATE COLLEGE
West Liberty, WV 26074

WEST VIRGINIA INST. OF TECH
Montgomery, WV 25136

WEST VIRGINIA WESLEYAN COLLEGE
Buckhannon, WV 26201

WHEELING JESUIT COLLEGE
Wheeling, WV 26003-6295

District 3

BARRY UNIVERSITY
Miami Shores, FL 33161

BARTON COLLEGE
Wilson, NC 27893

BELLARMINE COLLEGE
Louisville, KY 40205-0671

BELMONT ABBEY COLLEGE
Belmont, NC 28012-2795

CARSON-NEWMAN COLLEGE
Jefferson City, TN 37760

CATAWBA COLLEGE
Salisbury, NC 28144-2488

COKER COLLEGE
Hartsville, SC 29550

COLUMBUS COLLEGE
Columbus, GA 31907-2079

DELTA STATE UNIVERSITY
Cleveland, MS 38733

ECKERD COLLEGE
St. Petersburg, FL 33733

ELON COLLEGE
Elon College, NC 27244

ERSKINE COLLEGE
Due West, SC 29639

FAYETTEVILLE STATE
UNIVERSITY
Fayetteville, NC 28301-4298

FLORIDA SOUTHERN COLLEGE
Lakeland, FL 33801-5698

FRANCIS MARION UNIVERSITY
Florence, SC 29501-0547

GARDNER-WEBB UNIVERSITY
Boiling Springs, NC 28017

GEORGIA COLLEGE
Milledgeville, GA 31061

HIGH POINT UNIVERSITY
High Point, NC 27262-3598

JOHNSON C. SMITH UNIVERSITY
Charlotte, NC 28216

KENNESAW STATE COLLEGE
Marietta, GA 30061

KENTUCKY STATE UNIVERSITY
Frankfort, KY 40601

KENTUCKY WESLEYAN COLLEGE
Owensboro, KY 42302-1039

LEES-MCRAE COLLEGE
Banner Elk, NC 28604-0128

LENOIR-RHYNE COLLEGE
Hickory, NC 28603

LIMESTONE COLLEGE
Gaffney, SC 29340-3799

LINCOLN MEMORIAL UNIVERSITY
Harrogate, TN 37752

LONGWOOD COLLEGE
Farmville, VA 23909-1899

LYNN UNIVERSITY
Boca Raton, FL 33431

MARS HILL COLLEGE
Mars Hill, NC 28754

MISSISSIPPI COLLEGE
Clinton, MS 39058

MOUNT OLIVE COLLEGE
Mount Olive, NC 28365

NEWBERRY COLLEGE
Newberry, SC 29108

UNIVERSITY OF NORTH ALABAMA
Florence, AL 35632

UNIVERSITY OF NORTH FLORIDA
Jacksonville, FL 32224-2645

NORTHERN KENTUCKY
UNIVERSITY
Highland Heights, KY 41099

PEMBROKE STATE UNIVERSITY
Pembroke, NC 28372-1510

PFEIFFER COLLEGE
Misenheimer, NC 28109-0960

PRESBYTERIAN COLLEGE
Clinton, SC 29325-2998

QUEENS COLLEGE (NC)
Charlotte, NC 28274

ROLLINS COLLEGE
Winter Park, FL 32789

UNIV. OF SOUTH CAROLINA-
AIKEN
Aiken, SC 29801

ST. ANDREWS PRESBYTERIAN
COLL.
Laurinburg, NC 28352-5598

ST. AUGUSTINE'S COLLEGE
Raleigh, NC 27610

ST. PAUL'S COLLEGE
Lawrenceville, VA 23868

UNIVERSITY OF TAMPA
Tampa, FL 33606-1490

VALDOSTA STATE UNIVERSITY
Valdosta, GA 31698

VIRGINIA UNION UNIVERSITY
Richmond, VA 23220-1790

UNIVERSITY OF WEST FLORIDA
Pensacola, FL 32514

WINGATE UNIVERSITY
Wingate, NC 28174

District 4

ASHLAND UNIVERSITY
Ashland, OH 44805

BEMIDJI STATE UNIVERSITY
Bemidji, MN 56601-2699

FERRIS STATE UNIVERSITY
Big Rapids, MI 49307-2295

GRAND VALLEY STATE
UNIVERSITY
Allendale, MI 49401

HILLSDALE COLLEGE
Hillsdale, MI 49242-1298

INDIANA UNIV.-PURDUE UNIV.
Indianapolis, IN 46202

UNIVERSITY OF INDIANAPOLIS
Indianapolis, IN 46227

LEWIS UNIVERSITY
Romeoville, IL 60441

UNIV. OF MINNESOTA-MORRIS
Morris, MN 56267

NORTHERN MICHIGAN
UNIVERSITY
Marquette, MI 49855-5391

NORTHWOOD UNIVERSITY
Midland, MI 48640

OAKLAND CITY COLLEGE
Oakland City, IN 47660-1099

OAKLAND UNIVERSITY
Rochestser, MI 48309-4401

SAGINAW VALLEY STATE UNIV.
University Center, MI 48710

UNIV. OF SOUTHERN INDIANA
Evansville, IN 47712

COLLEGE OF ST. FRANCIS
Joliet, IL 60435

WAYNE STATE UNIVERSITY
Detroit, MI 48202

WINONA STATE UNIVERSITY
Winona, MN 55987-5838

UNIV. OF WISCONSIN-PARKSIDE
Kenosha, WI 53141-2000

District 5

CENTRAL MISSOURI STATE UNIV.
Warrensburg, MO 64093

DRURY COLLEGE
Springfield, MO 65802

LINCOLN UNIVERSITY
Jefferson City, MO 65102-0029

MANKATO STATE UNIVERSITY
Mankato, MN 56002-8400

MISSOURI SOUTHERN ST.
COLLEGE
Joplin, MO 64801-1595

MISSOURI WESTERN ST. COLLEGE
St. Joseph, MO 64507

UNIVERSITY OF MISSOURI
Rolla, MO 65401

UNIVERSITY OF MISSOURI
St. Louis, MO 63121-4499

UNIV. OF NEBRASKA at KEARNEY
Kearney, NE 68849

NORTH DAKOTA STATE
UNIVERSITY
Fargo, ND 58105

UNIVERSITY OF NORTH DAKOTA
Grand Forks, ND 58202

NORTHEAST MISSOURI STATE
UNIV.
Kirksville, MO 63501

UNIV. OF NORTHERN COLORADO
Greeley, CO 80639

NORTHERN STATE UNIVERSITY
Aberdeen, SD 57401

PITTSBURG STATE UNIVERSITY
Pittsburg, KS 66762

SOUTH DAKOTA STATE
UNIVERSITY
Brookings, SD 57007

SOUTHWEST BAPTIST
UNIVERSITY
Bolivar, MO 65613

ST. CLOUD STATE UNIVERSITY
St. Cloud, MN 56301-4498

WASHBURN UNIVERSITY
Topeka, KS 66621

WAYNE STATE COLLEGE
Wayne, NE 68787-1172

District 6

ABILENE CHRISTIAN UNIVERSITY
Abilene, TX 79699

CAMERON UNIVERSITY
Lawton, OK 73505-6377

UNIV. OF CENTRAL ARKANSAS
Conway, AR 72035-0001

UNIVERSITY OF CENTRAL
OKLAHOMA
Edmond, OK 73034

EAST TEXAS STATE UNIVERSITY
Commerce, TX 75429-3011

HENDERSON STATE UNIVERSITY
Arkadelphia, AR 71999-0001

WESTERN NEW MEXICO
UNIVERSITY
Silver City, NM 88061

District 7

ADAMS STATE COLLEGE
Alamosa, CO 81102

COLORADO CHRISTIAN
UNIVERSITY
Lakewood, CO 80226

COLORADO SCHOOL OF MINES
Golden, CO 80401

UNIV. OF COLORADO-COLO.
SPRINGS
Colorado Springs, CO 80933-7150

UNIVERSITY OF DENVER
Denver, CO 80208

FORT HAYS STATE UNIVERSITY
Hays, KS 67601

FORT LEWIS COLLEGE
Durango, CO 81301-3999

GRAND CANYON UNIVERSITY
Phoenix, AZ 85017

REGIS UNIVERSITY
Denver, CO 80221-1099

UNIV. OF SOUTHERN COLORADO
Pueblo, CO 81001-4901

District 8

UNIV. OF CALIFORNIA-DAVIS
Davis, CA 95616

CALIF. STATE U-DOMINGUEZ
HILLS
Carson, CA 90747

CALIF. STATE U.-SAN BERNARDINO
San Bernardino, CA 92407-2397

CALIF. STATE UNIV.-STANISLAUS
Turlock, CA 95382

UNIVERSITY OF HAWAII-HILO
Hilo, HI 96720-4091

PORTLAND STATE UNIVERSITY
Portland, OR 97207-0751

NCAA PROVISIONAL MEMBERS
District 2

WESTMINSTER COLLEGE
New Wilmington, PA 16172

District 3

ANDERSON COLLEGE
Anderson, SC 29621

CHRISTIAN BROTHERS
UNIVERSITY
Memphis, TN 38104

GEORGIA SOUTHWESTERN
COLLEGE
Americus, GA 31709-4693

LAMBUTH UNIVERSITY
Jackson, TN 38301

UNIVERSITY OF MONTEVALLO
Montevallo, AL 35115-6001

TUSCULUM COLLEGE
Greeneville, TN 37743

District 5

EAST CENTRAL UNIVERSITY
Ada, OK 74820

OKLAHOMA PANHANDLE ST. UNIV.
Goodwell, OK 73939

SOUTHEASTERN OKLA. ST. UNIV.
Durant, OK 74701

SOUTHWESTERN OKLAHOMA ST.
UNIV.
Weatherford, OK 73096

District 6

ARKANSAS TECH UNIVERSITY
Russellville, AR 72801-2222

UNIV. OF ARKANSAS-MONTICELLO
Monticello, AR 71656-3596

CONCORDIA UNIVERSITY at
AUSTIN
Austin, TX 78705-2799

HARDING UNIVERSITY
Searcy, AR 72149-0001

INCARNATE WORD COLLEGE
San Antonio, TX 78209

LYON COLLEGE
Batesville, AR 72503-2317

UNIV. OF MARY HARDIN-BAYLOR
Belton, TX 76513

OUACHITA BAPTIST UNIVERSITY
Arkadelphia, AR 71998-0001

SOUTHERN ARKANSAS
UNIVERSITY
Magnolia, AR 71753-5000

ST. EDWARD'S UNIVERSITY
Austin, TX 78704

ST. MARY'S UNIVERSITY
San Antonio, TX 78228-8572

TEXAS LUTHERAN COLLEGE
Seguin, TX 78155

TEXAS WESLEYAN UNIVERSITY
Fort Worth, TX 76105

District 8

ST. MARTIN'S COLLEGE
Lacey, WA 98503

WESTERN WASHINGTON UNIV.
Bellingham, WA 98225

WOMEN'S GOLF

DIVISION I
District 1

BOSTON COLLEGE
Chestnut Hill, MA 02167-3934

BOSTON UNIVERSITY
Boston, MA 02215

DARTMOUTH COLLEGE
Hanover, NH 03755

UNIVERSITY OF HARTFORD
West Hartford, CT 06117-1599

HARVARD UNIVERSITY
Cambridge, MA 02138-3800

UNIVERSITY OF NEW HAMPSHIRE
Durham, NH 03824

YALE UNIVERSITY
New Haven, CT 06520-7398

District 2

JAMES MADISON UNIVERSITY
Harrisonburg, VA 22807

PENNSYLVANIA STATE UNIV.
University Park, PA 16802

PRINCETON UNIVERSITY
Princeton, NJ 08544

RUTGERS UNIVERSITY
New Brunswick, NJ 08903

SIENA COLLEGE
Loudonville, NY 12211-1462

ST. FRANCIS COLLEGE
Loretto, PA 15940-0600

WAGNER COLLEGE
Staten Island, NY 10301-4495

COLLEGE OF WILLIAM & MARY
Williamsburg, VA 23187

District 3

ALABAMA STATE UNIVERSITY
Montgomery, AL 36101-0271

UNIV. OF ALABAMA at
TUSCALOOSA
Tuscaloosa, AL 35487

UNIV. OF ALABAMA at
BIRMINGHAM
Birmingham, AL 35294-0110

APPALACHIAN STATE UNIVERSITY
Boone, NC 28608

AUBURN UNIVERSITY
Auburn University, AL 36849-5113

CAMPBELL UNIVERSITY
Buies Creek, NC 27506

UNIVERSITY OF CENTRAL
FLORIDA
Orlando, FL 32816-0002

CHARLESTON SOUTHERN UNIV.
Charleston, SC 29423-8087

COLLEGE OF CHARLESTON
Charleston, SC 29424

COASTAL CAROLINA UNIVERSITY
Conway, SC 29526

DUKE UNIVERSITY
Durham, NC 27708-0555

EAST TENNESSEE STATE UNIV.
Johnson City, TN 37614

EASTERN KENTUCKY UNIVERSITY
Richmond, KY 40475-3101

FLORIDA ATLANTIC UNIVERSITY
Boca Raton, FL 33431-0991

FLORIDA INTERNATIONAL UNIV.
Miami, FL 33199

FLORIDA STATE UNIVERSITY
Tallahassee, FL 32306

UNIVERSITY OF FLORIDA
Gainesville, FL 32604

FURMAN UNIVERSITY
Greenville, SC 29613

GEORGIA STATE UNIVERSITY
Atlanta, GA 30303-3083

UNIVERSITY OF GEORGIA
Athens, GA 30613

JACKSONVILLE STATE
UNIVERSITY
Jacksonville, AL 36265-9982

JACKSONVILLE UNIVERSITY
Jacksonville, FL 32211-3394

UNIVERSITY OF KENTUCKY
Lexington, KY 40506-0032

LOUISIANA STATE UNIVERSITY
Baton Rouge, LA 70803

UNIVERSITY OF MEMPHIS
Memphis, TN 38152

MERCER UNIVERSITY
Macon, GA 31207

UNIVERSITY OF MIAMI
Coral Gables, FL 33124-6710

MISSISSIPPI STATE UNIVERSITY
Mississippi State, MS 39762-5509

UNIVERSITY OF MISSISSIPPI
University, MS 38677

MURRAY STATE UNIVERSITY
Murray, KY 42071-0009

UNIVERSITY OF NEW ORLEANS
New Orleans, LA 70148

UNIVERSITY OF NORTH
CAROLINA
Chapel Hill, NC 27514

UNIVERSITY OF NORTH
CAROLINA
Greensboro, NC 27412-5001

UNIVERSITY OF NORTH
CAROLINA
Wilmington, NC 28403-3297

RADFORD UNIVERSITY
Radford, VA 24142

SAMFORD UNIVERSITY
Birmingham, AL 35229

UNIVERSITY OF SOUTH ALABAMA
Mobile, AL 36688

UNIVERSITY OF SOUTH CAROLINA
Columbia, SC 29208

UNIVERSITY OF SOUTH FLORIDA
Tampa, FL 33620

UNIV. OF SOUTHERN MISSISSIPPI
Hattiesburg, MS 39406-5001

STETSON UNIVERSITY
De Land, FL 32720

TENNESSEE TECHNOLOGICAL
UNIV.
Cookeville, TN 38505-0001

THE UNIVERSITY OF TENNESSEE
Knoxville, TN 37996

TROY STATE UNIVERSITY
Troy, AL 36082

TULANE UNIVERSITY
New Orleans, LA 70118

VANDERBILT UNIVERSITY
Nashville, TN 37212

WAKE FOREST UNIVERSITY
Winston-Salem, NC 27109

WESTERN CAROLINA UNIVERSITY
Cullowhee, NC 28723

WESTERN KENTUCKY
UNIVERSITY
Bowling Green, KY 42101-3576

WINTHROP UNIVERSITY
Rock Hill, SC 29733

WOFFORD COLLEGE
Spartanburg, SC 29303-3663

District 4

BOWLING GREEN STATE UNIV.
Bowling Green, OH 43403

CHICAGO STATE UNIVERSITY
Chicago, IL 60628-1598

UNIVERSITY OF CINCINNATI
Cincinnati, OH 45221

UNIVERSITY OF DAYTON
Dayton, OH 45469

ILLINOIS STATE UNIVERSITY
Normal, IL 61761

UNIVERSITY OF ILLINOIS
Champaign, IL 61820

INDIANA UNIVERSITY
Bloomington, IN 47405

UNIVERSITY OF IOWA
Iowa City, IA 52242

LOYOLA UNIVERSITY
Chicago, IL 60626

MICHIGAN STATE UNIVERSITY
East Lansing, MI 48824

UNIVERSITY OF MICHIGAN
Ann Arbor, MI 48109-2201

UNIV. OF MINNESOTA-TWIN
CITIES
Minneapolis, MN 55455

NORTHEASTERN ILLINOIS UNIV.
Chicago, IL 60625-4699

NORTHERN ILLINOIS UNIVERSITY
De Kalb, IL 60115-2854

NORTHWESTERN UNIVERSITY
Evanston, IL 60208

UNIVERSITY OF NOTRE DAME
Notre Dame, IN 46556

OHIO STATE UNIVERSITY
Columbus, OH 43210

PURDUE UNIVERSITY
West Lafayette, IN 47907

UNIVERSITY OF TOLEDO
Toledo, OH 43606

UNIVERSITY OF WISCONSIN
Madison, WI 53711

XAVIER UNIVERSITY
Cincinnati, OH 45207-6114

District 5

BRADLEY UNIVERSITY
Peoria, IL 61625

UNIVERSITY OF COLORADO
Boulder, CO 80309

CREIGHTON UNIVERSITY
Omaha, NE 68178-0001

IOWA STATE UNIVERSITY
Ames, IA 50011

KANSAS STATE UNIVERSITY
Manhattan, KS 66506

UNIVERSITY OF KANSAS
Lawrence, KS 66045

UNIV. OF MISSOURI-COLUMBIA
Columbia, MO 65211

UNIV. OF MISSOURI-KANSAS CITY
Kansas City, MO 64110

UNIVERSITY OF NEBRASKA
Lincoln, NE 68588

UNIVERSITY OF NORTHERN IOWA
Cedar Falls, IA 50614

OKLAHOMA STATE UNIVERSITY
Stillwater, OK 74078

UNIVERSITY OF OKLAHOMA
Norman, OK 73019

ORAL ROBERTS UNIVERSITY
Tulsa, OK 74171

SOUTHERN ILLINOIS UNIVERSITY
Carbondale, IL 62901

SOUTHWEST MISSOURI STATE
UNIV.
Springfield, MO 65804

UNIVERSITY OF TULSA
Tulsa, OK 74104

WICHITA STATE UNIVERSITY
Wichita, KS 67260

District 6

ALCORN STATE UNIVERSITY
Lorman, MS 39096-9402

ARKANSAS STATE UNIVERSITY
State University, AR 72467

UNIVERSITY OF ARKANSAS
Fayetteville, AR 72701

UNIVERSITY OF ARKANSAS
Little Rock, AR 72204-1099

BAYLOR UNIVERSITY
Waco, TX 76798

GRAMBLING STATE UNIVERSITY
Grambling, LA 71245

JACKSON STATE UNIVERSITY
Jackson, MS 39217

LAMAR UNIVERSITY
Beaumont, TX 77710

MISSISSIPPI VALLEY ST. UNIV.
Itta Bena, MS 38941-1400

UNIVERSITY OF NORTH TEXAS
Denton, TX 76203-6737

PRAIRIE VIEW A&M UNIVERSITY
Prairie View, TX 77446

SOUTHERN METHODIST
UNIVERSITY
Dallas, TX 75275

SOUTHERN UNIVERSITY
Baton Rouge, LA 70813

UNIVERSITY OF TEXAS
Austin, TX 78712

TEXAS A&M UNIVERSITY
College Station, TX 77843-1228

TEXAS CHRISTIAN UNIVERSITY
Fort Worth, TX 76129-0001

UNIV. OF TEXAS-PAN AMERICAN
Edinburg, TX 78539-2999

TEXAS SOUTHERN UNIVERSITY
Houston, TX 77004

TEXAS TECH UNIVERSITY
Lubbock, TX 79409

District 7

BOISE STATE UNIVERSITY
Boise, ID 83725

BRIGHAM YOUNG UNIVERSITY
Provo, UT 84602

COLORADO STATE UNIVERSITY
Fort Collins, CO 80523-0100

GONZAGA UNIVERSITY
Spokane, WA 99258

UNIVERSITY OF HAWAII-MANOA
Honolulu, HI 96822-2370

IDAHO STATE UNIVERSITY
Pocatello, ID 83209

UNIVERSITY OF IDAHO
Moscow, ID 83843

MONTANA STATE UNIV-BOZEMAN
Bozeman, MT 59717-0338

THE UNIVERSITY OF MONTANA
Missoula, MT 59812-1291

UNIVERSITY OF NEW MEXICO
Albuquerque, NM 87131

NORTHERN ARIZONA UNIVERSITY
Flagstaff, AZ 86011

SAN DIEGO STATE UNIVERSITY
San Diego, CA 92182

UNIVERSITY OF TEXAS-EL PASO
El Paso, TX 79968

WEBER STATE UNIVERSITY
Ogden, UT 84408-2701

UNIVERSITY OF WYOMING
Laramie, WY 82071

District 8

ARIZONA STATE UNIVERSITY
Tempe, AZ 85287-2505

UNIVERSITY OF ARIZONA
Tucson, AZ 85721

UNIV. OF CALIFORNIA-BERKELEY
Berkeley, CA 94720

UNIV. OF CALIF.-LOS ANGELES
Los Angeles, CA 90095-1405

EASTERN WASHINGTON
UNIVERSITY
Cheney, WA 99004

LONG BEACH STATE UNIVERSITY
Long Beach, CA 90840-0118

NEW MEXICO STATE UNIVERSITY
Las Cruces, NM 88003

OREGON STATE UNIVERSITY
Corvallis, OR 97331

UNIVERSITY OF OREGON
Eugene, OR 97403-1226

PEPPERDINE UNIVERSITY
Malibu, CA 90263

UNIVERSITY OF SAN FRANCISCO
San Francisco, CA 94117-1080

SAN JOSE STATE UNIVERSITY
San Jose, CA 95192

SANTA CLARA UNIVERSITY
Santa Clara, CA 95053

UNIV. OF SOUTHERN CALIFORNIA
Los Angeles, CA 90089-0012

STANFORD UNIVERSITY
Stanford, CA 94305

WASHINGTON STATE UNIVERSITY
Pullman, WA 99164

UNIVERSITY OF WASHINGTON
Seattle, WA 98195

DIVISION II

District 1
SACRED HEART UNIVERSITY
Fairfield, CT 06432-1000

District 2
FAIRMONT STATE COLLEGE
Fairmont, WV 26554

District 3
BELLARMINE COLLEGE
Louisville, KY 40205-0671

FLORIDA SOUTHERN COLLEGE
Lakeland, FL 33801-5698

LONGWOOD COLLEGE
Farmville, VA 23909-1899

LYNN UNIVERSITY
Boca Raton, FL 33431

ROLLINS COLLEGE
Winter Park, FL 32789

District 4
FERRIS STATE UNIVERSITY
Big Rapids, MI 49307-2295

GRAND VALLEY STATE
UNIVERSITY
Allendale, MI 49401

UNIVERSITY OF INDIANAPOLIS
Indianapolis, IN 46227

LEWIS UNIVERSITY
Romeoville, IL 60441

UNIV. OF MINNESOTA-MORRIS
Morris, MN 56267

MOOREHEAD STATE UNIVERSITY
Moorhead, MN 56563-2996

OAKLAND CITY COLLEGE
Oakland City, IN 47660-1099

OAKLAND UNIVERSITY
Rochestser, MI 48309-4401

WINONA STATE UNIVERSITY
Winona, MN 55987-5838

District 5
CHADRON STATE COLLEGE
Chadron, NE 69337

MANKATO STATE UNIVERSITY
Mankato, MN 56002-8400

UNIV. OF NEBRASKA at KEARNEY
Kearney, NE 68849

UNIVERSITY OF NORTH DAKOTA
Grand Forks, ND 58202

NORTHEAST MISSOURI STATE
UNIV.
Kirksville, MO 63501

UNIV. OF NORTHERN COLORADO
Greeley, CO 80639

NORTHERN STATE UNIVERSITY
Aberdeen, SD 57401

SOUTH DAKOTA STATE
UNIVERSITY
Brookings, SD 57007

ST. CLOUD STATE UNIVERSITY
St. Cloud, MN 56301-4498

WAYNE STATE COLLEGE
Wayne, NE 68787-1172

District 6
WESTERN NEW MEXICO
UNIVERSITY
Silver City, NM 88061

District 7
UNIVERSITY OF DENVER
Denver, CO 80208

MESA STATE COLLEGE
Grand Junction, CO 81501

NCAA PROVISIONAL MEMBERS
District 3
UNIVERSITY OF MONTEVALLO
Montevallo, AL 35115-6001

District 8
WESTERN WASHINGTON UNIV.
Bellingham, WA 98225

MEN'S GYMNASTICS

DIVISION I

District 1

UNIV. OF MASSACHUSETTS-AMHERST
Amherst, MA 01003

UNIVERSITY OF VERMONT
Burlington, VT 05405

District 2

JAMES MADISON UNIVERSITY
Harrisonburg, VA 22807

PENNSYLVANIA STATE UNIV.
University Park, PA 16802

SYRACUSE UNIVERSITY
Syracuse, NY 13244

TEMPLE UNIVERSITY
Philadelphia, PA 19122

U.S. MILITARY ACADEMY
West Point, NY 10996

U.S. NAVAL ACADEMY
Annapolis, MD 21402

COLLEGE OF WILLIAM & MARY
Williamsburg, VA 23187

District 3

RADFORD UNIVERSITY
Radford, VA 24142

District 4

UNIVERSITY OF ILLINOIS
Champaign, IL 61820

UNIVERSITY OF ILLINOIS
Chicago, IL 60607

UNIVERSITY OF IOWA
Iowa City, IA 52242

MICHIGAN STATE UNIVERSITY
East Lansing, MI 48824

UNIVERSITY OF MICHIGAN
Ann Arbor, MI 48109-2201

UNIV. OF MINNESOTA-TWIN CITIES
Minneapolis, MN 55455

OHIO STATE UNIVERSITY
Columbus, OH 43210

WESTERN MICHIGAN UNIVERSITY
Kalamazoo, MI 49008-5134

District 5

UNIVERSITY OF NEBRASKA
Lincoln, NE 68588

UNIVERSITY OF OKLAHOMA
Norman, OK 73019

District 7

BRIGHAM YOUNG UNIVERSITY
Provo, UT 84602

UNIVERSITY OF NEW MEXICO
Albuquerque, NM 87131

U.S. AIR FORCE ACADEMY
USAF Academy, CO 80840-5461

District 8

UNIV. OF CALIFORNIA-BERKELEY
Berkeley, CA 94720

UNIV. OF CALIF-SANTA BARBARA
Santa Barbara, CA 93106

SAN JOSE STATE UNIVERSITY
San Jose, CA 95192

STANFORD UNIVERSITY
Stanford, CA 94305

DIVISION II

District 1

SOUTHERN CONNECTICUT ST. UNIV.
New Haven, CT 06515

WOMEN'S GYMNASTICS

DIVISION I

District 1

BROWN UNIVERSITY
Providence, RI 02912

UNIV. OF MASSACHUSETTS-AMHERST
Amherst, MA 01003

UNIVERSITY OF NEW HAMPSHIRE
Durham, NH 03824

NORTHEASTERN UNIVERSITY
Boston, MA 02115-5096

UNIVERSITY OF RHODE ISLAND
Kingston, RI 02881

UNIVERSITY OF VERMONT
Burlington, VT 05405

YALE UNIVERSITY
New Haven, CT 06520-7398

District 2

CORNELL UNIVERSITY
Ithaca, NY 14853

GEORGE WASHINGTON
UNIVERSITY
Washington, DC 20052

JAMES MADISON UNIVERSITY
Harrisonburg, VA 22807

PENNSYLVANIA STATE UNIV.
University Park, PA 16802

UNIVERSITY OF PENNSYLVANIA
Philadelphia, PA 19104-6380

UNIVERSITY OF PITTSBURGH
Pittsburgh, PA 15260

RUTGERS UNIVERSITY
New Brunswick, NJ 08903

TEMPLE UNIVERSITY
Philadelphia, PA 19122

TOWSON STATE UNIVERSITY
Towson, MD 21204

WEST VIRGINIA UNIVERSITY
Morgantown, WV 26506-6201

COLLEGE OF WILLIAM & MARY
Williamsburg, VA 23187

District 3

UNIV. OF ALABAMA at
TUSCALOOSA
Tuscaloosa, AL 3587

AUBURN UNIVERSITY
Auburn University, AL 36849-5113

UNIVERSITY OF FLORIDA
Gainesville, FL 32604

UNIVERSITY OF GEORGIA
Athens, GA 30613

UNIVERSITY OF KENTUCKY
Lexington, KY 40506-0032

LOUISIANA STATE UNIVERSITY
Baton Rouge, LA 70803

UNIVERSITY OF MARYLAND
College Park, MD 20740

UNIVERSITY OF NORTH
CAROLINA
Chapel Hill, NC 27514

NORTH CAROLINA STATE UNIV.
Raleigh, NC 27695-7001

RADFORD UNIVERSITY
Radford, VA 24142

District 4

BALL STATE UNIVERSITY
Muncie, IN 47306

BOWLING GREEN STATE UNIV.
Bowling Green, OH 43403

CENTRAL MICHIGAN UNIVERSITY
Mount Pleasant, MI 48859

EASTERN MICHIGAN UNIVERSITY
Ypsilanti, MI 48197

ILLINOIS STATE UNIVERSITY
Normal, IL 61761

UNIVERSITY OF ILLINOIS
Champaign, IL 61820

UNIVERSITY OF ILLINOIS
Chicago, IL 60607

UNIVERSITY OF IOWA
Iowa City, IA 52242

KENT STATE UNIVERSITY
Kent, OH 44242

MICHIGAN STATE UNIVERSITY
East Lansing, MI 48824

UNIVERSITY OF MICHIGAN
Ann Arbor, MI 48109-2201

UNIV. OF MINNESOTA-TWIN
CITIES
Minneapolis, MN 55455

NORTHERN ILLINOIS UNIVERSITY
De Kalb, IL 60115-2854

OHIO STATE UNIVERSITY
Columbus, OH 43210

WESTERN MICHIGAN UNIVERSITY
Kalamazoo, MI 49008-5134

District 5

IOWA STATE UNIVERSITY
Ames, IA 50011

UNIV. OF MISSOURI-COLUMBIA
Columbia, MO 65211

UNIVERSITY OF NEBRASKA
Lincoln, NE 68588

UNIVERSITY OF OKLAHOMA
Norman, OK 73019

SOUTHEAST MISSOURI STATE
UNIV.
Cape Girardeau, MO 63701-4799

District 6

CENTENARY COLLEGE
Shreveport, LA 71134-1188

District 7

BOISE STATE UNIVERSITY
Boise, ID 83725

BRIGHAM YOUNG UNIVERSITY
Provo, UT 84602

UNIVERSITY OF DENVER
Denver, CO 80208

SOUTHERN UTAH UNIVERSITY
Cedar City, UT 84720

UNIVERSITY OF UTAH
Salt Lake City, UT 84112

District 8

ARIZONA STATE UNIVERSITY
Tempe, AZ 85287-2505

UNIVERSITY OF ARIZONA
Tucson, AZ 85721

UNIV. OF CALIFORNIA-BERKELEY
Berkeley, CA 94720

UNIV. OF CALIFORNIA-DAVIS
Davis, CA 95616

UNIV. OF CALIF.-LOS ANGELES
Los Angeles, CA 90095-1405

UNIV. OF CALIF-SANTA BARBARA
Santa Barbara, CA 93106

CALIF. STATE UNIV.-FULLERTON
Fullerton, CA 92634-9480

CALIF. STATE UNIV.-SACRAMENTO
Sacramento, CA 95819

OREGON STATE UNIVERSITY
Corvallis, OR 97331

SAN JOSE STATE UNIVERSITY
San Jose, CA 95192

STANFORD UNIVERSITY
Stanford, CA 94305

UTAH STATE UNIVERSITY
Logan, UT 84322-7400

UNIVERSITY OF WASHINGTON
Seattle, WA 98195

DIVISION II

District 1

UNIVERSITY OF BRIDGEPORT
Bridgeport, CT 06601

SOUTHERN CONNECTICUT ST.
UNIV.
New Haven, CT 06515

District 2

INDIANA UNIV. OF PENNSYLVANIA
Indiana, PA 15705

WEST CHESTER UNIVERSITY
West Chester, PA 19383

District 4

WINONA STATE UNIVERSITY
Winona, MN 55987-5838

District 6

TEXAS WOMAN'S UNIVERSITY
Denton, TX 76204

District 7

U.S. AIR FORCE ACADEMY
USAF Academy, CO 80840-5461

District 8

UNIVERSITY OF ALASKA-
ANCHORAGE
Anchorage, AK 99508

SEATTLE PACIFIC UNIVERSITY
Seattle, WA 98119

MEN'S ICE HOCKEY

DIVISION I

District 1

BOSTON COLLEGE
Chestnut Hill, MA 02167-3934

BOSTON UNIVERSITY
Boston, MA 02215

BROWN UNIVERSITY
Providence, RI 02912

UNIVERSITY OF CONNECTICUT
Storrs, CT 06269

DARTMOUTH COLLEGE
Hanover, NH 03755

FAIRFIELD UNIVERSITY
Fairfield, CT 06430-5195

HARVARD UNIVERSITY
Cambridge, MA 02138-3800

COLLEGE OF THE HOLY CROSS
Worcester, MA 01610-2395

UNIVERSITY OF MAINE
Orono, ME 04469

UNIV. OF MASSACHUSETTS-
LOWELL
Lowell, MA 01854

UNIV. OF MASSACHUSETTS-
AMHERST
Amherst, MA 01003

MERRIMACK COLLEGE
North Andover, MA 01845

UNIVERSITY OF NEW HAMPSHIRE
Durham, NH 03824

NORTHEASTERN UNIVERSITY
Boston, MA 02115-5096

PROVIDENCE COLLEGE
Providence, RI 02918

UNIVERSITY OF VERMONT
Burlington, VT 05405

YALE UNIVERSITY
New Haven, CT 06520-7398

District 2

CANISIUS COLLEGE
Buffalo, NY 14208-1098

CLARKSON UNIVERSITY
Potsdam, NY 13699-5500

COLGATE UNIVERSITY
Hamilton, NY 13346-1304

CORNELL UNIVERSITY
Ithaca, NY 14853

IONA COLLEGE
New Rochelle, NY 10801

PRINCETON UNIVERSITY
Princeton, NJ 08544

FRENSSELAER POLYTECHNIC
INST.
Troy, NY 12180-3590

ST. LAWRENCE UNIVERSITY
Canton, NY 13617

U.S. MILITARY ACADEMY
West Point, NY 10996

UNION COLLEGE
Schenectady, NY 12308

VILLANOVA UNIVERSITY
Villanova, PA 19085

District 4

BOWLING GREEN STATE UNIV.
Bowling Green, OH 43403

FERRIS STATE UNIVERSITY
Big Rapids, MI 49307-2295

UNIVERSITY OF ILLINOIS
Chicago, IL 60607

LAKE SUPERIOR STATE
UNIVERSITY
Sault Sainte Marie, MI 49783

MIAMI UNIVERSITY
Oxford, OH 45056

MICHIGAN STATE UNIVERSITY
East Lansing, MI 48824

MICHIGAN TECHNOLOGICAL
UNIV.
Houghton, MI 49931-1295

UNIVERSITY OF MICHIGAN
Ann Arbor, MI 48109-2201

UNIV. OF MINNESOTA-DULUTH
Duluth, MN 55812

UNIV. OF MINNESOTA-TWIN
CITIES
Minneapolis, MN 55455

NORTHERN MICHIGAN
UNIVERSITY
Marquette, MI 49855-5391

UNIVERSITY OF NOTRE DAME
Notre Dame, IN 46556

OHIO STATE UNIVERSITY
Columbus, OH 43210

WESTERN MICHIGAN UNIVERSITY
Kalamazoo, MI 49008-5134

UNIVERSITY OF WISCONSIN
Madison, WI 53711

District 5

UNIVERSITY OF NORTH DAKOTA
Grand Forks, ND 58202

ST. CLOUD STATE UNIVERSITY
St. Cloud, MN 56301-4498

District 7

COLORADO COLLEGE
Colorado Springs, CO 80903

UNIVERSITY OF DENVER
Denver, CO 80208

U.S. AIR FORCE ACADEMY
USAF Academy, CO 80840-5461

District 8

UNIVERSITY OF ALASKA-
ANCHORAGE
Anchorage, AK 99508

UNIVERSITY OF ALASKA-
FAIRBANKS
Fairbanks, AK 99775-7500

DIVISION II

District 1

AMERICAN INTERNATIONAL
COLLEGE
Springfield, MA 01109-3189

ASSUMPTION COLLEGE
Worcester, MA 01615-0005

BENTLEY COLLEGE
Waltham, MA 02154-4705

NEW HAMPSHIRE COLLEGE
Hooksett, NH 03106-1045

QUINNIPIAC COLLEGE
Hamden, CT 06518-1940

SACRED HEART UNIVERSITY
Fairfield, CT 06432-1000

ST. ANSELM COLLEGE
Manchester, NH 03102-1310

ST. MICHAEL'S COLLEGE
Colchester, VT 05439

STONEHILL COLLEGE
North Easton, MA 02357

District 2

MERCYHURST COLLEGE
Erie, PA 16546

District 3

UNIV. OF ALABAMA-HUNTSVILLE
Huntsville, AL 35899

District 4

BEMIDJI STATE UNIVERSITY
Bemidji, MN 56601-2699

District 5

MANKATO STATE UNIVERSITY
Mankato, MN 56002-8400

MEN'S LACROSSE

DIVISION I

District 1

BOSTON COLLEGE
Chestnut Hill, MA 02167-3934

BOSTON UNIVERSITY
Boston, MA 02215

DARTMOUTH COLLEGE
Hanover, NH 03755

FAIRFIELD UNIVERSITY
Fairfield, CT 06430-5195

UNIVERSITY OF HARTFORD
West Hartford, CT 06117-1599

HARVARD UNIVERSITY
Cambridge, MA 02138-3800

COLLEGE OF THE HOLY CROSS
Worcester, MA 01610-2395

UNIV. OF MASSACHUSETTS-
AMHERST
Amherst, MA 01003

UNIVERSITY OF NEW HAMPSHIRE
Durham, NH 03824

PROVIDENCE COLLEGE
Providence, RI 02918

UNIVERSITY OF VERMONT
Burlington, VT 05405

YALE UNIVERSITY
New Haven, CT 06520-7398

District 2

BUCKNELL UNIVERSITY
Lewisburg, PA 17837

CANISIUS COLLEGE
Buffalo, NY 14208-1098

COLGATE UNIVERSITY
Hamilton, NY 13346-1304

CORNELL UNIVERSITY
Ithaca, NY 14853

UNIVERSITY OF DELAWARE
Newark, DE 19716

DREXEL UNIVERSITY
Philadelphia, PA 19104

GEORGETOWN UNIVERSITY
Washington, DC 20057

HOBART & WM. SMITH COLLEGES
Geneva, NY 14456

HOFSTRA UNIVERSITY
Hempstead, NY 11550

LAFAYETTE COLLEGE
Easton, PA 18042

LEHIGH UNIVERSITY
Bethlehem, PA 18015-3089

LOYOLA COLLEGE
Baltimore, MD 21210

MANHATTAN COLLEGE
Riverdale, NY 10471

MARIST COLLEGE
Poughkeepsie, NY 12601-1387

UNIV. OF MARYLAND-BALT. CO.
Baltimore, MD 21228-5398

MOUNT ST. MARY'S COLLEGE
Emmitsburg, MD 21727-7799

NIAGARA UNIVERSITY
Niagara University, NY 14109

PENNSYLVANIA STATE UNIV.
University Park, PA 16802

UNIVERSITY OF PENNSYLVANIA
Philadelphia, PA 19104-6380

PRINCETON UNIVERSITY
Princeton, NJ 08544

RUTGERS UNIVERSITY
New Brunswick, NJ 08903

SIENA COLLEGE
Loudonville, NY 12211-1462

St. JOHN'S UNIVERSITY
Jamaica, NY 11439

ST. JOSEPH'S UNIVERSITY
Philadelphia, PA 19131-1395

STATE UNIV. OF N.Y. at STONY
BROOK
Stony Brook, NY 11794

SYRACUSE UNIVERSITY
Syracuse, NY 13244

TOWSON STATE UNIVERSITY
Towson, MD 21204

U.S. MILITARY ACADEMY
West Point, NY 10996

U.S. NAVAL ACADEMY
Annapolis, MD 21402

VILLANOVA UNIVERSITY
Villanova, PA 19085

District 3

DUKE UNIVERSITY
Durham, NC 27708-0555

JOHNS HOPKINS UNIVERSITY
Baltimore, MD 21218-2684

UNIVERSITY OF MARYLAND
College Park, MD 20740

UNIVERSITY OF NORTH
CAROLINA
Chapel Hill, NC 27514

RADFORD UNIVERSITY
Radford, VA 24142

VIRGINIA MILITARY INSTITUTE
Lexington, VA 24450-0304

UNIVERSITY OF VIRGINIA
Charlottesville, VA 22903

District 4

BUTLER UNIVERSITY
Indianapolis, IN 46208

MICHIGAN STATE UNIVERSITY
East Lansing, MI 48824

UNIVERSITY OF NOTRE DAME
Notre Dame, IN 46556

OHIO STATE UNIVERSITY
Columbus, OH 43210

District 7

U.S. AIR FORCE ACADEMY
USAF Academy, CO 80840-5461

DIVISION II

District 1

AMERICAN INTERNATIONAL
COLLEGE
Springfield, MA 01109-3189

ASSUMPTION COLLEGE
Worcester, MA 01615-0005

BENTLEY COLLEGE
Waltham, MA 02154-4705

MERRIMACK COLLEGE
North Andover, MA 01845

NEW HAMPSHIRE COLLEGE
Hooksett, NH 03106-1045

UNIVERSITY OF NEW HAVEN
West Haven, CT 06516-1999

QUINNIPIAC COLLEGE
Hamden, CT 06518-1940

SACRED HEART UNIVERSITY
Fairfield, CT 06432-1000

ST. ANSELM COLLEGE
Manchester, NH 03102-1310

ST. MICHAEL'S COLLEGE
Colchester, VT 05439

District 2

ADELPHI UNIVERSITY
Garden City, NY 11530

STATE UNIV. OF N.Y. at ALBANY
Albany, NY 12222

DOWLING COLLEGE
Oakdale, NY 11769-1999

LE MOYNE COLLEGE
Syracuse, NY 13214-1399

LONG ISLAND U./C.W. POST
CAMPUS
Brookville, NY 11548

NEW YORK INSTITUTE OF TECH.
Old Westbury, NY 11568-8000

PACE UNIVERSITY
New York, NY 10038-1502

QUEENS COLLEGE (NY)
Flushing, NY 11367

SOUTHAMPTON CAMPUS OF L.I.U.
Southampton, NY 11968

WEST CHESTER UNIVERSITY
West Chester, PA 19383

District 3

CATAWBA COLLEGE
Salisbury, NC 28144-2488

LIMESTONE COLLEGE
Gaffney, SC 29340-3799

PFEIFFER COLLEGE
Misenheimer, NC 28109-0960

ST. ANDREWS PRESBYTERIAN
COLL.
Laurinburg, NC 28352-5598

District 4
NORTHWOOD UNIVERSITY
Midland, MI 48640

District 7
COLORADO SCHOOL OF MINES
Golden, CO 80401

UNIVERSITY OF DENVER
Denver, CO 80208

REGIS UNIVERSITY
Denver, CO 80221-1099

WOMEN'S LACROSSE

DIVISION I

District 1

BOSTON COLLEGE
Chestnut Hill, MA 02167-3934

BOSTON UNIVERSITY
Boston, MA 02215

BROWN UNIVERSITY
Providence, RI 02912

DARTMOUTH COLLEGE
Hanover, NH 03755

HARVARD UNIVERSITY
Cambridge, MA 02138-3800

COLLEGE OF THE HOLY CROSS
Worcester, MA 01610-2395

UNIV. OF MASSACHUSETTS-
AMHERST
Amherst, MA 01003

UNIVERSITY OF NEW HAMPSHIRE
Durham, NH 03824

UNIVERSITY OF VERMONT
Burlington, VT 05405

YALE UNIVERSITY
New Haven, CT 06520-7398

District 2

AMERICAN UNIVERSITY
Washington, DC 20016

BUCKNELL UNIVERSITY
Lewisburg, PA 17837

COLGATE UNIVERSITY
Hamilton, NY 13346-1304

COLUMBIA UNIV.-BARNARD
COLLEGE
New York, NY 10027

CORNELL UNIVERSITY
Ithaca, NY 14853

UNIVERSITY OF DELAWARE
Newark, DE 19716

DREXEL UNIVERSITY
Philadelphia, PA 19104

GEORGE MASON UNIVERSISTY
Fairfax, VA 22030

GEORGETOWN UNIVERSITY
Washington, DC 20057

HOFSTRA UNIVERSITY
Hempstead, NY 11550

JAMES MADISON UNIVERSITY
Harrisonburg, VA 22807

LAFAYETTE COLLEGE
Easton, PA 18042

LEHIGH UNIVERSITY
Bethlehem, PA 18015-3089

LOYOLA COLLEGE
Baltimore, MD 21210

MANHATTAN COLLEGE
Riverdale, NY 10471

UNIV. OF MARYLAND-BALT. CO.
Baltimore, MD 21228-5398

MONMOUTH UNIVERSITY
West Long Branch, NJ 07764

MOUNT ST. MARY'S COLLEGE
Emmitsburg, MD 21727-7799

NIAGARA UNIVERSITY
Niagara University, NY 14109

PENNSYLVANIA STATE UNIV.
University Park, PA 16802

UNIVERSITY OF PENNSYLVANIA
Philadelphia, PA 19104-6380

PRINCETON UNIVERSITY
Princeton, NJ 08544

RUTGERS UNIVERSITY
New Brunswick, NJ 08903

ST. JOSEPH'S UNIVERSITY
Philadelphia, PA 19131-1395

TEMPLE UNIVERSITY
Philadelphia, PA 19122

TOWSON STATE UNIVERSITY
Towson, MD 21204

VILLANOVA UNIVERSITY
Villanova, PA 19085

COLLEGE OF WILLIAM & MARY
Williamsburg, VA 23187

District 3

DAVIDSON COLLEGE
Davidson, NC 28036

DUKE UNIVERSITY
Durham, NC 27708-0555

UNIVERSITY OF MARYLAND
College Park, MD 20740

UNIVERSITY OF NORTH
CAROLINA
Chapel Hill, NC 27514

OLD DOMINION UNIVERSITY
Norfolk, VA 23529

UNIVERSITY OF RICHMOND
Richmond, VA 23173-1903

VANDERBILT UNIVERSITY
Nashville, TN 37212

VIRGINIA POLYTECHNIC
INSTITUTE
Blacksburg, VA 24061

UNIVERSITY OF VIRGINIA
Charlottesville, VA 22903

District 4

OHIO STATE UNIVERSITY
Columbus, OH 43210

District 8

STANFORD UNIVERSITY
Stanford, CA 94305

DIVISION II

District 1

SACRED HEART UNIVERSITY
Fairfield, CT 06432-1000

ST. MICHAEL'S COLLEGE
Colchester, VT 05439

District 2

STATE UNIV. OF N.Y. at ALBANY
Albany, NY 12222

BLOOMSBURG UNIVERSITY
Bloomsburg, PA 17815

EAST STROUDSBURG UNIVERSITY
East Stroudsburg, PA 18301

GANNON UNIVERSITY
Erie, PA 16541

LE MOYNE COLLEGE
Syracuse, NY 13214-1399

LOCK HAVEN UNIVERSITY
Lock Haven, PA 17745

MERCYHURST COLLEGE
Erie, PA 16546

MILLERSVILLE UNIVERSITY
Millersville, PA 17551-0302

PHILA. COLLEGE OF TEXT. & SCI.
Philadelphia, PA 19144-5497

SHIPPENSBURG UNIVERSITY
Shippensburg, PA 17257

WEST CHESTER UNIVERSITY
West Chester, PA 19383

District 3

LONGWOOD COLLEGE
Farmville, VA 23909-1899

District 7

UNIVERSITY OF DENVER
Denver, CO 80208

MEN'S RIFLE

DIVISION I

District 2

U.S. NAVAL ACADEMY
Annapolis, MD 21402

District 3

MOREHEAD STATE UNIVERSITY
Morehead, KY 40351-1689

VIRGINIA MILITARY INSTITUTE
Lexington, VA 24450-0304

District 5

ST. LOUIS UNIVERSITY
St. Louis, MO 63108

District 6

CENTENARY COLLEGE
Shreveport, LA 71134-1188

District 7

UNIVERSITY OF NEVADA
Reno, NV 89557

District 8

UNIVERSITY OF SAN FRANCISCO
San Francisco, CA 94117-1080

MEN'S SKIING ·

DIVISION I

District 1

BOSTON COLLEGE
Chestnut Hill, MA 02167-3934

DARTMOUTH COLLEGE
Hanover, NH 03755

HARVARD UNIVERSITY
Cambridge, MA 02138-3800

UNIV. OF MASSACHUSETTS-
AMHERST
Amherst, MA 01003

UNIVERSITY OF NEW HAMPSHIRE
Durham, NH 03824

UNIVERSITY OF VERMONT
Burlington, VT 05405

District 4

UNIVERSITY OF WISCONSIN
Green Bay, WI 54311-7001

District 5

UNIVERSITY OF COLORADO
Boulder, CO 80309

District 7

UNIVERSITY OF NEVADA
Reno, NV 89557

UNIVERSITY OF NEW MEXICO
Albuquerque, NM 87131

UNIVERSITY OF UTAH
Salt Lake City, UT 84112

DIVISION II

District 1

ST. ANSELM COLLEGE
Manchester, NH 03102-1310

ST. MICHAEL'S COLLEGE
Colchester, VT 05439

District 4

NORTHERN MICHIGAN
UNIVERSITY
Marquette, MI 49855-5391

District 7

UNIVERSITY OF DENVER
Denver, CO 80208

WESTERN STATE COLLEGE
Gunnison, CO 81231

District 8

UNIVERSITY OF ALASKA-
ANCHORAGE
Anchorage, AK 99508

UNIVERSITY OF ALASKA-
FAIRBANKS
Fairbanks, AK 99775-7500

MEN'S SOCCER

DIVISION I

District 1

BOSTON COLLEGE
Chestnut Hill, MA 02167-3934

BOSTON UNIVERSITY
Boston, MA 02215

BROWN UNIVERSITY
Providence, RI 02912

CENTRAL CONN. STATE UNIV.
New Britain, CT 06050-4010

DARTMOUTH COLLEGE
Hanover, NH 03755

FAIRFIELD UNIVERSITY
Fairfield, CT 06430-5195

UNIVERSITY OF HARTFORD
West Hartford, CT 06117-1599

HARVARD UNIVERSITY
Cambridge, MA 02138-3800

COLLEGE OF THE HOLY CROSS
Worcester, MA 01610-2395

UNIVERSITY OF MAINE
Orono, ME 04469

UNIV. OF MASSACHUSETTS-
AMHERST
Amherst, MA 01003

UNIVERSITY OF NEW HAMPSHIRE
Durham, NH 03824

NORTHEASTERN UNIVERSITY
Boston, MA 02115-5096

PROVIDENCE COLLEGE
Providence, RI 02918

UNIVERSITY OF RHODE ISLAND
Kingston, RI 02881

UNIVERSITY OF VERMONT
Burlington, VT 05405

YALE UNIVERSITY
New Haven, CT 06520-7398

District 2

ADELPHI UNIVERSITY
Garden City, NY 11530

AMERICAN UNIVERSITY
Washington, DC 20016

BUCKNELL UNIVERSITY
Lewisburg, PA 17837

STATE UNIV. OF N.Y. at BUFFALO
Buffalo, NY 14260

CANISIUS COLLEGE
Buffalo, NY 14208-1098

COLGATE UNIVERSITY
Hamilton, NY 13346-1304

COLUMBIA UNIV.-BARNARD
COLLEGE
New York, NY 10027

CORNELL UNIVERSITY
Ithaca, NY 14853

UNIVERSITY OF DELAWARE
Newark, DE 19716

DREXEL UNIVERSITY
Philadelphia, PA 19104

DUQUESNE UNIVERSITY
Pittsburgh, PA 15282

FAIRLEIGH DICKINSON-TEANECK
Teaneck, NJ 07666

FORDHAM UNIVERSITY
Bronx, NY 10458-5155

GEORGE MASON UNIVERSITY
Fairfax, VA 22030

GEORGE WASHINGTON
UNIVERSITY
Washington, DC 20052

GEORGETOWN UNIVERSITY
Washington, DC 20057

HARTWICK COLLEGE
Oneonta, NY 13820-4020

HOFSTRA UNIVERSITY
Hempstead, NY 11550

HOWARD UNIVERSITY
Washington, DC 20059

IONA COLLEGE
New Rochelle, NY 10801

JAMES MADISON UNIVERSITY
Harrisonburg, VA 22807

LA SALLE UNIVERSITY
Philadelphia, PA 19141-1199

LAFAYETTE COLLEGE
Easton, PA 18042

LEHIGH UNIVERSITY
Bethlehem, PA 18015-3089

LONG ISLAND UNIV.-BROOKLYN
Brooklyn, NY 11201

LOYOLA COLLEGE
Baltimore, MD 21210

MANHATTAN COLLEGE
Riverdale, NY 10471

MARIST COLLEGE
Poughkeepsie, NY 12601-1387

UNIV. OF MARYLAND-BALT. CO.
Baltimore, MD 21228-5398

U. OF MARYLAND-EASTERN
SHORE
Princess Anne, MD 21853-1299

MONMOUTH UNIVERSITY
West Long Branch, NJ 07764

MOUNT ST. MARY'S COLLEGE
Emmitsburg, MD 21727-7799

NIAGARA UNIVERSITY
Niagara University, NY 14109

STATE UNIV. COLLEGE at
ONEONTA
Oneonta, NY 13820-4015

PENNSYLVANIA STATE UNIV.
University Park, PA 16802

UNIVERSITY OF PENNSYLVANIA
Philadelphia, PA 19104-6380

PHILA. COLLEGE OF TEXT. & SCI.
Philadelphia, PA 19144-5497

UNIVERSITY OF PITTSBURGH
Pittsburgh, PA 15260

PRINCETON UNIVERSITY
Princeton, NJ 08544

RIDER UNIVERSITY
Lawrenceville, NJ 08648-3099

ROBERT MORRIS COLLEGE
Coraopolis, PA 15108-1189

RUTGERS UNIVERSITY
New Brunswick, NJ 08903

SETON HALL UNIVERSITY
South Orange, NJ 07079

SIENA COLLEGE
Loudonville, NY 12211-1462

ST. BONAVENTURE UNIVERSITY
St. Bonaventure, NY 14778

ST. FRANCIS COLLEGE
Brooklyn Heights, NY 11201

ST. FRANCIS COLLEGE
Loretto, PA 15940-0600

ST. JOHN'S UNIVERSITY
Jamaica, NY 11439

ST. JOSEPH'S UNIVERSITY
Philadelphia, PA 19131-1395

ST. PETER'S COLLEGE
Jersey City, NJ 07306

SYRACUSE UNIVERSITY
Syracuse, NY 13244

TEMPLE UNIVERSITY
Philadelphia, PA 19122

TOWSON STATE UNIVERSITY
Towson, MD 21204

U.S. MILITARY ACADEMY
West Point, NY 10996

U.S. NAVAL ACADEMY
Annapolis, MD 21402

VILLANOVA UNIVERSITY
Villanova, PA 19085

WEST VIRGINIA UNIVERSITY
Morgantown, WV 26506-6201

COLLEGE OF WILLIAM & MARY
Williamsburg, VA 23187

District 3

ALABAMA A&M UNIVERSITY
Normal, AL 35762

UNIV. OF ALABAMA at
BIRMINGHAM
Birmingham, AL 35294-0110

APPALACHIAN STATE UNIVERSITY
Boone, NC 28608

CAMPBELL UNIVERSITY
Buies Creek, NC 27506

UNIVERSITY OF CENTRAL
FLORIDA
Orlando, FL 32816-0002

CHARLESTON SOUTHERN UNIV.
Charleston, SC 29423-8087

COLLEGE OF CHARLESTON
Charleston, SC 29424

THE CITADEL
Charleston, SC 29409

CLEMSON UNIVERSITY
Clemson, SC 29632

COASTAL CAROLINA UNIVERSITY
Conway, SC 29526

DAVIDSON COLLEGE
Davidson, NC 28036

DUKE UNIVERSITY
Durham, NC 27708-0555

EAST CAROLINA UNIVERSITY
Greenville, NC 27858-4353

FLORIDA ATLANTIC UNIVERSITY
Boca Raton, FL 33431-0991

FLORIDA INTERNATIONAL UNIV.
Miami, FL 33199

FURMAN UNIVERSITY
Greenville, SC 29613

GEORGIA SOUTHERN UNIVERSITY
Statesboro, GA 30460-8033

GEORGIA STATE UNIVERSITY
Atlanta, GA 30303-3083

JACKSONVILLE UNIVERSITY
Jacksonville, FL 32211-3394

UNIVERSITY OF KENTUCKY
Lexington, KY 40506-0032

LIBERTY UNIVERSITY
Lynchburg, VA 24506

UNIVERSITY OF LOUISVILLE
Louisville, KY 40292

MARSHALL UNIVERSITY
Huntington, WV 25755

UNIVERSITY OF MARYLAND
College Park, MD 20740

UNIVERSITY OF MEMPHIS
Memphis, TN 38152

MERCER UNIVERSITY
Macon, GA 31207

UNIVERSITY OF NORTH
CAROLINA
Asheville, NC 28804-3299

UNIVERSITY OF NORTH
CAROLINA
Chapel Hill, NC 27514

UNIVERSITY OF NORTH
CAROLINA
Charlotte, NC 28223

UNIVERSITY OF NORTH
CAROLINA
Greensboro, NC 27412-5001

UNIVERSITY OF NORTH
CAROLINA
Wilmington, NC 28403-3297

NORTH CAROLINA STATE UNIV.
Raleigh, NC 27695-7001

OLD DOMINION UNIVERSITY
Norfolk, VA 23529

RADFORD UNIVERSITY
Radford, VA 24142

UNIVERSITY OF RICHMOND
Richmond, VA 23173-1903

UNIVERSITY OF SOUTH ALABAMA
Mobile, AL 36688

UNIVERSITY OF SOUTH CAROLINA
Columbia, SC 29208

UNIVERSITY OF SOUTH FLORIDA
Tampa, FL 33620

STETSON UNIVERSITY
De Land, FL 32720

VANDERBILT UNIVERSITY
Nashville, TN 37212

VIRGINIA COMMONWEALTH UNIV.
Richmond, VA 23284-2003

VIRGINIA MILITARY INSTITUTE
Lexington, VA 24450-0304

VIRGINIA POLYTECHNIC
INSTITUTE
Blacksburg, VA 24061

UNIVERSITY OF VIRGINIA
Charlottesville, VA 22903

WAKE FOREST UNIVERSITY
Winston-Salem, NC 27109

WESTERN KENTUCKY
UNIVERSITY
Bowling Green, KY 42101-3576

WINTHROP UNIVERSITY
Rock Hill, SC 29733

WOFFORD COLLEGE
Spartanburg, SC 29303-3663

District 4

UNIVERSITY OF AKRON
Akron, OH 44325

BOWLING GREEN STATE UNIV.
Bowling Green, OH 43403

BUTLER UNIVERSITY
Indianapolis, IN 46208

UNIVERSITY OF CINCINNATI
Cincinnati, OH 45221

CLEVELAND STATE UNIVERSITY
Cleveland, OH 44115

UNIVERSITY OF DAYTON
Dayton, OH 45469

DE PAUL UNIVERSITY
Chicago, IL 60604-2287

UNIVERSITY OF DETROIT-MERCY
Detroit, MI 48219-0900

EASTERN ILLINOIS UNIVERSITY
Charleston, IL 61920-3099

EASTERN MICHIGAN UNIVERSITY
Ypsilanti, MI 48197

UNIVERSITY OF EVANSVILLE
Evansville, IN 47722

UNIVERSITY OF ILLINOIS
Champaign, IL 61820

INDIANA UNIVERSITY
Bloomington, IN 47405

LOYOLA UNIVERSITY
Chicago, IL 60626

MARQUETTE UNIVERSITY
Milwaukee, WI 53201-1881

MIAMI UNIVERSITY
Oxford, OH 45056

MICHIGAN STATE UNIVERSITY
East Lansing, MI 48824

NORTHEASTERN ILLINOIS UNIV.
Chicago, IL 60625-4699

NORTHERN ILLINOIS UNIVERSITY
De Kalb, IL 60115-2854

NORTHWESTERN UNIVERSITY
Evanston, IL 60208

UNIVERSITY OF NOTRE DAME
Notre Dame, IN 46556

OHIO STATE UNIVERSITY
Columbus, OH 43210

QUINCY UNIVERSITY
Quincy, IL 62301-2699

SOUTHERN ILLINOIS UNIVERSITY
Edwardsville, IL 62026

VALPARAISO UNIVERSITY
Valparaiso, IN 46383-6493

WESTERN ILLINOIS UNIVERSITY
Macomb, IL 61455

WESTERN MICHIGAN UNIVERSITY
Kalamazoo, MI 49008-5134

UNIVERSITY OF WISCONSIN
Green Bay, WI 54311-7001

UNIVERSITY OF WISCONSIN
Madison, WI 53711

UNIVERSITY OF WISCONSIN
Milwaukee, WI 53201

WRIGHT STATE UNIVERSITY
Dayton, OH 45435-0001

XAVIER UNIVERSITY
Cincinnati, OH 45207-6114

District 5

BRADLEY UNIVERSITY
Peoria, IL 61625

CREIGHTON UNIVERSITY
Omaha, NE 68178-0001

DRAKE UNIVERSITY
Des Moines, IA 50311-4505

UNIV. OF MISSOURI-KANSAS CITY
Kansas City, MO 64110

ORAL ROBERTS UNIVERSITY
Tulsa, OK 74171

SOUTHEAST MISSOURI STATE UNIV.
Cape Girardeau, MO 63701-4799

ST. LOUIS UNIVERSITY
St. Louis, MO 63108

UNIVERSITY OF TULSA
Tulsa, OK 74104

District 6

UNIVERSITY OF ARKANSAS
Little Rock, AR 72204-1099

CENTENARY COLLEGE
Shreveport, LA 71134-1188

SOUTHERN METHODIST UNIVERSITY
Dallas, TX 75275

TEXAS CHRISTIAN UNIVERSITY
Fort Worth, TX 76129-0001

UNIV. OF TEXAS-PAN AMERICAN
Edinburg, TX 78539-2999

District 7

CALIF. STATE UNIV.-FRESNO
Fresno, CA 93740-0048

GONZAGA UNIVERSITY
Spokane, WA 99258

UNIVERSITY OF NEW MEXICO
Albuquerque, NM 87131

SAN DIEGO STATE UNIVERSITY
San Diego, CA 92182

U.S. AIR FORCE ACADEMY
USAF Academy, CO 80840-5461

District 8

UNIV. OF CALIFORNIA-BERKELEY
Berkeley, CA 94720

UNIV. OF CALIF.-LOS ANGELES
Los Angeles, CA 90095-1405

UNIV. OF CALIF.-SANTA BARBARA
Santa Barbara, CA 93106

UNIV. OF CALIFORNIA-IRVINE
Irvine, CA 92717

CALIF. POLYTECHNIC STATE UNIV.
San Luis Obispo, CA 93407

CALIF. STATE UNIV.-FULLERTON
Fullerton, CA 92634-9480

CALIF. STATE UNIV.-NORTHRIDGE
Northridge, CA 91330

CALIF. STATE UNIV.-SACRAMENTO
Sacramento, CA 95819

LOYOLA MARYMOUNT UNIVERSITY
Los Angeles, CA 90045-2699

UNIVERSITY OF NEVADA
Reno, NV 89557

OREGON STATE UNIVERSITY
Corvallis, OR 97331

UNIVERSITY OF PORTLAND
Portland, OR 97203-5798

UNIVERSITY OF SAN DIEGO
San Diego, CA 92110-2492

UNIVERSITY OF SAN FRANCISCO
San Francisco, CA 94117-1080

SAN JOSE STATE UNIVERSITY
San Jose, CA 95192

SANTA CLARA UNIVERSITY
Santa Clara, CA 95053

ST. MARY'S COLLEGE
Moraga, CA 94556

STANFORD UNIVERSITY
Stanford, CA 94305

UNIVERSITY OF WASHINGTON
Seattle, WA 98195

DIVISION II

District 1

AMERICAN INTERNATIONAL COLLEGE
Springfield, MA 01109-3189

ASSUMPTION COLLEGE
Worcester, MA 01615-0005

BENTLEY COLLEGE
Waltham, MA 02154-4705

UNIVERSITY OF BRIDGEPORT
Bridgeport, CT 06601

BRYANT COLLEGE
Smithfield, RI 02917-1284

FRANKLIN PIERCE COLLEGE
Rindge, NH 03461

KEENE STATE COLLEGE
Keene, NH 03431-4183

UNIV. OF MASSACHUSETTS-LOWELL
Lowell, MA 01854

MERRIMACK COLLEGE
North Andover, MA 01845

NEW HAMPSHIRE COLLEGE
Hooksett, NH 03106-1045

UNIVERSITY OF NEW HAVEN
West Haven, CT 06516-1999

QUINNIPIAC COLLEGE
Hamden, CT 06518-1940

SACRED HEART UNIVERSITY
Fairfield, CT 06432-1000

SOUTHERN CONNECTICUT ST.
UNIV.
New Haven, CT 06515

ST. ANSELM COLLEGE
Manchester, NH 03102-1310

ST. MICHAEL'S COLLEGE
Colchester, VT 05439

STONEHILL COLLEGE
North Easton, MA 02357

District 2

STATE UNIV. OF N.Y. at ALBANY
Albany, NY 12222

ALDERSON-BROADDUS COLLEGE
Philippi, WV 26416

BLOOMSBURG UNIVERSITY
Bloomsburg, PA 17815

CALIFORNIA UNIVERSITY
California, PA 15419

THE UNIVERSITY OF
CHARLESTON
Charleston, WV 25304

CONCORDIA COLLEGE
Bronxville, NY 10708

DAVIS AND ELKINS COLLEGE
Elkins, WV 26241

UNIV. OF DISTRICT OF COLUMBIA
Washington, DC 20008

DOWLING COLLEGE
Oakdale, NY 11769-1999

EAST STROUDSBURG UNIVERSITY
East Stroudsburg, PA 18301

GANNON UNIVERSITY
Erie, PA 16541

KUTZTOWN UNIVERSITY
Kutztown, PA 19530-0721

LE MOYNE COLLEGE
Syracuse, NY 13214-1399

LOCK HAVEN UNIVERSITY
Lock Haven, PA 17745

LONG ISLAND U./C.W. POST
CAMPUS
Brookville, NY 11548

MERCY COLLEGE
Dobbs Ferry, NY 10522

MERCYHURST COLLEGE
Erie, PA 16546

MILLERSVILLE UNIVERSITY
Millersville, PA 17551-0302

NEW YORK INSTITUTE OF TECH.
Old Westbury, NY 11568-8000

UNIVERSITY OF PITTSBURGH
Johnstown, PA 15904-2990

SALEM-TEIKYO UNIVERSITY
Salem, WV 26426

SHEPHERD COLLEGE
Shepherdstown, WV 25443

SHIPPENSBURG UNIVERSITY
Shippensburg, PA 17257

SLIPPERY ROCK UNIVERSITY
Slippery Rock, PA 16057

SOUTHAMPTON CAMPUS OF L.I.U.
Southampton, NY 11968

THE COLLEGE OF ST. ROSE
Albany, NY 12203

STATE UNIV. OF N.Y. at STONY
BROOK
Stony Brook, NY 11794

WEST CHESTER UNIVERSITY
West Chester, PA 19383

WEST VIRGINIA WESLEYAN
COLLEGE
Buckhannon, WV 26201

WHEELING JESUIT COLLEGE
Wheeling, WV 26003-6295

District 3

UNIV. OF ALABAMA-HUNTSVILLE
Huntsville, AL 35899

AUGUSTA COLLEGE
Augusta, GA 30910

BARRY UNIVERSITY
Miami Shores, FL 33161

BARTON COLLEGE
Wilson, NC 27893

BELLARMINE COLLEGE
Louisville, KY 40205-0671

BELMONT ABBEY COLLEGE
Belmont, NC 28012-2795

CARSON-NEWMAN COLLEGE
Jefferson City, TN 37760

CATAWBA COLLEGE
Salisbury, NC 28144-2488

COKER COLLEGE
Hartsville, SC 29550

ECKERD COLLEGE
St. Petersburg, FL 33733

ELON COLLEGE
Elon College, NC 27244

ERSKINE COLLEGE
Due West, SC 29639

FLORIDA INSTITUTE OF TECH.
Melbourne, FL 32901

FLORIDA SOUTHERN COLLEGE
Lakeland, FL 33801-5698

FRANCIS MARION UNIVERSITY
Florence, SC 29501-0547

GARDNER-WEBB UNIVERSITY
Boiling Springs, NC 28017

HIGH POINT UNIVERSITY
High Point, NC 27262-3598

KENTUCKY WESLEYAN COLLEGE
Owensboro, KY 42302-1039

LANDER UNIVERSITY
Greenwood, SC 29649-2099

LEES-MCRAE COLLEGE
Banner Elk, NC 28604-0128

LENOIR-RHYNE COLLEGE
Hickory, NC 28603

LIMESTONE COLLEGE
Gaffney, SC 29340-3799

LINCOLN MEMORIAL UNIVERSITY
Harrogate, TN 37752

LONGWOOD COLLEGE
Farmville, VA 23909-1899

LYNN UNIVERSITY
Boca Raton, FL 33431

MARS HILL COLLEGE
Mars Hill, NC 28754

MOUNT OLIVE COLLEGE
Mount Olive, NC 28365

NEWBERRY COLLEGE
Newberry, SC 29108

UNIVERSITY OF NORTH FLORIDA
Jacksonville, FL 32224-2645

NORTHERN KENTUCKY
UNIVERSITY
Highland Heights, KY 41099

PEMBROKE STATE UNIVERSITY
Pembroke, NC 28372-1510

PFEIFFER COLLEGE
Misenheimer, NC 28109-0960

PRESBYTERIAN COLLEGE
Clinton, SC 29325-2998

QUEENS COLLEGE (NC)
Charlotte, NC 28274

ROLLINS COLLEGE
Winter Park, FL 32789

UNIV. OF SOUTH CAROLINA-
AIKEN
Aiken, SC 29801

U. OF SO. CAROLINA-
SPARTANBURG
Spartanburg, SC 29303

ST. ANDREWS PRESBYTERIAN
COLL.
Laurinburg, NC 28352-5598

ST. LEO COLLEGE
Saint Leo, FL 33574

UNIVERSITY OF TAMPA
Tampa, FL 33606-1490

UNIVERSITY OF WEST FLORIDA
Pensacola, FL 32514

WINGATE UNIVERSITY
Wingate, NC 28174

District 4

ASHLAND UNIVERSITY
Ashland, OH 44805

INDIANA UNIV.-PURDUE UNIV.
Indianapolis, IN 46202

INDIANA UNIV.-PURDUE UNIV.
Fort Wayne, IN 46805-1499

UNIVERSITY OF INDIANAPOLIS
Indianapolis, IN 46227

LEWIS UNIVERSITY
Romeoville, IL 60441

OAKLAND UNIVERSITY
Rochestser, MI 48309-4401

SAGINAW VALLEY STATE UNIV.
University Center, MI 48710

UNIV. OF SOUTHERN INDIANA
Evansville, IN 47712

COLLEGE OF ST. FRANCIS
Joliet, IL 60435

SAINT JOSEPH'S COLLEGE
Rensselaer, IN 47978

UNIV. OF WISCONSIN-PARKSIDE
Kenosha, WI 53141-2000

District 5

DRURY COLLEGE
Springfield, MO 65802

LINCOLN UNIVERSITY
Jefferson City, MO 65102-0029

MISSOURI SOUTHERN ST.
COLLEGE
Joplin, MO 64801-1595

UNIVERSITY OF MISSOURI
Rolla, MO 65401

UNIVERSITY OF MISSOURI
St. Louis, MO 63121-4499

NORTHEAST MISSOURI STATE
UNIV.
Kirksville, MO 63501

SOUTHWEST BAPTIST
UNIVERSITY
Bolivar, MO 65613

District 6

WEST TEXAS A&M UNIVERSITY
Canyon, TX 79016-0999

District 7

COLORADO CHRISTIAN
UNIVERSITY
Lakewood, CO 80226

COLORADO SCHOOL OF MINES
Golden, CO 80401

UNIV. OF COLORADO-COLO.
SPRINGS
Colorado Springs, CO 80933-7150

UNIVERSITY OF DENVER
Denver, CO 80208

FORT LEWIS COLLEGE
Durango, CO 81301-3999

GRAND CANYON UNIVERSITY
Phoenix, AZ 85017

METROPOLITAN STATE COLLEGE
Denver, CO 80217-3362

REGIS UNIVERSITY
Denver, CO 80221-1099

UNIV. OF SOUTHERN COLORADO
Pueblo, CO 81001-4901

District 8

UNIV. OF CALIFORNIA-DAVIS
Davis, CA 95616

CALIF. POLYTECHNIC STATE UNIV.
San Luis Obispo, CA 93407

CALIF. STATE UNIV.-BAKERSFIELD
Bakersfield, CA 93311-1099

CALIF. STATE UNIV.-CHICO
Chico, CA 95929-0300

CALIF. STATE U-DOMINGUEZ
HILLS
Carson, CA 90747

CALIF. STATE UNIV.-HAYWARD
Hayward, CA 94542

CALIF. STATE UNIV.-LOS ANGELES
Los Angeles, CA 90032-8240

CALIF. STATE U.-SAN BERNARDINO
San Bernardino, CA 92407-2397

CALIF. STATE UNIV.-STANISLAUS
Turlock, CA 95382

HUMBOLDT STATE UNIVERSITY
Arcata, CA 95521

COLLEGE OF NOTRE DAME
Belmont, CA 94002-9974

SAN FRANCISCO STATE
UNIVERSITY
San Francisco, CA 94132

SEATTLE PACIFIC UNIVERSITY
Seattle, WA 98119

SONOMA STATE UNIVERSITY
Rohnert Park, CA 94928

NCAA PROVISIONAL MEMBERS

District 2

UNIV. OF PUERTO RICO-
MAYAGUEZ
Mayaguez, PR 00709

UNIVERSITY OF VIRGIN ISLANDS
St. Thomas, VI 00802

WESTMINSTER COLLEGE
New Wilmington, PA 16172

District 3

ANDERSON COLLEGE
Anderson, SC 29621

CHRISTIAN BROTHERS
UNIVERSITY
Memphis, TN 38104

CLAYTON STATE COLLEGE
Morrow, GA 30260

COLUMBIA UNION COLLEGE
Takoma Park, MD 20912

LAMBUTH UNIVERSITY
Jackson, TN 38301

UNIVERSITY OF MONTEVALLO
Montevallo, AL 35115-6001

TUSCULUM COLLEGE
Greeneville, TN 37743

District 5

ROCKHURST COLLEGE
Kansas City, MO 64110

District 6

CONCORDIA UNIVERSITY at
AUSTIN
Austin, TX 78705-2799

EAST TEXAS BAPTIST UNIVERSITY
Marshall, TX 75670-1498

INCARNATE WORD COLLEGE
San Antonio, TX 78209

UNIV. OF MARY HARDIN-BAYLOR
Belton, TX 76513

MIDWESTERN STATE UNIVERSITY
Wichita Falls, TX 76308

SCHREINER COLLEGE
Keerville, TX 78028

ST. EDWARD'S UNIVERSITY
Austin, TX 78704

ST. MARY'S UNIVERSITY
San Antonio, TX 78228-8572

TEXAS LUTHERAN COLLEGE
Seguin, TX 78155

TEXAS WESLEYAN UNIVERSITY
Fort Worth, TX 76105

District 8

CENTRAL WASHINGTON UNIV.
Ellensburg, WA 98926

HAWAII PACIFIC UNIVERSITY
Honolulu, HI 96813

WESTERN WASHINGTON UNIV.
Bellingham, WA 98225

WOMEN'S SOCCER

DIVISION I

District 1

BOSTON COLLEGE
Chestnut Hill, MA 02167-3934

BOSTON UNIVERSITY
Boston, MA 02215

BROWN UNIVERSITY
Providence, RI 02912

CENTRAL CONN. STATE UNIV.
New Britain, CT 06050-4010

UNIVERSITY OF CONNECTICUT
Storrs, CT 06269

DARTMOUTH COLLEGE
Hanover, NH 03755

FAIRFIELD UNIVERSITY
Fairfield, CT 06430-5195

UNIVERSITY OF HARTFORD
West Hartford, CT 06117-1599

HARVARD UNIVERSITY
Cambridge, MA 02138-3800

COLLEGE OF THE HOLY CROSS
Worcester, MA 01610-2395

UNIVERSITY OF MAINE
Orono, ME 04469

UNIV. OF MASSACHUSETTS-AMHERST
Amherst, MA 01003

UNIVERSITY OF NEW HAMPSHIRE
Durham, NH 03824

PROVIDENCE COLLEGE
Providence, RI 02918

UNIVERSITY OF RHODE ISLAND
Kingston, RI 02881

UNIVERSITY OF VERMONT
Burlington, VT 05405

YALE UNIVERSITY
New Haven, CT 06520-7398

District 2

AMERICAN UNIVERSITY
Washington, DC 20016

BUCKNELL UNIVERSITY
Lewisburg, PA 17837

STATE UNIV. OF N.Y. at BUFFALO
Buffalo, NY 14260

CANISIUS COLLEGE
Buffalo, NY 14208-1098

COLGATE UNIVERSITY
Hamilton, NY 13346-1304

COLUMBIA UNIV.-BARNARD COLLEGE
New York, NY 10027

CORNELL UNIVERSITY
Ithaca, NY 14853

UNIVERSITY OF DELAWARE
Newark, DE 19716

FORDHAM UNIVERSITY
Bronx, NY 10458-5155

GEORGE MASON UNIVERSITY
Fairfax, VA 22030

GEORGE WASHINGTON UNIVERSITY
Washington, DC 20052

GEORGETOWN UNIVERSITY
Washington, DC 20057

HOFSTRA UNIVERSITY
Hempstead, NY 11550

HOWARD UNIVERSITY
Washington, DC 20059

IONA COLLEGE
New Rochelle, NY 10801

JAMES MADISON UNIVERSITY
Harrisonburg, VA 22807

LA SALLE UNIVERSITY
Philadelphia, PA 19141-1199

LAFAYETTE COLLEGE
Easton, PA 18042

LEHIGH UNIVERSITY
Bethlehem, PA 18015-3089

LOYOLA COLLEGE
Baltimore, MD 21210

MANHATTAN COLLEGE
Riverdale, NY 10471

MARIST COLLEGE
Poughkeepsie, NY 12601-1387

UNIV. OF MARYLAND-BALT. CO.
Baltimore, MD 21228-5398

MONMOUTH UNIVERSITY
West Long Branch, NJ 07764

MOUNT ST. MARY'S COLLEGE
Emmitsburg, MD 21727-7799

NIAGARA UNIVERSITY
Niagara University, NY 14109

PENNSYLVANIA STATE UNIV.
University Park, PA 16802

UNIVERSITY OF PENNSYLVANIA
Philadelphia, PA 19104-6380

PRINCETON UNIVERSITY
Princeton, NJ 08544

ROBERT MORRIS COLLEGE
Coraopolis, PA 15108-1189

RUTGERS UNIVERSITY
New Brunswick, NJ 08903

SETON HALL UNIVERSITY
South Orange, NJ 07079

SIENA COLLEGE
Loudonville, NY 12211-1462

ST. BONAVENTURE UNIVERSITY
St. Bonaventure, NY 14778

ST. FRANCIS COLLEGE
Loretto, PA 15940-0600

ST. JOHN'S UNIVERSITY
Jamaica, NY 11439

ST. PETER'S COLLEGE
Jersey City, NJ 07306

STATE UNIV. OF N.Y. at STONY
BROOK
Stony Brook, NY 11794

SYRACUSE UNIVERSITY
Syracuse, NY 13244

TEMPLE UNIVERSITY
Philadelphia, PA 19122

TOWSON STATE UNIVERSITY
Towson, MD 21204

U.S. MILITARY ACADEMY
West Point, NY 10996

U.S. NAVAL ACADEMY
Annapolis, MD 21402

VILLANOVA UNIVERSITY
Villanova, PA 19085

WAGNER COLLEGE
Staten Island, NY 10301-4495

COLLEGE OF WILLIAM & MARY
Williamsburg, VA 23187

District 3

UNIV. OF ALABAMA at
TUSCALOOSA
Tuscaloosa, AL 35487

APPALACHIAN STATE UNIVERSITY
Boone, NC 28608

AUBURN UNIVERSITY
Auburn University AL 36849-5113

CAMPBELL UNIVERSITY
Buies Creek, NC 27506

UNIVERSITY OF CENTRAL
FLORIDA
Orlando, FL 32816-0002

CHARLESTON SOUTHERN UNIV.
Charleston, SC 29423-8087

COLLEGE OF CHARLESTON
Charleston, SC 29424

CLEMSON UNIVERSITY
Clemson, SC 29632

DAVIDSON COLLEGE
Davidson, NC 28036

DUKE UNIVERSITY
Durham, NC 27708-0555

EAST CAROLINA UNIVERSITY
Greenville, NC 27858-4353

FLORIDA ATLANTIC UNIVERSITY
Boca Raton, FL 33431-0991

FLORIDA INTERNATIONAL UNIV.
Miami, FL 33199

FURMAN UNIVERSITY
Greenville, SC 29613

GEORGIA SOUTHERN UNIVERSITY
Statesboro, GA 30460-8033

GEORGIA STATE UNIVERSITY
Atlanta, GA 30303-3083

UNIVERSITY OF GEORGIA
Athens, GA 30613

JACKSONVILLE STATE
UNIVERSITY
Jacksonville, AL 36265-9982

JACKSONVILLE UNIVERSITY
Jacksonville, FL 32211-3394

UNIVERSITY OF KENTUCKY
Lexington, KY 40506-0032

LIBERTY UNIVERSITY
Lynchburg, VA 24506

LOUISIANA STATE UNIVERSITY
Baton Rouge, LA 70803

UNIVERSITY OF LOUISVILLE
Louisville, KY 40292

UNIVERSITY OF MARYLAND
College Park, MD 20740

UNIVERSITY OF MEMPHIS
Memphis, TN 38152

MERCER UNIVERSITY
Macon, GA 31207

UNIVERSITY OF MISSISSIPPI
University, MS 38677

UNIVERSITY OF NORTH
CAROLINA
Asheville, NC 28804-3299

UNIVERSITY OF NORTH
CAROLINA
Chapel Hill, NC 27514

UNIVERSITY OF NORTH
CAROLINA
Charlotte, NC 28223

UNIVERSITY OF NORTH
CAROLINA
Greensboro, NC 27412-5001

UNIVERSITY OF NORTH
CAROLINA
Wilmington, NC 28403-3297

NORTH CAROLINA STATE UNIV.
Raleigh, NC 27695-7001

OLD DOMINION UNIVERSITY
Norfolk, VA 23529

RADFORD UNIVERSITY
Radford, VA 24142

UNIVERSITY OF SOUTH ALABAMA
Mobile, AL 36688

UNIVERSITY OF SOUTH CAROLINA
Columbia, SC 29208

UNIVERSITY OF SOUTH FLORIDA
Tampa, FL 33620

SOUTHEASTERN LOUISIANA UNIV.
Hammond, LA 70402

STETSON UNIVERSITY
De Land, FL 32720

VANDERBILT UNIVERSITY
Nashville, TN 37212

VIRGINIA COMMONWEALTH UNIV.
Richmond, VA 23284-2003

VIRGINIA POLYTECHNIC
INSTITUTE
Blacksburg, VA 24061

UNIVERSITY OF VIRGINIA
Charlottesville, VA 22903

WAKE FOREST UNIVERSITY
Winston-Salem, NC 27109

WOFFORD COLLEGE
Spartanburg, SC 29303-3663

District 4

BUTLER UNIVERSITY
Indianapolis, IN 46208

UNIVERSITY OF CINCINNATI
Cincinnati, OH 45221

UNIVERSITY OF DAYTON
Dayton, OH 45469

UNIVERSITY OF DETROIT-MERCY
Detroit, MI 48219-0900

EASTERN ILLINOIS UNIVERSITY
Charleston, IL 61920-3099

EASTERN MICHIGAN UNIVERSITY
Ypsilanti, MI 48197

UNIVERSITY OF EVANSVILLE
Evansville, IN 47722

INDIANA UNIVERSITY
Bloomington, IN 47405

LOYOLA UNIVERSITY
Chicago, IL 60626

MARQUETTE UNIVERSITY
Milwaukee, WI 53201-1881

MICHIGAN STATE UNIVERSITY
East Lansing, MI 48824

UNIVERSITY OF MICHIGAN
Ann Arbor, MI 48109-2201

UNIV. OF MINNESOTA-TWIN
CITIES
Minneapolis, MN 55455

NORTHERN ILLINOIS UNIVERSITY
De Kalb, IL 60115-2854

NORTHWESTERN UNIVERSITY
Evanston, IL 60208

UNIVERSITY OF NOTRE DAME
Notre Dame, IN 46556

OHIO STATE UNIVERSITY
Columbus, OH 43210

UNIVERSITY OF TOLEDO
Toledo, OH 43606

VALPARAISO UNIVERSITY
Valparaiso, IN 46383-6493

UNIVERSITY OF WISCONSIN
Green Bay, WI 54311-7001

UNIVERSITY OF WISCONSIN
Madison, WI 53711

UNIVERSITY OF WISCONSIN
Milwaukee, WI 53201

WRIGHT STATE UNIVERSITY
Dayton, OH 45435-0001

XAVIER UNIVERSITY
Cincinnati, OH 45207-6114

District 5

CREIGHTON UNIVERSITY
Omaha, NE 68178-0001

UNIVERSITY OF KANSAS
Lawrence, KS 66045

UNIVERSITY OF NEBRASKA
Lincoln, NE 68588

ORAL ROBERTS UNIVERSITY
Tulsa, OK 74171

UNIVERSITY OF TULSA
Tulsa, OK 74104

District 6

UNIVERSITY OF ARKANSAS
Fayetteville, AR 72701

UNIVERSITY OF ARKANSAS
Little Rock, AR 72204-1099

CENTENARY COLLEGE
Shreveport, LA 71134-1188

SOUTHERN METHODIST
UNIVERSITY
Dallas, TX 75275

STEPHEN F. AUSTIN STATE UNIV.
Nacogdoches, TX 75962

UNIVERSITY OF TEXAS
Austin, TX 78712

TEXAS A&M UNIVERSITY
College Station, TX 77843-1228

TEXAS CHRISTIAN UNIVERSITY
Fort Worth, TX 76129-0001

TEXAS TECH UNIVERSITY
Lubbock, TX 79409

District 7

BRIGHAM YOUNG UNIVERSITY
Provo, UT 84602

CALIF. STATE UNIV.-FRESNO
Fresno, CA 93740-0048

COLORADO COLLEGE
Colorado Springs, CO 80903

GONZAGA UNIVERSITY
Spokane, WA 99258

UNIVERSITY OF HAWAII-MANOA
Honolulu, HI 96822-2370

THE UNIVERSITY OF MONTANA
Missoula, MT 59812-1291

UNIVERSITY OF NEW MEXICO
Albuquerque, NM 87131

SAN DIEGO STATE UNIVERSITY
San Diego, CA 92182

UNIVERSITY OF UTAH
Salt Lake City, UT 84112

UNIVERSITY OF WYOMING
Laramie, WY 82071

District 8

UNIVERSITY OF ARIZONA
Tucscon, AZ 85721

UNIV. OF CALIFORNIA-BERKELEY
Berkeley, CA 94720

UNIV. OF CALIF.-LOS ANGELES
Los Angeles, CA 90095-1405

UNIV. OF CALIF.-SANTA BARBARA
Santa Barbara, CA 93106

UNIV. OF CALIFORNIA-IRVINE
Irvine, CA 92717

CALIF. POLYTECHNIC STATE UNIV.
San Luis Obispo, CA 93407

CALIF. STATE UNIV.-FULLERTON
Fullerton, CA 92634-9480

CALIF. STATE UNIV.-NORTHRIDGE
Northridge, CA 91330

CALIF. STATE UNIV.-SACRAMENTO
Sacramento, CA 95819

LOYOLA MARYMOUNT
UNIVERSITY
Los Angeles, CA 90045-2699

OREGON STATE UNIVERSITY
Corvallis, OR 97331

UNIVERSITY OF THE PACIFIC
Stockton, CA 95211

PEPPERDINE UNIVERSITY
Malibu, CA 90263

UNIVERSITY OF PORTLAND
Portland, OR 97203-5798

UNIVERSITY OF SAN DIEGO
San Diego, CA 92110-2492

UNIVERSITY OF SAN FRANCISCO
San Francisco, CA 94117-1080

SAN JOSE STATE UNIVERSITY
San Jose, CA 95192

SANTA CLARA UNIVERSITY
Santa Clara, CA 95053

UNIV. OF SOUTHERN CALIFORNIA
Los Angeles, CA 90089-0012

ST. MARY'S COLLEGE
Moraga, CA 94556

STANFORD UNIVERSITY
Stanford, CA 94305

WASHINGTON STATE UNIVERSITY
Pullman, WA 99164

UNIVERSITY OF WASHINGTON
Seattle, WA 98195

DIVISION II

District 1

AMERICAN INTERNATIONAL COLLEGE
Springfield, MA 01109-3189

ASSUMPTION COLLEGE
Worcester, MA 01615-0005

BENTLEY COLLEGE
Waltham, MA 02154-4705

UNIVERSITY OF BRIDGEPORT
Bridgeport, CT 06601

BRYANT COLLEGE
Smithfield, RI 02917-1284

FRANKLIN PIERCE COLLEGE
Rindge, NH 03461

KEENE STATE COLLEGE
Keene, NH 03431-4183

UNIV. OF MASSACHUSETTS-LOWELL
Lowell, MA 01854

MERRIMACK COLLEGE
North Andover, MA 01845

NEW HAMPSHIRE COLLEGE
Hooksett, NH 03106-1045

UNIVERSITY OF NEW HAVEN
West Haven, CT 06516-1999

QUINNIPIAC COLLEGE
Hamden, CT 06518-1940

SACRED HEART UNIVERSITY
Fairfield, CT 06432-1000

ST. ANSELM COLLEGE
Manchester, NH 03102-1310

ST. MICHAEL'S COLLEGE
Colchester, VT 05439

STONEHILL COLLEGE
North Easton, MA 02357

District 2

ADELPHI UNIVERSITY
Garden City, NY 11530

STATE UNIV. OF N.Y. at ALBANY
Albany, NY 12222

BLOOMSBURG UNIVERSITY
Bloomsburg, PA 17815

CALIFORNIA UNIVERSITY
California, PA 15419

THE UNIVERSITY OF CHARLESTON
Charleston, WV 25304

CONCORDIA COLLEGE
Bronxville, NY 10708

EAST STROUDSBURG UNIVERSITY
East Stroudsburg, PA 18301

GANNON UNIVERSITY
Erie, PA 16541

INDIANA UNIV. OF PENNSYLVANIA
Indiana, PA 15705

KUTZTOWN UNIVERSITY
Kutztown, PA 19530-0721

LE MOYNE COLLEGE
Syracuse, NY 13214-1399

LOCK HAVEN UNIVERSITY
Lock Haven, PA 17745

LONG ISLAND U./C.W. POST CAMPUS
Brookville, NY 11548

MERCYHURST COLLEGE
Erie, PA 16546

MILLERSVILLE UNIVERSITY
Millersville, PA 17551-0302

MOLLOY COLLEGE
Rockville Centre, NY 11570

NEW YORK INSTITUTE OF TECH.
Old Westbury, NY 11568-8000

PHILA. COLLEGE OF TEXT. & SCI.
Philadelphia, PA 19144-5497

SHIPPENSBURG UNIVERSITY
Shippensburg, PA 17257

SLIPPERY ROCK UNIVERSITY
Slippery Rock, PA 16057

SOUTHAMPTON CAMPUS OF L.I.U.
Southampton, NY 11968

THE COLLEGE OF ST. ROSE
Albany, NY 12203

WEST CHESTER UNIVERSITY
West Chester, PA 19383

WEST VIRGINIA WESLEYAN COLLEGE
Buckhannon, WV 26201

WHEELING JESUIT COLLEGE
Wheeling, WV 26003-6295

District 3

BARRY UNIVERSITY
Miami Shores, FL 33161

BARTON COLLEGE
Wilson, NC 27893

BELLARMINE COLLEGE
Louisville, KY 40205-0671

BELMONT ABBEY COLLEGE
Belmont, NC 28012-2795

CARSON-NEWMAN COLLEGE
Jefferson City, TN 37760

CATAWBA COLLEGE
Salisbury, NC 28144-2488

COKER COLLEGE
Hartsville, SC 29550

ELON COLLEGE
Elon College, NC 27244

ERSKINE COLLEGE
Due West, SC 29639

FRANCIS MARION UNIVERSITY
Florence, SC 29501-0547

GARDNER-WEBB UNIVERSITY
Boiling Springs, NC 28017

HIGH POINT UNIVERSITY
High Point, NC 27262-3598

KENTUCKY WESLEYAN COLLEGE
Owensboro, KY 42302-1039

LEES-MCRAE COLLEGE
Banner Elk, NC 28604-0128

LENOIR-RHYNE COLLEGE
Hickory, NC 28603

LINCOLN MEMORIAL UNIVERSITY
Harrogate, TN 37752

LONGWOOD COLLEGE
Farmville, VA 23909-1899

LYNN UNIVERSITY
Boca Raton, FL 33431

MARS HILL COLLEGE
Mars Hill, NC 28754

MOUNT OLIVE COLLEGE
Mount Olive, NC 28365

NEWBERRY COLLEGE
Newberry, SC 29108

PFEIFFER COLLEGE
Misenheimer, NC 28109-0960

PRESBYTERIAN COLLEGE
Clinton, SC 29325-2998

QUEENS COLLEGE (NC)
Charlotte, NC 28274

ST. ANDREWS PRESBYTERIAN
COLL.
Laurinburg, NC 28352-5598

UNIVERSITY OF WEST FLORIDA
Pensacola, FL 32514

WINGATE UNIVERSITY
Wingate, NC 28174

District 4

ASHLAND UNIVERSITY
Ashland, OH 44805

UNIVERSITY OF INDIANAPOLIS
Indianapolis, IN 46227

LEWIS UNIVERSITY
Romeoville, IL 60441

UNIV. OF MINNESOTA-DULUTH
Duluth, MN 55812

MOORHEAD STATE UNIVERSITY
Moorhead, MN 56563-2996

NORTHWOOD UNIVERSITY
Midland, MI 48640

OAKLAND UNIVERSITY
Rochestser, MI 48309-4401

QUINCY UNIVERSITY
Quincy, IL 62301-2699

SAGINAW VALLEY STATE UNIV.
University Center, MI 48710

SOUTHERN ILLINOIS UNIVERSITY
Edwardsville, IL 62026

COLLEGE OF ST. FRANCIS
Joliet, IL 60435

SAINT JOSEPH'S COLLEGE
Rensselaer, IN 47978

WINONA STATE UNIVERSITY
Winona, MN 55987-5838

UNIV. OF WISCONSIN-PARKSIDE
Kenosha, WI 53141-2000

District 5

CENTRAL MISSOURI STATE UNIV.
Warrensburg, MO 64093

DRURY COLLEGE
Springfield, MO 65802

MANKATO STATE UNIVERSITY
Mankato, MN 56002-8400

UNIVERSITY OF MISSOURI
Rolla, MO 65401

UNIVERSITY OF MISSOURI
St. Louis, MO 63121-4499

NORTH DAKOTA STATE
UNIVERSITY
Fargo, ND 58105

NORTHEAST MISSOURI STATE
UNIV.
Kirksville, MO 63501

UNIV. OF NORTHERN COLORADO
Greeley, CO 80639

SOUTHWEST BAPTIST
UNIVERSITY
Bolivar, MO 65613

ST. CLOUD STATE UNIVERSITY
St. Cloud, MN 56301-4498

District 6

ANGELO STATE UNIVERSITY
San Angelo, TX 76909

EAST TEXAS STATE UNIVERSITY
Commerce, TX 75429-3011

District 7

COLORADO CHRISTIAN
UNIVERSITY
Lakewood, CO 80226

UNIVERSITY OF DENVER
Denver, CO 80208

FORT LEWIS COLLEGE
Durango, CO 81301-3999

METROPOLITAN STATE COLLEGE
Denver, CO 80217-3362

REGIS UNIVERSITY
Denver, CO 80221-1099

UNIV. OF SOUTHERN COLORADO
Pueblo, CO 81001-4901

U.S. AIR FORCE ACADEMY
USAF Academy, CO 80840-5461

District 8

UNIV. OF CALIFORNIA-DAVIS
Davis, CA 95616

CALIF. STATE POLYTECHNIC UNIV.
Pomona, CA 91768

CALIF. STATE UNIV.-CHICO
Chico, CA 95929-0300

CALIF. STATE U.-DOMINGUEZ
HILLS
Carson, CA 90747

CALIF. STATE UNIV.-HAYWARD
Hayward, CA 94542

CALIF. STATE UNIV.-LOS ANGELES
Los Angeles, CA 90032-8240

CALIF. STATE U.-SAN BERNARDINO
San Bernardino, CA 92407-2397

HUMBOLDT STATE UNIVERSITY
Arcata, CA 95521

PORTLAND STATE UNIVERSITY
Portland, OR 97207-0751

SAN FRANCISCO STATE
UNIVERSITY
San Francisco, CA 94132

SONOMA STATE UNIVERSITY
Rohnert Park, CA 94928

NCAA PROVISIONAL MEMBERS

District 3

ANDERSON COLLEGE
Anderson, SC 29621

CHRISTIAN BROTHERS
UNIVERSITY
Memphis, TN 38104

LAMBUTH UNIVERSITY
Jackson, TN 38301

UNIVERSITY OF MONTEVALLO
Montevallo, AL 35115-6001

TUSCULUM COLLEGE
Greeneville, TN 37743

District 5

ROCKHURST COLLEGE
Kansas City, MO 64110

District 6

INCARNATE WORD COLLEGE
San Antonio, TX 78209

MIDWESTERN STATE UNIVERSITY
Wichita Falls, TX 76308

ST. EDWARD'S UNIVERSITY
Austin, TX 78704

ST. MARY'S UNIVERSITY
San Antonio, TX 78228-8572

TEXAS LUTHERAN COLLEGE
Seguin, TX 78155

District 8

CENTRAL WASHINGTON UNIV.
Ellensburg, WA 98926

HAWAII PACIFIC UNIVERSITY
Honolulu, HI 96813

WESTERN WASHINGTON UNIV.
Bellingham, WA 98225

WOMEN'S SOFTBALL

DIVISION I

District 1

BOSTON COLLEGE
Chestnut Hill, MA 02167-3934

BOSTON UNIVERSITY
Boston, MA 02215

BROWN UNIVERSITY
Providence, RI 02912

CENTRAL CONN. STATE UNIV.
New Britain, CT 06050-4010

UNIVERSITY OF CONNECTICUT
Storrs, CT 06269

DARTMOUTH COLLEGE
Hanover, NH 03755

FAIRFIELD UNIVERSITY
Fairfield, CT 06430-5195

UNIVERSITY OF HARTFORD
West Hartford, CT 06117-1599

HARVARD UNIVERSITY
Cambridge, MA 02138-3800

COLLEGE OF THE HOLY CROSS
Worcester, MA 01610-2395

UNIVERSITY OF MAINE
Orono, ME 04469

UNIV. OF MASSACHUSETTS-
AMHERST
Amherst, MA 01003

PROVIDENCE COLLEGE
Providence, RI 02918

UNIVERSITY OF RHODE ISLAND
Kingston, RI 02881

UNIVERSITY OF VERMONT
Burlington, VT 05405

YALE UNIVERSITY
New Haven, CT 06520-7398

District 2

BUCKNELL UNIVERSITY
Lewisburg, PA 17837

CANISIUS COLLEGE
Buffalo, NY 14208-1098

COLGATE UNIVERSITY
Hamilton, NY 13346-1304

CORNELL UNIVERSITY
Ithaca, NY 14853

DELAWARE STATE UNIVERSITY
Dover, DE 19901

UNIVERSITY OF DELAWARE
Newark, DE 19716

DREXEL UNIVERSITY
Philadelphia, PA 19104

FORDHAM UNIVERSITY
Bronx, NY 10458-5155

GEORGE MASON UNIVERSITY
Fairfax, VA 22030

HAMPTON UNIVERSITY
Hampton, VA 23668

HOFSTRA UNIVERSITY
Hempstead, NY 11550

IONA COLLEGE
New Rochelle, NY 10801

LA SALLE UNIVERSITY
Philadelphia, PA 19141-1199

LAFAYETTE COLLEGE
Easton, PA 18042

LEHIGH UNIVERSITY
Bethlehem, PA 18015-3089

LONG ISLAND UNIV.-BROOKLYN
Brooklyn, NY 11201

MANHATTAN COLLEGE
Riverdale, NY 10471

MARIST COLLEGE
Poughkeepsie, NY 12601-1387

UNIV. OF MARYLAND-BALT. CO.
Baltimore, MD 21228-5398

U. OF MARYLAND-EASTERN
SHORE
Princess Anne, MD 21853-1299

MONMOUTH UNIVERSITY
West Long Branch, NJ 07764

MORGAN STATE UNIVERSITY
Baltimore, MD 21239

MOUNT ST. MARY'S COLLEGE
Emmitsburg, MD 21727-7799

NIAGARA UNIVERSITY
Niagara University, NY 14109

PENNSYLVANIA STATE UNIV.
University Park, PA 16802

UNIVERSITY OF PENNSYLVANIA
Philadelphia, PA 19104-6380

PRINCETON UNIVERSITY
Princeton, NJ 08544

RIDER UNIVERSITY
Lawrenceville, NJ 08648-3099

ROBERT MORRIS COLLEGE
Coraopolis, PA 15108-1189

RUTGERS UNIVERSITY
New Brunswick, NJ 08903

SETON HALL UNIVERSITY
South Orange, NJ 07079

SIENA COLLEGE
Loudonville, NY 12211-1462

ST. BONAVENTURE UNIVERSITY
St. Bonaventure, NY 14778

ST. FRANCIS COLLEGE
Brooklyn Heights, NY 11201

ST. FRANCIS COLLEGE
Loretto, PA 15940-0600

ST. JOHN'S UNIVERSITY
Jamaica, NY 11439

ST. JOSEPH'S UNIVERSITY
Philadelphia, PA 19131-1395

ST. PETER'S COLLEGE
Jersey City, NJ 07306

TEMPLE UNIVERSITY
Philadelphia, PA 19122

TOWSON STATE UNIVERSITY
Towson, MD 21204

U.S. MILITARY ACADEMY
West Point, NY 10996

VILLANOVA UNIVERSITY
Villanova, PA 19085

WAGNER COLLEGE
Staten Island, NY 10301-4495

District 3

AUSTIN PEAY STATE UNIVERSITY
Clarksville, TN 37044-4576

BETHUNE-COOKMAN COLLEGE
Daytona Beach, FL 32114-3099

CAMPBELL UNIVERSITY
Buies Creek, NC 27506

CHARLESTON SOUTHERN UNIV.
Charleston, SC 29423-8087

COLLEGE OF CHARLESTON
Charleston, SC 29424

COASTAL CAROLINA UNIVERSITY
Conway, SC 29526

COPPIN STATE COLLEGE
Baltimore, MD 21216

EAST CAROLINA UNIVERSITY
Greenville, NC 27858-4353

EASTERN KENTUCKY UNIVERSITY
Richmond, KY 40475-3101

FLORIDA A&M UNIVERSITY
Tallahassee, FL 32307

FLORIDA ATLANTIC UNIVERSITY
Boca Raton, FL 33431-0991

FLORIDA STATE UNIVERSITY
Tallahassee, FL 32306

FURMAN UNIVERSITY
Greenville, SC 29613

GEORGIA INSTITUTE OF TECH.
Atlanta, GA 30332

GEORGIA SOUTHERN UNIVERSITY
Statesboro, GA 30460-8033

GEORGIA STATE UNIVERSITY
Atlanta, GA 30303-3083

JACKSONVILLE STATE
UNIVERSITY
Jacksonville, AL 36265-9982

LIBERTY UNIVERSITY
Lynchburg, VA 24506

MARSHALL UNIVERSITY
Huntington, WV 25755

UNIVERSITY OF MARYLAND
College Park, MD 20740

UNIVERSITY OF MEMPHIS
Memphis, TN 38152

MERCER UNIVERSITY
Macon, GA 31207

MIDDLE TENNESSEE STATE UNIV.
Murfreesboro, TN 37132

MOREHEAD STATE UNIVERSITY
Morehead, KY 40351-1689

UNIVERSITY OF NORTH
CAROLINA
Chapel Hill, NC 27514

UNIVERSITY OF NORTH
CAROLINA
Charlotte, NC 28223

UNIVERSITY OF NORTH
CAROLINA
Greensboro, NC 27412-5001

UNIVERSITY OF NORTH
CAROLINA
Wilmington, NC 28403-3297

NORTH CAROLINA A&T ST. UNIV.
Greensboro, NC 27411

RADFORD UNIVERSITY
Radford, VA 24142

SAMFORD UNIVERSITY
Birmingham, AL 35229

SOUTH CAROLINA STATE UNIV.
Orangeburg, SC 29117-0001

UNIVERSITY OF SOUTH CAROLINA
Columbia, SC 29208

UNIVERSITY OF SOUTH FLORIDA
Tampa, FL 33620

SOUTHEASTERN LOUISIANA UNIV.
Hammond, LA 70402

STETSON UNIVERSITY
De Land, FL 32720

TENNESSEE STATE UNIVERSITY
Nashville, TN 37209-1561

TENNESSEE TECHNOLOGICAL
UNIV.
Cookeville, TN 38505-0001

UNIVERSITY OF TENNESSEE
Chattanooga, TN 37403-2598

THE UNIVERSITY OF TENNESSEE
Knoxville, TN 37996

UNIV. OF TENNESSEE at MARTIN
Martin, TN 38238-5021

TROY STATE UNIVERSITY
Troy, AL 36082

VIRGINIA POLYTECHNIC INSTITUTE
Blacksburg, VA 24061

UNIVERSITY OF VIRGINIA
Charlottesville, VA 22903

WINTHROP UNIVERSITY
Rock Hill, SC 29733

District 4

UNIVERSITY OF AKRON
Akron, OH 44325

BALL STATE UNIVERSITY
Muncie, IN 47306

BOWLING GREEN STATE UNIV.
Bowling Green, OH 43403

BUTLER UNIVERSITY
Indianapolis, IN 46208

CENTRAL MICHIGAN UNIVERSITY
Mount Pleasant, MI 48859

CLEVELAND STATE UNIVERSITY
Cleveland, OH 44115

UNIVERSITY OF DAYTON
Dayton, OH 45469

DE PAUL UNIVERSITY
Chicago, IL 60604-2287

UNIVERSITY OF DETROIT-MERCY
Detroit, MI 48219-0900

EASTERN ILLINOIS UNIVERSITY
Charleston, IL 61920-3099

EASTERN MICHIGAN UNIVERSITY
Ypsilanti, MI 48197

UNIVERSITY OF EVANSVILLE
Evansville, IN 47722

ILLINOIS STATE UNIVERSITY
Normal, IL 61761

UNIVERSITY OF ILLINOIS
Chicago, IL 60607

INDIANA UNIVERSITY
Bloomington, IN 47405

UNIVERSITY OF IOWA
Iowa City, IA 52242

KENT STATE UNIVERSITY
Kent, OH 44242

LOYOLA UNIVERSITY
Chicago, IL 60626

MIAMI UNIVERSITY
Oxford, OH 45056

MICHIGAN STATE UNIVERSITY
East Lansing, MI 48824

UNIVERSITY OF MICHIGAN
Ann Arbor, MI 48109-2201

UNIV. OF MINNESOTA-TWIN CITIES
Minneapolis, MN 55455

NORTHEASTERN ILLINOIS UNIV.
Chicago, IL 60625-4699

NORTHERN ILLINOIS UNIVERSITY
De Kalb, IL 60115-2854

NORTHWESTERN UNIVERSITY
Evanston, IL 60208

UNIVERSITY OF NOTRE DAME
Notre Dame, IN 46556

OHIO STATE UNIVERSITY
Columbus, OH 43210

OHIO UNIVERSITY
Athens, OH 45701

PURDUE UNIVERSITY
West Lafayette, IN 47907

UNIVERSITY OF TOLEDO
Toledo, OH 43606

VALPARAISO UNIVERSITY
Valparaiso, IN 46383-6493

WESTERN ILLINOIS UNIVERSITY
Macomb, IL 61455

WESTERN MICHIGAN UNIVERSITY
Kalamazoo, MI 49008-5134

UNIVERSITY OF WISCONSIN
Green Bay, WI 54311-7001

UNIVERSITY OF WISCONSIN
Madison, WI 53711

WRIGHT STATE UNIVERSITY
Dayton, OH 45435-0001

YOUNGSTOWN STATE UNIVERSITY
Youngstown, OH 44555-0001

District 5

BRADLEY UNIVERSITY
Peoria, IL 61625

CREIGHTON UNIVERSITY
Omaha, NE 68178-0001

DRAKE UNIVERSITY
Des Moines, IA 50311-4505

INDIANA STATE UNIVERSITY
Terre Haute, IN 47809

IOWA STATE UNIVERSITY
Ames, IA 50011

UNIVERSITY OF KANSAS
Lawrence, KS 66045

UNIV. OF MISSOURI-COLUMBIA
Columbia, MO 65211

UNIV. OF MISSOURI-KANSAS CITY
Kansas City, MO 64110

UNIVERSITY OF NEBRASKA
Lincoln, NE 68588

UNIVERSITY OF NORTHERN IOWA
Cedar Falls, IA 50614

OKLAHOMA STATE UNIVERSITY
Stillwater, OK 74078

UNIVERSITY OF OKLAHOMA
Norman, OK 73019

SOUTHEAST MISSOURI STATE
UNIV.
Cape Girardeau, MO 63701-4799

SOUTHERN ILLINOIS UNIVERSITY
Carbondale, IL 62901

SOUTHWEST MISSOURI STATE
UNIV.
Springfield, MO 65804

ST. LOUIS UNIVERSITY
St. Louis, MO 63108

UNIVERSITY OF TULSA
Tulsa, OK 74104

WICHITA STATE UNIVERSITY
Wichita, KS 67260

District 6

BAYLOR UNIVERSITY
Waco, TX 76798

CENTENARY COLLEGE
Shreveport, LA 71134-1188

LOUISIANA TECH UNIVERSITY
Ruston, LA 71272

MCNESSE STATE UNIVERSITY
Lake Charles, LA 70609

NICHOLLS STATE UNIVERSITY
Thibodaux, LA 70310

NORTHEAST LOUISIANA
UNIVERSITY
Monroe, LA 71209-3000

NORTHWESTERN STATE
UNIVERSITY
Natchitoches, LA 71497-0003

SAM HOUSTON STATE
UNIVERSITY
Huntsville, TX 77341

SOUTHWEST TEXAS STATE UNIV.
San Marcos, TX 78666-4615

UNIV. OF SOUTHWESTERN LA.
Lafayette, LA 70504-1008

STEPHEN F. AUSTIN STATE UNIV.
Nacogdoches, TX 75962

UNIVERSITY OF TEXAS
Arlington, TX 76019

UNIVERSITY OF TEXAS
Austin, TX 78712

UNIVERSITY OF TEXAS
San Antonio, TX 78249

TEXAS A&M UNIVERSITY
College Station, TX 77843-1228

TEXAS TECH UNIVERSITY
Lubbock, TX 79409

District 7

CALIF. STATE UNIV.-FRESNO
Fresno, CA 93740-0048

COLORADO STATE UNIVERSITY
Fort Collins, CO 80523-0100

UNIVERSITY OF HAWAII-MANOA
Honolulu, HI 96822-2370

UNIVERSITY OF NEW MEXICO
Albuquerque, NM 87131

SAN DIEGO STATE UNIVERSITY
San Diego, CA 92182

SOUTHERN UTAH UNIVERSITY
Cedar City, UT 84720

UNIVERSITY OF UTAH
Salt Lake City, UT 84112

District 8

ARIZONA STATE UNIVERSITY
Tempe, AZ 85287-2505

UNIVERSITY OF ARIZONA
Tucson, AZ 85721

UNIV. OF CALIFORNIA-BERKELEY
Berkeley, CA 94720

UNIV. OF CALIF.-LOS ANGELES
Los Angeles, CA 90095-1405

UNIV. OF CALIF-SANTA BARBARA
Santa Barbara, CA 93106

CALIF. POLYTECHNIC STATE UNIV.
San Luis Obispo, CA 93407

CALIF. STATE UNIV.-FULLERTON
Fullerton, CA 92634-9480

CALIF. STATE UNIV.-NORTHRIDGE
Northridge, CA 91330

CALIF. STATE UNIV.-SACRAMENTO
Sacramento, CA 95819

LONG BEACH STATE UNIVERSITY
Long Beach, CA 90840-0118

LOYOLA MARYMOUNT
UNIVERSITY
Los Angeles, CA 90045-2699

UNIVERSITY OF NEVADA
Las Vegas, NV 89154

NEW MEXICO STATE UNIVERSITY
Las Cruces, NM 88003

OREGON STATE UNIVERSITY
Corvallis, OR 97331

UNIVERSITY OF OREGON
Eugene, OR 97403-1226

UNIVERSITY OF THE PACIFIC
Stockton, CA 95211

UNIVERSITY OF SAN DIEGO
San Diego, CA 92110-2492

SAN JOSE STATE UNIVERSITY
San Jose, CA 95192

SANTA CLARA UNIVERSITY
Santa Clara, CA 95053

ST. MARY'S COLLEGE
Moraga, CA 94556

STANFORD UNIVERSITY
Stanford, CA 94305

UTAH STATE UNIVERSITY
Logan, UT 84322-7400

UNIVERSITY OF WASHINGTON
Seattle, WA 98195

DIVISION II

District 1

AMERICAN INTERNATIONAL
COLLEGE
Springfield, MA 01109-3189

ASSUMPTION COLLEGE
Worcester, MA 01615-0005

BENTLEY COLLEGE
Waltham, MA 02154-4705

UNIVERSITY OF BRIDGEPORT
Bridgeport, CT 06601

BRYANT COLLEGE
Smithfield, RI 02917-1284

FRANKLIN PIERCE COLLEGE
Rindge, NH 03461

KEENE STATE COLLEGE
Keene, NH 03431-4183

UNIV. OF MASSACHUSETTS-
LOWELL
Lowell, MA 01854

MERRIMACK COLLEGE
North Andover, MA 01845

NEW HAMPSHIRE COLLEGE
Hooksett, NH 03106-1045

UNIVERSITY OF NEW HAVEN
West Haven, CT 06516-1999

QUINNIPIAC COLLEGE
Hamden, CT 06518-1940

SACRED HEART UNIVERSITY
Fairfield, CT 06432-1000

SOUTHERN CONNECTICUT ST.
UNIV.
New Haven, CT 06515

ST. ANSELM COLLEGE
Manchester, NH 03102-1310

ST. MICHAEL'S COLLEGE
Colchester, VT 05439

STONEHILL COLLEGE
North Easton, MA 02357

District 2

ADELPHI UNIVERSITY
Garden City, NY 11530

STATE UNIV. OF N.Y. at ALBANY
Albany, NY 12222

ALDERSON-BROADDUS COLLEGE
Philippi, WV 26416

BLOOMSBURG UNIVERSITY
Bloomsburg, PA 17815

BLUEFIELD STATE COLLEGE
Bluefield, WV 24701-2198

CALIFORNIA UNIVERSITY
California, PA 15419

THE UNIVERSITY OF
CHARLESTON
Charleston, WV 25304

CLARION UNIVERSITY
Clarion, PA 16214

CONCORD COLLEGE
Athens, WV 24712

CONCORDIA COLLEGE
Bronxville, NY 10708

DAVIS AND ELKINS COLLEGE
Elkins, WV 26241

DOWLING COLLEGE
Oakdale, NY 11769-1999

EAST STROUDSBURG UNIVERSITY
East Stroudsburg, PA 18301

EDINBORO UNIVERSITY
Edinboro, PA 16444-0001

FAIRMONT STATE COLLEGE
Fairmont, WV 26554

GANNON UNIVERSITY
Erie, PA 16541

INDIANA UNIV. OF PENNSYLVANIA
Indiana, PA 15705

KUTZTOWN UNIVERSITY
Kutztown, PA 19530-0721

LE MOYNE COLLEGE
Syracuse, NY 13214-1399

LOCK HAVEN UNIVERSITY
Lock Haven, PA 17745

LONG ISLAND U./C.W. POST CAMPUS
Brookville, NY 11548

MANSFIELD UNIVERSITY
Mansfield, PA 16933

MERCY COLLEGE
Dobbs Ferry, NY 10522

MERCYHURST COLLEGE
Erie, PA 16546

MILLERSVILLE UNIVERSITY
Millersville, PA 17551-0302

MOLLOY COLLEGE
Rockville Centre, NY 11570

NEW YORK INSTITUTE OF TECH.
Old Westbury, NY 11568-8000

PACE UNIVERSITY
New York, NY 10038-1502

PHILA. COLLEGE OF TEXT. & SCI.
Philadelphia, PA 19144-5497

QUEENS COLLEGE (NY)
Flushing, NY 11367

SALEM-TEIKYO UNIVERSITY
Salaem, OV 26426

SHEPHERD COLLEGE
Shepherdstown, WV 25443

SHIPPENSBURG UNIVERSITY
Shippensburg, PA 17257

SLIPPERY ROCK UNIVERSITY
Slippery Rock, PA 16057

SOUTHAMPTON CAMPUS OF L.I.U.
Southampton, NY 11968

THE COLLEGE OF ST. ROSE
Albany, NY 12203

STATE UNIV. OF N.Y. at STONY BROOK
Stony Brook, NY 11794

WEST CHESTER UNIVERSITY
West Chester, PA 19383

WEST LIBERTY STATE COLLEGE
West Liberty, WV 26074

WEST VIRGINIA INST. OF TECH
Montgomery, WV 25136

WEST VIRGINIA WESLEYAN COLLEGE
Buckhannon, WV 26201

District 3

UNIV. OF ALABAMA-HUNTSVILLE
Huntsville, AL 35899

AUGUSTA COLLEGE
Augusta, GA 30910

BARRY UNIVERSITY
Miami Shores, FL 33161

BARTON COLLEGE
Wilson, NC 27893

BELLARMINE COLLEGE
Louisville, KY 40205-0671

BELMONT ABBEY COLLEGE
Belmont, NC 28012-2795

BOWIE STATE UNIVERSITY
Bowie, MD 20715-9465

CARSON-NEWMAN COLLEGE
Jefferson City, TN 37760

CATAWBA COLLEGE
Salisbury, NC 28144-2488

COKER COLLEGE
Hartsville, SC 29550

COLUMBUS COLLEGE
Columbus, GA 31907-2079

DELTA STATE UNIVERSITY ·
Cleveland, MS 38733

ECKERD COLLEGE
St. Petersburg, FL 33733

ELIZABETH CITY STATE UNIV.
Elizabeth City, NC 27909

ELON COLLEGE
Elon College, NC 27244

ERSKINE COLLEGE
Due West, SC 29639

FAYETTEVILLE STATE UNIVERSITY
Fayetteville, NC 28301-4298

FLORIDA INSTITUTE OF TECH.
Melbourne, FL 32901

FLORIDA SOUTHERN COLLEGE
Lakeland, FL 33801-5698

FRANCIS MARION UNIVERSITY
Florence, SC 29501-0547

GARDNER-WEBB UNIVERSITY
Boiling Springs, NC 28017

GEORGIA COLLEGE
Milledgeville, GA 31061

JOHNSON C. SMITH UNIVERSITY
Charlotte, NC 28216

KENNESAW STATE COLLEGE
Marietta, GA 30061

KENTUCKY STATE UNIVERSITY
Frankfort, KY 40601

KENTUCKY WESLEYAN COLLEGE
Owensboro, KY 42302-1039

LANDER UNIVERSITY
Greenwood, SC 29649-2099

LENOIR-RHYNE COLLEGE
Hickory, NC 28603

LIMESTONE COLLEGE
Gaffney, SC 29340-3799

LINCOLN MEMORIAL UNIVERSITY
Harrogate, TN 37752

LONGWOOD COLLEGE
Farmville, VA 23909-1899

MARS HILL COLLEGE
Mars Hill, NC 28754

MISSISSIPPI COLLEGE
Clinton, MS 39058

MISSISSIPPI UNIV. FOR WOMEN
Columbus, MS 39701

MOUNT OLIVE COLLEGE
Mount Olive, NC 28365

NEWBERRY COLLEGE
Newberry, SC 29108

NORFOLK STATE UNIVERSITY
Norfolk, VA 23504

UNIVERSITY OF NORTH ALABAMA
Florence, AL 35632

NORTH CAROLINA CENTRAL
UNIV.
Durham, NC 27707

UNIVERSITY OF NORTH FLORIDA
Jacksonville, FL 32224-2645

NORTHERN KENTUCKY
UNIVERSITY
Highland Heights, KY 41099

PEMBROKE STATE UNIVERSITY
Pembroke, NC 28372-1510

PFEIFFER COLLEGE
Misenheimer, NC 28109-0960

QUEENS COLLEGE (NC)
Charlotte, NC 28274

ROLLINS COLLEGE
Winter Park, FL 32789

SHAW UNIVERSITY
Raleigh, NC 27611

UNIV. OF SOUTH CAROLINA-
AIKEN
Aiken, SC 29801

U. OF SO. CAROLINA-
SPARTANBURG
Spartanburg, SC 29303

ST. ANDREWS PRESBYTERIAN
COLL.
Laurinburg, NC 28352-5598

ST. AUGUSTINE'S COLLEGE
Raleigh, NC 27610

ST. LEO COLLEGE
Saint Leo, FL 33574

ST. PAUL'S COLLEGE
Lawrenceville, VA 23868

UNIVERSITY OF TAMPA
Tampa, FL 33606-1490

VALDOSTA STATE UNIVERSITY
Valdosta, GA 31698

VIRGINIA STATE UNIVERSITY
Petersburg, VA 23806

VIRGINIA UNION UNIVERSITY
Richmond, VA 23220-1790

UNIVERSITY OF WEST ALABAMA
Livingston, AL 35470

UNIVERSITY OF WEST FLORIDA
Pensacola, FL 32514

WEST GEORGIA COLLEGE
Carrollton, GA 30118

WINGATE UNIVERSITY
Wingate, NC 28174

WINSTON-SALEM STATE UNIV.
Winston-Salem, NC 27110

District 4

ASHLAND UNIVERSITY
Ashland, OH 44805

BEMIDJI STATE UNIVERSITY
Bemidji, MN 56601-2699

FERRIS STATE UNIVERSITY
Big Rapids, MI 49307-2295

GRAND VALLEY STATE
UNIVERSITY
Allendale, MI 49401

HILLSDALE COLLEGE
Hillsdale, MI 49242-1298

INDIANA UNIV.-PURDUE UNIV.
Indianapolis, IN 46202

INDIANA UNIV.-PURDUE UNIV.
Fort Wayne, IN 46805-1499

UNIVERSITY OF INDIANAPOLIS
Indianapolis, IN 46227

LAKE SUPERIOR STATE UNIV.
Sault Sainte Marie, MI 49783

LEWIS UNIVERSITY
Romeoville, IL 60441

UNIV. OF MINNESOTA-DULUTH
Duluth, MN 55812

UNIVERSITY OF MINNESOTA-
MORRIS
Morris, MN 56267

MOORHEAD STATE UNIVERSITY
Moorhead, MN 56563-2996

NORTHWOOD UNIVERSITY
Midland, MI 48640

OAKLAND UNIVERSITY
Rochestser, MI 48309-4401

QUINCY UNIVERSITY
Quincy, IL 62301-2699

SAGINAW VALLEY STATE UNIV.
University Center, MI 48710

SOUTHERN ILLINOIS UNIVERSITY
Edwardsville, IL 62026

UNIV. OF SOUTHERN INDIANA
Evansville, IN 47712

SOUTHWEST STATE UNIVERSITY
Marshall, MN 56258

COLLEGE OF ST. FRANCIS
Joliet, IL 60435

SAINT JOSEPH'S COLLEGE
Rensselaer, IN 47978

WAYNE STATE UNIVERSITY
Detroit, MI 48202

WINONA STATE UNIVERSITY
Winona, MN 55987-5838

UNIV. OF WISCONSIN-PARKSIDE
Kenosha, WI 53141-2000

District 5

AUGUSTANA COLLEGE
Sioux Falls, SD 57197

CENTRAL MISSOURI STATE UNIV.
Warrensburg, MO 64093

EMPORIA STATE UNIVERSITY
Emporia, KS 66801-5087

LINCOLN UNIVERSITY
Jefferson City, MO 65102-0029

MANKATO STATE UNIVERSITY
Mankato, MN 56002-8400

MISSOURI SOUTHERN ST.
COLLEGE
Joplin, MO 64801-1595

MISSOURI WESTERN ST. COLLEGE
St. Joseph, MO 64507

UNIVERSITY OF MISSOURI
Rolla, MO 65401

UNIVERSITY OF MISSOURI
St. Louis, MO 63121-4499

MORNINGSIDE COLLEGE
Sioux City, IA 51106-1751

UNIV. OF NEBRASKA at KEARNEY
Kearney, NE 68849

UNIV. OF NEBRASKA at OMAHA
Omaha, NE 68182

NORTH DAKOTA STATE
UNIVERSITY
Fargo, ND 58105

UNIVERSITY OF NORTH DAKOTA
Grand Forks, ND 58202

NORTHEAST MISSOURI STATE
UNIV.
Kirksville, MO 63501

NORTHERN STATE UNIVERSITY
Aberdeen, SD 57401

NORTHWEST MISSOURI STATE
UNIV.
Maryville, MO 64468-6001

PITTSBURG STATE UNIVERSITY
Pittsburg, KS 66762

SOUTH DAKOTA STATE
UNIVERSITY
Brookings, SD 57007

UNIVERSITY OF SOUTH DAKOTA
Vermillion, SD 57069-2390

SOUTHWEST BAPTIST
UNIVERSITY
Bolivar, MO 65613

ST. CLOUD STATE UNIVERSITY
St. Cloud, MN 56301-4498

WASHBURN UNIVERSITY
Topeka, KS 66621

WAYNE STATE COLLEGE
Wayne, NE 68787-1172

District 6

CAMERON UNIVERSITY
Lawton, OK 73505-6377

UNIV. OF CENTRAL ARKANSAS
Conway, AR 72035-0001

UNIVERSITY OF CENTRAL
OKLAHOMA
Edmond, OK 73034

TARLETON STATE UNIVERSITY
Stephenville, TX 76402

District 7

ADAMS STATE COLLEGE
Alamosa, CO 81102

COLORADO SCHOOL OF MINES
Golden, CO 80401

UNIV. OF COLORADO-COLO.
SPRINGS
Colorado Springs, CO 80933-7150

FORT LEWIS COLLEGE
Durango, CO 81301-3999

MESA STATE COLLEGE
Grand Junction, CO 81501

NEW MEXICO HIGHLANDS UNIV.
Las Vegas, NM 87701

REGIS UNIVERSITY
Denver, CO 80221-1099

UNIV. OF SOUTHERN COLORADO
Pueblo, CO 81001-4901

District 8

UNIV. OF CALIFORNIA-DAVIS
Davis, CA 95616

UNIV. OF CALIFORNIA-RIVERSIDE
Riverside, CA 92521

CALIF. STATE UNIV.-BAKERSFIELD
Bakersfield, CA 93311-1099

CALIF. STATE UNIV.-CHICO
Chico, CA 95929-0300

CALIF. STATE U-DOMINGUEZ
HILLS
Carson, CA 90747

CALIF. STATE UNIV.-HAYWARD
Hayward, CA 94542

CALIF. STATE U.-SAN BERNARDINO
San Bernardino, CA 92407-2397

CALIF. STATE UNIV.-STANISLAUS
Turlock, CA 95382

CHAMINADE UNIVERSITY
Honolulu, HI 96816

UNIVERSITY OF HAWAII-HILO
Hilo, HI 96720-4091

HUMBOLDT STATE UNIVERSITY
Arcata, CA 95521

COLLEGE OF NOTRE DAME
Belmont, CA 94002-9974

PORTLAND STATE UNIVERSITY
Portland, OR 97207-0751

SAN FRANCISCO STATE
UNIVERSITY
San Francisco, CA 94132

SONOMA STATE UNIVERSITY
Rohnert Park, CA 94928

NCAA PROVISIONAL MEMBERS

District 2

UNIV. OF PUERTO RICO-
MAYAGUEZ
Mayaguez, PR 00709

WEST VIRGINIA STATE COLLEGE
Institute, WV 25112-1000

WESTMINSTER COLLEGE
New Wilmington, PA 16172

District 3

ANDERSON COLLEGE
Anderson, SC 29621

CHRISTIAN BROTHERS
UNIVERSITY
Memphis, TN 38104

COLUMBIA UNION COLLEGE
Takoma Park, MD 20912

GEORGIA SOUTHWESTERN
COLLEGE
Americus, GA 31709-4693

LAMBUTH UNIVERSITY
Jackson, TN 38301

TUSCULUM COLLEGE
Greeneville, TN 37743

District 5

EAST CENTRAL UNIVERSITY
Ada, OK 74820

OKLAHOMA PANHANDLE ST. UNIV.
Goodwell, OK 73939

UNIV. OF SCIENCE & ARTS
Chickasha, OK 73018

SOUTHEASTERN OKLA. ST. UNIV.
Durant, OK 74701

District 6

UNIV. OF ARKANSAS-MONTICELLO
Monticello, AR 7166-3596

HOUSTON BAPTIST UNIVERSITY
Houston, TX 77074-3298

INCARNATE WORD COLLEGE
San Antonio, TX 78209

UNIV. OF MARY HARDIN-BAYLOR
Belton, TX 76513

SCHREINER COLLEGE
Keerville, TX 78028

ST. EDWARD'S UNIVERSITY
Austin, TX 78704

ST. MARY'S UNIVERSITY
San Antonio, TX 78228-8572

TEXAS LUTHERAN COLLEGE
Seguin, TX 78155

TEXAS WESLEYAN UNIVERSITY
Fort Worth, TX 76105

District 8

CENTRAL WASHINGTON UNIV.
Ellensburg, WA 98926

HAWAII PACIFIC UNIVERSITY
Honolulu, HI 96813

ST. MARTIN'S COLLEGE
Lacey, WA 98503

WESTERN WASHINGTON UNIV.
Bellingham, WA 98225

MEN'S SWIMMING

DIVISION I

District 1

BOSTON COLLEGE
Chestnut Hill, MA 02167-3934

BOSTON UNIVERSITY
Boston, MA 02215

BROWN UNIVERSITY
Providence, RI 02912

CENTRAL CONN. STATE UNIV.
New Britain, CT 06050-4010

UNIVERSITY OF CONNECTICUT
Storrs, CT 06269

DARTMOUTH COLLEGE
Hanover, NH 03755

FAIRFIELD UNIVERSITY
Fairfield, CT 06430-5195

HARVARD UNIVERSITY
Cambridge, MA 02138-3800

COLLEGE OF THE HOLY CROSS
Worcester, MA 01610-2395

UNIVERSITY OF MAINE
Orono, ME 04469

UNIV. OF MASSACHUSETTS-
AMHERST
Amherst, MA 01003

UNIVERSITY OF NEW HAMPSHIRE
Durham, NH 03824

NORTHEASTERN UNIVERSITY
Boston, MA 02115-5096

PROVIDENCE COLLEGE
Providence, RI 02918

UNIVERSITY OF RHODE ISLAND
Kingston, RI 02881

UNIVERSITY OF VERMONT
Burlington, VT 05405

YALE UNIVERSITY
New Haven, CT 06520-7398

District 2

AMERICAN UNIVERSITY
Washington, DC 20016

BUCKNELL UNIVERSITY
Lewisburg, PA 17837

STATE UNIV. OF N.Y. at BUFFALO
Buffalo, NY 14260

CANISIUS COLLEGE
Buffalo, NY 14208-1098

COLGATE UNIVERSITY
Hamilton, NY 13346-1304

COLUMBIA UNIV.-BARNARD
COLLEGE
New York, NY 10027

CORNELL UNIVERSITY
Ithaca, NY 14853

UNIVERSITY OF DELAWARE
Newark, DE 19716

DREXEL UNIVERSITY
Philadelphia, PA 19104

DUQUESNE UNIVERSITY
Pittsburgh, PA 15282

FORDHAM UNIVERSITY
Bronx, NY 10458-5155

GEORGE WASHINGTON
UNIVERSITY
Washington, DC 20052

GEORGETOWN UNIVERSITY
Washington, DC 20057

HOWARD UNIVERSITY
Washington, DC 20059

IONA COLLEGE
New Rochelle, NY 10801

JAMES MADISON UNIVERSITY
Harrisonburg, VA 22807

LA SALLE UNIVERSITY
Philadelphia, PA 19141-1199

LAFAYETTE COLLEGE
Easton, PA 18042

LEHIGH UNIVERSITY
Bethlehem, PA 18015-3089

LOYOLA COLLEGE
Baltimore, MD 21210

MARIST COLLEGE
Poughkeepsie, NY 12601-1387

UNIV. OF MARYLAND-BALT. CO.
Baltimore, MD 21228-5398

NIAGARA UNIVERSITY
Niagara University, NY 14109

PENNSYLVANIA STATE UNIV.
University Park, PA 16802

UNIVERSITY OF PENNSYLVANIA
Philadelphia, PA 19104-6380

UNIVERSITY OF PITTSBURGH
Pittsburgh, PA 15260

PRINCETON UNIVERSITY
Princeton, NJ 08544

RIDER UNIVERSITY
Lawrenceville, NJ 08648-3099

RUTGERS UNIVERSITY
New Brunswick, NJ 08903

SETON HALL UNIVERSITY
South Orange, NJ 07079

ST. BONAVENTURE UNIVERSITY
St. Bonaventure, NY 14778

ST. FRANCIS COLLEGE
Brooklyn Heights, NY 11201

ST. JOHN'S UNIVERSITY
Jamaica, NY 11439

ST. PETER'S COLLEGE
Jersey City, NJ 07306

SYRACUSE UNIVERSITY
Syracuse, NY 13244

TOWSON STATE UNIVERSITY
Towson, MD 21204

U.S. MILITARY ACADEMY
West Point, NY 10996

U.S. NAVAL ACADEMY
Annapolis, MD 21402

VILLANOVA UNIVERSITY
Villanova, PA 19085

WEST VIRGINIA UNIVERSITY
Morgantown, WV 26506-6201

COLLEGE OF WILLIAM & MARY
Williamsburg, VA 23187

District 3

UNIV. OF ALABAMA at
TUSCALOOSA
Tuscaloosa, AL 35487

AUBURN UNIVERSITY
Auburn University, AL 36849-5113

COLLEGE OF CHARLESTON
Charleston, SC 29424

CLEMSON UNIVERSITY
Clemson, SC 29632

DAVIDSON COLLEGE
Davidson, NC 28036

DUKE UNIVERSITY
Durham, NC 27708-0555

EAST CAROLINA UNIVERSITY
Greenville, NC 27858-4353

FLORIDA A&M UNIVERSITY
Tallahassee, FL 32307

FLORIDA ATLANTIC UNIVERSITY
Boca Raton, FL 33431-0991

FLORIDA STATE UNIVERSITY
Tallahassee, FL 32306

UNIVERSITY OF FLORIDA
Gainesville, FL 32604

GEORGIA INSTITUTE OF TECH.
Atlanta, GA 30332

GEORGIA SOUTHERN UNIVERSITY
Statesboro, GA 30460-8033

UNIVERSITY OF GEORGIA
Athens, GA 30613

UNIVERSITY OF KENTUCKY
Lexington, KY 40506-0032

LOUISIANA STATE UNIVERSITY
Baton Rouge, LA 70803

UNIVERSITY OF LOUISVILLE
Louisville, KY 40292

UNIVERSITY OF MARYLAND
College Park, MD 20740

MERCER UNIVERSITY
Macon, GA 31207

UNIVERSITY OF MIAMI
Coral Gables, FL 33124-6710

UNIVERSITY OF NORTH
CAROLINA
Chapel Hill, NC 27514

UNIVERSITY OF NORTH
CAROLINA
Wilmington, NC 28403-3297

NORTH CAROLINA STATE UNIV.
Raleigh, NC 27695-7001

OLD DOMINION UNIVERSITY
Norfolk, VA 23529

UNIVERSITY OF RICHMOND
Richmond, VA 23173-1903

UNIVERSITY OF SOUTH CAROLINA
Columbia, SC 29208

THE UNIVERSITY OF TENNESSEE
Knoxville, TN 37996

VIRGINIA MILITARY INSTITUTE
Lexington, VA 24450-0304

VIRGINIA POLYTECHNIC
INSTITUTE
Blacksburg, VA 24061

UNIVERSITY OF VIRGINIA
Charlottesville, VA 22903

WESTERN KENTUCKY
UNIVERSITY
Bowling Green, KY 42101-3576

District 4

BALL STATE UNIVERSITY
Muncie, IN 47306

BOWLING GREEN STATE UNIV.
Bowling Green, OH 43403

BUTLER UNIVERSITY
Indianapolis, IN 46208

UNIVERSITY OF CINCINNATI
Cincinnati, OH 45221

CLEVELAND STATE UNIVERSITY
Cleveland, OH 44115

EASTERN ILLINOIS UNIVERSITY
Charleston, IL 61920-3099

EASTERN MICHIGAN UNIVERSITY
Ypsilanti, MI 48197

UNIVERSITY OF EVANSVILLE
Evansville, IN 47722

UNIVERSITY OF ILLINOIS
Chicago, IL 60607

INDIANA UNIVERSITY
Bloomington, IN 47405

UNIVERSITY OF IOWA
Iowa City, IA 52242

MIAMI UNIVERSITY
Oxford, OH 45056

MICHIGAN STATE UNIVERSITY
East Lansing, MI 48824

UNIVERSITY OF MICHIGAN
Ann Arbor, MI 48109-2201

UNIV. OF MINNESOTA-TWIN
CITIES
Minneapolis, MN 55455

NORTHEASTERN ILLINOIS UNIV.
Chicago, IL 60625-4699

NORTHERN ILLINOIS UNIVERSITY
De Kalb, IL 60115-2854

NORTHWESTERN UNIVERSITY
Evanston, IL 60208

UNIVERSITY OF NOTRE DAME
Notre Dame, IN 46556

OHIO STATE UNIVERSITY
Columbus, OH 43210

OHIO UNIVERSITY
Athens, OH 45701

PURDUE UNIVERSITY
West Lafayette, IN 47907

UNIVERSITY OF TOLEDO
Toledo, OH 43606

VALPARAISO UNIVERSITY
Valparaiso, IN 46383-6493

WESTERN ILLINOIS UNIVERSITY
Macomb, IL 61455

UNIVERSITY OF WISCONSIN
Green Bay, WI 54311-7001

UNIVERSITY OF WISCONSIN
Madison, WI 53711

UNIVERSITY OF WISCONSIN
Milwaukee, WI 53201

WRIGHT STATE UNIVERSITY
Dayton, OH 45435-0001

XAVIER UNIVERSITY
Cincinnati, OH 45207-6114

District 5

BRADLEY UNIVERSITY
Peoria, IL 61625

IOWA STATE UNIVERSITY
Ames, IA 50011

UNIVERSITY OF KANSAS
Lawrence, KS 66045

UNIV. OF MISSOURI-COLUMBIA
Columbia, MO 65211

UNIVERSITY OF NEBRASKA
Lincoln, NE 68588

UNIVERSITY OF NORTHERN IOWA
Cedar Falls, IA 50614

SOUTHERN ILLINOIS UNIVERSITY
Carbondale, IL 62901

ST. LOUIS UNIVERSITY
St. Louis, MO 63108

District 6

UNIVERSITY OF ARKANSAS
Fayetteville, AR 72701

UNIVERSITY OF ARKANSAS
Little Rock, AR 72204-1099

NORTHEAST LOUISIANA
UNIVERSITY
Monroe, LA 71209-3000

RICE UNIVERSITY
Houston, TX 77251

SOUTHERN METHODIST
UNIVERSITY
Dallas, TX 75275

UNIVERSITY OF TEXAS
Austin, TX 78712

TEXAS A&M UNIVERSITY
College Station, TX 77843-1228

TEXAS CHRISTIAN UNIVERSITY
Fort Worth, TX 76129-0001

District 7

BRIGHAM YOUNG UNIVERSITY
Provo, UT 84602

UNIVERSITY OF HAWAII-MANOA
Honolulu, HI 96822-2370

UNIVERSITY OF NEW MEXICO
Albuquerque, NM 87131

NORTHERN ARIZONA UNIVERSITY
Flagstaff, AZ 86011

U.S. AIR FORCE ACADEMY
USAF Academy, CO 80840-5461

UNIVERSITY OF UTAH
Salt Lake City, UT 84112

UNIVERSITY OF WYOMING
Laramie, WY 82071

District 8

ARIZONA STATE UNIVERSITY
Tempe, AZ 8287-2505

UNIVERSITY OF ARIZONA
Tucson, AZ 85721

UNIV. OF CALIFORNIA-BERKELEY
Berkeley, CA 94720

UNIV. OF CALIF-SANTA BARBARA
Santa Barbara, CA 93106

UNIV. OF CALIFORNIA-IRVINE
Irvine, CA 92717

CALIF. POLYTECHNIC STATE UNIV.
San Luis Obispo, CA 93407

CALIF. STATE UNIV.-NORTHRIDGE
Northridge, CA 91330

UNIVERSITY OF NEVADA
Las Vegas, NV 89154

NEW MEXICO STATE UNIVERSITY
Las Cruces, NM 88003

UNIVERSITY OF THE PACIFIC
Stockton, CA 95211

UNIV. OF SOUTHERN CALIFORNIA
Los Angeles, CA 90089-0012

STANFORD UNIVERSITY
Stanford, CA 94305

UNIVERSITY OF WASHINGTON
Seattle, WA 98195

DIVISION II

District 1

BENTLEY COLLEGE
Waltham, MA 02154-4705

KEENE STATE COLLEGE
Keene, NH 03431-4183

SOUTHERN CONNECTICUT ST.
UNIV.
New Haven, CT 06515

ST. MICHAEL'S COLLEGE
Colchester, VT 05439

District 2

STATE UNIV. OF N.Y. at ALBANY
Albany, NY 12222

AMERICAN UNIV. OF PUERTO RICO
Bayamon, PR 00960-2037

BLOOMSBURG UNIVERSITY
Bloomsburg, PA 17815

CLARION UNIVERSITY
Clarion, PA 16214

EDINBORO UNIVERSITY
Edinboro, PA 16444-0001

FAIRMONT STATE COLLEGE
Fairmont, WV 26554

GANNON UNIVERSITY
Erie, PA 16541

INDIANA UNIV. OF PENNSYLVANIA
Indiana, PA 15705

KUTZTOWN UNIVERSITY
Kutztown, PA 19530-0721

LE MOYNE COLLEGE
Syracuse, NY 13214-1399

QUEENS COLLEGE (NY)
Flushing, NY 11367

SALEM-TEIKYO UNIVERSITY
Salem, WV 26426

SHIPPENSBURG UNIVERSITY
Shippensburg, PA 17257

SLIPPERY ROCK UNIVERSITY
Slippery Rock, PA 16057

THE COLLEGE OF ST. ROSE
Albany, NY 12203

STATE UNIV. OF N.Y. at STONY
BROOK
Stony Brook, NY 11794

WEST CHESTER UNIVERSITY
West Chester, PA 19383

WEST VIRGINIA WESLEYAN
COLLEGE
Buckhannon, WV 26201

WHEELING JESUIT COLLEGE
Wheeling, WV 26003-6295

District 3

DELTA STATE UNIVERSITY
Cleveland, MS 38733

ROLLINS COLLEGE
Winter Park, FL 32789

UNIVERSITY OF TAMPA
Tampa, FL 33606-1490

District 4

ASHLAND UNIVERSITY
Ashland, OH 44805

GRAND VALLEY STATE
UNIVERSITY
Allendale, MI 49401

UNIVERSITY OF INDIANAPOLIS
Indianapolis, IN 46227

OAKLAND UNIVERSITY
Rochester, MI 48309-4401

WAYNE STATE UNIVERSITY
Detroit, MI 48202

District 5

DRURY COLLEGE
Springfield, MO 65802

MANKATO STATE UNIVERSITY
Mankato, MN 56002-8400

UNIVERSITY OF MISSOURI
Rolla, MO 65401

UNIVERSITY OF NORTH DAKOTA
Grand Forks, ND 58202

NORTHEAST MISSOURI STATE
UNIV.
Kirksville, MO 63501

SOUTH DAKOTA STATE
UNIVERSITY
Brookings, SD 57007

UNIVERSITY OF SOUTH DAKOTA
Vermillion, SD 57069-2390

ST. CLOUD STATE UNIVERSITY
St. Cloud, MN 5630-4498

District 6

HENDERSON STATE UNIVERSITY
Arkadelphia, AR 71999-0001

District 7

COLORADO SCHOOL OF MINES
Golden, CO 80401

UNIVERSITY OF DENVER
Denver, CO 80208

METROPOLITAN STATE COLLEGE
Denver, CO 80217-3362

District 8

UNIVERSITY OF ALASKA-
ANCHORAGE
Anchorage, AK 99508

UNIV. OF CALIFORNIA-DAVIS
Davis, CA 95616

CALIF. STATE UNIV.-BAKERSFIELD
Bakersfield, CA 93311-1099

SAN FRANCISCO STATE
UNIVERSITY
San Francisco, CA 94132

NCAA PROVISIONAL MEMBERS
District 2
UNIV. OF PUERTO RICO-
MAYAGUEZ
Mayaguez, PR 00709

WESTMINSTER COLLEGE
New Wilmington, PA 16172

District 6

OUACHITA BAPTIST UNIVERSITY
Arkadelphia, AR 71998-0001

District 8

CENTRAL WASHINGTON UNIV.
Ellensburg, WA 98926

WOMEN'S SWIMMING

DIVISION I
District 1
BOSTON COLLEGE
Chestnut Hill, MA 02167-3934

BOSTON UNIVERSITY
Boston, MA 02215

BROWN UNIVERSITY
Providence, RI 02912

CENTRAL CONN. STATE UNIV.
New Britain, CT 06050-4010

UNIVERSITY OF CONNECTICUT
Storrs, CT 06269

DARTMOUTH COLLEGE
Hanover, NH 03755

FAIRFIELD UNIVERSITY
Fairfield, CT 06430-5195

HARVARD UNIVERSITY
Cambridge, MA 02138-3800

COLLEGE OF THE HOLY CROSS
Worcester, MA 01610-2395

UNIVERSITY OF MAINE
Orono, ME 04469

UNIV. OF MASSACHUSETTS-
AMHERST
Amherst, MA 01003

UNIVERSITY OF NEW HAMPSHIRE
Durham, NH 03824

NORTHEASTERN UNIVERSITY
Boston, MA 02115-5096

PROVIDENCE COLLEGE
Providence, RI 02918

UNIVERSITY OF RHODE ISLAND
Kingston, RI 02881

UNIVERSITY OF VERMONT
Burlington, VT 05405

YALE UNIVERSITY
New Haven, CT 06520-7398

District 2

AMERICAN UNIVERSITY
Washington, DC 20016

BUCKNELL UNIVERSITY
Lewisburg, PA 17837

STATE UNIV. OF N.Y. at BUFFALO
Buffalo, NY 14260

CANISIUS COLLEGE
Buffalo, NY 14208-1098

COLGATE UNIVERSITY
Hamilton, NY 13346-1304

COLUMBIA UNIV.-BARNARD
COLLEGE
New York, NY 10027

CORNELL UNIVERSITY
Ithaca, NY 14853

UNIVERSITY OF DELAWARE
Newark, DE 19716

DREXEL UNIVERSITY
Philadelphia, PA 19104

DUQUESNE UNIVERSITY
Pittsburgh, PA 15282

FORDHAM UNIVERSITY
Bronx, NY 10458-5155

GEORGE WASHINGTON
UNIVERSITY
Washington, DC 20052

GEORGETOWN UNIVERSITY
Washington, DC 20057

HOWARD UNIVERSITY
Washington, DC 20059

IONA COLLEGE
New Rochelle, NY 10801

JAMES MADISON UNIVERSITY
Harrisonburg, VA 22807

LA SALLE UNIVERSITY
Philadelphia, PA 19141-1199

LAFAYETTE COLLEGE
Easton, PA 18042

LEHIGH UNIVERSITY
Bethlehem, PA 18015-3089

LOYOLA COLLEGE
Baltimore, MD 21210

MARIST COLLEGE
Poughkeepsie, NY 12601-1387

UNIV. OF MARYLAND-BALT. CO.
Baltimore, MD 21228-5398

NIAGARA UNIVERSITY
Niagara University, NY 14109

PENNSYLVANIA STATE UNIV.
University Park, PA 16802

UNIVERSITY OF PENNSYLVANIA
Philadelphia, PA 19104-6380

UNIVERSITY OF PITTSBURGH
Pittsburgh, PA 15260

PRINCETON UNIVERSITY
Princeton, NJ 08544

RIDER UNIVERSITY
Lawrenceville, NJ 08648-3099

RUTGERS UNIVERSITY
New Brunswick, NJ 08903

SETON HALL UNIVERSITY
South Orange, NJ 07079

ST. BONAVENTURE UNIVERSITY
St. Bonaventure, NY 14778

ST. FRANCIS COLLEGE
Brooklyn Heights, NY 11201

ST. FRANCIS COLLEGE
Loretto, PA 15940-0600

ST. JOHN'S UNIVERSITY
Jamaica, NY 11439

ST. PETER'S COLLEGE
Jersey City, NJ 07306

SYRACUSE UNIVERSITY
Syracuse, NY 13244

TOWSON STATE UNIVERSITY
Towson, MD 21204

U.S. MILITARY ACADEMY
West Point, NY 10996

U.S. NAVAL ACADEMY
Annapolis, MD 21402

VILLANOVA UNIVERSITY
Villanova, PA 19085

WEST VIRGINIA UNIVERSITY
Morgantown, WV 26506-6201

COLLEGE OF WILLIAM & MARY
Williamsburg, VA 23187

District 3

UNIV. OF ALABAMA at
TUSCALOOSA
Tuscaloosa, AL 35487

AUBURN UNIVERSITY
Auburn University, AL 36849-5113

COLLEGE OF CHARLESTON
Charleston, SC 29424

CLEMSON UNIVERSITY
Clemson, SC 29632

DAVIDSON COLLEGE
Davidson, NC 28036

DUKE UNIVERSITY
Durham, NC 27708-0555

EAST CAROLINA UNIVERSITY
Greenville, NC 27858-4353

FLORIDA A&M UNIVERSITY
Tallahassee, FL 32307

FLORIDA ATLANTIC UNIVERSITY
Boca Raton, FL 33431-0991

FLORIDA STATE UNIVERSITY
Tallahassee, FL 32306

UNIVERSITY OF FLORIDA
Gainesville, FL 32604

GEORGIA SOUTHERN UNIVERSITY
Statesboro, GA 30460-8033

UNIVERSITY OF GEORGIA
Athens, GA 30613

UNIVERSITY OF KENTUCKY
Lexington, KY 40506-0032

LOUISIANA STATE UNIVERSITY
Baton Rouge, LA 70803

UNIVERSITY OF LOUISVILLE
Louisville, KY 40292

UNIVERSITY OF MARYLAND
College Park, MD 20740

MERCER UNIVERSITY
Macon, GA 31207

UNIVERSITY OF MIAMI
Coral Gables, FL 33124-6710

UNIVERSITY OF NORTH
CAROLINA
Chapel Hill, NC 27514

UNIVERSITY OF NORTH
CAROLINA
Wilmington, NC 28403-3297

NORTH CAROLINA STATE UNIV.
Raleigh, NC 27695-7001

OLD DOMINION UNIVERSITY
Norfolk, VA 23529

UNIVERSITY OF RICHMOND
Richmond, VA 23173-1903

UNIVERSITY OF SOUTH CAROLINA
Columbia, SC 29208

THE UNIVERSITY OF TENNESSEE
Knoxville, TN 37996

VIRGINIA POLYTECHNIC
INSTITUTE
Blacksburg, VA 24061

UNIVERSITY OF VIRGINIA
Charlottesville, VA 22903

District 4

BALL STATE UNIVERSITY
Muncie, IN 47306

BOWLING GREEN STATE UNIV.
Bowling Green, OH 43403

BUTLER UNIVERSITY
Indianapolis, IN 46208

UNIVERSITY OF CINCINNATI
Cincinnati, OH 45221

CLEVELAND STATE UNIVERSITY
Cleveland, OH 44115

EASTERN ILLINOIS UNIVERSITY
Charleston, IL 61920-3099

EASTERN MICHIGAN UNIVERSITY
Ypsilanti, MI 48197

UNIVERSITY OF EVANSVILLE
Evansville, IN 47722

ILLINOIS STATE UNIVERSITY
Normal, IL 61761

UNIVERSITY OF ILLINOIS
Champaign, IL 61820

UNIVERSITY OF ILLINOIS
Chicago, IL 60607

INDIANA UNIVERSITY
Bloomington, IN 47405

UNIVERSITY OF IOWA
Iowa City, IA 52242

MIAMI UNIVERSITY
Oxford, OH 45056

MICHIGAN STATE UNIVERSITY
East Lansing, MI 48824

UNIVERSITY OF MICHIGAN
Ann Arbor, MI 48109-2201

UNIV. OF MINNESOTA-TWIN
CITIES
Minneapolis, MN 55455

NORTHEASTERN ILLINOIS UNIV.
Chicago, IL 60625-4699

NORTHERN ILLINOIS UNIVERSITY
De Kalb, IL 60115-2854

NORTHWESTERN UNIVERSITY
Evanston, IL 60208

UNIVERSITY OF NOTRE DAME
Notre Dame, IN 46556

OHIO STATE UNIVERSITY
Columbus, OH 43210

OHIO UNIVERSITY
Athens, OH 45701

PURDUE UNIVERSITY
West Lafayette, IN 47907

UNIVERSITY OF TOLEDO
Toledo, OH 43606

VALPARAISO UNIVERSITY
Valparaiso, IN 46383-6493

WESTERN ILLINOIS UNIVERSITY
Macomb, IL 61455

UNIVERSITY OF WISCONSIN
Green Bay, WI 54311-7001

UNIVERSITY OF WISCONSIN
Madison, WI 53711

UNIVERSITY OF WISCONSIN
Milwaukee, WI 53201

WRIGHT STATE UNIVERSITY
Dayton, OH 45435-0001

XAVIER UNIVERSITY
Cincinnati, OH 45207-6114

District 5

BRADLEY UNIVERSITY
Peoria, IL 61625

IOWA STATE UNIVERSITY
Ames, IA 50011

UNIVERSITY OF KANSAS
Lawrence, KS 66045

UNIV. OF MISSOURI-COLUMBIA
Columbia, MO 65211

UNIVERSITY OF NEBRASKA
Lincoln, NE 68588

UNIVERSITY OF NORTHERN IOWA
Cedar Falls, IA 50614

SOUTHERN ILLINOIS UNIVERSITY
Carbondale, IL 62901

ST. LOUIS UNIVERSITY
St. Louis, MO 63108

District 6

UNIVERSITY OF ARKANSAS
Fayetteville, AR 72701

UNIVERSITY OF ARKANSAS
Little Rock, AR 72204-1099

UNIVERSITY OF HOUSTON
Houston, TX 77204

RICE UNIVERSITY
Houston, TX 77251

SOUTHERN METHODIST
UNIVERSITY
Dallas, TX 75275

UNIVERSITY OF TEXAS
Austin, TX 78712

TEXAS A&M UNIVERSITY
College Station, TX 77843-1228

TEXAS CHRISTIAN UNIVERSITY
Fort Worth, TX 76129-0001

District 7

BRIGHAM YOUNG UNIVERSITY
Provo, UT 84602

CALIF. STATE UNIV.-FRESNO
Fresno, CA 93740-0048

COLORADO STATE UNIVERSITY
Fort Collins, CO 80523-0100

UNIVERSITY OF HAWAII-MANOA
Honolulu, HI 96822-2370

UNIVERSITY OF NEVADA
Reno, NV 89557

UNIVERSITY OF NEW MEXICO
Albuquerque, NM 87131

NORTHERN ARIZONA UNIVERSITY
Flagstaff, AZ 86011

SAN DIEGO STATE UNIVERSITY
San Diego, CA 92182

UNIVERSITY OF UTAH
Salt Lake City, UT 84112

UNIVERSITY OF WYOMING
Laramie, WY 82071

District 8

ARIZONA STATE UNIVERSITY
Tempe, AZ 85287-2505

UNIVERSITY OF ARIZONA
Tucson, AZ 85721

UNIV. OF CALIFORNIA-BERKELEY
Berkeley, CA 94720

UNIV. OF CALIF.-LOS ANGELES
Los Angeles, CA 90095-1405

UNIV. OF CALIF-SANTA BARBARA
Santa Barbara, CA 93106

UNIV. OF CALIFORNIA-IRVINE
Irvine, CA 92717

CALIF. POLYTECHNIC STATE UNIV.
San Luis Obispo, CA 93407

CALIF. STATE UNIV.-NORTHRIDGE
Northridge, CA 91330

LOYOLA MARYMOUNT
UNIVERSITY
Los Angeles, CA 90045-2699

UNIVERSITY OF NEVADA
Las Vegas, NV 89154

NEW MEXICO STATE UNIVERSITY
Las Cruces, NM 88003

OREGON STATE UNIVERSITY
Corvallis, OR 97331

UNIVERSITY OF THE PACIFIC
Stockton, CA 95211

PEPPERDINE UNIVERSITY
Malibu, CA 90263

UNIVERSITY OF SAN DIEGO
San Diego, CA 92110-2492

SAN JOSE STATE UNIVERSITY
San Jose, CA 95192

UNIV. OF SOUTHERN CALIFORNIA
Los Angeles, CA 90089-0012

STANFORD UNIVERSITY
Stanford, CA 94305

WASHINGTON STATE UNIVERSITY
Pullman, WA 99164

UNIVERSITY OF WASHINGTON
Seattle, WA 98195

DIVISION II

District 1

BENTLEY COLLEGE
Waltham, MA 02154-4705

KEENE STATE COLLEGE
Keene, NH 03431-4183 ·

SOUTHERN CONNECTICUT ST.
UNIV.
New Haven, CT 06515

ST. MICHAEL'S COLLEGE
Colchester, VT 05439

District 2

ADELPHI UNIVERSITY
Garden City, NY 11530

STATE UNIV. OF N.Y. at ALBANY
Albany, NY 12222

BLOOMSBURG UNIVERSITY
Bloomsburg, PA 17815

CLARION UNIVERSITY
Clarion, PA 16214

EAST STROUDSBURG UNIVERSITY
East Stroudsburg, PA 18301

EDINBORO UNIVERSITY
Edinboro, PA 16444-0001

FAIRMONT STATE COLLEGE
Fairmont, WV 26554

GANNON UNIVERSITY
Erie, PA 16541

INDIANA UNIV. OF PENNSYLVANIA
Indiana, PA 15705

KUTZTOWN UNIVERSITY
Kutztown, PA 19530-0721

LE MOYNE COLLEGE
Syracuse, NY 13214-1399

LOCK HAVEN UNIVERSITY
Lock Haven, PA 17745

MANSFIELD UNIVERSITY
Mansfield, PA 16933

MILLERSVILLE UNIVERSITY
Millersville, PA 17551-0302

QUEENS COLLEGE (NY)
Flushing, NY 11367

SALEM-TEIKYO UNIVERSITY
Salem, WV 26426

SHIPPENSBURG UNIVERSITY
Shippensburg, PA 17257

SLIPPERY ROCK UNIVERSITY
Slippery Rock, PA 16057

THE COLLEGE OF ST. ROSE
Albany, NY 12203

STATE UNIV. OF N.Y. at STONY
BROOK
Stony Brook, NY 11794

WEST CHESTER UNIVERSITY
West Chester, PA 19383

WEST VIRGINIA WESLEYAN
COLLEGE
Buckhannon, WV 26201

WHEELING JESUIT COLLEGE
Wheeling, WV 26003-6295

District 3

CATAWBA COLLEGE
Salisbury, NC 28144-2488

DELTA STATE UNIVERSITY
Cleveland, MS 38733

PFEIFFER COLLEGE
Misenheimer, NC 28109-0960

ROLLINS COLLEGE
Winter Park, FL 32789

UNIVERSITY OF TAMPA
Tampa, FL 33606-1490

District 4

ASHLAND UNIVERSITY
Ashland, OH 44805

GRAND VALLEY STATE
UNIVERSITY
Allendale, MI 49401

HILLSDALE COLLEGE
Hillsdale, MI 49242-1298

UNIVERSITY OF INDIANAPOLIS
Indianapolis, IN 46227

NORTHERN MICHIGAN
UNIVERSITY
Marquette, MI 49855-5391

OAKLAND UNIVERSITY
Rochestser, MI 48309-4401

WAYNE STATE UNIVERSITY
Detroit, MI 48202

District 5

DRURY COLLEGE
Springfield, MO 65802

MANKATO STATE UNIVERSITY
Mankato, MN 56002-8400

UNIV. OF NEBRASKA at KEARNEY
Kearney, NE 68849

UNIVERSITY OF NORTH DAKOTA
Grand Forks, ND 58202

NORTHEAST MISSOURI STATE
UNIV.
Kirksville, MO 63501

UNIV. OF NORTHERN COLORADO
Greeley, CO 80639

SOUTH DAKOTA STATE
UNIVERSITY
Brookings, SD 57007

UNIVERSITY OF SOUTH DAKOTA
Vermillion, SD 57069-2390

ST. CLOUD STATE UNIVERSITY
St. Cloud, MN 56301-4498

District 6

HENDERSON STATE UNIVERSITY
Arkadelphia, AR 71999-0001.

District 7

COLORADO SCHOOL OF MINES
Golden, CO 80401

UNIVERSITY OF DENVER
Denver, CO 80208

METROPOLITAN STATE COLLEGE
Denver, CO 80217-3362

U.S. AIR FORCE ACADEMY
USAF Academy, CO 80840-5461

District 8

UNIV. OF CALIFORNIA-DAVIS
Davis, CA 95616

CALIF. STATE UNIV.-BAKERSFIELD
Bakersfield, CA 93311-1099

CALIF. STATE UNIV.-HAYWARD
Hayward, CA 94542

SAN FRANCISCO STATE
UNIVERSITY
San Francisco, CA 94132

NCAA PROVISIONAL MEMBERS
District 2

UNIV. OF PUERTO RICO-
MAYAGUEZ
Mayaguez, PR 00709

WESTMINSTER COLLEGE
New Wilmington, PA 16172

District 6

OUACHITA BAPTIST UNIVERSITY
Arkadelphia, AR 71998-0001

District 8

CENTRAL WASHINGTON UNIV.
Ellensburg, WA 98926

MEN'S TENNIS

DIVISION I
District 1

BOSTON COLLEGE
Chestnut Hill, MA 02167-3934

BOSTON UNIVERSITY
Boston, MA 02215

BROWN UNIVERSITY
Providence, RI 02912

CENTRAL CONN. STATE UNIV.
New Britain, CT 06050-4010

UNIVERSITY OF CONNECTICUT
Storrs, CT 06269

DARTMOUTH COLLEGE
Hanover, NH 03755

FAIRFIELD UNIVERSITY
Fairfield, CT 06430-5195

UNIVERSITY OF HARTFORD
West Hartford, CT 06117-1599

HARVARD UNIVERSITY
Cambridge, MA 02138-3800

COLLEGE OF THE HOLY CROSS
Worcester, MA 01610-2395

UNIV. OF MASSACHUSETTS-
AMHERST
Amherst, MA 01003

UNIVERSITY OF NEW HAMPSHIRE
Durham, NH 03824

NORTHEASTERN UNIVERSITY
Boston, MA 02115-5096

PROVIDENCE COLLEGE
Providence, RI 02918

UNIVERSITY OF RHODE ISLAND
Kingston, RI 02881

UNIVERSITY OF VERMONT
Burlington, VT 05405

YALE UNIVERSITY
New Haven, CT 06520-7398

District 2

AMERICAN UNIVERSITY
Washington, DC 20016

BUCKNELL UNIVERSITY
Lewisburg, PA 17837

STATE UNIV. OF N.Y. at BUFFALO
Buffalo, NY 14260

CANISIUS COLLEGE
Buffalo, NY 14208-1098

COLGATE UNIVERSITY
Hamilton, NY 13346-1304

COLUMBIA UNIV.-BARNARD
COLLEGE
New York, NY 10027

CORNELL UNIVERSITY
Ithaca, NY 14853

DELAWARE STATE UNIVERSITY
Dover, DE 19901

UNIVERSITY OF DELAWARE
Newark, DE 19716

DREXEL UNIVERSITY
Philadelphia, PA 19104

DUQUESNE UNIVERSITY
Pittsburgh, PA 15282

FAIRLEIGH DICKINSON-TEANECK
Teaneck, NJ 07666

FORDHAM UNIVERSITY
Bronx, NY 10458-5155

GEORGE MASON UNIVERSITY
Fairfax, VA 22030

GEORGE WASHINGTON
UNIVERSITY
Washington, DC 20052

GEORGETOWN UNIVERSITY
Washington, DC 20057

HAMPTON UNIVERSITY
Hampton, VA 23668

HOFSTRA UNIVERSITY
Hempstead, NY 11550

HOWARD UNIVERSITY
Washington, DC 20059

IONA COLLEGE
New Rochelle, NY 10801

JAMES MADISON UNIVERSITY
Harrisonburg, VA 22807

LA SALLE UNIVERSITY
Philadelphia, PA 19141-1199

LAFAYETTE COLLEGE
Easton, PA 18042

LEHIGH UNIVERSITY
Bethlehem, PA 18015-3089

LOYOLA COLLEGE
Baltimore, MD 21210

MANHATTAN COLLEGE
Riverdale, NY 10471

MARIST COLLEGE
Poughkeepsie, NY 12601-1387

UNIV. OF MARYLAND-BALT. CO.
Baltimore, MD 21228-5398

U. OF MARYLAND-EASTERN
SHORE
Princess Anne, MD 21853-1299

MONMOUTH UNIVERSITY
West Long Branch, NJ 07764

MORGAN STATE UNIVERSITY
Baltimore, MD 21239

MOUNT ST. MARY'S COLLEGE
Emmitsburg, MD 21727-7799

NIAGARA UNIVERSITY
Niagara University, NY 14109

PENNSYLVANIA STATE UNIV.
University Park, PA 16802

UNIVERSITY OF PENNSYLVANIA
Philadelphia, PA 19104-6380

PRINCETON UNIVERSITY
Princeton, NJ 08544

RIDER UNIVERSITY
Lawrenceville, NJ 08648-3099

ROBERT MORRIS COLLEGE
Coraopolis, PA 15108-1189

RUTGERS UNIVERSITY
New Brunswick, NJ 08903

SETON HALL UNIVERSITY
South Orange, NJ 07079

SIENA COLLEGE
Loudonville, NY 12211-1462

ST. BONAVENTURE UNIVERSITY
St. Bonaventure, NY 14778

ST. FRANCIS COLLEGE
Brooklyn Heights, NY 11201

ST. FRANCIS COLLEGE
Loretto, PA 15940-0600

ST. JOHN'S UNIVERSITY
Jamaica, NY 11439

ST. JOSEPH'S UNIVERSITY
Philadelphia, PA 19131-1395

ST. PETER'S COLLEGE
Jersey City, NJ 07306

TEMPLE UNIVERSITY
Philadelphia, PA 19122

TOWSON STATE UNIVERSITY
Towson, MD 21204

U.S. MILITARY ACADEMY
West Point, NY 10996

U.S. NAVAL ACADEMY
Annapolis, MD 21402

VILLANOVA UNIVERSITY
Villanova, PA 19085

WAGNER COLLEGE
Staten Island, NY 10301-4495

WEST VIRGINIA UNIVERSITY
Morgantown, WV 26506-6201

COLLEGE OF WILLIAM & MARY
Williamsburg, VA 23187

District 3

ALABAMA STATE UNIVERSITY
Montgomery, AL 36101-0271

UNIV. OF ALABAMA at
TUSCALOOSA
Tuscaloosa, AL 35487

UNIV. OF ALABAMA at
BIRMINGHAM
Birmingham, AL 35294-0110

APPALACHIAN STATE UNIVERSITY
Boone, NC 28608

AUBURN UNIVERSITY
Auburn University, AL 36849-5113

AUSTIN PEAY STATE UNIVERSITY
Clarksville, TN 37044-4576

BETHUNE-COOKMAN COLLEGE
Daytona Beach, FL 32114-3099

CAMPBELL UNIVERSITY
Buies Creek, NC 27506

UNIVERSITY OF CENTRAL
FLORIDA
Orlando, FL 32816-0002

CHARLESTON SOUTHERN UNIV.
Charleston, SC 29423-8087

COLLEGE OF CHARLESTON
Charleston, SC 29424

THE CITADEL
Charleston, SC 29409

CLEMSON UNIVERSITY
Clemson, SC 29632

COASTAL CAROLINA UNIVERSITY
Conway, SC 29526

COPPIN STATE COLLEGE
Baltimore, MD 21216

DAVIDSON COLLEGE
Davidson, NC 28036

DUKE UNIVERSITY
Durham, NC 27708-0555

EAST CAROLINA UNIVERSITY
Greenville, NC 27858-4353

EAST TENNESSEE STATE UNIV.
Johnson City, TN 37614

EASTERN KENTUCKY UNIVERSITY
Richmond, KY 40475-3101

FLORIDA A&M UNIVERSITY
Tallahassee, FL 32307

FLORIDA ATLANTIC UNIVERSITY
Boca Raton, FL 33431-0991

FLORIDA INTERNATIONAL UNIV.
Miami, FL 33199

FLORIDA STATE UNIVERSITY
Tallahassee, FL 32306

UNIVERSITY OF FLORIDA
Gainesville, FL 32604

FURMAN UNIVERSITY
Greenville, SC 29613

GEORGIA INSTITUTE OF TECH.
Atlanta, GA 30332

GEORGIA SOUTHERN UNIVERSITY
Statesboro, GA 30460-8033

GEORGIA STATE UNIVERSITY
Atlanta, GA 30303-3083

UNIVERSITY OF GEORGIA
Athens, GA 30613

JACKSONVILLE STATE
UNIVERSITY
Jacksonville, AL 36265-9982

JACKSONVILLE UNIVERSITY
Jacksonville, FL 32211-3394

UNIVERSITY OF KENTUCKY
Lexington, KY 40506-0032

LIBERTY UNIVERSITY
Lynchburg, VA 24506

LOUISIANA STATE UNIVERSITY
Baton Rouge, LA 70803

UNIVERSITY OF LOUISVILLE
Louisville, KY 40292

UNIVERSITY OF MARYLAND
College Park, MD 20740

UNIVERSITY OF MEMPHIS
Memphis, TN 38152

MERCER UNIVERSITY
Macon, GA 31207

UNIVERSITY OF MIAMI
Coral Gables, FL 33124-6710

MIDDLE TENNESSEE STATE UNIV.
Murfreesboro, TN 37132

MISSISSIPPI STATE UNIVERSITY
Mississippi State, MS 39762-5509

UNIVERSITY OF MISSISSIPPI
University, MS 38677

MOREHEAD STATE UNIVERSITY
Morehead, KY 40351-1689

MURRAY STATE UNIVERSITY
Murray, KY 42071-0009

UNIVERSITY OF NEW ORLEANS
New Orleans, LA 70148

UNIVERSITY OF NORTH
CAROLINA
Asheville, NC 28804-3299

UNIVERSITY OF NORTH
CAROLINA
Chapel Hill, NC 27514

UNIVERSITY OF NORTH
CAROLINA
Charlotte, NC 28223

UNIVERSITY OF NORTH
CAROLINA
Greensboro, NC 27412-5001

UNIVERSITY OF NORTH
CAROLINA
Wilmington, NC 28403-3297

NORTH CAROLINA A&T ST. UNIV.
Greensboro, NC 27411

NORTH CAROLINA STATE UNIV.
Raleigh, NC 27695-7001

OLD DOMINION UNIVERSITY
Norfolk, VA 23529

RADFORD UNIVERSITY
Radford, VA 24142

UNIVERSITY OF RICHMOND
Richmond, VA 23173-1903

SAMFORD UNIVERSITY
Birmingham, AL 35229

UNIVERSITY OF SOUTH ALABAMA
Mobile, AL 36688

SOUTH CAROLINA STATE UNIV.
Orangeburg, SC 29117-0001

UNIVERSITY OF SOUTH CAROLINA
Columbia, SC 29208

UNIVERSITY OF SOUTH FLORIDA
Tampa, FL 33620

SOUTHEASTERN LOUISIANA UNIV.
Hammond, LA 70402

UNIV. OF SOUTHERN MISSISSIPPI
Hattiesburg, MS 39406-5001

STETSON UNIVERSITY
De Land, FL 32720

TENNESSEE STATE UNIVERSITY
Nashville, TN 37209-1561

TENNESSEE TECHNOLOGICAL
UNIV.
Cookeville, TN 38505-0001

UNIVERSITY OF TENNESSEE
Chattanooga, TN 37403-2598

THE UNIVERSITY OF TENNESSEE
Knoxville, TN 37996

UNIV. OF TENNESSEE at MARTIN
Martin, TN 38238-5021

TROY STATE UNIVERSITY
Troy, AL 36082

TULANE UNIVERSITY
New Orleans, LA 70118

VANDERBILT UNIVERSITY
Nashville, TN 37212

VIRGINIA COMMONWEALTH UNIV.
Richmond, VA 23284-2003

VIRGINIA MILITARY INSTITUTE
Lexington, VA 24450-0304

VIRGINIA POLYTECHNIC
INSTITUTE
Blacksburg, VA 24061

UNIVERSITY OF VIRGINIA
Charlottesville, VA 22903

WAKE FOREST UNIVERSITY
Winston-Salem, NC 27109

WESTERN KENTUCKY
UNIVERSITY
Bowling Green, KY 42101-3576

WINTHROP UNIVERSITY
Rock Hill, SC 29733

WOFFORD COLLEGE
Spartanburg, SC 29303-3663

District 4

UNIVERSITY OF AKRON
Akron, OH 44325

BALL STATE UNIVERSITY
Muncie, IN 47306

BOWLING GREEN STATE UNIV.
Bowling Green, OH 43403

BUTLER UNIVERSITY
Indianapolis, IN 46208

CHICAGO STATE UNIVERSITY
Chicago, IL 60628-1598

UNIVERSITY OF CINCINNATI
Cincinnati, OH 45221

UNIVERSITY OF DAYTON
Dayton, OH 45469

DE PAUL UNIVERSITY
Chicago, IL 60604-2287

EASTERN ILLINOIS UNIVERSITY
Charleston, IL 61920-3099

EASTERN MICHIGAN UNIVERSITY
Ypsilanti, MI 48197

UNIVERSITY OF EVANSVILLE
Evansville, IN 47722

ILLINOIS STATE UNIVERSITY
Normal, IL 61761

UNIVERSITY OF ILLINOIS
Champaign, IL 61820

UNIVERSITY OF ILLINOIS
Chicago, IL 60607

INDIANA UNIVERSITY
Bloomington, IN 47405

UNIVERSITY OF IOWA
Iowa City, IA 52242

MARQUETTE UNIVERSITY
Milwaukee, WI 53201-1881

MIAMI UNIVERSITY
Oxford, OH 45056

MICHIGAN STATE UNIVERSITY
East Lansing, MI 48824

UNIVERSITY OF MICHIGAN
Ann Arbor, MI 48109-2201

UNIV. OF MINNESOTA-TWIN
CITIES
Minneapolis, MN 55455

NORTHEASTERN ILLINOIS UNIV.
Chicago, IL 60625-4699

NORTHERN ILLINOIS UNIVERSITY
De Kalb, IL 60115-2854

NORTHWESTERN UNIVERSITY
Evanston, IL 60208

UNIVERSITY OF NOTRE DAME
Notre Dame, IN 46556

OHIO STATE UNIVERSITY
Columbus, OH 43210

PURDUE UNIVERSITY
West Lafayette, IN 47907

UNIVERSITY OF TOLEDO
Toledo, OH 43606

VALPARAISO UNIVERSITY
Valparaiso, IN 46383-6493

WESTERN ILLINOIS UNIVERSITY
Macomb, IL 61455

WESTERN MICHIGAN UNIVERSITY
Kalamazoo, MI 49008-5134

UNIVERSITY OF WISCONSIN
Green Bay, WI 54311-7001

UNIVERSITY OF WISCONSIN
Madison, WI 53711

WRIGHT STATE UNIVERSITY
Dayton, OH 45435-0001

XAVIER UNIVERSITY
Cincinnati, OH 45207-6114

YOUNGSTOWN STATE
UNIVERSITY
Youngstown, OH 44555-0001

District 5

BRADLEY UNIVERSITY
Peoria, IL 61625

UNIVERSITY OF COLORADO
Boulder, CO 80309

CREIGHTON UNIVERSITY
Omaha, NE 68178-0001

DRAKE UNIVERSITY
Des Moines, IA 50311-4505

INDIANA STATE UNIVERSITY
Terre Haute, IN 47809

UNIVERSITY OF KANSAS
Lawrence, KS 66045

UNIV. OF MISSOURI-COLUMBIA
Columbia, MO 65211

UNIV. OF MISSOURI-KANSAS CITY
Kansas City, MO 64110

UNIVERSITY OF NEBRASKA
Lincoln, NE 68588

UNIVERSITY OF NORTHERN IOWA
Cedar Falls, IA 50614

OKLAHOMA STATE UNIVERSITY
Stillwater, OK 74078

UNIVERSITY OF OKLAHOMA
Norman, OK 73019

ORAL ROBERTS UNIVERSITY
Tulsa, OK 74171

SOUTHERN ILLINOIS UNIVERSITY
Carbondale, IL 62901

SOUTHWEST MISSOURI STATE
UNIV.
Springfield, MO 65804

ST. LOUIS UNIVERSITY
St. Louis, MO 63108

UNIVERSITY OF TULSA
Tulsa, OK 74104

WICHITA STATE UNIVERSITY
Wichita, KS 67260

District 6

ALCORN STATE UNIVERSITY
Lorman, MS 39096-9402

UNIVERSITY OF ARKANSAS
Fayetteville, AR 72701

UNIVERSITY OF ARKANSAS
Little Rock, AR 72204-1099

BAYLOR UNIVERSITY
Waco, TX 76798

CENTENARY COLLEGE
Shreveport, LA 71134-1188

GRAMBLING STATE UNIVERSITY
Grambling, LA 71245

JACKSON STATE UNIVERSITY
Jackson, MS 39217

LAMAR UNIVERSITY
Beaumont, TX 77710

MISSISSIPPI VALLEY ST. UNIV.
Itta Bena, MS 38941-1400

UNIVERSITY OF NORTH TEXAS
Denton, TX 76203-6737

NORTHEAST LOUISIANA
UNIVERSITY
Monroe, LA 71209-3000

PRAIRIE VIEW A&M UNIVERSITY
Prairie View, TX 77446

RICE UNIVERSITY
Houston, TX 77251

SOUTHERN METHODIST
UNIVERSITY
Dallas, TX 75275

SOUTHERN UNIVERSITY
Baton Rouge, LA 70813

SOUTHWEST TEXAS STATE UNIV.
San Marcos, TX 78666-4615

UNIV. OF SOUTHWESTERN LA.
Lafayette, LA 70504-1008

UNIVERSITY OF TEXAS
Arlington, TX 76019

UNIVERSITY OF TEXAS
Austin, TX 78712

UNIVERSITY OF TEXAS
San Antonio, TX 78249

TEXAS A&M UNIVERSITY
College Station, TX 77843-1228

TEXAS CHRISTIAN UNIVERSITY
Fort Worth, TX 76129-0001

UNIV. OF TEXAS-PAN AMERICAN
Edinburg, TX 78539-2999

TEXAS SOUTHERN UNIVERSITY
Houston, TX 77004

TEXAS TECH UNIVERSITY
Lubbock, TX 79409

District 7

BOISE STATE UNIVERSITY
Boise, ID 83725

BRIGHAM YOUNG UNIVERSITY
Provo, UT 84602

CALIF. STATE UNIV.-FRESNO
Fresno, CA 93740-0048

COLORADO STATE UNIVERSITY
Fort Collins, CO 80523-0100

GONZAGA UNIVERSITY
Spokane, WA 99258

UNIVERSITY OF HAWAII-MANOA
Honolulu, HI 96822-2370

IDAHO STATE UNIVERSITY
Pocatello, ID 83209

UNIVERSITY OF IDAHO
Moscow, ID 83843

MONTANA STATE UNIV-BOZEMAN
Bozeman, MT 59717-0338

THE UNIVERSITY OF MONTANA
Missoula, MT 59812-1291

UNIVERSITY OF NEVADA
Reno, NV 89557

UNIVERSITY OF NEW MEXICO
Albuquerque, NM 87131

NORTHERN ARIZONA UNIVERSITY
Flagstaff, AZ 86011

SAN DIEGO STATE UNIVERSITY
San Diego, CA 92182

UNIVERSITY OF TEXAS-EL PASO
El Paso, TX 79968

U.S. AIR FORCE ACADEMY
USAF Academy, CO 80840-5461

UNIVERSITY OF UTAH
Salt Lake City, UT 84112

WEBER STATE UNIVERSITY
Ogden, UT 84408-2701

District 8

ARIZONA STATE UNIVERSITY
Tempe, AZ 85287-2505

UNIVERSITY OF ARIZONA
Tucson, AZ 85721

UNIV. OF CALIFORNIA-BERKELEY
Berkeley, CA 94720

UNIV. OF CALIF.-LOS ANGELES
Los Angeles, CA 90095-1405

UNIV. OF CALIF-SANTA BARBARA
Santa Barbara, CA 93106

UNIV. OF CALIFORNIA-IRVINE
Irvine, CA 92717

CALIF. POLYTECHNIC STATE UNIV.
San Luis Obispo, CA 93407

CALIF. STATE UNIV.-SACRAMENTO
Sacramento, CA 95819

EASTERN WASHINGTON
UNIVERSITY
Cheney, WA 99004

LOYOLA MARYMOUNT
UNIVERSITY
Los Angeles, CA 90045-2699

UNIVERSITY OF NEVADA
Las Vegas, NV 89154

NEW MEXICO STATE UNIVERSITY
Las Cruces, NM 88003

UNIVERSITY OF OREGON
Eugene, OR 97403-1226

UNIVERSITY OF THE PACIFIC
Stockton, CA 95211

PEPPERDINE UNIVERSITY
Malibu, CA 90263

UNIVERSITY OF PORTLAND
Portland, OR 97203-5798

UNIVERSITY OF SAN DIEGO
San Diego, CA 92110-2492

UNIVERSITY OF SAN FRANCISCO
San Francisco, CA 94117-1080

SAN JOSE STATE UNIVERSITY
San Jose, CA 95192

SANTA CLARA UNIVERSITY
Santa Clara, CA 95053

UNIV. OF SOUTHERN CALIFORNIA
Los Angeles, CA 90089-0012

ST. MARY'S COLLEGE
Moraga, CA 94556

STANFORD UNIVERSITY
Stanford, CA 94305

UTAH STATE UNIVERSITY
Logan, UT 84322-7400

UNIVERSITY OF WASHINGTON
Seattle, WA 98195

DIVISION II

District 1

AMERICAN INTERNATIONAL
COLLEGE
Springfield, MA 01109-3189

ASSUMPTION COLLEGE
Worcester, MA 01615-0005

BENTLEY COLLEGE
Waltham, MA 02154-4705

BRYANT COLLEGE
Smithfield, RI 02917-1284

FRANKLIN PIERCE COLLEGE
Rindge, NH 03461

UNIV. OF MASSACHUSETTS-
LOWELL
Lowell, MA 01854

MERRIMACK COLLEGE
North Andover, MA 01845

QUINNIPIAC COLLEGE
Hamden, CT 06518-1940

SACRED HEART UNIVERSITY
Fairfield, CT 06432-1000

ST. ANSELM COLLEGE
Manchester, NH 03102-1310

ST. MICHAEL'S COLLEGE
Colchester, VT 05439

STONEHILL COLLEGE
North Easton, MA 02357

District 2

ADELPHI UNIVERSITY
Garden City, NY 11530

STATE UNIV. OF N.Y. at ALBANY
Albany, NY 12222

BLOOMSBURG UNIVERSITY
Bloomsburg, PA 17815

BLUEFIELD STATE COLLEGE
Bluefield, WV 24701-2198

THE UNIVERSITY OF
CHARLESTON
Charleston, WV 25304

CHEYNEY UNIVERSITY
Cheyney, PA 19319

CONCORD COLLEGE
Athens, WV 24712

CONCORDIA COLLEGE
Bronxville, NY 10708

DAVIS AND ELKINS COLLEGE
Elkins, WV 26241

UNIV. OF DISTRICT OF COLUMBIA
Washington, DC 20008

DOWLING COLLEGE
Oakdale, NY 11769-1999

EAST STROUDSBURG UNIVERSITY
East Stroudsburg, PA 18301

EDINBORO UNIVERSITY
Edinboro, PA 16444-0001

FAIRMONT STATE COLLEGE
Fairmont, WV 26554

GANNON UNIVERSITY
Erie, PA 16541

KUTZTOWN UNIVERSITY
Kutztown, PA 19530-0721

LE MOYNE COLLEGE
Syracuse, NY 13214-1399

MERCY COLLEGE
Dobbs Ferry, NY 10522

MERCYHURST COLLEGE
Erie, PA 16546

MILLERSVILLE UNIVERSITY
Millersville, PA 17551-0302

PACE UNIVERSITY
New York, NY 10038-1502

PHILA. COLLEGE OF TEXT. & SCI.
Philadelphia, PA 19144-5497

QUEENS COLLEGE (NY)
Flushing, NY 11367

SALEM-TEIKYO UNIVERSITY
Salem, WV 26426

SHEPHERD COLLEGE
Shepherdstown, WV 25443

SLIPPERY ROCK UNIVERSITY
Slippery Rock, PA 16057

THE COLLEGE OF ST. ROSE
Albany, NY 12203

STATE UNIV. OF N.Y. at STONY
BROOK
Stony Brook, NY 11794

WEST CHESTER UNIVERSITY
West Chester, PA 19383

WEST LIBERTY STATE COLLEGE
West Liberty, WV 26074

WEST VIRGINIA INST. OF TECH
Montgomery, WV 25136

WEST VIRGINIA WESLEYAN
COLLEGE
Buckhannon, WV 26201

District 3

ALABAMA A&M UNIVERSITY
Normal, AL 35762

UNIV. OF ALABAMA-HUNTSVILLE
Huntsville, AL 35899

ARMSTRONG STATE COLLEGE
Savannah, GA 31419-1997

AUGUSTA COLLEGE
Augusta, GA 30910

BARRY UNIVERSITY
Miami Shores, FL 33161

BARTON COLLEGE
Wilson, NC 27893

BELLARMINE COLLEGE
Louisville, KY 40205-0671

BELMONT ABBEY COLLEGE
Belmont, NC 28012-2795

CARSON-NEWMAN COLLEGE
Jefferson City, TN 37760

CATAWBA COLLEGE
Salisbury, NC 28144-2488

CLARK ATLANTA UNIVERSITY
Atlanta, GA 30314

COKER COLLEGE
Hartsville, SC 29550

COLUMBUS COLLEGE
Columbus, GA 31907-2079

DELTA STATE UNIVERSITY
Cleveland, MS 38733

ECKERD COLLEGE
St. Petersburg, FL 33733

ELON COLLEGE
Elon College, NC 27244

ERSKINE COLLEGE
Due West, SC 29639

FLORIDA INSTITUTE OF TECH.
Melbourne, FL 32901

FLORIDA SOUTHERN COLLEGE
Lakeland, FL 33801-5698

FORT VALLEY STATE COLLEGE
Fort Valley, GA 31030

FRANCIS MARION UNIVERSITY
Florence, SC 29501-0547

GARDNER-WEBB UNIVERSITY
Boiling Springs, NC 28017

GEORGIA COLLEGE
Milledgeville, GA 31061

HIGH POINT UNIVERSITY
High Point, NC 27262-3598

JOHNSON C. SMITH UNIVERSITY
Charlotte, NC 28216

KENTUCKY STATE UNIVERSITY
Frankfort, KY 40601

KENTUCKY WESLEYAN COLLEGE
Owensboro, KY 42302-1039

LANDER UNIVERSITY
Greenwood, SC 29649-2099

LANE COLLEGE
Jackson, TN 38301

LEES-MCRAE COLLEGE
Banner Elk, NC 28604-0128

LENOIR-RHYNE COLLEGE
Hickory, NC 28603

LIMESTONE COLLEGE
Gaffney, SC 29340-3799

LINCOLN MEMORIAL UNIVERSITY
Harrogate, TN 37752

LONGWOOD COLLEGE
Farmville, VA 23909-1899

LYNN UNIVERSITY
Boca Raton, FL 33431

MARS HILL COLLEGE
Mars Hill, NC 28754

MISSISSIPPI COLLEGE
Clinton, MS 39058

MOREHOUSE COLLEGE
Atlanta, GA 30314

MORRIS BROWN COLLEGE
Atlanta, GA 30314

MOUNT OLIVE COLLEGE
Mount Olive, NC 28365

NEWBERRY COLLEGE
Newberry, SC 29108

NORFOLK STATE UNIVERSITY
Norfolk, VA 23504

UNIVERSITY OF NORTH ALABAMA
Florence, AL 35632

NORTH CAROLINA CENTRAL
UNIV.
Durham, NC 27707

UNIVERSITY OF NORTH FLORIDA
Jacksonville, FL 32224-2645

NORTHERN KENTUCKY
UNIVERSITY
Highland Heights, KY 41099

PFEIFFER COLLEGE
Misenheimer, NC 28109-0960

PRESBYTERIAN COLLEGE
Clinton, SC 29325-2998

QUEENS COLLEGE (NC)
Charlotte, NC 28274

ROLLINS COLLEGE
Winter Park, FL 32789

SHAW UNIVERSITY
Raleigh, NC 27611

UNIV. OF SOUTH CAROLINA-
AIKEN
Aiken, SC 29801

U. OF SO. CAROLINA-
SPARTANBURG
Spartanburg, SC 29303

ST. ANDREWS PRESBYTERIAN
COLL.
Laurinburg, NC 28352-5598

ST. AUGUSTINE'S COLLEGE
Raleigh, NC 27610

ST. LEO COLLEGE
Saint Leo, FL 33574

ST. PAUL'S COLLEGE
Lawrenceville, VA 23868

UNIVERSITY OF TAMPA
Tampa, FL 33606-1490

TUSKEGEE UNIVERSITY
Tuskegee, AL 36088

VALDOSTA STATE UNIVERSITY
Valdosta, GA 31698

VIRGINIA STATE UNIVERSITY
Petersburg, VA 23806

VIRGINIA UNION UNIVERSITY
Richmond, VA 23220-1790

UNIVERSITY OF WEST ALABAMA
Livingston, AL 35470

UNIVERSITY OF WEST FLORIDA
Pensacola, FL 32514

WEST GEORGIA COLLEGE
Carrollton, GA 30118

WINGATE UNIVERSITY
Wingate, NC 28174

WINSTON-SALEM STATE UNIV.
Winston-Salem, NC 27110

District 4

ASHLAND UNIVERSITY
Ashland, OH 44805

FERRIS STATE UNIVERSITY
Big Rapids, MI 49307-2295

GRAND VALLEY STATE
UNIVERSITY
Allendale, MI 49401

HILLSDALE COLLEGE
Hillsdale, MI 49242-1298

INDIANA UNIV.-PURDUE UNIV.
Indianapolis, IN 46202

INDIANA UNIV.-PURDUE UNIV.
Fort Wayne, IN 46805-1499

UNIVERSITY OF INDIANAPOLIS
Indianapolis, IN 46227

LAKE SUPERIOR STATE UNIV.
Sault Sainte Marie, MI 49783

LEWIS UNIVERSITY
Romeoville, IL 60441

MICHIGAN TECHNOLOGICAL
UNIV.
Houghton, MI 49931-1295

UNIV. OF MINNESOTA-DULUTH
Duluth, MN 55812

UNIV. OF MINNESOTA-MORRIS
Morris, MN 56267

NORTHWOOD UNIVERSITY
Midland, MI 48640

QUINCY UNIVERSITY
Quincy, IL 62301-2699

SOUTHERN ILLINOIS UNIVERSITY
Edwardsville, IL 62026

UNIV. OF SOUTHERN INDIANA
Evansville, IN 47712

COLLEGE OF ST. FRANCIS
Joliet, IL 60435

SAINT JOSEPH'S COLLEGE
Rensselaer, IN 47978

WAYNE STATE UNIVERSITY
Detroit, MI 48202

WINONA STATE UNIVERSITY
Winona, MN 55987-5838

District 5

AUGUSTANA COLLEGE
Sioux Falls, SD 57197

DRURY COLLEGE
Springfield, MO 65802

EMPORIA STATE UNIVERSITY
Emporia, KS 66801-5087

MANKATO STATE UNIVERSITY
Mankato, MN 56002-8400

UNIVERSITY OF MISSOURI
Rolla, MO 65401

UNIVERSITY OF MISSOURI
St. Louis, MO 63121-4499

UNIV. OF NEBRASKA at KEARNEY
Kearney, NE 68849

NORTHEAST MISSOURI STATE
UNIV.
Kirksville, MO 63501

UNIV. OF NORTHERN COLORADO
Greeley, CO 80639

NORTHERN STATE UNIVERSITY
Aberdeen, SD 57401

NORTHWEST MISSOURI STATE
UNIV.
Maryville, MO 64468-6001

SOUTH DAKOTA STATE
UNIVERSITY
Brookings, SD 57007

UNIVERSITY OF SOUTH DAKOTA
Vermillion, SD 57069-2390

SOUTHWEST BAPTIST
UNIVERSITY
Bolivar, MO 65613

ST. CLOUD STATE UNIVERSITY
St. Cloud, MN 56301-4498

WASHBURN UNIVERSITY
Topeka, KS 66621

District 6

ABILENE CHRISTIAN UNIVERSITY
Abilene, TX 79699

CAMERON UNIVERSITY
Lawton, OK 73505-6377

UNIVERSITY OF CENTRAL
OKLAHOMA
Edmond, OK 73034

HENDERSON STATE UNIVERSITY
Arkadelphia, AR 71999-0001

WEST TEXAS A&M UNIVERSITY
Canyon, TX 79016-0999

WESTERN NEW MEXICO
UNIVERSITY
Silver City, NM 88061

District 7

COLORADO CHRISTIAN
UNIVERSITY
Lakewood, CO 80226

COLORADO SCHOOL OF MINES
Golden, CO 80401

UNIV. OF COLORADO-COLO.
SPRINGS
Colorado Springs, CO 80933-7150

UNIVERSITY OF DENVER
Denver, CO 80208

MESA STATE COLLEGE
Grand Junction, CO 81501

METROPOLITAN STATE COLLEGE
Denver, CO 80217-3362

MONTANA STATE UNIVERSITY
Billings, MT 59101-0298

UNIV. OF SOUTHERN COLORADO
Pueblo, CO 81001-4901

District 8

UNIV. OF CALIFORNIA-DAVIS
Davis, CA 95616

UNIV. OF CALIFORNIA-RIVERSIDE
Riverside, CA 92521

CALIF. STATE POLYTECHNIC UNIV.
Pomona, CA 91768

CALIF. STATE UNIV.-LOS ANGELES
Los Angeles, CA 90032-8240

CHAMINADE UNIVERSITY
Honolulu, HI 96816

UNIVERSITY OF HAWAII-HILO
Hilo, HI 96720-4091

COLLEGE OF NOTRE DAME
Belmont, CA 94002-9974

NCAA PROVISIONAL MEMBER
District 2

UNIV. OF PUERTO RICO-
MAYAGUEZ
Mayaguez, PR 00709

UNIVERSITY OF VIRGIN ISLANDS
St. Thomas, VI 00802

WEST VIRGINIA STATE COLLEGE
Institute, WV 25112-1000

WESTMINSTER COLLEGE
New Wilmington, PA 16172

District 3

ANDERSON COLLEGE
Anderson, SC 29621

CHRISTIAN BROTHERS
UNIVERSITY
Memphis, TN 38104

GEORGIA SOUTHWESTERN
COLLEGE
Americus, GA 31709-4693

LAMBUTH UNIVERSITY
Jackson, TN 38301

TUSCULUM COLLEGE
Greeneville, TN 37743

District 5

EAST CENTRAL UNIVERSITY
Ada, OK 74820

NORTHWESTERN OKLAHOMA ST.
U.
Alva, OK 73717

ROCKHURST COLLEGE
Kansas City, MO 64110

UNIV. OF SCIENCE & ARTS
Chickasha, OK 73018

SOUTHEASTERN OKLA. ST. UNIV.
Durant, OK 74701

SOUTHWESTERN OKLAHOMA ST.
UNIV.
Weatherford, OK 73096

District 6

CONCORDIA UNIVERSITY at
AUSTIN
Austin, TX 78705-2799

HARDING UNIVERSITY
Searcy, AR 72149-0001

INCARNATE WORD COLLEGE
San Antonio, TX 78209

LYON COLLEGE
Batesville, AR 72503-2317

UNIV. OF MARY HARDIN-BAYLOR
Belton, TX 76513

MIDWESTERN STATE UNIVERSITY
Wichita Falls, TX 76308

OUACHITA BAPTIST UNIVERSITY
Arkadelphia, AR 71998-0001

SCHREINER COLLEGE
Keerville, TX 78028

ST. EDWARD'S UNIVERSITY
Austin, TX 78704

ST. MARY'S UNIVERSITY
San Antonio, TX 78228-8572

TEXAS LUTHERAN COLLEGE
Seguin, TX 78155

TEXAS WESLEYAN UNIVERSITY
Fort Worth, TX 76105

District 7

LEWIS-CLARK STATE COLLEGE
Lewiston, ID 83501

District 8

BRIGHAM YOUNG UNIVERSITY
Laie, HI 96762-1294

HAWAII PACIFIC UNIVERSITY
Honolulu, HI 96813

WESTERN WASHINGTON UNIV.
Bellingham, WA 98225

WOMEN'S TENNIS

DIVISION I

District 1

BOSTON COLLEGE
Chestnut Hill, MA 02167-3934

BOSTON UNIVERSITY
Boston, MA 02215

BROWN UNIVERSITY
Providence, RI 02912

CENTRAL CONN. STATE UNIV.
New Britain, CT 06050-4010

UNIVERSITY OF CONNECTICUT
Storrs, CT 06269

DARTMOUTH COLLEGE
Hanover, NH 03755

FAIRFIELD UNIVERSITY
Fairfield, CT 06430-5195

UNIVERSITY OF HARTFORD
West Hartford, CT 06117-1599

HARVARD UNIVERSITY
Cambridge, MA 02138-3800

COLLEGE OF THE HOLY CROSS
Worcester, MA 01610-2395

UNIVERSITY OF MAINE
Orono, ME 04469

UNIV. OF MASSACHUSETTS-
AMHERST
Amherst, MA 01003

UNIVERSITY OF NEW HAMPSHIRE
Durham, NH 03824

PROVIDENCE COLLEGE
Providence, RI 0298

UNIVERSITY OF RHODE ISLAND
Kingston, RI 02881

UNIVERSITY OF VERMONT
Burlington, VT 05405

YALE UNIVERSITY
New Haven, CT 06520-7398

District 2

AMERICAN UNIVERSITY
Washington, DC 20016

BUCKNELL UNIVERSITY
Lewisburg, PA 17837

STATE UNIV. OF N.Y. at BUFFALO
Buffalo, NY 14260

CANISIUS COLLEGE
Buffalo, NY 14208-1098

COLGATE UNIVERSITY
Hamilton, NY 13346-1304

COLUMBIA UNIV.-BARNARD
COLLEGE
New York, NY 10027

CORNELL UNIVERSITY
Ithaca, NY 14853

DELAWARE STATE UNIVERSITY
Dover, DE 19901

UNIVERSITY OF DELAWARE
Newark, DE 19716

DREXEL UNIVERSITY
Philadelphia, PA 19104

DUQUESNE UNIVERSITY
Pittsburgh, PA 15282

FAIRLEIGH DICKINSON-TEANECK
Teaneck, NJ 07666

FORDHAM UNIVERSITY
Bronx, NY 10458-5155

GEORGE MASON UNIVERSITY
Fairfax, VA 22030

GEORGE WASHINGTON
UNIVERSITY
Washington, DC 20052

GEORGETOWN UNIVERSITY
Washington, DC 20057

HAMPTON UNIVERSITY
Hampton, VA 23668

HOFSTRA UNIVERSITY
Hempstead, NY 11550

HOWARD UNIVERSITY
Washington, DC 20059

IONA COLLEGE
New Rochelle, NY 10801

JAMES MADISON UNIVERSITY
Harrisonburg, VA 22807

LA SALLE UNIVERSITY
Philadelphia, PA 19141-1199

LAFAYETTE COLLEGE
Easton, PA 18042

LEHIGH UNIVERSITY
Bethlehem, PA 18015-3089

LONG ISLAND UNIV.-BROOKLYN
Brooklyn, NY 11201

LOYOLA COLLEGE
Baltimore, MD 21210

MANHATTAN COLLEGE
Riverdale, NY 10471

MARIST COLLEGE
Poughkeepsie, NY 12601-1387

UNIV. OF MARYLAND-BALT. CO.
Baltimore, MD 21228-5398

U. OF MARYLAND-EASTERN
SHORE
Princess Anne, MD 21853-1299

MONMOUTH UNIVERSITY
West Long Branch, NJ 07764

MORGAN STATE UNIVERSITY
Baltimore, MD 21239

MOUNT ST. MARY'S COLLEGE
Emmitsburg, MD 21727-7799

NIAGARA UNIVERSITY
Niagara University, NY 14109

PENNSYLVANIA STATE UNIV.
University Park, PA 16802

UNIVERSITY OF PENNSYLVANIA
Philadelphia, PA 19104-6380

UNIVERSITY OF PITTSBURGH
Pittsburgh, PA 15260

PRINCETON UNIVERSITY
Princeton, NJ 08544

RIDER UNIVERSITY
Lawrenceville, NJ 08648-3099

ROBERT MORRIS COLLEGE
Coraopolis, PA 15108-1189

RUTGERS UNIVERSITY
New Brunswick, NJ 08903

SETON HALL UNIVERSITY
South Orange, NJ 07079

SIENA COLLEGE
Loudonville, NY 12211-1462

ST. BONAVENTURE UNIVERSITY
St. Bonaventure, NY 14778

ST. FRANCIS COLLEGE
Brooklyn Heights, NY 11201

ST. FRANCIS COLLEGE
Loretto, PA 15940-0600

ST. JOHN'S UNIVERSITY
Jamaica, NY 11439

ST. JOSEPH'S UNIVERSITY
Philadelphia, PA 19131-1395

ST. PETER'S COLLEGE
Jersey City, NJ 07306

SYRACUSE UNIVERSITY
Syracuse, NY 13244

TEMPLE UNIVERSITY
Philadelphia, PA 19122

TOWSON STATE UNIVERSITY
Towson, MD 21204

U.S. MILITARY ACADEMY
West Point, NY 10996

VILLANOVA UNIVERSITY
Villanova, PA 19085

WAGNER COLLEGE
Staten Island, NY 10301-4495

WEST VIRGINIA UNIVERSITY
Morgantown, WV 26506-6201

COLLEGE OF WILLIAM & MARY
Williamsburg, VA 23187

District 3

ALABAMA STATE UNIVERSITY
Montgomery, AL 36101-0271

UNIV. OF ALABAMA at
TUSCALOOSA
Tuscaloosa, AL 35487

UNIV. OF ALABAMA at
BIRMINGHAM
Birmingham, AL 35294-0110

APPALACHIAN STATE UNIVERSITY
Boone, NC 28608

AUBURN UNIVERSITY
Auburn University, AL 36849-5113

AUSTIN PEAY STATE UNIVERSITY
Clarksville, TN 37044-4576

BETHUNE-COOKMAN COLLEGE
Daytona Beach, FL 32114-3099

CAMPBELL UNIVERSITY
Buies Creek, NC 27506

UNIVERSITY OF CENTRAL
FLORIDA
Orlando, FL 32816-0002

CHARLESTON SOUTHERN UNIV.
Charleston, SC 29423-8087

COLLEGE OF CHARLESTON
Charleston, SC 29424

CLEMSON UNIVERSITY
Clemson, SC 29632

COASTAL CAROLINA UNIVERSITY
Conway, SC 29526

COPPIN STATE COLLEGE
Baltimore, MD 21216

DAVIDSON COLLEGE
Davidson, NC 28036

DUKE UNIVERSITY
Durham, NC 27708-0555

EAST CAROLINA UNIVERSITY
Greenville, NC 27858-4353

EAST TENNESSEE STATE UNIV.
Johnson City, TN 37614

EASTERN KENTUCKY UNIVERSITY
Richmond, KY 40475-3101

FLORIDA A&M UNIVERSITY
Tallahassee, FL 32307

FLORIDA ATLANTIC UNIVERSITY
Boca Raton, FL 33431-0991

FLORIDA INTERNATIONAL UNIV.
Miami, FL 33199

FLORIDA STATE UNIVERSITY
Tallahassee, FL 32306

UNIVERSITY OF FLORIDA
Gainesville, FL 32604

FURMAN UNIVERSITY
Greenville, SC 29613

GEORGIA INSTITUTE OF TECH.
Atlanta, GA 30332

GEORGIA SOUTHERN UNIVERSITY
Statesboro, GA 30460-8033

GEORGIA STATE UNIVERSITY
Atlanta, GA 30303-3083

UNIVERSITY OF GEORGIA
Athens, GA 30613

JACKSONVILLE STATE
UNIVERSITY
Jacksonville, AL 36265-9982

JACKSONVILLE UNIVERSITY
Jacksonville, FL 32211-3394

UNIVERSITY OF KENTUCKY
Lexington, KY 40506-0032

LOUISIANA STATE UNIVERSITY
Baton Rouge, LA 70803

UNIVERSITY OF LOUISVILLE
Louisville, KY 40292

MARSHALL UNIVERSITY
Huntington, WV 25755

UNIVERSITY OF MARYLAND
College Park, MD 20740

UNIVERSITY OF MEMPHIS
Memphis, TN 38152

MERCER UNIVERSITY
Macon, GA 31207

UNIVERSITY OF MIAMI
Coral Gables, FL 33124-6710

MIDDLE TENNESSEE STATE UNIV.
Murfreesboro, TN 37132

MISSISSIPPI STATE UNIVERSITY
Mississippi State, MS 39762-5509

UNIVERSITY OF MISSISSIPPI
University, MS 38677

MOREHEAD STATE UNIVERSITY
Morehead, KY 40351-1689

MURRAY STATE UNIVERSITY
Murray, KY 42071-0009

UNIVERSITY OF NEW ORLEANS
New Orleans, LA 70148

UNIVERSITY OF NORTH
CAROLINA
Asheville, NC 28804-3299

UNIVERSITY OF NORTH
CAROLINA
Chapel Hill, NC 27514

UNIVERSITY OF NORTH
CAROLINA
Charlotte, NC 28223

UNIVERSITY OF NORTH
CAROLINA
Greensboro, NC 27412-5001

UNIVERSITY OF NORTH
CAROLINA
Wilmington, NC 28403-3297

NORTH CAROLINA A&T ST. UNIV.
Greensboro, NC 27411

NORTH CAROLINA STATE UNIV.
Raleigh, NC 27695-7001

OLD DOMINION UNIVERSITY
Norfolk, VA 23529

RADFORD UNIVERSITY
Radford, VA 24142

UNIVERSITY OF RICHMOND
Richmond, VA 23173-1903

SAMFORD UNIVERSITY
Birmingham, AL 35229

UNIVERSITY OF SOUTH ALABAMA
Mobile, AL 36688

SOUTH CAROLINA STATE UNIV.
Orangeburg, SC 29117-0001

UNIVERSITY OF SOUTH CAROLINA
Columbia, SC 29208

UNIVERSITY OF SOUTH FLORIDA
Tampa, FL 33620

SOUTHEASTERN LOUISIANA UNIV.
Hammond, LA 70402

UNIV. OF SOUTHERN MISSISSIPPI
Hattiesburg, MS 39406-5001

STETSON UNIVERSITY
De Land, FL 32720

TENNESSEE STATE UNIVERSITY
Nashville, TN 37209-1561

TENNESSEE TECHNOLOGICAL
UNIV.
Cookeville, TN 38505-0001

UNIVERSITY OF TENNESSEE
Chattanooga, TN 37403-2598

THE UNIVERSITY OF TENNESSEE
Knoxville, TN 37996

UNIV. OF TENNESSEE at MARTIN
Martin, TN 38238-5021

TROY STATE UNIVERSITY
Troy, AL 36082

TULANE UNIVERSITY
New Orleans, LA 70118

VANDERBILT UNIVERSITY
Nashville, TN 37212

VIRGINIA COMMONWEALTH UNIV.
Richmond, VA 23284-2003

VIRGINIA POLYTECHNIC
INSTITUTE
Blacksburg, VA 24061

UNIVERSITY OF VIRGINIA
Charlottesville, VA 22903

WAKE FOREST UNIVERSITY
Winston-Salem, NC 27109

WESTERN CAROLINA UNIVERSITY
Cullowhee, NC 28723

WESTERN KENTUCKY
UNIVERSITY
Bowling Green, KY 42101-3576

WINTHROP UNIVERSITY
Rock Hill, SC 29733

WOFFORD COLLEGE
Spartanburg, SC 29303-3663

District 4

UNIVERSITY OF AKRON
Akron, OH 44325

BALL STATE UNIVERSITY
Muncie, IN 47306

BOWLING GREEN STATE UNIV.
Bowling Green, OH 43403

BUTLER UNIVERSITY
Indianapolis, IN 46208

CHICAGO STATE UNIVERSITY
Chicago, IL 60628-1598

UNIVERSITY OF CINCINNATI
Cincinnati, OH 45221

CLEVELAND STATE UNIVERSITY
Cleveland, OH 44115

UNIVERSITY OF DAYTON
Dayton, OH 45469

DE PAUL UNIVERSITY
Chicago, IL 60604-2287

UNIVERSITY OF DETROIT-MERCY
Detroit, MI 48219-0900

EASTERN ILLINOIS UNIVERSITY
Charleston, IL 61920-3099

EASTERN MICHIGAN UNIVERSITY
Ypsilanti, MI 48197

UNIVERSITY OF EVANSVILLE
Evansville, IN 47722

ILLINOIS STATE UNIVERSITY
Normal, IL 61761

UNIVERSITY OF ILLINOIS
Champaign, IL 61820

UNIVERSITY OF ILLINOIS
Chicago, IL 60607

INDIANA UNIVERSITY
Bloomington, IN 47405

UNIVERSITY OF IOWA
Iowa City, IA 52242

MARQUETTE UNIVERSITY
Milwaukee, WI 53201-1881

MIAMI UNIVERSITY
Oxford, OH 45056

MICHIGAN STATE UNIVERSITY
East Lansing, MI 48824

UNIVERSITY OF MICHIGAN
Ann Arbor, MI 48109-2201

UNIV. OF MINNESOTA-TWIN
CITIES
Minneapolis, MN 55455

NORTHEASTERN ILLINOIS UNIV.
Chicago, IL 60625-4699

NORTHERN ILLINOIS UNIVERSITY
De Kalb, IL 60115-2854

NORTHWESTERN UNIVERSITY
Evanston, IL 60208

UNIVERSITY OF NOTRE DAME
Notre Dame, IN 46556

OHIO STATE UNIVERSITY
Columbus, OH 43210

PURDUE UNIVERSITY
West Lafayette, IN 47907

UNIVERSITY OF TOLEDO
Toledo, OH 43606

VALPARAISO UNIVERSITY
Valparaiso, IN 46383-6493

WESTERN ILLINOIS UNIVERSITY
Macomb, IL 61455

WESTERN MICHIGAN UNIVERSITY
Kalamazoo, MI 49008-5134

UNIVERSITY OF WISCONSIN
Green Bay, WI 54311-7001

UNIVERSITY OF WISCONSIN
Madison, WI 53711

UNIVERSITY OF WISCONSIN
Milwaukee, WI 53201

WRIGHT STATE UNIVERSITY
Dayton, OH 45435-0001

XAVIER UNIVERSITY
Cincinnati, OH 45207-6114

YOUNGSTOWN STATE
UNIVERSITY
Youngstown, OH 44555-0001

District 5

BRADLEY UNIVERSITY
Peoria, IL 61625

UNIVERSITY OF COLORADO
Boulder, CO 80309

CREIGHTON UNIVERSITY
Omaha, NE 68178-0001

DRAKE UNIVERSITY
Des Moines, IA 50311-4505

INDIANA STATE UNIVERSITY
Terre Haute, IN 47809

IOWA STATE UNIVERSITY
Ames, IA 50011

KANSAS STATE UNIVERSITY
Manhattan, KS 66506

UNIVERSITY OF KANSAS
Lawrence, KS 66045

UNIV. OF MISSOURI-COLUMBIA
Columbia, MO 65211

UNIV. OF MISSOURI-KANSAS CITY
Kansas City, MO 64110

UNIVERSITY OF NEBRASKA
Lincoln, NE 68588

UNIVERSITY OF NORTHERN IOWA
Cedar Falls, IA 50614

OKLAHOMA STATE UNIVERSITY
Stillwater, OK 74078

UNIVERSITY OF OKLAHOMA
Norman, OK 73019

ORAL ROBERTS UNIVERSITY
Tulsa, OK 74171

SOUTHEAST MISSOURI STATE UNIV.
Cape Girardeau, MO 63701-4799

SOUTHERN ILLINOIS UNIVERSITY
Carbondale, IL 62901

SOUTHWEST MISSOURI STATE UNIV.
Springfield, MO 65804

ST. LOUIS UNIVERSITY
St. Louis, MO 63108

UNIVERSITY OF TULSA
Tulsa, OK 74104

WICHITA STATE UNIVERSITY
Wichita, KS 67260

District 6

ALCORN STATE UNIVERSITY
Lorman, MS 39096-9402

ARKANSAS STATE UNIVERSITY
State University, AR 72467

UNIVERSITY OF ARKANSAS
Fayetteville, AR 72701

UNIVERSITY OF ARKANSAS
Little Rock, AR 72204-1099

BAYLOR UNIVERSITY
Waco, TX 76798

CENTENARY COLLEGE
Shreveport, LA 71134-1188

GRAMBLING STATE UNIVERSITY
Grambling, LA 71245

UNIVERSITY OF HOUSTON
Houston, TX 77204

JACKSON STATE UNIVERSITY
Jackson, MS 39217

LAMAR UNIVERSITY
Beaumont, TX 77710

LOUISIANA TECH UNIVERSITY
Ruston, LA 71272

MCNESSE STATE UNIVERSITY
Lake Charles, LA 70609

MISSISSIPPI VALLEY ST. UNIV.
Itta Bena, MS 38941-1400

NICHOLLS STATE UNIVERSITY
Thibodaux, LA 70310

UNIVERSITY OF NORTH TEXAS
Denton, TX 76203-6737

NORTHEAST LOUISIANA UNIVERSITY
Monroe, LA 71209-3000

NORTHWESTERN STATE UNIVERSITY
Natchitoches, LA 71497-0003

PRAIRIE VIEW A&M UNIVERSITY
Prairie View, TX 77446

RICE UNIVERSITY
Houston, TX 77251

SAM HOUSTON STATE UNIVERSITY
Huntsville, TX 77341

SOUTHERN METHODIST UNIVERSITY
Dallas, TX 75275

SOUTHERN UNIVERSITY
Baton Rouge, LA 70813

SOUTHWEST TEXAS STATE UNIV.
San Marcos, TX 78666-4615

UNIV. OF SOUTHWESTERN LA.
Lafayette, LA 70504-1008

STEPHEN F. AUSTIN STATE UNIV.
Nacogdoches, TX 75962

UNIVERSITY OF TEXAS
Arlington, TX 76019

UNIVERSITY OF TEXAS
Austin, TX 78712

UNIVERSITY OF TEXAS
San Antonio, TX 78249

TEXAS A&M UNIVERSITY
College Station, TX 77843-1228

TEXAS CHRISTIAN UNIVERSITY
Fort Worth, TX 76129-0001

UNIV. OF TEXAS-PAN AMERICAN
Edinburg, TX 78539-2999

TEXAS SOUTHERN UNIVERSITY
Houston, TX 77004

TEXAS TECH UNIVERSITY
Lubbock, TX 79409

District 7

BOISE STATE UNIVERSITY
Boise, ID 83725

BRIGHAM YOUNG UNIVERSITY
Provo, UT 84602

CALIF. STATE UNIV.-FRESNO
Fresno, CA 93740-0048

COLORADO STATE UNIVERSITY
Fort Collins, CO 80523-0100

GONZAGA UNIVERSITY
Spokane, WA 99258

UNIVERSITY OF HAWAII-MANOA
Honolulu, HI 96822-2370

IDAHO STATE UNIVERSITY
Pocatello, ID 83209

UNIVERSITY OF IDAHO
Moscow, ID 83843

MONTANA STATE UNIV-BOZEMAN
Bozeman, MT 59717-0338

THE UNIVERSITY OF MONTANA
Missoula, MT 59812-1291

UNIVERSITY OF NEVADA
Reno, NV 89557

UNIVERSITY OF NEW MEXICO
Albuquerque, NM 87131

NORTHERN ARIZONA UNIVERSITY
Flagstaff, AZ 86011

SAN DIEGO STATE UNIVERSITY
San Diego, CA 92182

SOUTHERN UTAH UNIVERSITY
Cedar City, UT 84720

UNIVERSITY OF TEXAS-EL PASO
El Paso, TX 79968

UNIVERSITY OF UTAH
Salt Lake City, UT 84112

WEBER STATE UNIVERSITY
Ogden, UT 84408-2701

District 8

ARIZONA STATE UNIVERSITY
Tempe, AZ 85287-2505

UNIVERSITY OF ARIZONA
Tucson, AZ 85721

UNIV. OF CALIFORNIA-BERKELEY
Berkeley, CA 94720

UNIV. OF CALIF.-LOS ANGELES
Los Angeles, CA 90095-1405

UNIV. OF CALIF-SANTA BARBARA
Santa Barbara, CA 93106

UNIV. OF CALIFORNIA-IRVINE
Irvine, CA 92717

CALIF. POLYTECHNIC STATE UNIV.
San Luis Obispo, CA 93407

CALIF. STATE UNIV.-FULLERTON
Fullerton, CA 92634-9480

CALIF. STATE UNIV.-NORTHRIDGE
Northridge, CA 91330

CALIF. STATE UNIV.-SACRAMENTO
Sacramento, CA 95819

EASTERN WASHINGTON
UNIVERSITY
Cheney, WA 99004

LONG BEACH STATE UNIVERSITY
Long Beach, CA 90840-0118

LOYOLA MARYMOUNT
UNIVERSITY
Los Angeles, CA 90045-2699

UNIVERSITY OF NEVADA
Las Vegas, NV 89154

NEW MEXICO STATE UNIVERSITY
Las Cruces, NM 88003

UNIVERSITY OF OREGON
Eugene, OR 97403-1226

UNIVERSITY OF THE PACIFIC
Stockton, CA 95211

PEPPERDINE UNIVERSITY
Malibu, CA 90263

UNIVERSITY OF PORTLAND
Portland, OR 97203-5798

UNIVERSITY OF SAN DIEGO
San Diego, CA 92110-2492

UNIVERSITY OF SAN FRANCISCO
San Francisco, CA 94117-1080

SAN JOSE STATE UNIVERSITY
San Jose, CA 95192

SANTA CLARA UNIVERSITY
Santa Clara, CA 95053

UNIV. OF SOUTHERN CALIFORNIA
Los Angeles, CA 90089-0012

ST. MARY'S COLLEGE
Moraga, CA 94556

STANFORD UNIVERSITY
Stanford, CA 94305

UTAH STATE UNIVERSITY
Logan, UT 84322-7400

WASHINGTON STATE UNIVERSITY
Pullman, WA 99164

UNIVERSITY OF WASHINGTON
Seattle, WA 98195

DIVISION II

District 1

AMERICAN INTERNATIONAL
COLLEGE
Springfield, MA 01109-3189

ASSUMPTION COLLEGE
Worcester, MA 01615-0005

BENTLEY COLLEGE
Waltham, MA 02154-4705

BRYANT COLLEGE
Smithfield, RI 02917-1284

FRANKLIN PIERCE COLLEGE
Rindge, NH 03461

UNIV. OF MASSACHUSETTS-
LOWELL
Lowell, MA 01854

MERRIMACK COLLEGE
North Andover, MA 01845

UNIVERSITY OF NEW HAVEN
West Haven, CT 06516-1999

QUINNIPIAC COLLEGE
Hamden, CT 06518-1940

SACRED HEART UNIVERSITY
Fairfield, CT 06432-1000

ST. ANSELM COLLEGE
Manchester, NH 03102-1310

ST. MICHAEL'S COLLEGE
Colchester, VT 05439

STONEHILL COLLEGE
North Easton, MA 02357

District 2

ADELPHI UNIVERSITY
Garden City, NY 11530

STATE UNIV. OF N.Y. at ALBANY
Albany, NY 12222

BLOOMSBURG UNIVERSITY
Bloomsburg, PA 17815

BLUEFIELD STATE COLLEGE
Bluefield, WV 24701-2198

CALIFORNIA UNIVERSITY
California, PA 15419

THE UNIVERSITY OF
CHARLESTON
Charleston, WV 25304

CHEYNEY UNIVERSITY
Cheyney, PA 19319

CLARION UNIVERSITY
Clarion, PA 16214

CONCORD COLLEGE
Athens, WV 24712

CONCORDIA COLLEGE
Bronxville, NY 10708

DAVIS AND ELKINS COLLEGE
Elkins, WV 26241

UNIV. OF DISTRICT OF COLUMBIA
Washington, DC 20008

DOWLING COLLEGE
Oakdale, NY 11769-1999

EAST STROUDSBURG UNIVERSITY
East Stroudsburg, PA 18301

EDINBORO UNIVERSITY
Edinboro, PA 16444-0001

FAIRMONT STATE COLLEGE
Fairmont, WV 26554

GANNON UNIVERSITY
Erie, PA 16541

GLENVILLE STATE COLLEGE
Glenville, WV 26351

INDIANA UNIV. OF PENNSYLVANIA
Indiana, PA 15705

KUTZTOWN UNIVERSITY
Kutztown, PA 19530-0721

LE MOYNE COLLEGE
Syracuse, NY 13214-1399

LONG ISLAND U./C.W. POST
CAMPUS
Brookville, NY 11548

MERCYHURST COLLEGE
Erie, PA 16546

MILLERSVILLE UNIVERSITY
Millersville, PA 17551-0302

MOLLOY COLLEGE
Rockville Centre, NY 11570

PACE UNIVERSITY
New York, NY 10038-1502

PHILA. COLLEGE OF TEXT. & SCI.
Philadelphia, PA 19144-5497

QUEENS COLLEGE (NY)
Flushing, NY 11367

SALEM-TEIKYO UNIVERSITY
Salem, WV 26426

SHEPHERD COLLEGE
Shepherdstown, WV 25443

SHIPPENSBURG UNIVERSITY
Shippensburg, PA 17257

SLIPPERY ROCK UNIVERSITY
Slippery Rock, PA 16057

THE COLLEGE OF ST. ROSE
Albany, NY 12203

STATE UNIV. OF N.Y. at STONY
BROOK
Stony Brook, NY 11794

WEST CHESTER UNIVERSITY
West Chester, PA 19383

WEST LIBERTY STATE COLLEGE
West Liberty, WV 26074

WEST VIRGINIA INST. OF TECH
Montgomery, WV 25136

WEST VIRGINIA WESLEYAN
COLLEGE
Buckhannon, WV 26201

District 3

UNIV. OF ALABAMA-HUNTSVILLE
Huntsville, AL 35899

ARMSTRONG STATE COLLEGE
Savannah, GA 31419-1997

AUGUSTA COLLEGE
Augusta, GA 30910

BARRY UNIVERSITY
Miami Shores, FL 33161

BARTON COLLEGE
Wilson, NC 27893

BELLARMINE COLLEGE
Louisville, KY 40205-0671

BELMONT ABBEY COLLEGE
Belmont, NC 28012-2795

CARSON-NEWMAN COLLEGE
Jefferson City, TN 37760

CATAWBA COLLEGE
Salisbury, NC 28144-2488

CLARK ATLANTA UNIVERSITY
Atlanta, GA 30314

COKER COLLEGE
Hartsville, SC 29550

COLUMBUS COLLEGE
Columbus, GA 31907-2079

DELTA STATE UNIVERSITY
Cleveland, MS 38733

ECKERD COLLEGE
St. Petersburg, FL 33733

ELON COLLEGE
Elon College, NC 27244

ERSKINE COLLEGE
Due West, SC 29639

FLORIDA SOUTHERN COLLEGE
Lakeland, FL 33801-5698

FORT VALLEY STATE COLLEGE
Fort Valley, GA 31030

FRANCIS MARION UNIVERSITY
Florence, SC 29501-0547

GARDNER-WEBB UNIVERSITY
Boiling Springs, NC 28017

GEORGIA COLLEGE
Milledgeville, GA 31061

HIGH POINT UNIVERSITY
High Point, NC 27262-3598

KENNESAW STATE COLLEGE
Marietta, GA 30061

KENTUCKY STATE UNIVERSITY
Frankfort, KY 40601

KENTUCKY WESLEYAN COLLEGE
Owensboro, KY 42302-1039

LANDER UNIVERSITY
Greenwood, SC 29649-2099

LANE COLLEGE
Jackson, TN 38301

LEES-MCRAE COLLEGE
Banner Elk, NC 28604-0128

LENOIR-RHYNE COLLEGE
Hickory, NC 28603

LIMESTONE COLLEGE
Gaffney, SC 29340-3799

LINCOLN MEMORIAL UNIVERSITY
Harrogate, TN 37752

LONGWOOD COLLEGE
Farmville, VA 23909-1899

LYNN UNIVERSITY
Boca Raton, FL 33431

MARS HILL COLLEGE
Mars Hill, NC 28754

MISSISSIPPI COLLEGE
Clinton, MS 39058

MISSISSIPPI UNIV. FOR WOMEN
Columbus, MS 39701

MORRIS BROWN COLLEGE
Atlanta, GA 30314

MOUNT OLIVE COLLEGE
Mount Olive, NC 28365

NEWBERRY COLLEGE
Newberry, SC 29108

UNIVERSITY OF NORTH ALABAMA
Florence, AL 35632

UNIVERSITY OF NORTH FLORIDA
Jacksonville, FL 32224-2645

NORTHERN KENTUCKY
UNIVERSITY
Highland Heights, KY 41099

PFEIFFER COLLEGE
Misenheimer, NC 28109-0960

PRESBYTERIAN COLLEGE
Clinton, SC 29325-2998

QUEENS COLLEGE (NC)
Charlotte, NC 28274

ROLLINS COLLEGE
Winter Park, FL 32789

SAVANNAH STATE COLLEGE
Savannah, GA 31404

U. OF SO. CAROLINA-
SPARTANBURG
Spartanburg, SC 29303

ST. ANDREWS PRESBYTERIAN
COLL.
Laurinburg, NC 28352-5598

ST. LEO COLLEGE
Saint Leo, FL 33574

UNIVERSITY OF TAMPA
Tampa, FL 33606-1490

TUSKEGEE UNIVERSITY
Tuskegee, AL 36088

VALDOSTA STATE UNIVERSITY
Valdosta, GA 31698

VIRGINIA STATE UNIVERSITY
Petersburg, VA 23806

UNIVERSITY OF WEST ALABAMA
Livingston, AL 35470

UNIVERSITY OF WEST FLORIDA
Pensacola, FL 32514

WEST GEORGIA COLLEGE
Carrollton, GA 30118

WINGATE UNIVERSITY
Wingate, NC 28174

District 4

ASHLAND UNIVERSITY
Ashland, OH 44805

BEMIDJI STATE UNIVERSITY
Bemidji, MN 56601-2699

FERRIS STATE UNIVERSITY
Big Rapids, MI 49307-2295

GRAND VALLEY STATE
UNIVERSITY
Allendale, MI 49401

HILLSDALE COLLEGE
Hillsdale, MI 49242-1298

INDIANA UNIV.-PURDUE UNIV.
Indianapolis, IN 46202

INDIANA UNIV.-PURDUE UNIV.
Fort Wayne, IN 46805-1499

UNIVERSITY OF INDIANAPOLIS
Indianapolis, IN 46227

LAKE SUPERIOR STATE UNIV.
Sault Sainte Marie, MI 49783

LEWIS UNIVERSITY
Romeoville, IL 60441

MICHIGAN TECHNOLOGICAL
UNIV.
Houghton, MI 49931-1295

UNIV. OF MINNESOTA-DULUTH
Duluth, MN 55812

UNIV. OF MINNESOTA-MORRIS
Morris, MN 56267

MOORHEAD STATE UNIVERSITY
Moorhead, MN 56563-2996

NORTHERN MICHIGAN
UNIVERSITY
Marquette, MI 49855-5391

NORTHWOOD UNIVERSITY
Midland, MI 48640

OAKLAND UNIVERSITY
Rochestser, MI 48309-4401

QUINCY UNIVERSITY
Quincy, IL 62301-2699

SAGINAW VALLEY STATE UNIV.
University Center, MI 48710

SOUTHERN ILLINOIS UNIVERSITY
Edwardsville, IL 62026

UNIV. OF SOUTHERN INDIANA
Evansville, IN 47712

SOUTHWEST STATE UNIVERSITY
Marshall, MN 56258

COLLEGE OF ST. FRANCIS
Joliet, IL 60435

SAINT JOSEPH'S COLLEGE
Rensselaer, IN 47978

WAYNE STATE UNIVERSITY
Detroit, MI 48202

WINONA STATE UNIVERSITY
Winona, MN 55987-5838

District 5

AUGUSTANA COLLEGE
Sioux Falls, SD 57197

DRURY COLLEGE
Springfield, MO 65802

EMPORIA STATE UNIVERSITY
Emporia, KS 66801-5087

LINCOLN UNIVERSITY
Jefferson City, MO 65102-0029

MANKATO STATE UNIVERSITY
Mankato, MN 56002-8400

MISSOURI SOUTHERN ST.
COLLEGE
Joplin, MO 64801-1595

MISSOURI WESTERN ST. COLLEGE
St. Joseph, MO 64507

UNIV. OF NEBRASKA at KEARNEY
Kearney, NE 68849

NORTHEAST MISSOURI STATE
UNIV.
Kirksville, MO 63501

UNIV. OF NORTHERN COLORADO
Greeley, CO 80639

NORTHERN STATE UNIVERSITY
Aberdeen, SD 57401

NORTHWEST MISSOURI STATE
UNIV.
Maryville, MO 64468-6001

SOUTH DAKOTA STATE
UNIVERSITY
Brookings, SD 57007

UNIVERSITY OF SOUTH DAKOTA
Vermillion, SD 57069-2390

SOUTHWEST BAPTIST
UNIVERSITY
Bolivar, MO 65613

ST. CLOUD STATE UNIVERSITY
St. Cloud, MN 56301-4498

WASHBURN UNIVERSITY
Topeka, KS 66621

District 6

ABILENE CHRISTIAN UNIVERSITY
Abilene, TX 79699

CAMERON UNIVERSITY
Lawton, OK 73505-6377

UNIV. OF CENTRAL ARKANSAS
Conway, AR 72035-0001

UNIVERSITY OF CENTRAL
OKLAHOMA
Edmond, OK 73034

EASTERN NEW MEXICO
UNIVERSITY
Portales, NM 88130

HENDERSON STATE UNIVERSITY
Arkadelphia, AR 71999-0001

TARLETON STATE UNIVERSITY
Stephenville, TX 76402

TEXAS WOMEN'S UNIVERSITY
Denton, TX 76204

WEST TEXAS A&M UNIVERSITY
Canyon, TX 79016-0999

WESTERN NEW MEXICO
UNIVERSITY
Silver City, NM 88061

District 7

COLORADO CHRISTIAN
UNIVERSITY
Lakewood, CO 80226

UNIV. OF COLORADO-COLO.
SPRINGS
Colorado Springs, CO 80933-7150

UNIVERSITY OF DENVER
Denver, CO 80208

FORT HAYS STATE UNIVERSITY
Hays, KS 67601

GRAND CANYON UNIVERSITY
Phoenix, AZ 85017

MESA STATE COLLEGE
Grand Junction, CO 81501

METROPOLITAN STATE COLLEGE
Denver, CO 80217-3362

MONTANA STATE UNIVERSITY
Billings, MT 59101-0298

REGIS UNIVERSITY
Denver, CO 80221-1099

UNIV. OF SOUTHERN COLORADO
Pueblo, CO 81001-4901

U.S. AIR FORCE ACADEMY
USAF Academy, CO 80840-5461

District 8

UNIV. OF CALIFORNIA-DAVIS
Davis, CA 95616

UNIV. OF CALIFORNIA-RIVERSIDE
Riverside, CA 92521

CALIF. STATE POLYTECHNIC UNIV.
Pomona, CA 91768

CALIF. STATE UNIV.-BAKERSFIELD
Bakersfield, CA 93311-1099

CALIF. STATE UNIV.-LOS ANGELES
Los Angeles, CA 90032-8240

CALIF. STATE U.-SAN BERNARDINO
San Bernardino, CA 92407-2397

CHAMINADE UNIVERSITY
Honolulu, HI 96816

UNIVERSITY OF HAWAII-HILO
Hilo, HI 96720-4091

COLLEGE OF NOTRE DAME
Belmont, CA 94002-9974

PORTLAND STATE UNIVERSITY
Portland, OR 97207-0751

**NCAA PROVISIONAL MEMBER
District 2**

UNIV. OF PUERTO RICO-
MAYAGUEZ
Mayaguez, PR 00709

UNIV. OF PUERTO RICO-BAYAMON
Bayamon, PR 00619-1919

UNIVERSITY OF VIRGIN ISLANDS
St. Thomas, VI 00802

WEST VIRGINIA STATE COLLEGE
Institute, WV 25112-1000

WESTMINSTER COLLEGE
New Wilmington, PA 16172

District 3

ANDERSON COLLEGE
Anderson, SC 29621

CHRISTIAN BROTHERS
UNIVERSITY
Memphis, TN 38104

GEORGIA SOUTHWESTERN
COLLEGE
Americus, GA 31709-4693

LAMBUTH UNIVERSITY
Jackson, TN 38301

UNIVERSITY OF MONTEVALLO
Montevallo, AL 35115-6001

TUSCULUM COLLEGE
Greeneville, TN 37743

District 5

EAST CENTRAL UNIVERSITY
Ada, OK 74820

NORTHWESTERN OKLAHOMA ST. U.
Alva, OK 73717

ROCKHURST COLLEGE
Kansas City, MO 64110

UNIV. OF SCIENCE & ARTS
Chickasha, OK 73018

SOUTHEASTERN OKLA. ST. UNIV.
Durant, OK 74701

SOUTHWESTERN OKLAHOMA ST. UNIV.
Weatherford, OK 73096

District 6

ARKANSAS TECH UNIVERSITY
Russellville, AR 72801-2222

UNIV. OF ARKANSAS-MONTICELLO
Monticello, AR 71656-3596

CONCORDIA UNIVERSITY at AUSTIN
Austin, TX 78705-2799

EAST TEXAS BAPTIST UNIVERSITY
Marshall, TX 75670-1498

HARDING UNIVERSITY
Searcy, AR 72149-0001

INCARNATE WORD COLLEGE
San Antonio, TX 78209

LYON COLLEGE
Batesville, AR 72503-2317

UNIV. OF MARY HARDIN-BAYLOR
Belton, TX 76513

MIDWESTERN STATE UNIVERSITY
Wichita Falls, TX 76308

OUACHITA BAPTIST UNIVERSITY
Arkadelphia, AR 71998-0001

SCHREINER COLLEGE
Keerville, TX 78028

SOUTHERN ARKANSAS UNIVERSITY
Magnolia, AR 71753-5000

ST. EDWARD'S UNIVERSITY
Austin, TX 78704

ST. MARY'S UNIVERSITY
San Antonio, TX 78228-8572

TEXAS LUTHERAN COLLEGE
Seguin, TX 78155

TEXAS WESLEYAN UNIVERSITY
Fort Worth, TX 76105

District 7

LEWIS-CLARK STATE COLLEGE
Lewiston, ID 83501

District 8

BRIGHAM YOUNG UNIVERSITY
Laie, HI 96762-1294

HAWAII PACIFIC UNIVERSITY
Honolulu, HI 96813

WESTERN WASHINGTON UNIV.
Bellingham, WA 98225

MEN'S VOLLEYBALL

DIVISION I

District 1

HARVARD UNIVERSITY
Cambridge, MA 02138-3800

District 2

GEORGE MASON UNIVERSITY
Fairfax, VA 22030

PENNSYLVANIA STATE UNIV.
University Park, PA 16802

PRINCETON UNIVERSITY
Princeton, NJ 08544

RUTGERS UNIVERSITY
Newark, NJ 07102

ST. FRANCIS COLLEGE
Loretto, PA 15940-0600

District 3

FLORIDA ATLANTIC UNIVERSITY
Boca Raton, FL 33431-0991

District 4

BALL STATE UNIVERSITY
Muncie, IN 47306

LOYOLA UNIVERSITY
Chicago, IL 60626

OHIO STATE UNIVERSITY
Columbus, OH 43210

UNIVERSITY OF WISCONSIN
Milwaukee, WI 53201

District 7

BRIGHAM YOUNG UNIVERSITY
Provo, UT 84602

UNIVERSITY OF HAWAII-MANOA
Honolulu, HI 96822-2370

SAN DIEGO STATE UNIVERSITY
San Diego, CA 92182

District 8

UNIV. OF CALIF.-LOS ANGELES
Los Angeles, CA 90095-1405

UNIV. OF CALIF-SANTA BARBARA
Santa Barbara, CA 93106

UNIV. OF CALIFORNIA-IRVINE
Irvine, CA 92717

CALIF. STATE UNIV.-NORTHRIDGE
Northridge, CA 91330

LONG BEACH STATE UNIVERSITY
Long Beach, CA 90840-0118

LOYOLA MARYMOUNT
UNIVERSITY
Los Angeles, CA 90045-2699

UNIVERSITY OF THE PACIFIC
Stockton, CA 95211

PEPPERDINE UNIVERSITY
Malibu, CA 90263

UNIV. OF SOUTHERN CALIFORNIA
Los Angeles, CA 90089-0012

STANFORD UNIVERSITY
Stanford, CA 94305

NCAA PROVISIONAL MEMBERS
District 2

UNIV. OF PUERTO RICO-
MAYAGUEZ
Mayaguez, PR 00709

DIVISION II
District 1

SACRED HEART UNIVERSITY
Fairfield, CT 06432-1000

District 2

AMERICAN UNIV. OF PUERTO RICO
Bayamon, PR 00960-2037

CONCORDIA COLLEGE
Bronxville, NY 10708

EAST STROUDSBURG UNIVERSITY
East Stsroudsburg, PA 18301

QUEENS COLLEGE (NY)
Flushing, NY 11367

SOUTHAMPTON CAMPUS OF L.I.U.
Southampton, NY 11968

District 4

INDIANA UNIV.-PURDUE UNIV.
Fort Wayne, IN 46805-1499

LEWIS UNIVERSITY
Romeoville, IL 60441

QUINCY UNIVERSITY
Quincy, IL 62301-2699

District 7

MONTANA STATE UNIVERSITY
Billings, MT 59101-0298

District 8

CALIF. STATE U.-SAN BERNARDINO
San Bernardino, CA 92407-2397

NCAA PROVISIONAL MEMBERS
District 2

UNIV. OF PUERTO RICO-BAYAMON
Bayamon, PR 00619-1919

UNIVERSITY OF VIRGIN ISLANDS
St. Thomas, VI 00802

District 3

COLUMBIA UNION COLLEGE
Takoma Park, MD 20912

District 6

CONCORDIA UNIVERSITY at
AUSTIN
Austin, TX 78705-2799

WOMEN'S VOLLEYBALL

DIVISION I
District 1

BOSTON COLLEGE
Chestnut Hill, MA 02167-3934

BROWN UNIVERSITY
Providence, RI 02912

CENTRAL CONN. STATE UNIV.
New Britain, CT 06050-4010

UNIVERSITY OF CONNECTICUT
Storrs, CT 06269

DARTMOUTH COLLEGE
Hanover, NH 03755

FAIRFIELD UNIVERSITY
Fairfield, CT 06430-5195

UNIVERSITY OF HARTFORD
West Hartford, CT 06117-1599

HARVARD UNIVERSITY
Cambridge, MA 02138-3800

COLLEGE OF THE HOLY CROSS
Worcester, MA 01610-2395

UNIV. OF MASSACHUSETTS-
AMHERST
Amherst, MA 01003

UNIVERSITY OF NEW HAMPSHIRE
Durham, NH 03824

NORTHEASTERN UNIVERSITY
Boston, MA 02115-5096

PROVIDENCE COLLEGE
Providence, RI 02918

UNIVERSITY OF RHODE ISLAND
Kingston, RI 02881

UNIVERSITY OF VERMONT
Burlington, VT 05405

YALE UNIVERSITY
New Haven, CT 06520-7398

District 2

AMERICAN UNIVERSITY
Washington, DC 20016

BUCKNELL UNIVERSITY
Lewisburg, PA 17837

STATE UNIV. OF N.Y. at BUFFALO
Buffalo, NY 14260

CANISIUS COLLEGE
Buffalo, NY 14208-1098

COLGATE UNIVERSITY
Hamilton, NY 13346-1304

COLUMBIA UNIV.-BARNARD
COLLEGE
New York, NY 10027

CORNELL UNIVERSITY
Ithaca, NY 14853

DELAWARE STATE UNIVERSITY
Dover, DE 19901

UNIVERSITY OF DELAWARE
Newark, DE 19716

DREXEL UNIVERSITY
Philadelphia, PA 19104

DUQUESNE UNIVERSITY
Pittsburgh, PA 15282

FAIRLEIGH DICKINSON-TEANECK
Teaneck, NJ 07666

FORDHAM UNIVERSITY
Bronx, NY 10458-5155

GEORGE MASON UNIVERSITY
Fairfax, VA 22030

GEORGE WASHINGTON
UNIVERSITY
Washington, DC 20052

GEORGETOWN UNIVERSITY
Washington, DC 20057

HAMPTON UNIVERSITY
Hampton, VA 23668

HOFSTRA UNIVERSITY
Hempstead, NY 11550

HOWARD UNIVERSITY
Washington, DC 20059

IONA COLLEGE
New Rochelle, NY 10801

JAMES MADISON UNIVERSITY
Harrisonburg, VA 22807

LA SALLE UNIVERSITY
Philadelphia, PA 19141-1199

LAFAYETTE COLLEGE
Easton, PA 18042

LEHIGH UNIVERSITY
Bethlehem, PA 18015-3089

LONG ISLAND UNIV.-BROOKLYN
Brooklyn, NY 11201

LOYOLA COLLEGE
Baltimore, MD 21210

MANHATTAN COLLEGE
Riverdale, NY 10471

MARIST COLLEGE
Poughkeepsie, NY 12601-1387

UNIV. OF MARYLAND-BALT. CO.
Baltimore, MD 21228-5398

U. OF MARYLAND-EASTERN
SHORE
Princess Anne, MD 21853-1299

MORGAN STATE UNIVERSITY
Baltimore, MD 21239

NIAGARA UNIVERSITY
Niagara University, NY 14109

PENNSYLVANIA STATE UNIV.
University Park, PA 16802

UNIVERSITY OF PENNSYLVANIA
Philadelphia, PA 19104-6380

UNIVERSITY OF PITTSBURGH
Pittsburgh, PA 15260

PRINCETON UNIVERSITY
Princeton, NJ 08544

RIDER UNIVERSITY
Lawrenceville, NJ 08648-3099

ROBERT MORRIS COLLEGE
Coraopolis, PA 15108-1189

RUTGERS UNIVERSITY
New Brunswick, NJ 08903

SETON HALL UNIVERSITY
South Orange, NJ 07079

SIENA COLLEGE
Loudonville, NY 12211-1462

ST. BONAVENTURE UNIVERSITY
St. Bonaventure, NY 14778

ST. FRANCIS COLLEGE
Brooklyn Heights, NY 11201

ST. FRANCIS COLLEGE
Loretto, PA 15940-0600

ST. JOHN'S UNIVERSITY
Jamaica, NY 11439

ST. PETER'S COLLEGE
Jersey City, NJ 07306

SYRACUSE UNIVERSITY
Syracuse, NY 13244

TEMPLE UNIVERSITY
Philadelphia, PA 19122

TOWSON STATE UNIVERSITY
Towson, MD 21204

U.S. MILITARY ACADEMY
West Point, NY 10996

U.S. NAVAL ACADEMY
Annapolis, MD 21402

VILLANOVA UNIVERSITY
Villanova, PA 19085

WAGNER COLLEGE
Staten Island, NY 10301-4495

WEST VIRGINIA UNIVERSITY
Morgantown, WV 26506-6201

COLLEGE OF WILLIAM & MARY
Williamsburg, VA 23187

District 3

ALABAMA STATE UNIVERSITY
Montgomery, AL 36101-0271

UNIV. OF ALABAMA at
TUSCALOOSA
Tuscaloosa, AL 35487

UNIV. OF ALABAMA at
BIRMINGHAM
Birmingham, AL 35294-0110

APPALACHIAN STATE UNIVERSITY
Boone, NC 28608

AUBURN UNIVERSITY
Auburn University, AL 36849-5113

AUSTIN PEAY STATE UNIVERSITY
Clarksville, TN 37044-4576

BETHUNE-COOKMAN COLLEGE
Daytona Beach, FL 32114-3099

CAMPBELL UNIVERSITY
Buies Creek, NC 27506

UNIVERSITY OF CENTRAL
FLORIDA
Orlando, FL 32816-0002

CHARLESTON SOUTHERN UNIV.
Charleston, SC 29423-8087

COLLEGE OF CHARLESTON
Charleston, SC 29424

CLEMSON UNIVERSITY
Clemson, SC 29632

COASTAL CAROLINA UNIVERSITY
Conway, SC 29526

COPPIN STATE COLLEGE
Baltimore, MD 21216

DAVIDSON COLLEGE
Davidson, NC 28036

DUKE UNIVERSITY
Durham, NC 27708-0555

EAST CAROLINA UNIVERSITY
Greenville, NC 27858-4353

EAST TENNESSEE STATE UNIV.
Johnson City, TN 37614

EASTERN KENTUCKY UNIVERSITY
Richmond, KY 40475-3101

FLORIDA A&M UNIVERSITY
Tallahassee, FL 32307

FLORIDA ATLANTIC UNIVERSITY
Boca Raton, FL 33431-0991

FLORIDA INTERNATIONAL UNIV.
Miami, FL 33199

FLORIDA STATE UNIVERSITY
Tallahassee, FL 32306

UNIVERSITY OF FLORIDA
Gainesville, FL 32604

FURMAN UNIVERSITY
Greenville, SC 29613

GEORGIA INSTITUTE OF TECH.
Atlanta, GA 30332

GEORGIA SOUTHERN UNIVERSITY
Statesboro, GA 30460-8033

GEORGIA STATE UNIVERSITY
Atlanta, GA 30303-3083

UNIVERSITY OF GEORGIA
Athens, GA 30613

JACKSONVILLE STATE
UNIVERSITY
Jacksonville, AL 36265-9982

JACKSONVILLE UNIVERSITY
Jacksonville, FL 32211-3394

UNIVERSITY OF KENTUCKY
Lexington, KY 40506-0032

LIBERTY UNIVERSITY
Lynchburg, VA 24506

LOUISIANA STATE UNIVERSITY
Baton Rouge, LA 70803

UNIVERSITY OF LOUISVILLE
Louisville, KY 40292

MARSHALL UNIVERSITY
Huntington, WV 25755

UNIVERSITY OF MARYLAND
College Park, MD 20740

UNIVERSITY OF MEMPHIS
Memphis, TN 38152

MERCER UNIVERSITY
Macon, GA 31207

MIDDLE TENNESSEE STATE UNIV.
Murfreesboro, TN 37132

MISSISSIPPI STATE UNIVERSITY
Mississippi State, MS 39762-5509

UNIVERSITY OF MISSISSIPPI
University, MS 38677

MOREHEAD STATE UNIVERSITY
Morehead, KY 40351-1689

MURRAY STATE UNIVERSITY
Murray, KY 42071-0009

UNIVERSITY OF NEW ORLEANS
New Orleans, LA 70148

UNIVERSITY OF NORTH
CAROLINA
Asheville, NC 28804-3299

UNIVERSITY OF NORTH
CAROLINA
Chapel Hill, NC 27514

UNIVERSITY OF NORTH
CAROLINA
Charlotte, NC 28223

UNIVERSITY OF NORTH
CAROLINA
Greensboro, NC 27412-5001

UNIVERSITY OF NORTH
CAROLINA
Wilmington, NC 28403-3297

NORTH CAROLINA A&T ST. UNIV.
Greensboro, NC 27411

NORTH CAROLINA STATE UNIV.
Raleigh, NC 27695-7001

RADFORD UNIVERSITY
Radford, VA 24142

SAMFORD UNIVERSITY
Birmingham, AL 35229

UNIVERSITY OF SOUTH ALABAMA
Mobile, AL 36688

SOUTH CAROLINA STATE UNIV.
Orangeburg, SC 29117-0001

UNIVERSITY OF SOUTH CAROLINA
Columbia, SC 29208

UNIVERSITY OF SOUTH FLORIDA
Tampa, FL 33620

SOUTHEASTERN LOUISIANA UNIV.
Hammond, LA 70402

UNIV. OF SOUTHERN MISSISSIPPI
Hattiesburg, MS 39406-5001

STETSON UNIVERSITY
De Land, FL 32720

TENNESSEE STATE UNIVERSITY
Nashville, TN 37209-1561

TENNESSEE TECHNOLOGICAL
UNIV.
Cookeville, TN 38505-0001

UNIVERSITY OF TENNESSEE
Chattanooga, TN 37403-2598

THE UNIVERSITY OF TENNESSEE
Knoxville, TN 37996

UNIV. OF TENNESSEE at MARTIN
Martin, TN 38238-5021

TROY STATE UNIVERSITY
Troy, AL 36082

TULANE UNIVERSITY
New Orleans, LA 70118

VIRGINIA COMMONWEALTH UNIV.
Richmond, VA 23284-2003

VIRGINIA POLYTECHNIC
INSTITUTE
Blacksburg, VA 24061

UNIVERSITY OF VIRGINIA
Charlottesville, VA 22903

WESTERN CAROLINA UNIVERSITY
Cullowhee, NC 28723

WESTERN KENTUCKY
UNIVERSITY
Bowling Green, KY 42101-3576

WINTHROP UNIVERSITY
Rock Hill, SC 29733

WOFFORD COLLEGE
Spartanburg, SC 29303-3663

District 4

UNIVERSITY OF AKRON
Akron, OH 44325

BALL STATE UNIVERSITY
Muncie, IN 47306

BOWLING GREEN STATE UNIV.
Bowling Green, OH 43403

BUTLER UNIVERSITY
Indianapolis, IN 46208

CENTRAL MICHIGAN UNIVERSITY
Mount Pleasant, MI 48859

CHICAGO STATE UNIVERSITY
Chicago, IL 60628-1598

UNIVERSITY OF CINCINNATI
Cincinnati, OH 45221

CLEVELAND STATE UNIVERSITY
Cleveland, OH 44115

UNIVERSITY OF DAYTON
Dayton, OH 45469

DE PAUL UNIVERSITY
Chicago, IL 60604-2287

EASTERN ILLINOIS UNIVERSITY
Charleston, IL 61920-3099

EASTERN MICHIGAN UNIVERSITY
Ypsilanti, MI 48197

UNIVERSITY OF EVANSVILLE
Evansville, IN 47722

ILLINOIS STATE UNIVERSITY
Normal, IL 61761

UNIVERSITY OF ILLINOIS
Champaign, IL 61820

UNIVERSITY OF ILLINOIS
Chicago, IL 60607

INDIANA UNIVERSITY
Bloomington, IN 47405

UNIVERSITY OF IOWA
Iowa City, IA 52242

KENT STATE UNIVERSITY
Kent, OH 44242

LOYOLA UNIVERSITY
Chicago, IL 60626

MARQUETTE UNIVERSITY
Milwaukee, WI 53201-1881

MIAMI UNIVERSITY
Oxford, OH 45056

MICHIGAN STATE UNIVERSITY
East Lansing, MI 48824

UNIVERSITY OF MICHIGAN
Ann Arbor, MI 48109-2201

UNIV. OF MINNESOTA-TWIN
CITIES
Minneapolis, MN 55455

NORTHEASTERN ILLINOIS UNIV.
Chicago, IL 60625-4699

NORTHERN ILLINOIS UNIVERSITY
De Kalb, IL 60115-2854

NORTHWESTERN UNIVERSITY
Evanston, IL 60208

UNIVERSITY OF NOTRE DAME
Notre Dame, IN 46556

OHIO STATE UNIVERSITY
Columbus, OH 43210

PURDUE UNIVERSITY
West Lafayette, IN 47907

UNIVERSITY OF TOLEDO
Toledo, OH 43606

VALPARAISO UNIVERSITY
Valparaiso, IN 46383-6493

WESTERN ILLINOIS UNIVERSITY
Macomb, IL 61455

WESTERN MICHIGAN UNIVERSITY
Kalamazoo, MI 49008-5134

UNIVERSITY OF WISCONSIN
Green Bay, WI 54311-7001

UNIVERSITY OF WISCONSIN
Madison, WI 53711

UNIVERSITY OF WISCONSIN
Milwaukee, WI 53201

WRIGHT STATE UNIVERSITY
Dayton, OH 45435-0001

XAVIER UNIVERSITY
Cincinnati, OH 45207-6114

YOUNGSTOWN STATE
UNIVERSITY
Youngstown, OH 44555-0001

District 5

BRADLEY UNIVERSITY
Peoria, IL 61625

UNIVERSITY OF COLORADO
Boulder, CO 80309

CREIGHTON UNIVERSITY
Omaha, NE 68178-0001

DRAKE UNIVERSITY
Des Moines, IA 50311-4505

INDIANA STATE UNIVERSITY
Terre Haute, IN 47809

IOWA STATE UNIVERSITY
Ames, IA 50011

KANSAS STATE UNIVERSITY
Manhattan, KS 66506

UNIVERSITY OF KANSAS
Lawrence, KS 66045

UNIV. OF MISSOURI-COLUMBIA
Columbia, MO 65211

UNIV. OF MISSOURI-KANSAS CITY
Kansas City, MO 64110

UNIVERSITY OF NEBRASKA
Lincoln, NE 68588

UNIVERSITY OF NORTHERN IOWA
Cedar Falls, IA 50614

UNIVERSITY OF OKLAHOMA
Norman, OK 73019

ORAL ROBERTS UNIVERSITY
Tulsa, OK 74171

SOUTHEAST MISSOURI STATE
UNIV.
Cape Girardeau, MO 63701-4799

SOUTHERN ILLINOIS UNIVERSITY
Carbondale, IL 62901

SOUTHWEST MISSOURI STATE
UNIV.
Springfield, MO 65804

ST. LOUIS UNIVERSITY
St. Louis, MO 63108

UNIVERSITY OF TULSA
Tulsa, OK 74104

WICHITA STATE UNIVERSITY
Wichita, KS 67260

District 6

ALCORN STATE UNIVERSITY
Lorman, MS 39096-9402

ARKANSAS STATE UNIVERSITY
State University, AR 72467

UNIVERSITY OF ARKANSAS
Fayetteville, AR 72701

UNIVERSITY OF ARKANSAS
Little Rock, AR 72204-1099

BAYLOR UNIVERSITY
Waco, TX 76798

CENTENARY COLLEGE
Shreveport, LA 71134-1188

GRAMBLING STATE UNIVERSITY
Grambling, LA 71245

UNIVERSITY OF HOUSTON
Houston, TX 77204

JACKSON STATE UNIVERSITY
Jackson, MS 39217

LAMAR UNIVERSITY
Beaumont, TX 77710

LOUISIANA TECH UNIVERSITY
Ruston, LA 71272

MCNESSE STATE UNIVERSITY
Lake Charles, LA 70609

MISSISSIPPI VALLEY ST. UNIV.
Itta Bena, MS 38941-1400

NICHOLLS STATE UNIVERSITY
Thibodaux, LA 70310

UNIVERSITY OF NORTH TEXAS
Denton, TX 76203-6737

NORTHEAST LOUISIANA
UNIVERSITY
Monroe, LA 71209-3000

NORTHWESTERN STATE
UNIVERSITY
Natchitoches, LA 71497-0003

PRAIRIE VIEW A&M UNIVERSITY
Prairie View, TX 77446

RICE UNIVERSITY
Houston, TX 77251

SAM HOUSTON STATE
UNIVERSITY
Huntsville, TX 77341

SOUTHERN UNIVERSITY
Baton Rouge, LA 70813

SOUTHWEST TEXAS STATE UNIV.
San Marcos, TX 78666-4615

UNIV. OF SOUTHWESTERN LA.
Lafayette, LA 70504-1008

STEPHEN F. AUSTIN STATE UNIV.
Nacogdoches, TX 75962

UNIVERSITY OF TEXAS
Arlington, TX 76019

UNIVERSITY OF TEXAS
Austin, TX 78712

UNIVERSITY OF TEXAS
San Antonio, TX 78249

TEXAS A&M UNIVERSITY
College Station, TX 77843-1228

UNIV. OF TEXAS-PAN AMERICAN
Edinburg, TX 78539-2999

TEXAS SOUTHERN UNIVERSITY
Houston, TX 77004

TEXAS TECH UNIVERSITY
Lubbock, TX 79409

District 7

BOISE STATE UNIVERSITY
Boise, ID 83725

BRIGHAM YOUNG UNIVERSITY
Provo, UT 84602

CALIF. STATE UNIV.-FRESNO
Fresno, CA 93740-0048

COLORADO STATE UNIVERSITY
Fort Collins, CO 80523-0100

GONZAGA UNIVERSITY
Spokane, WA 99258

UNIVERSITY OF HAWAII-MANOA
Honolulu, HI 96822-2370

IDAHO STATE UNIVERSITY
Pocatello, ID 83209

UNIVERSITY OF IDAHO
Moscow, ID 83843

MONTANA STATE UNIV-BOZEMAN
Bozeman, MT 59717-0338

THE UNIVERSITY OF MONTANA
Missoula, MT 59812-1291

UNIVERSITY OF NEVADA
Reno, NV 89557

UNIVERSITY OF NEW MEXICO
Albuquerque, NM 87131

NORTHERN ARIZONA UNIVERSITY
Flagstaff, AZ 86011

SAN DIEGO STATE UNIVERSITY
San Diego, CA 92182

UNIVERSITY OF TEXAS-EL PASO
El Paso, TX 79968

UNIVERSITY OF UTAH
Salt Lake City, UT 84112

WEBER STATE UNIVERSITY
Ogden, UT 84408-2701

UNIVERSITY OF WYOMING
Laramie, WY 82071

District 8

ARIZONA STATE UNIVERSITY
Tempe, AZ 85287-2505

UNIVERSITY OF ARIZONA
Tucson, AZ 85721

UNIV. OF CALIFORNIA-BERKELEY
Berkeley, CA 94720

UNIV. OF CALIF.-LOS ANGELES
Los Angeles, CA 90095-1405

UNIV. OF CALIF-SANTA BARBARA
Santa Barbara, CA 93106

UNIV. OF CALIFORNIA-IRVINE
Irvine, CA 92717

CALIF. POLYTECHNIC STATE UNIV.
San Luis Obispo, CA 93407

CALIF. STATE UNIV.-FULLERTON
Fullerton, CA 92634-9480

CALIF. STATE UNIV.-NORTHRIDGE
Northridge, CA 91330

CALIF. STATE UNIV.-SACRAMENTO
Sacramento, CA 95819

EASTERN WASHINGTON
UNIVERSITY
Cheney, WA 99004

LONG BEACH STATE UNIVERSITY
Long Beach, CA 90840-0118

LOYOLA MARYMOUNT
UNIVERSITY
Los Angeles, CA 90045-2699

NEW MEXICO STATE UNIVERSITY
Las Cruces, NM 88003

OREGON STATE UNIVERSITY
Corvallis, OR 97331

UNIVERSITY OF OREGON
Eugene, OR 97403-1226

UNIVERSITY OF THE PACIFIC
Stockton, CA 95211

PEPPERDINE UNIVERSITY
Malibu, CA 90263

UNIVERSITY OF PORTLAND
Portland, OR 97203-5798

UNIVERSITY OF SAN DIEGO
San Diego, CA 92110-2492

UNIVERSITY OF SAN FRANCISCO
San Francisco, CA 94117-1080

SAN JOSE STATE UNIVERSITY
San Jose, CA 95192

SANTA CLARA UNIVERSITY
Santa Clara, CA 95053

UNIV. OF SOUTHERN CALIFORNIA
Los Angeles, CA 90089-0012

ST. MARY'S COLLEGE
Moraga, CA 94556

STANFORD UNIVERSITY
Stanford, CA 94305

UTAH STATE UNIVERSITY
Logan, UT 84322-7400

WASHINGTON STATE UNIVERSITY
Pullman, WA 99164

UNIVERSITY OF WASHINGTON
Seattle, WA 98195

DIVISION II

District 1

AMERICAN INTERNATIONAL
COLLEGE
Springfield, MA 01109-3189

ASSUMPTION COLLEGE
Worcester, MA 01615-0005

BENTLEY COLLEGE
Waltham, MA 02154-4705

BRYANT COLLEGE
Smithfield, RI 02917-1284

FRANKLIN PIERCE COLLEGE
Rindge, NH 03461

KEENE STATE COLLEGE
Keene, NH 03431-4183

UNIV. OF MASSACHUSETTS-
LOWELL
Lowell, MA 01854

MERRIMACK COLLEGE
North Andover, MA 01845

NEW HAMPSHIRE COLLEGE
Hooksett, NH 03106-1045

UNIVERSITY OF NEW HAVEN
West Haven, CT 06516-1999

QUINNIPIAC COLLEGE
Hamden, CT 06518-1940

SACRED HEART UNIVERSITY
Fairfield, CT 06432-1000

SOUTHERN CONNECTICUT ST.
UNIV.
New Haven, CT 06515

ST. ANSELM COLLEGE
Manchester, NH 03102-1310

ST. MICHAEL'S COLLEGE
Colchester, VT 05439

STONEHILL COLLEGE
North Easton, MA 02357

District 2

ADELPHI UNIVERSITY
Garden City, NY 11530

STATE UNIV. OF N.Y. at ALBANY
Albany, NY 12222

ALDERSON-BROADDUS COLLEGE
Philippi, WV 26416

AMERICAN UNIV. OF PUERTO RICO
Bayamon, PR 00960-2037

CALIFORNIA UNIVERSITY
California, PA 15419

THE UNIVERSITY OF
CHARLESTON
Charleston, WV 25304

CHEYNEY UNIVERSITY
Cheyney, PA 19319

CLARION UNIVERSITY
Clarion, PA 16214

CONCORD COLLEGE
Athens, WV 24712

CONCORDIA COLLEGE
Bronxville, NY 10708

UNIV. OF DISTRICT OF COLUMBIA
Washington, DC 20008

DOWLING COLLEGE
Oakdale, NY 11769-1999

EAST STROUDSBURG UNIVERSITY
East Stroudsburg, PA 18301

EDINBORO UNIVERSITY
Edinboro, PA 16444-0001

FAIRMONT STATE COLLEGE
Fairmont, WV 26554

GANNON UNIVERSITY
Erie, PA 16541

GLENVILLE STATE COLLEGE
Glenville, WV 26351

INDIANA UNIV. OF PENNSYLVANIA
Indiana, PA 15705

KUTZTOWN UNIVERSITY
Kutztown, PA 19530-0721

LE MOYNE COLLEGE
Syracuse, NY 13214-1399

LOCK HAVEN UNIVERSITY
Lock Haven, PA 17745

LONG ISLAND U./C.W. POST
CAMPUS
Brookville, NY 11548

MERCY COLLEGE
Dobbs Ferry, NY 10522

MERCYHURST COLLEGE
Erie, PA 16546

MILLERSVILLE UNIVERSITY
Millersville, PA 17551-0302

MOLLOY COLLEGE
Rockville Centre, NY 11570

NEW YORK INSTITUTE OF TECH.
Old Westbury, NY 11568-8000

PACE UNIVERSITY
New York, NY 10038-1502

UNIVERSITY OF PITTSBURGH
Johnstown, PA 15904-2990

QUEENS COLLEGE (NY)
Flushing, NY 11367

SALEM-TEIKYO UNIVERSITY
Salem, WV 26426

SHEPHERD COLLEGE
Shepherdstown, WV 25443

SHIPPENSBURG UNIVERSITY
Shippensburg, PA 17257

SLIPPERY ROCK UNIVERSITY
Slippery Rock, PA 16057

SOUTHAMPTON CAMPUS OF L.I.U.
Southampton, NY 11968

THE COLLEGE OF ST. ROSE
Albany, NY 12203

STATE UNIV. OF N.Y. at STONY
BROOK
Stony Brook, NY 11794

WEST CHESTER UNIVERSITY
West Chester, PA 19383

WEST LIBERTY STATE COLLEGE
West Liberty, WV 26074

WEST VIRGINIA INST. OF TECH
Montgomery, WV 25136

WEST VIRGINIA WESLEYAN
COLLEGE
Buckhannon, WV 26201

WHEELING JESUIT COLLEGE
Wheeling, WV 26003-6295

District 3

ALABAMA A&M UNIVERSITY
Normal, AL 35762

UNIV. OF ALABAMA-HUNTSVILLE
Huntsville, AL 35899

ALBANY STATE COLLEGE
Albany, GA 31705

ARMSTRONG STATE COLLEGE
Savannah, GA 31419-1997

AUGUSTA COLLEGE
Augusta, GA 30910

BARRY UNIVERSITY
Miami Shores, FL 33161

BARTON COLLEGE
Wilson, NC 27893

BELLARMINE COLLEGE
Louisville, KY 40205-0671

BELMONT ABBEY COLLEGE
Belmont, NC 28012-2795

BOWIE STATE UNIVERSITY
Bowie, MD 20715-9465

CARSON-NEWMAN COLLEGE
Jefferson City, TN 37760

CATAWBA COLLEGE
Salisbury, NC 28144-2488

CLARK ATLANTA UNIVERSITY
Atlanta, GA 30314

COKER COLLEGE
Hartsville, SC 29550

ECKERD COLLEGE
St. Petersburg, FL 33733

ELIZABETH CITY STATE UNIV.
Elizabeth City, NC 27909

ELON COLLEGE
Elon College, NC 27244

ERSKINE COLLEGE
Due West, SC 29639

FAYETTEVILLE STATE
UNIVERSITY
Fayetteville, NC 28301-4298

FLORIDA INSTITUTE OF TECH.
Melbourne, FL 32901

FLORIDA SOUTHERN COLLEGE
Lakeland, FL 33801-5698

FORT VALLEY STATE COLLEGE
Fort Valley, GA 31030

FRANCIS MARION UNIVERSITY
Florence, SC 29501-0547

GARDNER-WEBB UNIVERSITY
Boiling Springs, NC 28017

HIGH POINT UNIVERSITY
High Point, NC 27262-3598

JOHNSON C. SMITH UNIVERSITY
Charlotte, NC 28216

KENTUCKY STATE UNIVERSITY
Frankfort, KY 40601

KENTUCKY WESLEYAN COLLEGE
Owensboro, KY 42302-1039

LANE COLLEGE
Jackson, TN 38301

LE MOYNE-OWEN COLLEGE
Memphis, TN 38126

LEES-MCRAE COLLEGE
Banner Elk, NC 28604-0128

LENOIR-RHYNE COLLEGE
Hickory, NC 28603

LIMESTONE COLLEGE
Gaffney, SC 29340-3799

LINCOLN MEMORIAL UNIVERSITY
Harrogate, TN 37752

LIVINGSTONE COLLEGE
Salisbury, NC 28144

MARS HILL COLLEGE
Mars Hill, NC 28754

MILES COLLEGE
Birmingham, AL 35208

MISSISSIPPI COLLEGE
Clinton, MS 39058

MISSISSIPPI UNIV. FOR WOMEN
Columbus, MS 39701

MORRIS BROWN COLLEGE
Atlanta, GA 30314

MOUNT OLIVE COLLEGE
Mount Olive, NC 28365

NEWBERRY COLLEGE
Newberry, SC 29108

NORFOLK STATE UNIVERSITY
Norfolk, VA 23504

UNIVERSITY OF NORTH ALABAMA
Florence, AL 35632

NORTH CAROLINA CENTRAL
UNIV.
Durham, NC 27707

UNIVERSITY OF NORTH FLORIDA
Jacksonville, FL 32224-2645

NORTHERN KENTUCKY
UNIVERSITY
Highland Heights, KY 41099

PAINE COLLEGE
Augusta, GA 30901-3182

PEMBROKE STATE UNIVERSITY
Pembroke, NC 28372-1510

PFEIFFER COLLEGE
Misenheimer, NC 28109-0960

PRESBYTERIAN COLLEGE
Clinton, SC 29325-2998

QUEENS COLLEGE (NC)
Charlotte, NC 28274

ROLLINS COLLEGE
Winter Park, FL 32789

SAVANNAH STATE COLLEGE
Savannah, GA 31404

SHAW UNIVERSITY
Raleigh, NC 27611

UNIV. OF SOUTH CAROLINA-AIKEN
Aiken, SC 29801

U. OF SO. CAROLINA-SPARTANBURG
Spartanburg, SC 29303

ST. ANDREWS PRESBYTERIAN COLL.
Laurinburg, NC 28352-5598

ST. AUGUSTINE'S COLLEGE
Raleigh, NC 27610

ST. LEO COLLEGE
Saint Leo, FL 33574

ST. PAUL'S COLLEGE
Lawrenceville, VA 23868

UNIVERSITY OF TAMPA
Tampa, FL 33606-1490

TUSKEGEE UNIVERSITY
Tuskegee, AL 36088

VALDOSTA STATE UNIVERSITY
Valdosta, GA 31698

VIRGINIA STATE UNIVERSITY
Petersburg, VA 23806

VIRGINIA UNION UNIVERSITY
Richmond, VA 23220-1790

UNIVERSITY OF WEST ALABAMA
Livingston, AL 35470

WEST GEORGIA COLLEGE
Carrollton, GA 30118

WINGATE UNIVERSITY
Wingate, NC 28174

WINSTON-SALEM STATE UNIV.
Winston-Salem, NC 27110

District 4

ASHLAND UNIVERSITY
Ashland, OH 44805

BEMIDJI STATE UNIVERSITY
Bemidji, MN 56601-2699

FERRIS STATE UNIVERSITY
Big Rapids, MI 49307-2295

GRAND VALLEY STATE UNIVERSITY
Allendale, MI 49401

HILLSDALE COLLEGE
Hillsdale, MI 49242-1298

INDIANA UNIV.-PURDUE UNIV.
Indianapolis, IN 46202

INDIANA UNIV.-PURDUE UNIV.
Fort Wayne, IN 46805-1499

UNIVERSITY OF INDIANAPOLIS
Indianapolis, IN 46227

LAKE SUPERIOR STATE UNIV.
Sault Sainte Marie, MI 49783

LEWIS UNIVERSITY
Romeoville, IL 60441

MICHIGAN TECHNOLOGICAL UNIV.
Houghton, MI 49931-1295

UNIV. OF MINNESOTA-DULUTH
Duluth, MN 55812

UNIV. OF MINNESOTA-MORRIS
Morris, MN 56267

MOORHEAD STATE UNIVERSITY
Moorhead, MN 56563-2996

NORTHERN MICHIGAN UNIVERSITY
Marquette, MI 49855-5391

NORTHWOOD UNIVERSITY
Midland, MI 48640

OAKLAND CITY COLLEGE
Oakland City, IN 47660-1099

OAKLAND UNIVERSITY
Rochestser, MI 48309-4401

QUINCY UNIVERSITY
Quincy, IL 62301-2699

SAGINAW VALLEY STATE UNIV.
University Center, MI 48710

SOUTHERN ILLINOIS UNIVERSITY
Edwardsville, IL 62026

UNIV. OF SOUTHERN INDIANA
Evansville, IN 47712

SOUTHWEST STATE UNIVERSITY
Marshall, MN 56258

COLLEGE OF ST. FRANCIS
Joliet, IL 60435

SAINT JOSEPH'S COLLEGE
Rensselaer, IN 47978

WAYNE STATE UNIVERSITY
Detroit, MI 48202

WINONA STATE UNIVERSITY
Winona, MN 55987-5838

UNIV. OF WISCONSIN-PARKSIDE
Kenosha, WI 53141-2000

District 5

AUGUSTANA COLLEGE
Sioux Falls, SD 57197

CENTRAL MISSOURI STATE UNIV.
Warrensburg, MO 64093

CHADRON STATE COLLEGE
Chadron, NE 69337

DRURY COLLEGE
Springfield, MO 65802

EMPORIA STATE UNIVERSITY
Emporia, KS 66801-5087

MANKATO STATE UNIVERSITY
Mankato, MN 56002-8400

MISSOURI SOUTHERN ST.
COLLEGE
Joplin, MO 64801-1595

MISSOURI WESTERN ST. COLLEGE
St. Joseph, MO 64507

UNIVERSITY OF MISSOURI
St. Louis, MO 63121-4499

MORNINGSIDE COLLEGE
Sioux City, IA 51106-1751

UNIV. OF NEBRASKA at KEARNEY
Kearney, NE 68849

UNIV. OF NEBRASKA at OMAHA
Omaha, NE 68182

NORTH DAKOTA STATE
UNIVERSITY
Fargo, ND 58105

UNIVERSITY OF NORTH DAKOTA
Grand Forks, ND 58202

NORTHEAST MISSOURI STATE
UNIV.
Kirksville, MO 63501

UNIV. OF NORTHERN COLORADO
Greeley, CO 80639

NORTHERN STATE UNIVERSITY
Aberdeen, SD 57401

NORTHWEST MISSOURI STATE
UNIV.
Maryville, MO 64468-6001

PITTSBURG STATE UNIVERSITY
Pittsburg, KS 66762

SOUTH DAKOTA STATE
UNIVERSITY
Brookings, SD 57007

UNIVERSITY OF SOUTH DAKOTA
Vermillion, SD 57069-2390

SOUTHWEST BAPTIST
UNIVERSITY
Bolivar, MO 65613

ST. CLOUD STATE UNIVERSITY
St. Cloud, MN 56301-4498

WASHBURN UNIVERSITY
Topeka, KS 66621

WAYNE STATE COLLEGE
Wayne, NE 68787-1172

District 6

ABILENE CHRISTIAN UNIVERSITY
Abilene, TX 79699

ANGELO STATE UNIVERSITY
San Angelo, TX 76909

CAMERON UNIVERSITY
Lawton, OK 73505-6377

UNIV. OF CENTRAL ARKANSAS
Conway, AR 72035-0001

UNIVERSITY OF CENTRAL
OKLAHOMA
Edmond, OK 73034

EAST TEXAS STATE UNIVERSITY
Commerce, TX 75429-3011

EASTERN NEW MEXICO
UNIVERSITY
Portales, NM 88130

HENDERSON STATE UNIVERSITY
Arkadelphia, AR 71999-0001

TARLETON STATE UNIVERSITY
Stephenville, TX 76402

TEXAS A&M UNIV.-KINGSVILLE
Kingsville, TX 78363

TEXAS WOMAN'S UNIVERSITY
Denton, TX 76204

WEST TEXAS A&M UNIVERSITY
Canyon, TX 79016-0999

WESTERN NEW MEXICO
UNIVERSITY
Silver City, NM 88061

District 7

ADAMS STATE COLLEGE
Alamosa, CO 81102

COLORADO CHRISTIAN
UNIVERSITY
Lakewood, CO 80226

COLORADO SCHOOL OF MINES
Golden, CO 80401

UNIV. OF COLORADO-COLO.
SPRINGS
Colorado Springs, CO 80933-7150

UNIVERSITY OF DENVER
Denver, CO 80208

FORT HAYS STATE UNIVERSITY
Hays, KS 67601

FORT LEWIS COLLEGE
Durango, CO 81301-3999

GRAND CANYON UNIVERSITY
Phoenix, AZ 85017

MESA STATE COLLEGE
Grand Junction, CO 81501

METROPOLITAN STATE COLLEGE
Denver, CO 80217-3362

MONTANA STATE UNIVERSITY
Billings, MT 59101-0298

NEW MEXICO HIGHLANDS UNIV.
Las Vegas, NM 87701

REGIS UNIVERSITY
Denver, CO 80221-1099

UNIV. OF SOUTHERN COLORADO
Pueblo, CO 81001-4901

U.S. AIR FORCE ACADEMY
USAF Academy, CO 80840-5461

WESTERN STATE COLLEGE
Gunnison, CO 81231

District 8

UNIVERSITY OF ALASKA-
ANCHORAGE
Anchorage, AK 99508

UNIVERSITY OF ALASKA-
FAIRBANKS
Fairbanks, AK 99775-7500

UNIV. OF CALIFORNIA-DAVIS
Davis, CA 95616

UNIV. OF CALIFORNIA-RIVERSIDE
Riverside, CA 92521

CALIF. STATE POLYTECHNIC UNIV.
Pomona, CA 91768

CALIF. STATE UNIV.-BAKERSFIELD
Bakersfield, CA 93311-1099

CALIF. STATE UNIV.-CHICO
Chico, CA 95929-0300

CALIF. STATE U.-DOMINGUEZ
HILLS
Carson, CA 90747

CALIF. STATE UNIV.-HAYWARD
Hayward, CA 94542

CALIF. STATE UNIV.-LOS ANGELES
Los Angeles, CA 90032-8240

CALIF. STATE U.-SAN BERNARDINO
San Bernardino, CA 92407-2397

CALIF. STATE UNIV.-STANISLAUS
Turlock, CA 95382

CHAMINADE UNIVERSITY
Honolulu, HI 96816

UNIVERSITY OF HAWAII-HILO
Hilo, HI 96720-4091

HUMBOLDT STATE UNIVERSITY
Arcata, CA 95521

COLLEGE OF NOTRE DAME
Belmont, CA 94002-9974

PORTLAND STATE UNIVERSITY
Portland, OR 97207-0751

SAN FRANCISCO STATE
UNIVERSITY
San Francisco, CA 94132

SEATTLE PACIFIC UNIVERSITY
Seattle, WA 98119

SONOMA STATE UNIVERSITY
Rohnert Park, CA 94928

NCAA PROVISIONAL MEMBERS
District 2

UNIV. OF PUERTO RICO-
MAYAGUEZ
Mayaguez, PR 00709

UNIV. OF PUERTO RICO-BAYAMON
Bayamon, PR 00619-1919

UNIVERSITY OF VIRGIN ISLANDS
St. Thomas, VI 00802

WEST VIRGINIA STATE COLLEGE
Institute, WV 25112-1000

WESTMINSTER COLLEGE
New Wilmington, PA 16172

District 3

ANDERSON COLLEGE
Anderson, SC 29621

CHRISTIAN BROTHERS
UNIVERSITY
Memphis, TN 38104

COLUMBIA UNION COLLEGE
Takoma Park, MD 20912

GEORGIA SOUTHWESTERN
COLLEGE
Americus, GA 31709-4693

LAMBUTH UNIVERSITY
Jackson, TN 38301

UNIVERSITY OF MONTEVALLO
Montevallo, AL 35115-6001

TUSCULUM COLLEGE
Greeneville, TN 37743

District 5

ROCKHURST COLLEGE
Kansas City, MO 64110

District 6

ARKANSAS TECH UNIVERSITY
Russellville, AR 72801-2222

HARDING UNIVERSITY
Searcy, AR 72149-0001

HOUSTON BAPTIST UNIVERSITY
Houston, TX 77074-3298

INCARNATE WORD COLLEGE
San Antonio, TX 78209

LYON COLLEGE
Batesville, AR 72503-2317

UNIV. OF MARY HARDIN-BAYLOR
Belton, TX 76513

MIDWESTERN STATE UNIVERSITY
Wichita Falls, TX 76308

OUACHITA BAPTIST UNIVERSITY
Arkadelphia, AR 71998-0001

SCHREINER COLLEGE
Keerville, TX 78028

SOUTHERN ARKANSAS
UNIVERSITY
Magnolia, AR 71753-5000

ST. EDWARD'S UNIVERSITY
Austin, TX 78704

ST. MARY'S UNIVERSITY
San Antonio, TX 78228-8572

TEXAS LUTHERAN COLLEGE
Seguin, TX 78155

TEXAS WESLEYAN UNIVERSITY
Fort Worth, TX 76105

District 7

LEWIS-CLARK STATE COLLEGE
Lewiston, ID 83501

District 8

BRIGHAM YOUNG UNIVERSITY
Laie, HI 96762-1294

CENTRAL WASHINGTON UNIV.
Ellensburg, WA 98926

HAWAII PACIFIC UNIVERSITY
Honolulu, HI 96813

ST. MARTIN'S COLLEGE
Lacey, WA 98503

WESTERN WASHINGTON UNIV.
Bellingham, WA 98225

WOMEN'S ARCHERY

DIVISION I

District 2

COLUMBIA UNIV.-BARNARD
COLLEGE
New York, NY 10027

JAMES MADISON UNIVERSITY
Harrisonburg, VA 22807

WOMEN'S RIFLE

DIVISION I

District 3

AUSTIN PEAY STATE UNIVERSITY
Clarksville, TN 37044-4576

MOREHEAD STATE UNIVERSITY
Morehead, KY 40351-1689

District 6

CENTENARY COLLEGE
Shreveport, LA 71134-1188

TEXAS CHRISTIAN UNIVERSITY
Fort Worth, TX 76129-0001

District 7

UNIVERSITY OF NEVADA
Reno, NV 89557

UNIVERSITY OF TEXAS-EL PASO
El Paso, TX 79968

District 8

UNIVERSITY OF SAN FRANCISCO
San Francisco, CA 94117-1080

DIVISION II

District 6

EASTERN NEW MEXICO
UNIVERSITY
Portales, NM 88130

WOMEN'S ICE HOCKEY

DIVISION I

District 1

BOSTON COLLEGE
Chestnut Hill, MA 02167-3934

BROWN UNIVERSITY
Providence, RI 02912

DARTMOUTH COLLEGE
Hanover, NH 03755

HARVARD UNIVERSITY
Cambridge, MA 02138-3800

UNIVERSITY OF NEW HAMPSHIRE
Durham, NH 03824

NORTHEASTERN UNIVERSITY
Boston, MA 02115-5096

PROVIDENCE COLLEGE
Providence, RI 02918

YALE UNIVERSITY
New Haven, CT 06520-7398

District 2

CORNELL UNIVERSITY
Ithaca, NY 14853

PRINCETON UNIVERSITY
Princeton, NJ 08544

WOMEN'S BOWLING

DIVISION II

District 1

SACRED HEART UNIVERSITY
Fairfield, CT 06432-1000

BASEBALL

DIVISION I

District 1

BOSTON COLLEGE
Chestnut Hill, MA 02167-3934

BOSTON UNIVERSITY
Boston, MA 02215

BROWN UNIVERSITY
Providence, RI 02912

CENTRAL CONN. STATE UNIV.
New Britain, CT 06050-4010

UNIVERSITY OF CONNECTICUT
Storrs, CT 06269

DARTMOUTH COLLEGE
Hanover, NH 03755

FAIRFIELD UNIVERSITY
Fairfield, CT 06430-5195

UNIVERSITY OF HARTFORD
West Hartford, CT 06117-1599

HARVARD UNIVERSITY
Cambridge, MA 02138-3800

COLLEGE OF THE HOLY CROSS
Worcester, MA 01610-2395

UNIVERSITY OF MAINE
Orono, ME 04469

UNIVERSITY OF MASSACHUSETTS
Amherst, MA 01003

UNIVERSITY OF NEW HAMPSHIRE
Durham, NH 03824

NORTHEASTERN UNIVERSITY
Boston, MA 02115-5096

PROVIDENCE COLLEGE
Providence, RI 02918

UNIVERSITY OF RHODE ISLAND
Kingston, RI 02881

UNIVERSITY OF VERMONT
Burlington, VT 05405

YALE UNIVERSITY
New Haven, CT 06520-7398

District 2

BUCKNELL UNIVERSITY
Lewisburg, PA 17837

CANISIUS COLLEGE
Buffalo, NY 14208-1098

COLGATE UNIVERSITY
Hamilton, NY 13346-1304

COLUMBIA UNIV.-BARNARD
COLLEGE
New York, NY 10027

CORNELL UNIVERSITY
Ithaca, NY 14853

DELAWARE STATE UNIVERSITY
Dover, DE 19901

UNIVERSITY OF DELAWARE
Newark, DE 19716

DREXEL UNIVERSITY
Philadelphia, PA 19104

DUQUESNE UNIVERSITY
Pittsburgh, PA 15282

FAIRLEIGH DICKINSON-TEANECK
Teaneck, NJ 07666

FORDHAM UNIVERSITY
Bronx, NY 10458-5155

GEORGE MASON UNIVERSITY
Fairfax, VA 22030

GEORGE WASHINGTON
UNIVERSITY
Washington, DC 20052

GEORGETOWN UNIVERSITY
Washington, DC 20057

HAMPTON UNIVERSITY
Hampton, VA 23668

HOFSTRA UNIVERSITY
Hempstead, NY 11550

HOWARD UNIVERSITY
Washington, DC 20059

IONA COLLEGE
New Rochelle, NY 10801

JAMES MADISON UNIVERSITY
Harrisonburg, VA 22807

LA SALLE UNIVERSITY
Philadelphia, PA 19141-1199

LAFAYETTE COLLEGE
Easton, PA 18042

LE MOYNE COLLEGE
Syracuse, NY 13214-1399

LEHIGH UNIVERSITY
Bethlehem, PA 18015-3089

LONG ISLAND UNIV.-BROOKLYN
Brooklyn, NY 11201

LONG ISLAND U./C. W. POST
CAMPUS
Brookville, NY 11548

MANHATTAN COLLEGE
Riverdale, NY 10471

MARIST COLLEGE
Poughkeepsie, NY 12601-1387

UNIV. OF MARYLAND-BALT. CO.
Baltimore, MD 212228-5398

MONMOUTH UNIVERSITY
WES LONG BRANCE, NJ 07764

MOUNT ST. MARY'S COLLEGE
EMIITSBURG, MD 21727-7799

NEW YORK INSTITUTE OF TECH.
Old Westbury, NY 11568-8000

NIAGARA UNIVERSITY
Niagara University, NY 14109

PACE UNIVERSITY
New York, NY 10038-1502

PENNSYLVANIA STATE UNIV.
University Park, PA 16802

UNIVERSITY OF PENNSYLVANIA
Philadelphia, PA 19104-6380

UNIVERSITY OF PITTSBURGH
Pittsburgh, PA 15260

PRINCETON UNIVERSITY
Princeton, NJ 08544

RIDER UNIVERSITY
Lawrenceville, NJ 08648-3099

RUTGERS UNIVERSITY
New Brunswick, NJ 08903

SETON HALL UNIVERSITY
South Orange, NJ 07079

SIENA COLLEGE
Loudonville, NY 12211-1462

ST. BONAVENTURE UNIVERSITY
St. Bonaventure, NY 14778

ST. FRANCIS COLLEGE
Brooklyn Heights, NY 11201

ST. JOHN'S UNIVERSITY
Jamaica, NY 11439

ST. JOSEPH'S UNIVERSITY
Philadelphia, PA 19131-1395

ST. PETER'S COLLEGE
Jersey City, NJ 07306

TEMPLE UNIVERSITY
Philadelphia, PA 19122

TOWSON STATE UNIVERSITY
Towson, MD 21204

U.S. MILITARY ACADEMY
West Point, NY 10996

U.S. NAVAL ACADEMY
Annapolis, MD 21402

VILLANOVA UNIVERSITY
Villanova, PA 19085

WAGNER COLLEGE
Staten Island, NY 10301-4495

WEST VIRGINIA UNIVERSITY
Morgantown, WV 26505-6201

COLLEGE OF WILLIAM & MARY
Williamsburg, VA 23187

District 3

ALABAMA STATE UNIVERSITY
Montgomery, AL 36101-0271

UNIV. OF ALABAMA at
TUSCALOOSA
Tuscaloosa, AL 35487

UNIV. OF ALABAMA at
BIRMINGHAM
Birmingham, AL 35294-0110

APPALACHIAN STATE UNIVERSITY
Boone, NC 28608

AUBURN UNIVERSITY
Auburn University., AL 36849-5113

AUSTIN PEAY STATE UNIVERSITY
Clarksville, TN 37044-4576

BETHUNE-COOKMAN COLLEGE
Daytona Beach, FL 32114-3099

CAMPBELL UNIVERSITY
Buies Creek, NC 27506

UNIVERSITY OF CENTRAL
FLORIDA
Orlando, FL 32816-0002

CHARLESTON SOUTHERN UNIV.
Charleston, SC 29423-8087

COLLEGE OF CHARLESTON
Charleston, SC 29424

THE CITADEL
Charleston, SC 29409

CLEMSON UNIVERSITY
Clemson, SC ·29634-000

COASTAL CAROLINA UNIVERSITY
Conway, SC 29526

COPPIN STATE COLLEGE
Baltimore, MD 21216

DAVIDSON COLLEGE
Davidson, NC 28036

DUKE UNIVERSITY
Durham, NC 27708-0555

EAST CAROLINA UNIVERSITY
Greenville, NC 27858-4353

EAST TENNESSEE STATE UNIV.
Johnson City, TN 37614

EASTERN KENTUCKY UNIVERSITY
Richmond, KY 40475-3101

FLORIDA A&M UNIVERSITY
Tallahassee, FL 32307

FLORIDA ATLANTIC UNIVERSITY
Boca Raton, FL 33431-0991

FLORIDA INTERNATIONAL UNIV.
Miami, FL 33199

FLORIDA STATE UNIVERSITY
Tallahassee, FL 32306

UNIVERSITY OF FLORIDA
Gainesville, FL 32604

FURMAN UNIVERSITY
Greenville, SC 29613

GEORGIA INSTITUTE OF TECH.
Atlanta, GA 30332

GEORGIA SOUTHERN UNIVERSITY
Statesboro, GA 30460-8033

GEORGIA STATE UNIVERSITY
Atlanta, GA 30303-3083

UNIVERSITY OF GEORGIA
Athens, GA 30613

JACKSONVILLE STATE
UNIVERSITY
Jacksonville, AL 36265-9982

JACKSONVILLE UNIVERSITY
Jacksonville, FL 32211-3394

UNIVERSITY OF KENTUCKY
Lexington, KY 40506-0032

LIBERTY UNIVERSITY
Lynchburg, VA 24506

LOUISIANA STATE UNIVERSITY
Baton Rouge, LA 70803

UNIVERSITY OF LOUISVILLE
Louisville, KY 40292

MARSHALL UNIVERSITY
Huntington, WV 25755

UNIVERSITY OF MARYLAND
College Park, MD 20740

UNIVERSITY OF MEMPHIS
Memphis, TN 38152

MERCER UNIVERSITY
Macon, GA 31207

UNIVERSITY OF MIAMI
Coral Gables, FL 33124-6710

MIDDLE TENNESSEE STATE UNIV.
Murfreesboro, TN 37132

MISSISSIPPI STATE UNIVERSITY
Mississippi State, MS 39762-5509

UNIVERSITY OF MISSISSIPPI
University, MS 38677

MOREHEAD STATE UNIVERSITY
Morehead, KY 40351-1689

MURRAY STATE UNIVERSITY
Murray, KY 42071-0009

UNIVERSITY OF NEW ORLEANS
New Orleans, LA 70148

UNIVERSITY OF NORTH
CAROLINA
Asheville, NC 28804-3299

UNIVERSITY OF NORTH
CAROLINA
Chapel Hill, NC 27514

UNIVERSITY OF NORTH
CAROLINA
Charlotte, NC 28223

UNIVERSITY OF NORTH
CAROLINA
Greensboro, NC 27412-5001

UNIVERSITY OF NORTH
CAROLINA
Wilmington, NC 28403-3297

NORTH CAROLINA A&T ST. UNIV.
Greensboro, NC 27411

NORTH CAROLINA STATE UNIV.
Raleigh, NC 27695-7001

OLD DOMINION UNIVERSITY
Norfolk, VA 23529

RADFORD UNIVERSITY
Radford, VA 24142

UNIVERSITY OF RICHMOND
Richmond, VA 23173-1903

SAMFORD UNIVERSITY
Birmingham, AL 35229

UNIVERSITY OF SOUTH ALABAMA
Mobile, AL 36688

UNIVERSITY OF SOUTH CAROLINA
Columbia, SC 29208

UNIVERSITY OF SOUTH FLORIDA
Tampa, FL 33620

SOUTHEASTERN LOUISIANA UNIV.
Hammond, LA 70402

UNIV. OF SOUTHERN MISSISSIPPI
Hattiesburg, MS 39406-5001

STETSON UNIVERSITY
De Land, FL 32720

TENNESSEE TECHNOLOGICAL
UNIV.
Cookeville, TN 38505-0001

THE UNIVERSITY OF TENNESSEE
Knoxville, TN 37996

UNIV. OF TENNESSEE at MARTIN
Martin, TN 38238-5021

TROY STATE UNIVERSITY
Troy, AL 36082

TULANE UNIVERSITY
New Orleans, LA 70118

VANDERBILT UNIVERSITY
Nashville, TN 37212

VIRGINIA COMMONWEALTH UNIV.
Richmond, VA 23284-2003

VIRGINIA MILITARY INSTITUTE
Lexington, VA 24450-0304

VIRGINIA POLYTECHNIC
INSTITUTE
Blacksburg, VA 24061

UNIVERSITY OF VIRGINIA
Charlottesville, VA 22903

WAKE FOREST UNIVERSITY
Winston-Salem, NC 27109

WESTERN CAROLINA UNIVERSITY
Cullowhee, NC 28723

WESTERN KENTUCKY
UNIVERSITY
Bowling Green, KY 42101-3576

WINTHROP UNIVERSITY
Rock Hill, SC 29733

WOFFORD COLLEGE
Spartanburg, SC 29303-3663

District 4

UNIVERSITY OF AKRON
Akron, OH 44325

BALL STATE UNIVERSITY
Muncie, IN 47306

BOWLING GREEN STATE UNIV.
Bowling Green, OH 43403

BUTLER UNIVERSITY
Indianapolis, IN 46208

CENTRAL MICHIGAN UNIVERSITY
Mount Pleasant, MI 48859

CHICAGO STATE UNIVERSITY
Chicago, IL 60628-1598

UNIVERSITY OF CINCINNATI
Cincinnati, OH 45221

CLEVELAND STATE UNIVERSITY
Cleveland, OH 44115

UNIVERSITY OF DAYTON
Dayton, OH 45469

UNIVERSITY OF DETROIT MERCY
Detroit, MI 48219-0900

EASTERN ILLINOIS UNIVERSITY
Charleston, IL 61920-3099

EASTERN MICHIGAN UNIVERSITY
Ypsilanti, MI 48197

UNIVERSITY OF EVANSVILLE
Evansville, IN 47722

ILLINOIS STATE UNIVERSITY
Normal, IL 61761

UNIVERSITY OF ILLINOIS
Champaign, IL 61820

UNIVERSITY OF ILLINOIS
Chicago, IL 60607

INDIANA UNIVERSITY
Bloomington, IN 47405

UNIVERSITY OF IOWA
Iowa City, IA 52242

KENT STATE UNIVERSITY
Kent, OH 44242

MIAMI UNIVERSITY
Oxford, OH 45056

MICHIGAN STATE UNIVERSITY
East Lansing, MI 48824

UNIVERSITY OF MICHIGAN
Ann Arbor, MI 48109-2201

UNIV. OF MINNESOTA-TWIN
CITIES
Minneapolis, MN 55455

NORTHEASTERN ILLINOIS UNIV.
Chicago, IL 60625-4699

NORTHERN ILLINOIS UNIVERSITY
De Kalb, IL 60115-2854

NORTHWESTERN UNIVERSITY
Evanston, IL 60208

UNIVERSITY OF NOTRE DAME
Notre Dame, IN 46556

OHIO STATE UNIVERSITY
Columbus, OH 43210

OHIO UNIVERSITY
Athens, OH 45701

PURDUE UNIVERSITY
West Lafayette, IN 47907

UNIVERSITY OF TOLEDO
Toledo, OH 43606

VALPARAISO UNIVERSITY
Valparaiso, IN 46383-6493

WESTERN ILLINOIS UNIVERSITY
Macomb, IL 61455

WESTERN MICHIGAN UNIVERSITY
Kalamazoo, MI 49008-5134

UNIVERSITY OF WISCONSIN
Milwaukee, WI 53201

WRIGHT STATE UNIVERSITY
Dayton, OH 45435-0001

XAVIER UNIVERSITY
Cincinnati, OH 45207-6114

YOUNGSTOWN STATE
UNIVERSITY
Youngstown, OH 44555-0001

District 5

BRADLEY UNIVERSITY
Peoria, IL 61625

CREIGHTON UNIVERSITY
Omaha, NE 68178-0001

INDIANA STATE UNIVERSITY
Terre Haute, IN 47809

IOWA STATE UNIVERSITY
Ames, IA 50011

KANSAS STATE UNIVERSITY
Manhattan, KS 66506

UNIVERSITY OF KANSAS
Lawrence, KS 66045

UNIVERSITY OF MISSOURI-
COLUMBIA
Columbia, MO 65211

UNIVERSITY OF NEBRASKA
Lincoln, NE 68588

UNIVERSITY OF NORTHERN IOWA
Cedar Falls, IA 50614

OKLAHOMA STATE UNIVERSITY
Stillwater, OK 74078

UNIVERSITY OF OKLAHOMA
Norman, OK 73019

ORAL ROBERTS UNIVERSITY
Tulsa, OK 74171

SOUTHEAST MISSOURI STATE
UNIV.
Cape Girardeau, MO 63701-4799

SOUTHERN ILLINOIS UNIVERSITY
Carbondale, IL 62901

SOUTHWEST MISSOURI STATE
UNIV.
Springfield, MO 65804

ST. LOUIS UNIVERSITY
St. Louis, MO 63108

WICHITA STATE UNIVERSITY
Wichita, KS 67260

District 6

ALCORN STATE UNIVERSITY
Lorman, MS 39096-9402

ARKANSAS STATE UNIVERSITY
State University, AR 72467

UNIVERSITY OF ARKANSAS
Fayetteville, AR 72701

UNIVERSITY OF ARKANSAS
Little Rock, AR 72204-1099

BAYLOR UNIVERSITY
Waco, TX 76798

CENTENARY COLLEGE
Shreveport, LA 71134-1188

GRAMBLING STATE UNIVERSITY
Grambling, LA 71245

UNIVERSITY OF HOUSTON
Houston, TX 77204

JACKSON STATE UNIVERSITY
Jackson, MS 39217

LAMAR UNIVERSITY
Beaumont, TX 77710

LOUISIANA TECH UNIVERSITY
Ruston, LA 71272

MCNEESE STATE UNIVERSITY
Lake Charles, LA 70609

MISSISSIPPI VALLEY ST. UNIV.
Itta Bena, MS 38941-1400

NICHOLLS STATE UNIVERSITY
Thibodaux, LA 70310

NORTHEAST LOUISIANA
UNIVERSITY
Monroe, LA 71209-3000

NORTHWESTERN STATE
UNIVERSITY
Natchitoches, LA 71497-0003

PRAIRIE VIEW A&M UNIVERSITY
Prairie View, TX 77446

RICE UNIVERSITY
Houston, TX 77251

SAM HOUSTON STATE
UNIVERSITY
Huntsville, TX 77341

SOUTHERN UNIVERSITY
Baton Rouge, LA 70813

SOUTHWEST TEXAS STATE UNIV.
San Marcos, TX 78666-4615

UNIV. OF SOUTHWESTERN LA.
Lafayette, LA 70504-1008

STEPHEN F. AUSTIN STATE UNIV.
Nacogdoches, TX 75962

UNIVERSITY OF TEXAS
Arlington, TX 76019

UNIVERSITY OF TEXAS
Austin, TX 78712

UNIVERSITY OF TEXAS
San Antonio, TX 78249

TEXAS A&M UNIVERSITY
College Station, TX 77843-1228

TEXAS CHRISTIAN UNIVERSITY
Fort Worth, TX 76129-0001

UNIV. OF TEXAS-PAN AMERICAN
Edinburg, TX 78539-2999-2999

TEXAS SOUTHERN UNIVERSITY
Houston, TX 77004

TEXAS TECH UNIVERSITY
Lubbock, TX 79409

District 7

BRIGHAM YOUNG UNIVERSITY
Provo, UT 84602

CALIF. STATE UNIV.-FRESNO
Fresno, CA 93740-0048

GONZAGA UNIVERSITY
Spokane, WA 99258

GRAND CANYON UNIVERSITY
Phoenix, AZ 85017

UNIVERSITY OF HAWAII-MANOA
Honolulu, HI 96822-2370

UNIVERSITY OF NEVADA
Reno, NV 89557

UNIVERSITY OF NEW MEXICO
Albuquerque, NM 87131

SAN DIEGO STATE UNIVERSITY
San Diego, CA 92182

SOUTHERN UTAH UNIVERSITY
Cedar City, UT 84720

U.S. AIR FORCE ACADEMY
USAF Academy, CO 80840-5461

UNIVERSITY OF UTAH
Salt Lake City, UT 84112

UNIVERSITY OF WYOMING
Laramie, WY 82071

District 8

ARIZONA STATE UNIVERSITY
Tempe, AZ 85287-2505

UNIVERSITY OF ARIZONA
Tucson, AZ 85721

UNIV. OF CALIFORNIA-BERKELEY
Berkeley, CA 94720

UNIV. OF CALIF.-LOS ANGELES
Los Angeles, CA 90095-1405

UNIV. OF CALIF-SANTA BARBARA
Santa Barbara, CA 93106

CALIF. POLYTECHNIC STATE UNIV.
San Luis Obispo, CA 93407

CALIF. STATE UNIV.-FULLERTON
Fullerton, CA 92634-9480

CALIF. STATE UNIV.-NORTHRIDGE
Northridge, CA 91330

CALIF. STATE UNIV.-SACRAMENTO
Sacramento, CA 95819

UNIVERSITY OF HAWAII-HILO
Hilo, HI 96720-4091

LONG BEACH STATE UNIVERSITY
Long Beach, CA 90840-0118

LOYOLA MARYMOUNT
UNIVERSITY
Los Angeles, CA 90045-2699

UNIVERSITY OF NEVADA
Las Vegas, NV 89154

NEW MEXICO STATE UNIVERSITY
Las Cruces, NM 88003

OREGON STATE UNIVERSITY
Corvallis, OR 97331

UNIVERSITY OF THE PACIFIC
Stockton, CA 95211

PEPPERDINE UNIVERSITY
Malibu, CA 90263

PORTLAND STATE UNIVERSITY
Portland, OR 97207-0751

UNIVERSITY OF PORTLAND
Portland, OR 97203-5798

UNIVERSITY OF SAN DIEGO
San Diego, CA 92110-2492

UNIVERSITY OF SAN FRANCISCO
San Francisco, CA 94117-1080

SAN JOSE STATE UNIVERSITY
San Jose, CA 95192

SANTA CLARA UNIVERSITY
Santa Clara, CA 95053

UNIV. OF SOUTHERN CALIFORNIA
Los Angeles, CA 90089-0012

ST. MARY'S COLLEGE
Moraga, CA 94556

STANFORD UNIVERSITY
Stanford, CA 94305

WASHINGTON STATE UNIVERSITY
Pullman, WA 99164

UNIVERSITY OF WASHINGTON
Seattle, WA 98195

DIVISION II
District 1
AMERICAN INTERNATIONAL
COLLEGE
Springfield, MA 01109-3189

ASSUMPTION COLLEGE
Worcester, MA 01615-0005

BENTLEY COLLEGE
Waltham, MA 02154-4705

UNIVERSITY OF BRIDGEPORT
Bridgeport, CT 06601

BRYANT COLLEGE
Smithfield, RI 02917-1284

FRANKLIN PIERCE COLLEGE
Rindge, NH 03461

KEENE STATE COLLEGE
Keene, NH 03431-3183

UNIV. OF MASSACHUSETTS-
LOWELL
Lowell, MA 01854

MERRIMACK COLLEGE
North Andover, MA 01845

NEW HAMPSHIRE COLLEGE
Hooksett, NH 03106-1045

UNIVERSITY OF NEW HAVEN
West Haven, CT 06516-1999

QUINNIPIAC COLLEGE
Hamden, CT 06518-1940

SACRED HEART UNIVERSITY
Fairfield, CT 06432-1000

SOUTHERN CONNECTICUT ST.
UNIV.
New Haven, CT 06515

ST. ANSELM COLLEGE
Manchester, NH 03102-1310

ST. MICHAEL'S COLLEGE
Colchester, VT 05439

STONEHILL COLLEGE
North Easton, MA 02357

District 2
ADELPHI UNIVERSITY
Garden City, NY 11530

STATE UNIV. OF N.Y. AT ALBANY
Albany, NY 12222

ALDERSON-BROADDUS COLLEGE
Philippi, WV 26416

BLOOMSBURG UNIVERSITY
Bloomsburg, PA 17815

BLUEFIELD STATE COLLEGE
Bluefield, WV 24701-2198

CALIFORNIA UNIVERSITY
California, PA 15419

THE UNIVERSITY OF
CHARLESTON
Charleston, WV 25304

CLARION UNIVERSITY
Clarion, PA 16214

CONCORD COLLEGE
Athens, WV 24712

CONCORDIA COLLEGE
Bronxville, NY 10708

DAVIS AND ELKINS COLLEGE
Elkins, WV 26241

DOWLING COLLEGE
Oakdale, NY 11769-1999

EAST STROUDSBURG UNIVERSITY
East Stroudsburg, PA 18301

EDINBORO UNIVERSITY
Edinboro, PA 16444-0001

FAIRMONT STATE COLLEGE
Fairmont, WV 26554

GANNON UNIVERSITY
Erie, PA 16541

INDIANA UNIV. OF PENNSYLVANIA
Indiana, PA 15705

KUTZTOWN UNIVERSITY
Kutztown, PA 19530-0721

LOCK HAVEN UNIVERSITY
Lock Haven, PA 17745

MANSFIELD UNIVERSITY
Mansfield, PA 16933

MERCY COLLEGE
Dobbs Ferry, NY 10522

MERCYHURST COLLEGE
Erie, PA 16546

MILLERSVILLE UNIVERSITY
Millersville, PA 17551-0302

MOLLOY COLLEGE
Rockville Centre, NY 11570

PHILA. COLLEGE OF TEXT. & SCI.
Philadelphia, PA 19144-5497

UNIVERSITY OF PITTSBURGH
Johnstown, PA 15904-2990

QUEENS COLLEGE (NY)
Flushing, NY 11367

SALEM-TEIKYO UNIVERSITY
Salem, WV 26426

SHEPHERD COLLEGE
Shepherdstown, WV 25443

SHIPPENSBURG UNIVERSITY
Shippensburg, PA 17257

SLIPPERY ROCK UNIVERSITY
Slippery Rock, PA 16057

THE COLLEGE OF ST. ROSE
Albany, NY 12203

STATE UNIV. OF N.Y. at STONY
BROOK
Stony Brook, NY 11794

WEST CHESTER UNIVERSITY
West Chester, PA 19383

WEST LIBERTY STATE COLLEGE
West Liberty, WV 26074

WEST VIRGINIA INST. OF TECH
Montgomery, WV 25136

WEST VIRGINIA WESLEYAN
COLLEGE
Buckhannon, WV 26201

District 3

ALABAMA A&M UNIVERSITY
Normal, AL 35762

ALBANY STATE COLLEGE
Albany, GA 31705

ARMSTRONG STATE COLLEGE
Savannah, GA 31419-1997

AUGUSTA COLLEGE
Augusta, GA 30910

BARRY UNIVERSITY
Miami Shores, FL 33161

BARTON COLLEGE
Wilson, NC 27893

BELLARMINE COLLEGE
Louisville, KY 40205-0671

BELMONT ABBEY COLLEGE
Belmont, NC 28012-2795

BOWIE STATE UNIVERSITY
Bowie, MD 20715-9465

CARSON-NEWMAN COLLEGE
Jefferson City, TN 37760

CATAWBA COLLEGE
Salisbury, NC 28144-2488

CLARK ATLANTA UNIVERSITY
Atlanta, GA 30314

COKER COLLEGE
Hartsville, SC 29550

COLUMBUS COLLEGE
Columbus, GA 31907-2079

DELTA STATE UNIVERSITY
Cleveland, MS 38733

ECKERD COLLEGE
St. Petersburg, FL 33733

ELIZABETH CITY STATE UNIV.
Elizabeth City, NC 27909

ELON COLLEGE
Elon College, NC 27244

ERSKINE COLLEGE
Due West, SC 29639

FLORIDA INSTITUTE OF TECH.
Melbourne, FL 32901

FLORIDA SOUTHERN COLLEGE
Lakeland, FL 33801-5698

FRANCIS MARION UNIVERSITY
Florence, SC 29501-0547

GARDNER-WEBB UNIVERSITY
Boiling Springs, NC 28017

GEORGIA COLLEGE
Milledgeville, GA 31061

HIGH POINT UNIVERSITY
High Point, NC 27262-3598

KENNESAW STATE COLLEGE
Marietta, GA 30061

KENTUCKY STATE UNIVERSITY
Frankfort, KY 40601

KENTUCKY WESLEYAN COLLEGE
Owensboro, KY 42302-1039

LANE COLLEGE
Jackson, TN 38301

LE MOYNE-OWEN COLLEGE
Memphis, TN 38126

LENOIR-RHYNE COLLEGE
Hickory, NC 28603

LIMESTONE COLLEGE
Gaffney, SC 29340-3799

LINCOLN MEMORIAL UNIVERSITY
Harrogate, TN 37752

LONGWOOD COLLEGE
Farmville, VA 23909-1899

LYNN UNIVERSITY
Boca Raton, FL 33431

MARS HILL COLLEGE
Mars Hill, NC 28754

MILES COLLEGE
Birmingham, AL 35208

MISSISSIPPI COLLEGE
Clinton, MS 39058

MOUNT OLIVE COLLEGE
Mount Olive, NC 28365

NEWBERRY COLLEGE
Newberry, SC 29108

NORFOLK STATE UNIVERSITY
Norfolk, VA 23504

UNIVERSITY OF NORTH ALABAMA
Florence, AL 35632

UNIVERSITY OF NORTH FLORIDA
Jacksonville, FL 32224-2645

NORTHERN KENTUCKY
UNIVERSITY
Highland Heights, KY 41099

PAINE COLLEGE
Augusta, GA 30901-3182

PEMBROKE STATE UNIVERSITY
Pembroke, NC 28372-1510

PFEIFFER COLLEGE
Misenheimer, NC 28109-0960

PRESBYTERIAN COLLEGE
Clinton, SC 29325-2998

ROLLINS COLLEGE
Winter Park, FL 32789

SAVANNAH STATE COLLEGE
Savannah, GA 31404

SHAW UNIVERSITY
Raleigh, NC 27611

UNIV. OF SOUTH CAROLINA-
AIKEN
Aiken, SC 29801

U. OF SO. CAROLINA-
SPARTANBURG
Spartanburg, SC 29303

ST. ANDREWS PRESBYTERIAN
COLL
Laurinburg, NC 28352-5598

ST. AUGUSTINE'S COLLEGE
Raleigh, NC 27610

ST. LEO COLLEGE
Saint Leo, FL 33574

ST. PAUL'S COLLEGE
Lawrenceville, VA 23868

UNIVERSITY OF TAMPA
Tampa, FL 33606-1490

TUSKEGEE UNIVERSITY
Tuskegee, AL 36088

VALDOSTA STATE UNIVERSITY
Valdosta, GA 31698

VIRGINIA STATE UNIVERSITY
Petersburg, VA 23806

UNIVERSITY OF WEST ALABAMA
Livingston, AL 35470

UNIVERSITY OF WEST FLORIDA
Pensacola, FL 32514

WEST GEORGIA COLLEGE
Carrollton, GA 30118

WINGATE UNIVERSITY
Wingate, NC 28174

District 4

ASHLAND UNIVERSITY
Ashland, OH 44805

BEMIDJI STATE UNIVERSITY
Bemidji, MN 56601-2699

GRAND VALLEY STATE
UNIVERSITY
Allendale, MI 49401

HILLSDALE COLLEGE
Hillsdale, MI 49242-1298

INDIANA UNIV.-PURDUE UNIV.
Indianapolis, IN 46202

INDIANA UNIV.-PURDUE UNIV.
Fort Wayne, IN 46805-1499

UNIVERSITY OF INDIANAPOLIS
Indianapolis, IN 46227

LEWIS UNIVERSITY
Romeoville, IL 60441

UNIV. OF MINNESOTA-DULUTH
Duluth, MN 55812

UNIV. OF MINNESOTA-MORRIS
Morris, MN 56267

NORTHWOOD UNIVERSITY
Midland, MI 48640

OAKLAND CITY COLLEGE
Oakland City, IN 47660-1099

OAKLAND UNIVERSITY
Rochestser, MI 48309-4401

QUINCY UNIVERSITY
Quincy, IL 62301-2699

SAGINAW VALLEY STATE UNIV.
University Center, MI 48710

SOUTHERN ILLINOIS UNIVERSITY
Edwardsville, IL 62026

UNIV. OF SOUTHERN INDIANA
Evansville, IN 47712

SOUTHWEST STATE UNIVERSITY
Marshall, MN 56258

COLLEGE OF ST. FRANCIS
Joliet, IL 60435

SAINT JOSEPH'S COLLEGE
Rensselaer, IN 47978

WAYNE STATE UNIVERSITY
Detroit, MI 48202

WINONA STATE UNIVERSITY
Winona, MN 55987-5838

UNIV. OF WISCONSIN-PARKSIDE
Kenosha, WI 53141-2000

District 5

AUGUSTANA COLLEGE
Sioux Falls, SD 57197

CENTRAL MISSOURI STATE UNIV.
Warrensburg, MO 64093

EMPORIA STATE UNIVERSITY
Emporia, KS 66801-5087

LINCOLN UNIVERSITY
Jefferson City, MO 65102-0029

MANKATO STATE UNIVERSITY
Mankato, MN 56002-8400

MISSOURI SOUTHERN ST.
COLLEGE
Joplin, MO 64801-1595

MISSOURI WESTERN ST. COLLEGE
St. Joseph, MO 64507

UNIVERSITY OF MISSOURI
Rolla, MO 65401

UNIVERSITY OF MISSOURI
St. Louis, MO 63121-4499

MORNINGSIDE COLLEGE
Sioux City, IA 51106-1751

UNIV. OF NEBRASKA at KEARNEY
Kearney, NE 68849

UNIV. OF NEBRAKSA at OMAHA
Omaha, NE 68182

NORTH DAKOTA STATE
UNIVERSITY
Fargo, ND 58105

UNIVERSITY OF NORTH DAKOTA
Grand Forks, ND 58202

NORTHEAST MISSOURI STATE
UNIV.
Kirksville, MO 63501

UNIV. OF NORTHERN COLORADO
Greeley, CO 80639

NORTHERN STATE UNIVERSITY
Aberdeen, SD 57401

NORTHWEST MISSOURI STATE
UNIV.
Maryville, MO 64468-6001

PITTSBURG STATE UNIVERSITY
Pittsburg, KS 66762

SOUTH DAKOTA STATE
UNIVERSITY
Brookings, SD 57007

UNIVERSITY OF SOUTH DAKOTA
Vermillion, SD 57069-2390

SOUTHWEST BAPTIST
UNIVERSITY
Bolivar, MO 65613

ST. CLOUD STATE UNIVERSITY
St. Cloud, MN 56301-4498

WASHBURN UNIVERSITY
Topeka, KS 66621

WAYNE STATE COLLEGE
Wayne, NE 68787-1172

District 6

ABILENE CHRISTIAN UNIVERSITY
Abilene, TX 79699

CAMERON UNIVERSITY
Lawton, OK 73505-6377

UNIV. OF CENTRAL ARKANSAS
Conway, AR 72035-0001

UNIVERSITY OF CENTRAL
OKLAHOMA
Edmond, OK 73034

EASTERN NEW MEXICO
UNIVERSITY
Portales, NM 88130

HENDERSON STATE UNIVERSITY
Arkadelphia, AR 71999-0001

TARLETON STATE UNIVERSITY
Stephenville, TX 76402

TEXAS A&M UNIV.-KINGSVILLE
Kingsville, TX 78363

WEST TEXAS A&M UNIVERSITY
Canyon, TX 79016-0999

District 7

COLORADO SCHOOL OF MINES
Golden, CO 80401

UNIVERSITY OF DENVER
Denver, CO 80208

FORT HAYS STATE UNIVERSITY
Hays, KS 67601

MESA STATE COLLEGE
Grand Junction, CO 81501

METROPOLITAN STATE COLLEGE
Denver, CO 80217-3362

NEW MEXICO HIGHLANDS UNIV.
Las Vegas, NM 87701

REGIS UNIVERSITY
Denver, CO 80221-1099

UNIV. OF SOUTHERN COLORADO
Pueblo, CO 81001-4901

District 8

UNIV. OF CALIFORNIA-DAVIS
Davis, CA 95616

UNIV. OF CALIFORNIA-RIVERSIDE
Riverside, CA 92521

CALIF. STATE POLYTECHNIC UNIV.
Pomona, CA 91768

CALIF. STATE UNIV.-CHICO
Chico, CA 95929-0300

CALIF. STATE U.-DOMINGUEZ
HILLS
Carson, CA 90747

CALIF. STATE UNIV.-HAYWARD
Hayward, CA 94542

CALIF. STATE UNIV.-LOS ANGELES
Los Angeles, CA 90032-8240

CALIF. STATE U.-SAN BERNARDINO
San Bernardino, CA 92407-2397

CALIF. STATE UNIV.-STANISLAUS
Turlock, CA 95382

SAN FRANCISCO STATE UNIV.
San Francisco, CA 94132

SONOMA STATE UNIVERSITY
Rohnert Park, CA 94928

NCAA PROVISIONAL MEMBERS
District 2

UNIV. OF PUERTO RICO-
MAYAGUEZ
Mayabues, PR

WEST VIRGINIA STATE COLLEGE
Institute, WV 25112-1000

WESTMINSTER COLLEGE
New Wilmington, PA 16172

District 3

ANDERSON COLLEGE
Anderson, SC 29621

CHRISTIAN BROTHERS
UNIVERSITY
Memphis, TN 38104

COLUMBIA UNION COLLEGE
Takoma Park, MD 20912

GEORGIA SOUTHWESTERN
COLLEGE
Americus, GA 31709-4693

LAMBUTH UNIVERSITY
Jackson, TN 38301

UNIVERSITY OF MONTEVALLO
Montevallo, AL 35115-6001

TUSCULUM COLLEGE
Greeneville, TN 37743

District 5

EAST CENTRAL UNIVERSITY
Ada, OK 74820

NORTHWESTERN OKLAHOMA ST.
U.
Alva, OK 73717

ROCKHURST COLLEGE
Kansas City, MO 64110

UNIV. OF SCIENCE & ARTS
Chickasha, OK 73018

SOUTHEASTERN OKLA. ST. UNIV.
Durant, OK 74701

SOUTHWESTERN OKLAHOMA ST.
UNIV.
Weatherford, OK 73096

District 6

ARKANSAS TECH UNIVERSITY
Russellville, AR 72801-2222

UNIV. OF ARKANSAS-MONTICELLO
Monticello, AR 71656-3596

CONCORDIA UNIVERSITY at
AUSTIN
Austin, TX 78705-2799

EAST TEXAS BAPTIST UNIVERSITY
Marshall, TX 75670-1498

HARDING UNIVERSITY
Searcy, AR 72149-0001

HOUSTON BAPTIST UNIVERSITY
Houston, TX 77074-3298

INCARNATE WORD COLLEGE
San Antonio, TX 78209

LYON COLLEGE
Batesville, AR 72503-2317

UNIV. OF MARY HARDIN-
BAYLOR
Belton, TX 76513

OUACHITA BAPTIST
UNIVERSITY
Arkadelphia, AR 71998-0001

SCHREINER COLLEGE
Keerville, TX 78028

SOUTHERN ARKANSAS
UNIVERSITY
Magnolia, AR 71753-5000

ST. EDWARD'S UNIVERSITY
Austin, TX 78704

ST. MARY'S UNIVERSITY
San Antonio, TX 78228-8572

TEXAS LUTHERAN COLLEGE
Seguin, TX 78155

TEXAS WESLEYAN UNIVERSITY
Fort Worth, TX 76105

District 7

LEWIS-CLARK STATE COLLEGE
Lewiston, ID 83501

District 8

CENTRAL WASHINGTON UNIV.
Ellensburg, WA 98926

HAWAII PACIFIC UNIVERSITY
Honolulu, HI 96813

MEN'S TRACK, OUTDOOR

DIVISION I

District 1

BOSTON COLLEGE
Chestnut Hill, MA 02167-3934

BOSTON UNIVERSITY
Boston, MA 02215

BROWN UNIVERSITY
Providence, RI 02912

CENTRAL CONN. STATE UNIV.
New Britain, CT 06050-4010

UNIVERSITY OF CONNECTICUT
Storrs, CT 06269

DARTMOUTH COLLEGE
Hanover, NH 03755

UNIVERSITY OF HARTFORD
West Hartford, CT 06117-1599

HARVARD UNIVERSITY
Cambridge, MA 02138-3800

COLLEGE OF THE HOLY CROSS
Worcester, MA 01610-2395

UNIVERSITY OF MAINE
Orono, ME 04469

UNIVERSITY OF MASSACHUSETTS
Amherst, MA 01003

UNIVERSITY OF NEW HAMPSHIRE
Durham, NH 03824

NORTHEASTERN UNIVERSITY
Boston, MA 02115-5096

PROVIDENCE COLLEGE
Providence, RI 02918

UNIVERSITY OF RHODE ISLAND
Kingston, RI 02881

UNIVERSITY OF VERMONT
Burlington, VT 05405

YALE UNIVERSITY
New Haven, CT 06520-7398

District 2

BUCKNELL UNIVERSITY
Lewisburg, PA 17837

STATE UNIV. OF N.Y. at BUFFALO
Buffalo, NY 14260

CANISIUS COLLEGE
Buffalo, NY 14208-1098

COLGATE UNIVERSITY
Hamilton, NY 13346-1304

COLUMBIA UNIV.-BARNARD
COLLEGE
New York, NY 10027

CORNELL UNIVERSITY
Ithaca, NY 14853

DELAWARE STATE UNIVERSITY
Dover, DE 19901

UNIVERSITY OF DELAWARE
Newark, DE 19716

FAIRLEIGH DICKINSON-TEANECK
Teaneck, NJ 07666

FORDHAM UNIVERSITY
Bronx, NY 10458-5155

GEORGE MASON UNIVERSITY
Fairfax, VA 22030

GEORGETOWN UNIVERSITY
Washington, DC 20057

HAMPTON UNIVERSITY
Hampton, VA 23668

HOWARD UNIVERSITY
Washington, DC 20059

IONA COLLEGE
New Rochelle, NY 10801

JAMES MADISON UNIVERSITY
Harrisonburg, VA 22807

LA SALLE UNIVERSITY
Philadelphia, PA 19141-1199

LAFAYETTE COLLEGE
Easton, PA 18042

LEHIGH UNIVERSITY
Bethlehem, PA 18015-3089

LONG ISLAND UNIV.-BROOKLYN
Brooklyn, NY 11201

MANHATTAN COLLEGE
Riverdale, NY 10471

MARIST COLLEGE
Poughkeepsie, NY 12601-1387

UNIV. OF MARYLAND-BALT. CO.
Baltimore, MD 21228-5398

U. OF MARYLAND-EASTERN
SHORE
Princess Anne, MD 21853-1299

MONMOUTH UNIVERSITY
West Long Branch, NJ 07764

MORGAN STATE UNIVERSITY
Baltimore, MD 21239

MOUNT ST. MARY'S COLLEGE
Emmitsburg, MD 21727-7799

PENNSYLVANIA STATE UNIV.
University Park, PA 16802

UNIVERSITY OF PENNSYLVANIA
Philadelphia, PA 19104-6380

UNIVERSITY OF PITTSBURGH
Pittsburgh, PA 15260

PRINCETON UNIVERSITY
Princeton, NJ 08544

RIDER UNIVERSITY
Lawrenceville, NJ 08648-3099

ROBERT MORRIS COLLEGE
Coraopolis, PA 15108-1189

RUTGERS UNIVERSITY
New Brunswick, NJ 08903

SETON HALL UNIVERSITY
South Orange, NJ 07079

ST. FRANCIS COLLEGE
Brooklyn Heights, NY 11201

ST. FRANCIS COLLEGE
Loretto, PA 15940-0600

ST. JOHN'S UNIVERSITY
Jamaica, NY 11439

ST. JOSEPH'S UNIVERSITY
Philadelphia, PA 19131-1395

ST. PETER'S COLLEGE
Jersey City, NJ 07306

SYRACUSE UNIVERSITY
Syracuse, NY 13244

TEMPLE UNIVERSITY
Philadelphia, PA 19122

TOWSON STATE UNIVERSITY
Towson, MD 21204

U.S. MILITARY ACADEMY
West Point, NY 10996

U.S. NAVAL ACADEMY
Annapolis, MD 21402

VILLANOVA UNIVERSITY
Villanova, PA 19085

WAGNER COLLEGE
Staten Island, NY 10301-4495

WEST VIRGINIA UNIVERSITY
Morgantown, WV 26505-6201

COLLEGE OF WILLIAM & MARY
Williamsburg, VA 23187

District 3

ALABAMA STATE UNIVERSITY
Montgomery, AL 36101-0271

UNIV. OF ALABAMA at
TUSCALOOSA
Tuscaloosa, AL 35487

UNIV. OF ALABAMA at
BIRMINGHAM
Birmingham, AL 35294-0110

APPALACHIAN STATE UNIVERSITY
Boone, NC 28608

AUBURN UNIVERSITY
Auburn University, AL 36849-5113

BETHUNE-COOKMAN COLLEGE
Daytona Beach, FL 32114-3099

CAMPBELL UNIVERSITY
Buies Creek, NC 27506

CHARLESTON SOUTHERN UNIV.
Charleston, SC 29423-8087

THE CITADEL
Charleston, SC 29409

CLEMSON UNIVERSITY
Clemson, SC 29634-000

COASTAL CAROLINA UNIVERSITY
Conway, SC 29526

COPPIN STATE COLLEGE
Baltimore, MD 21216

DAVIDSON COLLEGE
Davidson, NC 28036

DUKE UNIVERSITY
Durham, NC 27708-0555

EAST CAROLINA UNIVERSITY
Greenville, NC 27858-4353

EAST TENNESSEE STATE UNIV.
Johnson City, TN 37614

EASTERN KENTUCKY UNIVERSITY
Richmond, KY 40475-3101

FLORIDA A&M UNIVERSITY
Tallahassee, FL 32307

FLORIDA INTERNATIONAL UNIV.
Miami, FL 33199

FLORIDA STATE UNIVERSITY
Tallahassee, FL 32306

UNIVERSITY OF FLORIDA
Gainesville, FL 32604

FURMAN UNIVERSITY
Greenville, SC 29613

GEORGIA INSTITUTE OF TECH.
Atlanta, GA 30332

UNIVERSITY OF GEORGIA
Athens, GA 30613

JACKSONVILLE UNIVERSITY
Jacksonville, FL 32211-3394

UNIVERSITY OF KENTUCKY
Lexington, KY 40506-0032

LIBERTY UNIVERSITY
Lynchburg, VA 24506

LOUISIANA STATE UNIVERSITY
Baton Rouge, LA 70803

UNIVERSITY OF LOUISVILLE
Louisville, KY 40292

MARSHALL UNIVERSITY
Huntington, WV 25755

UNIVERSITY OF MARYLAND
College Park, MD 20740

UNIVERSITY OF MEMPHIS
Memphis, TN 38152

UNIVERSITY OF MIAMI
Coral Gables, FL 33124-6710

MIDDLE TENNESSEE STATE UNIV.
Murfreesboro, TN 37132

MISSISSIPPI STATE UNIVERSITY
Mississippi State, MS 39762-5509

UNIVERSITY OF MISSISSIPPI
University, MS 38677

MURRAY STATE UNIVERSITY
Murray, KY 42071-0009

UNIVERSITY OF NEW ORLEANS
New Orleans, LA 70148

UNIVERSITY OF NORTH
CAROLINA
Asheville, NC 28804-3299

UNIVERSITY OF NORTH
CAROLINA
Chapel Hill, NC 27514

UNIVERSITY OF NORTH
CAROLINA
Charlotte, NC 28223

UNIVERSITY OF NORTH
CAROLINA
Wilmington, NC 28403-3297

NORTH CAROLINA A&T ST. UNIV.
Greensboro, NC 27411

NORTH CAROLINA STATE UNIV.
Raleigh, NC 27695-7001

UNIVERSITY OF RICHMOND
Richmond, VA 23173-1903

SAMFORD UNIVERSITY
Birmingham, AL 35229

UNIVERSITY OF SOUTH ALABAMA
Mobile, AL 36688

SOUTH CAROLINA STATE UNIV.
Orangeburg, SC 29117-0001

UNIVERSITY OF SOUTH CAROLINA
Columbia, SC 29208

UNIVERSITY OF SOUTH FLORIDA
Tampa, FL 33620

SOUTHEASTERN LOUISIANA UNIV.
Hammond, LA 70402

UNIV. OF SOUTHERN MISSISSIPPI
Hattiesburg, MS 39406-5001

TENNESSEE STATE UNIVERSITY
Nashville, TN 37209-1561

UNIVERSITY OF TENNESSEE
Chattanooga, TN 37403-2598

THE UNIVERSITY OF TENNESSEE
Knoxville, TN 37996

TROY STATE UNIVERSITY
Troy, AL 36082

TULANE UNIVERSITY
New Orleans, LA 70118

VIRGINIA COMMONWEALTH UNIV.
Richmond, VA 23284-2003

VIRGINIA MILITARY INSTITUTE
Lexington, VA 24450-0304

VIRGINIA POLYTECHNIC
INSTITUTE
Blacksburg, VA 24061

UNIVERSITY OF VIRGINIA
Charlottesville, VA 22903

WAKE FOREST UNIVERSITY
Winston-Salem, NC 27109

WESTERN CAROLINA UNIVERSITY
Cullowhee, NC 28723

WESTERN KENTUCKY
UNIVERSITY
Bowling Green, KY 42101-3576

WINTHROP UNIVERSITY
Rock Hill, SC 29733

District 4

UNIVERSITY OF AKRON
Akron, OH 44325

BALL STATE UNIVERSITY
Muncie, IN 47306

BOWLING GREEN STATE UNIV.
Bowling Green, OH 43403

BUTLER UNIVERSITY
Indianapolis, IN 46208

CENTRAL MICHIGAN UNIVERSITY
Mount Pleasant, MI 48859

CHICAGO STATE UNIVERSITY
Chicago, IL 60628-1598

UNIVERSITY OF CINCINNATI
Cincinnati, OH 45221

DE PAUL UNIVERSITY
Chicago, IL 60604-2287

UNIVERSITY OF DETROIT-MERCY
Detroit, MI 48219-0900

EASTERN ILLINOIS UNIVERSITY
Charleston, IL 61920-3099

EASTERN MICHIGAN UNIVERSITY
Ypsilanti, MI 48197

ILLINOIS STATE UNIVERSITY
Normal, IL 61761

UNIVERSITY OF ILLINOIS
Champaign, IL 61820

INDIANA UNIVERSITY
Bloomington, IN 47405

UNIVERSITY OF IOWA
Iowa City, IA 52242

KENT STATE UNIVERSITY
Kent, OH 44242

LOYOLA UNIVERSITY
Chicago, IL 60626

MARQUETTE UNIVERSITY
Milwaukee, WI 53201-1881

MIAMI UNIVERSITY
Oxford, OH 45056

MICHIGAN STATE UNIVERSITY
East Lansing, MI 48824

UNIVERSITY OF MICHIGAN
Ann Arbor, MI 48109-2201

UNIV. OF MINNESOTA-TWIN
CITIES
Minneapolis, MN 55455

UNIVERSITY OF NOTRE DAME
Notre Dame, IN 46556

OHIO STATE UNIVERSITY
Columbus, OH 43210

OHIO UNIVERSITY
Athens, OH 45701

PURDUE UNIVERSITY
West Lafayette, IN 47907

UNIVERSITY OF TOLEDO
Toledo, OH 43606

VALPARAISO UNIVERSITY
Valparaiso, IN 46383-6493

WESTERN ILLINOIS UNIVERSITY
Macomb, IL 61455

WESTERN MICHIGAN UNIVERSITY
Kalamazoo, MI 49008-5134

UNIVERSITY OF WISCONSIN
Madison, WI 53711

UNIVERSITY OF WISCONSIN
Milwaukee, WI 53201

YOUNGSTOWN STATE
UNIVERSITY
Youngstown, OH 44555-0001

District 5

BRADLEY UNIVERSITY
Peoria, IL 61625

UNIVERSITY OF COLORADO
Boulder, CO 80309

DRAKE UNIVERSITY
Des Moines, IA 50311-4505

INDIANA STATE UNIVERSITY
Terre Haute, IN 47809

IOWA STATE UNIVERSITY
Ames, IA 50011

KANSAS STATE UNIVERSITY
Manhattan, KS 66506

UNIVERSITY OF KANSAS
Lawrence, KS 66045

UNIV. OF MISSOURI-COLUMBIA
Columbia, MO 65211

UNIV. OF MISSOURI-KANSAS CITY
Kansas City, MO 64110

UNIVERSITY OF NEBRASKA
Lincoln, NE 68588

UNIVERSITY OF NORTHERN IOWA
Cedar Falls, IA 50614

OKLAHOMA STATE UNIVERSITY
Stillwater, OK 74078

UNIVERSITY OF OKLAHOMA
Norman, OK 73019

ORAL ROBERTS UNIVERSITY
Tulsa, OK 74171

SOUTHEAST MISSOURI STATE
UNIV.
Cape Girardeau, MO 63701-4799

SOUTHERN ILLINOIS UNIVERSITY
Carbondale, IL 62901

SOUTHWEST MISSOURI STATE
UNIV.
Springfield, MO 65804

UNIVERSITY OF TULSA
Tulsa, OK 74104

WICHITA STATE UNIVERSITY
Wichita, KS 67260

District 6

ALCORN STATE UNIVERSITY
Lorman, MS 39096-9402

ARKANSAS STATE UNIVERSITY
State University, AR 72467

UNIVERSITY OF ARKANSAS
Fayetteville, AR 72701

UNIVERSITY OF ARKANSAS
Little Rock, AR 72204-1099

BAYLOR UNIVERSITY
Waco, TX 76798

GRAMBLING STATE UNIVERSITY
Grambling, LA 71245

UNIVERSITY OF HOUSTON
Houston, TX 77204

JACKSON STATE UNIVERSITY
Jackson, MS 39217

LAMAR UNIVERSITY
Beaumont, TX 77710

LOUISIANA TECH UNIVERSITY
Ruston, LA 71272

MCNEESE STATE UNIVERSITY
Lake Charles, LA 70609

MISSISSIPPI VALLEY ST. UNIV.
Itta Bena, MS 38941-1400

NICHOLLS STATE UNIVERSITY
Thibodaux, LA 70310

UNIVERSITY OF NORTH TEXAS
Denton, TX 76203-6737

NORTHEAST LOUISIANA
UNIVERSITY
Monroe, LA 71209-3000

NORTHWESTERN STATE
UNIVERSITY
Natchitoches, LA 71497-0003

PRAIRIE VIEW A&M UNIVERSITY
Prairie View, TX 77446

RICE UNIVERSITY
Houston, TX 77251

SAM HOUSTON STATE
UNIVERSITY
Huntsville, TX 77341

SOUTHERN METHODIST
UNIVERSITY
Dallas, TX 75275

SOUTHERN UNIVERSITY
Baton Rouge, LA 70813

SOUTHWEST TEXAS STATE UNIV.
San Marcos, TX 78666-4615

UNIV. OF SOUTHWESTERN LA.
Lafayette, LA 70504-1008

STEPHEN F. AUSTIN STATE UNIV.
Nacogdoches, TX 75962

UNIVERSITY OF TEXAS
Arlington, TX 76019

UNIVERSITY OF TEXAS
Austin, TX 78712

UNIVERSITY OF TEXAS
San Antonio, TX 78249

TEXAS A&M UNIVERSITY
College Station, TX 77843-1228

TEXAS CHRISTIAN UNIVERSITY
Fort Worth, TX 76129-0001

UNIV. OF TEXAS-PAN AMERICAN
Edinburg, TX 78539-2999

TEXAS SOUTHERN UNIVERSITY
Houston, TX 77004

TEXAS TECH UNIVERSITY
Lubbock, TX 79409

District 7

BOISE STATE UNIVERSITY
Boise, ID 83725

BRIGHAM YOUNG UNIVERSITY
Provo, UT 84602

CALIF. STATE UNIV.-FRESNO
Fresno, CA 93740-0048

COLORADO STATE UNIVERSITY
Fort Collins, CO 80523-0100

IDAHO STATE UNIVERSITY
Pocatello, ID 83209

UNIVERSITY OF IDAHO
Moscow, ID 83843

MONTANA STATE UNIV-BOZEMAN
Bozeman, MT 59717-0338

THE UNIVERSITY OF MONTANA
Missoula, MT 59812-1291

UNIVERSITY OF NEW MEXICO
Albuquerque, NM 87131

NORTHERN ARIZONA UNIVERSITY
Flagstaff, AZ 86011

SOUTHERN UTAH UNIVERSITY
Cedar City, UT 84720

UNIVERSITY OF TEXAS-EL PASO
El Paso, TX 79968

U.S. AIR FORCE ACADEMY
USAF Academy, CO 80840-5461

UNIVERSITY OF UTAH
Salt Lake City, UT 84112

WEBER STATE UNIVERSITY
Ogden, UT 84408-2701

UNIVERSITY OF WYOMING
Laramie, WY 82071

District 8

ARIZONA STATE UNIVERSITY
Tempe, AZ 85287-2505

UNIVERSITY OF ARIZONA
Tucson, AZ 85721

UNIV. OF CALIFORNIA-BERKELEY
Berkeley, CA 94720

UNIV. OF CALIF.-LOS ANGELES
Los Angeles, CA 90095-1405

UNIV. OF CALIF-SANTA BARBARA
Santa Barbara, CA 93106

UNIV. OF CALIFORNIA-IRVINE
Irvine, CA 92717

CALIF. POLYTECHNIC STATE UNIV.
San Luis Obispo, CA 93407

CALIF. STATE UNIV.-FULLERTON
Fullerton, CA 92634-9480

CALIF. STATE UNIV.-NORTHRIDGE
Northridge, CA 91330

CALIF. STATE UNIV.-SACRAMENTO
Sacramento, CA 95819

EASTERN WASHINGTON
UNIVERSITY
Cheney, WA 99004

LONG BEACH STATE UNIVERSITY
Long Beach, CA 90840-0118

NEW MEXICO STATE UNIVERSITY
Las Cruces, NM 88003

UNIVERSITY OF OREGON
Eugene, OR 97403-1226

UNIVERSITY OF PORTLAND
Portland, OR 97203-5798

UNIV. OF SOUTHERN CALIFORNIA
Los Angeles, CA 90089-0012

STANFORD UNIVERSITY
Stanford, CA 94305

UTAH STATE UNIVERSITY
Logan, UT 84322-7400

WASHINGTON STATE UNIVERSITY
Pullman, WA 99164

UNIVERSITY OF WASHINGTON
Seattle, WA 98195

NCAA PROVISIONAL MEMBERS
District 6

UNIV. OF ARKANSAS-PINE BLUFF
Pine Bluff, AR 71601

DIVISION II
District 1

BENTLEY COLLEGE
Waltham, MA 02154-4705

BRYANT COLLEGE
Smithfield, RI 02917-1284

KEENE STATE COLLEGE
Keene, NH 03431-4183

UNIV. OF MASSACHUSETTS-
LOWELL
Lowell, MA 01854

UNIVERSITY OF NEW HAVEN
West Haven, CT 06516-1999

SACRED HEART UNIVERSITY
Fairfield, CT 06432-1000

SOUTHERN CONNECTICUT ST.
UNIV.
New Haven, CT 06515

STONEHILL COLLEGE
North Easton, MA 02357

District 2

STATE UNIV. OF N.Y. at ALBANY
Albany, NY 12222

AMERICAN UNIV. OF PUERTO RICO
Bayamon, PR 00960-2037

BLOOMSBURG UNIVERSITY
Bloomsburg, PA 17815

CALIFORNIA UNIVERSITY
California, PA 15419

CHEYNEY UNIVERSITY
Cheyney, PA 19319

CLARION UNIVERSITY
Clarion, PA 16214

EAST STROUDSBURG UNIVERSITY
East Stroudsburg, PA 18301

EDINBORO UNIVERSITY
Edinboro, PA 16444-0001

GLENVILLE STATE COLLEGE
Glenville, WV 26351

INDIANA UNIV. OF PENNSYLVANIA
Indiana, PA 15705

KUTZTOWN UNIVERSITY
Kutztown, PA 19530-0721

LOCK HAVEN UNIVERSITY
Lock Haven, PA 17745

LONG ISLAND U./C.W. POST
CAMPUS
Brookville, NY 11548

MANSFIELD UNIVERSITY
Mansfield, PA 16933

MILLERSVILLE UNIVERSITY
Millersville, PA 17551-0302

NEW YORK INSTITUTE OF TECH.
Old Westbury, NY 11568-8000

PACE UNIVERSITY
New York, NY 10038-1502

QUEENS COLLEGE (NY)
Flushing, NY 11367

SHIPPENSBURG UNIVERSITY
Shippensburg, PA 17257

SLIPPERY ROCK UNIVERSITY
Slippery Rock, PA 16057

THE COLLEGE OF ST. ROSE
Albany, NY 12203

STATE UNIV. OF N.Y. at STONY
BROOK
Stony Brook, NY 11794

WEST CHESTER UNIVERSITY
West Chester, PA 19383

WEST LIBERTY STATE COLLEGE
West Liberty, WV 26074

WEST VIRGINIA WESLEYAN
COLLEGE
Buckhannon, WV 26201

WHEELING JESUIT COLLEGE
Wheeling, WV 26003-6295

District 3

ALABAMA A&M UNIVERSITY
Normal, AL 35762

ALBANY STATE COLLEGE
Albany, GA 31705

BELLARMINE COLLEGE
Louisville, KY 40205-0671

BOWIE STATE UNIVERSITY
Bowie, MD 20715-9465

CARSON-NEWMAN COLLEGE
Jefferson City, TN 37760

CLARK ATLANTA UNIVERSITY
Atlanta, GA 30314

ELIZABETH CITY STATE UNIV.
Elizabeth City, NC 27909

FORT VALLEY STATE COLLEGE
Fort Valley, GA 31030

FRANCIS MARION UNIVERSITY
Florence, SC 29501-0547

HIGH POINT UNIVERSITY
High Point, NC 27262-3598

JOHNSON C. SMITH UNIVERSITY
Charlotte, NC 28216

KENTUCKY STATE UNIVERSITY
Frankfort, KY 40601

LANE COLLEGE
Jackson, TN 38301

LE MOYNE-OWEN COLLEGE
Memphis, TN 38126

LIVINGSTONE COLLEGE
Salisbury, NC 28144

MILES COLLEGE
Birmingham, AL 35208

MISSISSIPPI COLLEGE
Clinton, MS 39058

MOREHOUSE COLLEGE
Atlanta, GA 30314

MORRIS BROWN COLLEGE
Atlanta, GA 30314

NORFOLK STATE UNIVERSITY
Norfolk, VA 23504

NORTH CAROLINA CENTRAL
UNIV.
Durham, NC 27707

UNIVERSITY OF NORTH FLORIDA
Jacksonville, FL 32224-2645

PAINE COLLEGE
Augusta, GA 30901-3182

PEMBROKE STATE UNIVERSITY
Pembroke, NC 28372-1510

SAVANNAH STATE COLLEGE
Savannah, GA 31404

SHAW UNIVERSITY
Raleigh, NC 27611

ST. ANDREWS PRESBYTERIAN
COLL
Laurinburg, NC 28352-5598

ST. AUGUSTINE'S COLLEGE
Raleigh, NC 27610

ST. PAUL'S COLLEGE
Lawrenceville, VA 23868

TUSKEGEE UNIVERSITY
Tuskegee, AL 36088

VIRGINIA STATE UNIVERSITY
Petersburg, VA 23806

VIRGINIA UNION UNIVERSITY
Richmond, VA 23220-1790

WEST GEORGIA COLLEGE
Carrollton, GA 30118

WINSTON-SALEM STATE UNIV.
Winston-Salem, NC 27110

District 4
ASHLAND UNIVERSITY
Ashland, OH 44805

BEMIDJI STATE UNIVERSITY
Bemidji, MN 56601-2699

GRAND VALLEY STATE
UNIVERSITY
Allendale, MI 49401

HILLSDALE COLLEGE
Hillsdale, MI 49242-1298

UNIVERSITY OF INDIANAPOLIS
Indianapolis, IN 46227

LAKE SUPERIOR STATE UNIV.
Sault Sainte Marie, MI 49783

LEWIS UNIVERSITY
Romeoville, IL 60441

MICHIGAN TECHNOLOGICAL
UNIV.
Houghton, MI 49931-1295

UNIV. OF MINNESOTA-DULUTH
Duluth, MN 55812

UNIV. OF MINNESOTA-MORRIS
Morris, MN 56267

MOORHEAD STATE UNIVERSITY
Moorhead, MN 56563-2996

NORTHWOOD UNIVERSITY
Midland, MI 48640

SAGINAW VALLEY STATE UNIV.
University Center, MI 48710

SOUTHERN ILLINOIS UNIVERSITY
Edwardsville, IL 62026

UNIV. OF SOUTHERN INDIANA
Evansville, IN 47712

ST. JOSEPH'S COLLEGE
Rensselaer, IN 47978

UNIV. OF WISCONSIN-PARKSIDE
Kenosha, WI 53141-2000

District 5
AUGUSTANA COLLEGE
Sioux Falls, SD 57197

CENTRAL MISSOURI STATE UNIV.
Warrensburg, MO 64093

CHADRON STATE COLLEGE
Chadron, NE 69337

EMPORIA STATE UNIVERSITY
Emporia, KS 66801-5087

LINCOLN UNIVERSITY
Jefferson City, MO 65102-0029

MANKATO STATE UNIVERSITY
Mankato, MN 56002-8400

MISSOURI SOUTHERN ST.
COLLEGE
Joplin, MO 64801-1595

UNIVERSITY OF MISSOURI
Rolla, MO 65401

MORNINGSIDE COLLEGE
Sioux City, IA 51106-1751

UNIV. OF NEBRASKA at KEARNEY
Kearney, NE 68849

NORTH DAKOTA STATE
UNIVERSITY
Fargo, ND 58105

UNIVERSITY OF NORTH DAKOTA
Grand Forks, ND 58202

NORTHEAST MISSOURI STATE
UNIV.
Kirksville, MO 63501

UNIV. OF NORTHERN COLORADO
Greeley, CO 80639

NORTHERN STATE UNIVERSITY
Aberdeen, SD 57401

NORTHWEST MISSOURI STATE
UNIV.
Maryville, MO 64468-6001

PITTSBURG STATE UNIVERSITY
Pittsburg, KS 66762

SOUTH DAKOTA STATE
UNIVERSITY
Brookings, SD 57007

UNIVERSITY OF SOUTH DAKOTA
Vermillion, SD 57069-2390

SOUTHWEST BAPTIST
UNIVERSITY
Bolivar, MO 65613

ST. CLOUD STATE UNIVERSITY
St. Cloud, MN 56301-4498

WAYNE STATE COLLEGE
Wayne, NE 68787-1172

District 6

ABILENE CHRISTIAN UNIVERSITY
Abilene, TX 79699

ANGELO STATE UNIVERSITY
San Angelo, TX 76909

UNIVERSITY OF CENTRAL
OKLAHOMA
Edmond, OK 73034

EAST TEXAS STATE UNIVERSITY
Commerce, TX 75429-3011

TARLETON STATE UNIVERSITY
Stephenville, TX 76402

TEXAS A&M UNIV.-KINGSVILLE
Kingsville, TX 78363

District 7

ADAMS STATE COLLEGE
Alamosa, CO 81102

COLORADO SCHOOL OF MINES
Golden, CO 80401

FORT HAYS STATE UNIVERSITY
Hays, KS 67601

GRAND CANYON UNIVERSITY
Phoenix, AZ 85017

WESTERN STATE COLLEGE
Gunnison, CO 81231

District 8

UNIV. OF CALIFORNIA-DAVIS
Davis, CA 95616

UNIV. OF CALIFORNIA-RIVERSIDE
Riverside, CA 92521

CALIF. STATE POLYTECHNIC UNIV.
Pomona, CA 91768

CALIF. STATE UNIV.-BAKERSFIELD
Bakersfield, CA 93311-1099

CALIF. STATE UNIV.-CHICO
Chico, CA 95929-0300

CALIF. STATE UNIV.-LOS ANGELES
Los Angeles, CA 90032-8240

CALIF. STATE UNIV.-STANISLAUS
Turlock, CA 95382

HUMBOLDT STATE UNIVERSITY
Arcata, CA 95521

COLLEGE OF NOTRE DAME
Belmont, CA 94002-9974

PORTLAND STATE UNIVERSITY
Portland, OR 97207-0751

SAN FRANCISCO STATE UNIV.
San Francisco, CA 94132

SEATTLE PACIFIC UNIVERSITY
Seattle, WA 98119

**NCAA PROVISIONAL MEMBERS
DISTRICT 2**

UNIV. OF PUERTO RICO-
MAYAGUEZ
Mayaguez, PR 00709

UNIV. OF PUERTO RICO-BAYAMON
Bayamon, PR 00619-1919

UNIVERSITY OF VIRGIN ISLANDS
St. Thomas, VI 00802

WEST VIRGINIA STATE COLLEGE
Institute, WV 25112-1000

WESTMINSTER COLLEGE
New Wilmington, PA 16172

District 3

COLUMBIA UNION COLLEGE
Takoma Park, MD 20912

District 5

EAST CENTRAL UNIVERSITY
Ada, OK 74820

LANGSTON UNIVERSITY
Langston, OK 73050

NORTHWESTERN OKLAHOMA ST.
U.
Alva, OK 73717

SOUTHEASTERN OKLA. ST. UNIV.
Durant, OK 74701

SOUTHWESTERN OKLAHOMA ST.
UNIV.
Weatherford, OK 73096

District 6

HARDING UNIVERSITY
Searcy, AR 72149-0001

OUACHITA BAPTIST UNIVERSITY
Arkadelphia, AR 71998-0001

SOUTHERN ARKANSAS
UNIVERSITY
Magnolia, AR 71753-5000

District 8
CENTRAL WASHINGTON UNIV.
Ellensburg, WA 98926

WESTERN WASHINGTON UNIV.
Bellingham, WA 98225

MEN'S TRACK, INDOOR

DIVISION I
District 1

BOSTON COLLEGE
Chestnut Hill, MA 02167-3934

BOSTON UNIVERSITY
Boston, MA 02215

BROWN UNIVERSITY
Providence, RI 02912

CENTRAL CONN. STATE UNIV.
New Britain, CT 06050-4010

UNIVERSITY OF CONNECTICUT
Storrs, CT 06269

DARTMOUTH COLLEGE
Hanover, NH 03755

UNIVERSITY OF HARTFORD
West Hartford, CT 06117-1599

HARVARD UNIVERSITY
Cambridge, MA 02138-3800

COLLEGE OF THE HOLY CROSS
Worcester, MA 01610-2395

UNIVERSITY OF MAINE
Orono, ME 04469

UNIVERSITY OF MASSACHUSETTS
Amherst, MA 01003

UNIVERSITY OF NEW HAMPSHIRE
Durham, NH 03824

NORTHEASTERN UNIVERSITY
Boston, MA 02115-5096

PROVIDENCE COLLEGE
Providence, RI 02918

UNIVERSITY OF RHODE ISLAND
Kingston, RI 02881

UNIVERSITY OF VERMONT
Burlington, VT 05405

YALE UNIVERSITY
New Haven, CT 06520-7398

District 2

BUCKNELL UNIVERSITY
Lewisburg, PA 17837

STATE UNIV. OF N.Y. at BUFFALO
Buffalo, NY 14260

CANISIUS COLLEGE
Buffalo, NY 14208-1098

COLGATE UNIVERSITY
Hamilton, NY 13346-1304

COLUMBIA UNIV.-BARNARD
COLLEGE
New York, NY 10027

CORNELL UNIVERSITY
Ithaca, NY 14853

DELAWARE STATE UNIVERSITY
Dover, DE 19901

UNIVERSITY OF DELAWARE
Newark, DE 19716

FAIRLEIGH DICKINSON-TEANECK
Teaneck, NJ 07666

FORDHAM UNIVERSITY
Bronx, NY 10458-5155

GEORGE MASON UNIVERSITY
Fairfax, VA 22030

GEORGETOWN UNIVERSITY
Washington, DC 20057

HAMPTON UNIVERSITY
Hampton, VA 23668

HOWARD UNIVERSITY
Washington, DC 20059

IONA COLLEGE
New Rochelle, NY 10801

JAMES MADISON UNIVERSITY
Harrisonburg, VA 22807

LA SALLE UNIVERSITY
Philadelphia, PA 19141-1199

LAFAYETTE COLLEGE
Easton, PA 18042

LEHIGH UNIVERSITY
Bethlehem, PA 18015-3089

LONG ISLAND UNIV.-BROOKLYN
Brooklyn, NY 11201

MANHATTAN COLLEGE
Riverdale, NY 10471

MARIST COLLEGE
Poughkeepsie, NY 12601-1387

UNIV. OF MARYLAND-BALT. CO.
Baltimore, MD 21228-5398

U. OF MARYLAND-EASTERN
SHORE
Princess Anne, MD 21853-1299

MONMOUTH UNIVERSITY
West Long Branch, NJ 07764

MORGAN STATE UNIVERSITY
Baltimore, MD 21239

MOUNT ST. MARY'S COLLEGE
Emmitsburg, MD 21727-7799

PENNSYLVANIA STATE UNIV.
University Park, PA 16802

UNIVERSITY OF PENNSYLVANIA
Philadelphia, PA 19104-6380

UNIVERSITY OF PITTSBURGH
Pittsburgh, PA 15260

PRINCETON UNIVERSITY
Princeton, NJ 08544

RIDER UNIVERSITY
Lawrenceville, NJ 08648-3099

ROBERT MORRIS COLLEGE
Coraopolis, PA 15108-1189

RUTGERS UNIVERSITY
New Brunswick, NJ 08903

SETON HALL UNIVERSITY
South Orange, NJ 07079

ST. FRANCIS COLLEGE
Brooklyn Heights, NY 11201

ST. JOHN'S UNIVERSITY
Jamaica, NY 11439

ST. JOSEPH'S UNIVERSITY
Philadelphia, PA 19131-1395

ST. PETER'S COLLEGE
Jersey City, NJ 07306

SYRACUSE UNIVERSITY
Syracuse, NY 13244

TEMPLE UNIVERSITY
Philadelphia, PA 19122

U.S. MILITARY ACADEMY
West Point, NY 10996

U.S. NAVAL ACADEMY
Annapolis, MD 21402

VILLANOVA UNIVERSITY
Villanova, PA 19085

WAGNER COLLEGE
Staten Island, NY 10301 4495

WEST VIRGINIA UNIVERSITY
Morgantown, WV 26505-6201

COLLEGE OF WILLIAM & MARY
Williamsburg, VA 23187

District 3

ALABAMA STATE UNIVERSITY
Montgomery, AL 36101-0271

UNIV. OF ALABAMA at
TUSCALOOSA
Tuscaloosa, AL 35487

UNIV. OF ALABAMA at
BIRMINGHAM
Birmingham, AL 35294-0110

APPALACHIAN STATE UNIVERSITY
Boone, NC 28608

AUBURN UNIVERSITY
Auburn University, AL 36849-5113

BETHUNE-COOKMAN COLLEGE
Daytona Beach, FL 32114-3099

CHARLESTON SOUTHERN UNIV.
Charleston, SC 29423-8087

THE CITADEL
Charleston, SC 29409

CLEMSON UNIVERSITY
Clemson, SC 29634-000

COASTAL CAROLINA UNIVERSITY
Conway, SC 29526

COPPIN STATE COLLEGE
Baltimore, MD 21216

DAVIDSON COLLEGE
Davidson, NC 28036

DUKE UNIVERSITY
Durham, NC 27708-0555

EAST CAROLINA UNIVERSITY
Greenville, NC 27858-4353

EAST TENNESSEE STATE UNIV.
Johnson City, TN 37614

EASTERN KENTUCKY UNIVERSITY
Richmond, KY 40475-3101

FLORIDA A&M UNIVERSITY
Tallahassee, FL 32307

FLORIDA INTERNATIONAL UNIV.
Miami, FL 33199

FLORIDA STATE UNIVERSITY
Tallahassee, FL 32306

UNIVERSITY OF FLORIDA
Gainesville, FL 32604

GEORGIA INSTITUTE OF TECH.
Atlanta, GA 30332

UNIVERSITY OF GEORGIA
Athens, GA 30613

UNIVERSITY OF KENTUCKY
Lexington, KY 40506-0032

LIBERTY UNIVERSITY
Lynchburg, VA 24506

LOUISIANA STATE UNIVERSITY
Baton Rouge, LA 70803

UNIVERSITY OF LOUISVILLE
Louisville, KY 40292

MARSHALL UNIVERSITY
Huntington, WV 25755

UNIVERSITY OF MARYLAND
College Park, MD 20740

UNIVERSITY OF MEMPHIS
Memphis, TN 38152

UNIVERSITY OF MIAMI
Coral Gables, FL 33124-6710

MIDDLE TENNESSEE STATE UNIV.
Murfreesboro, TN 37132

MISSISSIPPI STATE UNIVERSITY
Mississippi State, MS 39762-5509

UNIVERSITY OF MISSISSIPPI
University, MS 38677

MURRAY STATE UNIVERSITY
Murray, KY 42071-0009

UNIVERSITY OF NEW ORLEANS
New Orleans, LA 70148

UNIVERSITY OF NORTH
CAROLINA
Asheville, NC 28804-3299

UNIVERSITY OF NORTH
CAROLINA
Chapel Hill, NC 27514

UNIVERSITY OF NORTH
CAROLINA
Wilmington, NC 28403-3297

NORTH CAROLINA A&T ST. UNIV.
Greensboro, NC 27411

NORTH CAROLINA STATE UNIV.
Raleigh, NC 27695-7001

UNIVERSITY OF RICHMOND
Richmond, VA 23173-1903

SAMFORD UNIVERSITY
Birmingham, AL 35229

UNIVERSITY OF SOUTH ALABAMA
Mobile, AL 36688

SOUTH CAROLINA STATE UNIV.
Orangeburg, SC 29117-0001

UNIVERSITY OF SOUTH CAROLINA
Columbia, SC 29208

UNIVERSITY OF SOUTH FLORIDA
Tampa, FL 33620

SOUTHEASTERN LOUISIANA UNIV.
Hammond, LA 70402

UNIV. OF SOUTHERN MISSISSIPPI
Hattiesburg, MS 39406-5001

TENNESSEE STATE UNIVERSITY
Nashville, TN 37209-1561

UNIVERSITY OF TENNESSEE
Chattanooga, TN 37403-2598

THE UNIVERSITY OF TENNESSEE
Knoxville, TN 37996

TULANE UNIVERSITY
New Orleans, LA 70118

VIRGINIA COMMONWEALTH UNIV.
Richmond, VA 23284-2003

VIRGINIA MILITARY INSTITUTE
Lexington, VA 24450-0304

VIRGINIA POLYTECHNIC
INSTITUTE
Blacksburg, VA 24061

UNIVERSITY OF VIRGINIA
Charlottesville, VA 22903

WAKE FOREST UNIVERSITY
Winston-Salem, NC 27109

WESTERN CAROLINA UNIVERSITY
Cullowhee, NC 28723

WESTERN KENTUCKY
UNIVERSITY
Bowling Green, KY 42101-3576

District 4

UNIVERSITY OF AKRON
Akron, OH 44325

BALL STATE UNIVERSITY
Muncie, IN 47306

BOWLING GREEN STATE UNIV.
Bowling Green, OH 43403

BUTLER UNIVERSITY
Indianapolis, IN 46208

CENTRAL MICHIGAN UNIVERSITY
Mount Pleasant, MI 48859

CHICAGO STATE UNIVERSITY
Chicago, IL 60628-1598

UNIVERSITY OF CINCINNATI
Cincinnati, OH 45221

DE PAUL UNIVERSITY
Chicago, IL 60604-2287

UNIVERSITY OF DETROIT-MERCY
Detroit, MI 48219-0900

EASTERN ILLINOIS UNIVERSITY
Charleston, IL 61920-3099

EASTERN MICHIGAN UNIVERSITY
Ypsilanti, MI 48197

ILLINOIS STATE UNIVERSITY
Normal, IL 61761

UNIVERSITY OF ILLINOIS
Champaign, IL 61820

INDIANA UNIVERSITY
Bloomington, IN 47405

UNIVERSITY OF IOWA
Iowa City, IA 52242

KENT STATE UNIVERSITY
Kent, OH 44242

LOYOLA UNIVERSITY
Chicago, IL 60626

MARQUETTE UNIVERSITY
Milwaukee, WI 53201-1881

MIAMI UNIVERSITY
Oxford, OH 45056

MICHIGAN STATE UNIVERSITY
East Lansing, MI 48824

UNIVERSITY OF MICHIGAN
Ann Arbor, MI 48109-2201

UNIV. OF MINNESOTA-TWIN CITIES
Minneapolis, MN 55455

UNIVERSITY OF NOTRE DAME
Notre Dame, IN 46556

OHIO STATE UNIVERSITY
Columbus, OH 43210

OHIO UNIVERSITY
Athens, OH 45701

PURDUE UNIVERSITY
West Lafayette, IN 47907

UNIVERSITY OF TOLEDO
Toledo, OH 43606

VALPARAISO UNIVERSITY
Valparaiso, IN 46383-6493

WESTERN ILLINOIS UNIVERSITY
Macomb, IL 61455

WESTERN MICHIGAN UNIVERSITY
Kalamazoo, MI 49008-5134

UNIVERSITY OF WISCONSIN
Madison, WI 53711

UNIVERSITY OF WISCONSIN
Milwaukee, WI 53201

YOUNGSTOWN STATE UNIVERSITY
Youngstown, OH 44555-0001

District 5

BRADLEY UNIVERSITY
Peoria, IL 61625

UNIVERSITY OF COLORADO
Boulder, CO 80309

DRAKE UNIVERSITY
Des Moines, IA 50311-4505

INDIANA STATE UNIVERSITY
Terre Haute, IN 47809

IOWA STATE UNIVERSITY
Ames, IA 50011

KANSAS STATE UNIVERSITY
Manhattan, KS 66506

UNIVERSITY OF KANSAS
Lawrence, KS 66045

UNIVERSITY OF MISSOURI-COLUMBIA
Columbia, MO 65211

UNIVERSITY OF NEBRASKA
Lincoln, NE 68588

UNIVERSITY OF NORTHERN IOWA
Cedar Falls, IA 50614

OKLAHOMA STATE UNIVERSITY
Stillwater, OK 74078

UNIVERSITY OF OKLAHOMA
Norman, OK 73019

ORAL ROBERTS UNIVERSITY
Tulsa, OK 74171

SOUTHEAST MISSOURI STATE UNIV.
Cape Girardeau, MO 63701-4799

SOUTHERN ILLINOIS UNIVERSITY
Carbondale, IL 62901

SOUTHWEST MISSOURI STATE UNIV.
Springfield, MO 65804

UNIVERSITY OF TULSA
Tulsa, OK 74104

WICHITA STATE UNIVERSITY
Wichita, KS 67260

District 6

ALCORN STATE UNIVERSITY
Lorman, MS 39096-9402

ARKANSAS STATE UNIVERSITY
State University, AR 72467

UNIVERSITY OF ARKANSAS
Fayetteville, AR 72701

UNIVERSITY OF ARKANSAS
Little Rock, AR 72204-1099

BAYLOR UNIVERSITY
Waco, TX 76798

GRAMBLING STATE UNIVERSITY
Grambling, LA 71245

UNIVERSITY OF HOUSTON
Houston, TX 77204

JACKSON STATE UNIVERSITY
Jackson, MS 39217

LAMAR UNIVERSITY
Beaumont, TX 77710

LOUISIANA TECH UNIVERSITY
Ruston, LA 71272

MCNEESE STATE UNIVERSITY
Lake Charles, LA 70609

MISSISSIPPI VALLEY ST. UNIV.
Itta Bena, MS 38941-1400

NICHOLLS STATE UNIVERSITY
Thibodaux, LA 70310

UNIVERSITY OF NORTH TEXAS
Denton, TX 76203-6737

NORTHEAST LOUISIANA
UNIVERSITY
Monroe, LA 71209-3000

NORTHWESTERN STATE
UNIVERSITY
Natchitoches, LA 71497-0003

PRAIRIE VIEW A&M UNIVERSITY
Prairie View, TX 77446

RICE UNIVERSITY
Houston, TX 77251

SAM HOUSTON STATE
UNIVERSITY
Huntsville, TX 77341

SOUTHERN METHODIST
UNIVERSITY
Dallas, TX 75275

SOUTHERN UNIVERSITY
Baton Rouge, LA 70813

SOUTHWEST TEXAS STATE UNIV.
San Marcos, TX 78666-4615

UNIV. OF SOUTHWESTERN LA.
Lafayette, LA 70504-1008

STEPHEN F. AUSTIN STATE UNIV.
Nacogdoches, TX 75962

UNIVERSITY OF TEXAS
Arlington, TX 76019

UNIVERSITY OF TEXAS
Austin, TX 78712

UNIVERSITY OF TEXAS
San Antonio, TX 78249

TEXAS A&M UNIVERSITY
College Station, TX 77843-1228

TEXAS CHRISTIAN UNIVERSITY
Fort Worth, TX 76129-0001

UNIV. OF TEXAS-PAN AMERICAN
Edinburg, TX 78539-2999

TEXAS SOUTHERN UNIVERSITY
Houston, TX 77004

TEXAS TECH UNIVERSITY
Lubbock, TX 79409

District 7

BOISE STATE UNIVERSITY
Boise, ID 83725

BRIGHAM YOUNG UNIVERSITY
Provo, UT 84602

CALIF. STATE UNIV.-FRESNO
Fresno, CA 93740-0048

COLORADO STATE UNIVERSITY
Fort Collins, CO 80523-0100

IDAHO STATE UNIVERSITY
Pocatello, ID 83209

UNIVERSITY OF IDAHO
Moscow, ID 83843

MONTANA STATE UNIV-BOZEMAN
Bozeman, MT 59717-0338

THE UNIVERSITY OF MONTANA
Missoula, MT 59812-1291

UNIVERSITY OF NEW MEXICO
Albuquerque, NM 87131

NORTHERN ARIZONA UNIVERSITY
Flagstaff, AZ 86011

SOUTHERN UTAH UNIVERSITY
Cedar City, UT 84720

UNIVERSITY OF TEXAS-EL PASO
El Paso, TX 79968

U.S. AIR FORCE ACADEMY
USAF Academy, CO 80840-5461

UNIVERSITY OF UTAH
Salt Lake City, UT 84112

WEBER STATE UNIVERSITY
Ogden, UT 84408-2701

UNIVERSITY OF WYOMING
Laramie, WY 82071

District 8

ARIZONA STATE UNIVERSITY
Tempe, AZ 85287-2505

UNIVERSITY OF ARIZONA
Tucson, AZ 85721

UNIV. OF CALIFORNIA-BERKELEY
Berkeley, CA 94720

UNIV. OF CALIF.-LOS ANGELES
Los Angeles, CA 90095-1405

CALIF. STATE UNIV.-NORTHRIDGE
Northridge, CA 91330

CALIF. STATE UNIV.-SACRAMENTO
Sacramento, CA 95819

EASTERN WASHINGTON
UNIVERSITY
Cheney, WA 99004

UNIVERSITY OF PORTLAND
Portland, OR 97203-5798

STANFORD UNIVERSITY
Stanford, CA 94305

UTAH STATE UNIVERSITY
Logan, UT 84322-7400

WASHINGTON STATE UNIVERSITY
Pullman, WA 99164

UNIVERSITY OF WASHINGTON
Seattle, WA 98195

NCAA PROVISIONAL MEMBERS
District 6

UNIV. OF ARKANSAS-PINE BLUFF
Pine Bluff, AR 71601

DIVISION II
District 1

BENTLEY COLLEGE
Waltham, MA 02154-4705

BRYANT COLLEGE
Smithfield, RI 02917-1284

KEENE STATE COLLEGE
Keene, NH 03431-4183

UNIV. OF MASSACHUSETTS-
LOWELL
Lowell, MA 01854

UNIVERSITY OF NEW HAVEN
West Haven, CT 06516-1999

SACRED HEART UNIVERSITY
Fairfield, CT 06432-1000

SOUTHERN CONNECTICUT ST.
UNIV.
New Haven, CT 06515

STONEHILL COLLEGE
North Easton, MA 02357

District 2

STATE UNIV. OF N.Y. AT ALBANY
Albany, NY 12222

CHEYNEY UNIVERSITY
Cheyney, PA 19319

EAST STROUDSBURG UNIVERSITY
East Stroudsburg, PA 18301

EDINBORO UNIVERSITY
Edinboro, PA 16444-0001

GLENVILLE STATE COLLEGE
Glenville, WV 26351

INDIANA UNIV. OF PENNSYLVANIA
Indiana, PA 15705

KUTZTOWN UNIVERSITY
Kutztown, PA 19530-0721

LOCK HAVEN UNIVERSITY
Lock Haven, PA 17745

LONG ISLAND U./C.W. POST
CAMPUS
Brookville, NY 11548

MANSFIELD UNIVERSITY
Mansfield, PA 16933

MILLERSVILLE UNIVERSITY
Millersville, PA 17551-0302

NEW YORK INSTITUTE OF TECH.
Old Westbury, NY 11568-8000

PACE UNIVERSITY
New York, NY 10038-1502

QUEENS COLLEGE (NY)
Flushing, NY 11367

SHIPPENSBURG UNIVERSITY
Shippensburg, PA 17257

SLIPPERY ROCK UNIVERSITY
Slippery Rock, PA 16057

THE COLLEGE OF ST. ROSE
Albany, NY 12203

STATE UNIV. OF N.Y. at STONY
BROOK
Stony Brook, NY 11794

WEST CHESTER UNIVERSITY
West Chester, PA 19383

District 3

ALABAMA A&M UNIVERSITY
Normal, AL 35762

BOWIE STATE UNIVERSITY
Bowie, MD 20715-9465

ELIZABETH CITY STATE UNIV.
Elizabeth City, NC 27909

HIGH POINT UNIVERSITY
High Point, NC 27262-3598

KENTUCKY STATE UNIVERSITY
Frankfort, KY 40601

MISSISSIPPI COLLEGE
Clinton, MS 39058

MORRIS BROWN COLLEGE
Atlanta, GA 30314

NORFOLK STATE UNIVERSITY
Norfolk, VA 23504

NORTH CAROLINA CENTRAL
UNIV.
Durham, NC 27707

UNIVERSITY OF NORTH FLORIDA
Jacksonville, FL 32224-2645

PEMBROKE STATE UNIVERSITY
Pembroke, NC 28372-1510

SHAW UNIVERSITY
Raleigh, NC 27611

ST. AUGUSTINE'S COLLEGE
Raleigh, NC 27610

ST. PAUL'S COLLEGE
Lawrenceville, VA 23868

VIRGINIA STATE UNIVERSITY
Petersburg, VA 23806

District 4

ASHLAND UNIVERSITY
Ashland, OH 44805

BEMIDJI STATE UNIVERSITY
Bemidji, MN 56601-2699

GRAND VALLEY STATE
UNIVERSITY
Allendale, MI 49401

HILLSDALE COLLEGE
Hillsdale, MI 49242-1298

UNIVERSITY OF INDIANAPOLIS
Indianapolis, IN 46227

LAKE SUPERIOR STATE UNIV.
Sault Sainte Marie, MI 49783

LEWIS UNIVERSITY
Romeoville, IL 60441

UNIV. OF MINNESOTA-DULUTH
Duluth, MN 55812

UNIV. OF MINNESOTA-MORRIS
Morris, MN 56267

MOORHEAD STATE UNIVERSITY
Moorhead, MN 56563-2996

NORTHWOOD UNIVERSITY
Midland, MI 48640

SAGINAW VALLEY STATE UNIV.
University Center, MI 48710

SOUTHERN ILLINOIS UNIVERSITY
Edwardsville, IL 62026

UNIV. OF SOUTHERN INDIANA
Evansville, IN 47712

ST. JOSEPH'S COLLEGE
Rensselaer, IN 47978

UNIV. OF WISCONSIN-PARKSIDE
Kenosha, WI 53141-2000

District 5

AUGUSTANA COLLEGE
Sioux Falls, SD 57197

CENTRAL MISSOURI STATE UNIV.
Warrensburg, MO 64093

CHADRON STATE COLLEGE
Chadron, NE 69337

EMPORIA STATE UNIVERSITY
Emporia, KS 66801-5087

LINCOLN UNIVERSITY
Jefferson City, MO 65102-0029

MANKATO STATE UNIVERSITY
Mankato, MN 56002-8400

MISSOURI SOUTHERN ST.
COLLEGE
Joplin, MO 64801-1595

UNIVERSITY OF MISSOURI
Rolla, MO 65401

MORNINGSIDE COLLEGE
Sioux City, IA 51106-1751

UNIV. OF NEBRASKA at KEARNEY
Kearney, NE 68849

NORTH DAKOTA STATE
UNIVERSITY
Fargo, ND 58105

UNIVERSITY OF NORTH DAKOTA
Grand Forks, ND 58202

NORTHEAST MISSOURI STATE
UNIV.
Kirksville, MO 63501

UNIV. OF NORTHERN COLORADO
Greeley, CO 80639

NORTHERN STATE UNIVERSITY
Aberdeen, SD 57401

NORTHWEST MISSOURI STATE
UNIV.
Maryville, MO 64468-6001

PITTSBURG STATE UNIVERSITY
Pittsburg, KS 66762

SOUTH DAKOTA STATE
UNIVERSITY
Brookings, SD 57007

UNIVERSITY OF SOUTH DAKOTA
Vermillion, SD 57069-2390

SOUTHWEST BAPTIST
UNIVERSITY
Bolivar, MO 65613

ST. CLOUD STATE UNIVERSITY
St. Cloud, MN 56301-4498

WAYNE STATE COLLEGE
Wayne, NE 68787-1172

District 6

ABILENE CHRISTIAN UNIVERSITY
Abilene, TX 79699

UNIVERSITY OF CENTRAL
OKLAHOMA
Edmond, OK 73034

District 7

ADAMS STATE COLLEGE
Alamosa, CO 81102

COLORADO SCHOOL OF MINES
Golden, CO 80401

FORT HAYS STATE UNIVERSITY
Hays, KS 67601

GRAND CANYON UNIVERSITY
Phoenix, AZ 85017

WESTERN STATE COLLEGE
Gunnison, CO 81231

District 8

UNIV. OF CALIFORNIA-DAVIS
Davis, CA 95616

UNIV. OF CALIFORNIA-RIVERSIDE
Riverside, CA 92521

CALIF. STATE UNIV.-BAKERSFIELD
Bakersfield, CA 93311-1099

CALIF. STATE UNIV.-LOS ANGELES
Los Angeles, CA 90032-8240

PORTLAND STATE UNIVERSITY
Portland, OR 97207-0751

SEATTLE PACIFIC UNIVERSITY
Seattle, WA 98119

**NCAA PROVISIONAL MEMBERS
DISTRICT 2**

UNIVERSITY OF VIRGIN ISLANDS
St. Thomas, VI 00802

WESTMINSTER COLLEGE
New Wilmington, PA 16172

District 3

COLUMBIA UNION COLLEGE
Takoma Park, MD 20912

District 6

HARDING UNIVERSITY
Searcy, AR 72149-0001

WOMEN'S TRACK, INDOOR

DIVISION I

District 1

BOSTON COLLEGE
Chestnut Hill, MA 02167-3934

BOSTON UNIVERSITY
Boston, MA 02215

BROWN UNIVERSITY
Providence, RI 02912

CENTRAL CONN. STATE UNIV.
New Britain, CT 06050-4010

UNIVERSITY OF CONNECTICUT
Storrs, CT 06269

DARTMOUTH COLLEGE
Hanover, NH 03755

UNIVERSITY OF HARTFORD
West Hartford, CT 06117-1599

HARVARD UNIVERSITY
Cambridge, MA 02138-3800

COLLEGE OF THE HOLY CROSS
Worcester, MA 01610-2395

UNIVERSITY OF MAINE
Orono, ME 04469

UNIVERSITY OF MASSACHUSETTS
Amherst, MA 01003

UNIVERSITY OF NEW HAMPSHIRE
Durham, NH 03824

NORTHEASTERN UNIVERSITY
Boston, MA 02115-5096

PROVIDENCE COLLEGE
Providence, RI 02918

UNIVERSITY OF RHODE ISLAND
Kingston, RI 02881

UNIVERSITY OF VERMONT
Burlington, VT 05405

YALE UNIVERSITY
New Haven, CT 06520-7398

District 2

BUCKNELL UNIVERSITY
Lewisburg, PA 17837

STATE UNIV. OF N.Y. at BUFFALO
Buffalo, NY 14260

CANISIUS COLLEGE
Buffalo, NY 14208-1098

COLGATE UNIVERSITY
Hamilton, NY 13346-1304

COLUMBIA UNIV.-BARNARD
COLLEGE
New York, NY 10027

CORNELL UNIVERSITY
Ithaca, NY 14853

DELAWARE STATE UNIVERSITY
Dover, DE 19901

UNIVERSITY OF DELAWARE
Newark, DE 19716

DUQUESNE UNIVERSITY
Pittsburgh, PA 15282

FAIRLEIGH DICKINSON-TEANECK
Teaneck, NJ 07666

FORDHAM UNIVERSITY
Bronx, NY 10458-5155

GEORGE MASON UNIVERSITY
Fairfax, VA 22030

GEORGETOWN UNIVERSITY
Washington, DC 20057

HAMPTON UNIVERSITY
Hampton, VA 23668

HOWARD UNIVERSITY
Washington, DC 20059

JAMES MADISON UNIVERSITY
Harrisonburg, VA 22807

LA SALLE UNIVERSITY
Philadelphia, PA 19141-1199

LAFAYETTE COLLEGE
Easton, PA 18042

LEHIGH UNIVERSITY
Bethlehem, PA 18015-3089

LONG ISLAND UNIV.-BROOKLYN
Brooklyn, NY 11201

MANHATTAN COLLEGE
Riverdale, NY 10471

MARIST COLLEGE
Poughkeepsie, NY 12601-1387

UNIV. OF MARYLAND-BALT. CO.
Baltimore, MD 21228-5398

U. OF MARYLAND-EASTERN
SHORE
Princess Anne, MD 21853-1299

MONMOUTH UNIVERSITY
West Long Branch, NJ 07764

MORGAN STATE UNIVERSITY
Baltimore, MD 21239

MOUNT ST. MARY'S COLLEGE
Emmitsburg, MD 21727-7799

PENNSYLVANIA STATE UNIV.
University Park, PA 16802

UNIVERSITY OF PENNSYLVANIA
Philadelphia, PA 19104-6380

UNIVERSITY OF PITTSBURGH
Pittsburgh, PA 15260

PRINCETON UNIVERSITY
Princeton, NJ 08544

RIDER UNIVERSITY
Lawrenceville, NJ 08648-3099

ROBERT MORRIS COLLEGE
Coraopolis, PA 15108-1189

RUTGERS UNIVERSITY
New Brunswick, NJ 08903

SETON HALL UNIVERSITY
South Orange, NJ 07079

ST. FRANCIS COLLEGE
Brooklyn Heights, NY 11201

ST. JOHN'S UNIVERSITY
Jamaica, NY 11439

ST. JOSEPH'S UNIVERSITY
Philadelphia, PA 19131-1395

ST. PETER'S COLLEGE
Jersey City, NJ 07306

SYRACUSE UNIVERSITY
Syracuse, NY 13244

TEMPLE UNIVERSITY
Philadelphia, PA 19122

U.S. MILITARY ACADEMY
West Point, NY 10996

U.S. NAVAL ACADEMY
Annapolis, MD 21402

VILLANOVA UNIVERSITY
Villanova, PA 19085

WAGNER COLLEGE
Staten Island, NY 10301-4495

WEST VIRGINIA UNIVERSITY
Morgantown, WV 26505-6201

COLLEGE OF WILLIAM & MARY
Williamsburg, VA 23187

District 3

ALABAMA STATE UNIVERSITY
Montgomery, AL 36101-0271

UNIV. OF ALABAMA at
TUSCALOOSA
Tuscaloosa, AL 35487

UNIV. OF ALABAMA at
BIRMINGHAM
Birmingham, AL 35294-0110

APPALACHIAN STATE UNIVERSITY
Boone, NC 28608

AUBURN UNIVERSITY
Auburn University, AL 36849-5113

AUSTIN PEAY STATE UNIVERSITY
Clarksville, TN 37044-4576

BETHUNE-COOKMAN COLLEGE
Daytona Beach, FL 32114-3099

UNIVERSITY OF CENTRAL
FLORIDA
Orlando, FL 32816-0002

CHARLESTON SOUTHERN UNIV.
Charleston, SC 29423-8087

CLEMSON UNIVERSITY
Clemson, SC 29634-000

COASTAL CAROLINA UNIVERSITY
Conway, SC 29526

COPPIN STATE COLLEGE
Baltimore, MD 21216

DAVIDSON COLLEGE
Davidson, NC 28036

DUKE UNIVERSITY
Durham, NC 27708-0555

EAST CAROLINA UNIVERSITY
Greenville, NC 27858-4353

EAST TENNESSEE STATE UNIV.
Johnson City, TN 37614

EASTERN KENTUCKY UNIVERSITY
Richmond, KY 40475-3101

FLORIDA A&M UNIVERSITY
Tallahassee, FL 32307

FLORIDA INTERNATIONAL UNIV.
Miami, FL 33199

FLORIDA STATE UNIVERSITY
Tallahassee, FL 32306

UNIVERSITY OF FLORIDA
Gainesville, FL 32604

FURMAN UNIVERSITY
Greenville, SC 29613

GEORGIA INSTITUTE OF TECH.
Atlanta, GA 30332

UNIVERSITY OF GEORGIA
Athens, GA 30613

JACKSONVILLE UNIVERSITY
Jacksonville, FL 32211-3394

UNIVERSITY OF KENTUCKY
Lexington, KY 40506-0032

LIBERTY UNIVERSITY
Lynchburg, VA 24506

LOUISIANA STATE UNIVERSITY
Baton Rouge, LA 70803

UNIVERSITY OF LOUISVILLE
Louisville, KY 40292

MARSHALL UNIVERSITY
Huntington, WV 25755

UNIVERSITY OF MARYLAND
College Park, MD 20740

UNIVERSITY OF MEMPHIS
Memphis, TN 38152

UNIVERSITY OF MIAMI
Coral Gables, FL 33124-6710

MIDDLE TENNESSEE STATE UNIV.
Murfreesboro, TN 37132

MISSISSIPPI STATE UNIVERSITY
Mississippi State, MS 39762-5509

UNIVERSITY OF MISSISSIPPI
University, MS 38677

MOREHEAD STATE UNIVERSITY
Morehead, KY 40351-1689

MURRAY STATE UNIVERSITY
Murray, KY 42071-0009

UNIVERSITY OF NEW ORLEANS
New Orleans, LA 70148

UNIVERSITY OF NORTH
CAROLINA
Asheville, NC 28804-3299

UNIVERSITY OF NORTH
CAROLINA
Chapel Hill, NC 27514

UNIVERSITY OF NORTH
CAROLINA
Wilmington, NC 28403-3297

NORTH CAROLINA A&T ST. UNIV.
Greensboro, NC 27411

NORTH CAROLINA STATE UNIV.
Raleigh, NC 27695-7001

OLD DOMINION UNIVERSITY
Norfolk, VA 23529

UNIVERSITY OF RICHMOND
Richmond, VA 23173-1903

SAMFORD UNIVERSITY
Birmingham, AL 35229

UNIVERSITY OF SOUTH ALABAMA
Mobile, AL 36688

SOUTH CAROLINA STATE UNIV.
Orangeburg, SC 29117-0001

UNIVERSITY OF SOUTH CAROLINA
Columbia, SC 29208

UNIVERSITY OF SOUTH FLORIDA
Tampa, FL 33620

SOUTHEASTERN LOUISIANA UNIV.
Hammond, LA 70402

UNIV. OF SOUTHERN MISSISSIPPI
Hattiesburg, MS 39406-5001

TENNESSEE STATE UNIVERSITY
Nashville, TN 37209-1561

TENNESSEE TECHNOLOGICAL
UNIV.
Cookeville, TN 38505-0001

UNIVERSITY OF TENNESSEE
Chattanooga, TN 37403-2598

THE UNIVERSITY OF TENNESSEE
Knoxville, TN 37996

UNIV. OF TENNESSEE at MARTIN
Martin, TN 38238-5021

TROY STATE UNIVERSITY
Troy, AL 36082

TULANE UNIVERSITY
New Orleans, LA 70118

VANDERBILT UNIVERSITY
Nashville, TN 37212

VIRGINIA COMMONWEALTH UNIV.
Richmond, VA 23284-2003

VIRGINIA POLYTECHNIC
INSTITUTE
Blacksburg, VA 24061

UNIVERSITY OF VIRGINIA
Charlottesville, VA 22903

WAKE FOREST UNIVERSITY
Winston-Salem, NC 27109

WESTERN CAROLINA UNIVERSITY
Cullowhee, NC 28723

WESTERN KENTUCKY
UNIVERSITY
Bowling Green, KY 42101-3576

District 4

UNIVERSITY OF AKRON
Akron, OH 44325

BALL STATE UNIVERSITY
Muncie, IN 47306

BOWLING GREEN STATE UNIV.
Bowling Green, OH 43403

BUTLER UNIVERSITY
Indianapolis, IN 46208

CENTRAL MICHIGAN UNIVERSITY
Mount Pleasant, MI 48859

CHICAGO STATE UNIVERSITY
Chicago, IL 60628-1598

UNIVERSITY OF CINCINNATI
Cincinnati, OH 45221

UNIVERSITY OF DAYTON
Dayton, OH 45469

DE PAUL UNIVERSITY
Chicago, IL 60604-2287

UNIVERSITY OF DETROIT-MERCY
Detroit, MI 48219-0900

EASTERN ILLINOIS UNIVERSITY
Charleston, IL 61920-3099

EASTERN MICHIGAN UNIVERSITY
Ypsilanti, MI 48197

ILLINOIS STATE UNIVERSITY
Normal, IL 61761

UNIVERSITY OF ILLINOIS
Champaign, IL 61820

INDIANA UNIVERSITY
Bloomington, IN 47405

UNIVERSITY OF IOWA
Iowa City, IA 52242

KENT STATE UNIVERSITY
Kent, OH 44242

LOYOLA UNIVERSITY
Chicago, IL 60626

MARQUETTE UNIVERSITY
Milwaukee, WI 53201-1881

MIAMI UNIVERSITY
Oxford, OH 45056

MICHIGAN STATE UNIVERSITY
East Lansing, MI 48824

UNIVERSITY OF MICHIGAN
Ann Arbor, MI 48109-2201

UNIV. OF MINNESOTA-TWIN
CITIES
Minneapolis, MN 55455

UNIVERSITY OF NOTRE DAME
Notre Dame, IN 46556

OHIO STATE UNIVERSITY
Columbus, OH 43210

OHIO UNIVERSITY
Athens, OH 45701

PURDUE UNIVERSITY
West Lafayette, IN 47907

UNIVERSITY OF TOLEDO
Toledo, OH 43606

VALPARAISO UNIVERSITY
Valparaiso, IN 46383-6493

WESTERN ILLINOIS UNIVERSITY
Macomb, IL 61455

WESTERN MICHIGAN UNIVERSITY
Kalamazoo, MI 49008-5134

UNIVERSITY OF WISCONSIN
Madison, WI 53711

UNIVERSITY OF WISCONSIN
Milwaukee, WI 53201

YOUNGSTOWN STATE
UNIVERSITY
Youngstown, OH 44555-0001

District 5

BRADLEY UNIVERSITY
Peoria, IL 61625

UNIVERSITY OF COLORADO
Boulder, CO 80309

DRAKE UNIVERSITY
Des Moines, IA 50311-4505

INDIANA STATE UNIVERSITY
Terre Haute, IN 47809

IOWA STATE UNIVERSITY
Ames, IA 50011

KANSAS STATE UNIVERSITY
Manhattan, KS 66506

UNIVERSITY OF KANSAS
Lawrence, KS 66045

UNIVERSITY OF MISSOURI-
COLUMBIA
Columbia, MO 65211

UNIVERSITY OF NEBRASKA
Lincoln, NE 68588

UNIVERSITY OF NORTHERN IOWA
Cedar Falls, IA 50614

OKLAHOMA STATE UNIVERSITY
Stillwater, OK 74078

UNIVERSITY OF OKLAHOMA
Norman, OK 73019

ORAL ROBERTS UNIVERSITY
Tulsa, OK 74171

SOUTHEAST MISSOURI STATE
UNIV.
Cape Girardeau, MO 63701-4799

SOUTHERN ILLINOIS UNIVERSITY
Carbondale,·IL 62901

SOUTHWEST MISSOURI STATE
UNIV.
Springfield, MO 65804

UNIVERSITY OF TULSA
Tulsa, OK 74104

WICHITA STATE UNIVERSITY
Wichita, KS 67260

District 6

ALCORN STATE UNIVERSITY
Lorman, MS 39096-9402

ARKANSAS STATE UNIVERSITY
State University, AR 72467

UNIVERSITY OF ARKANSAS
Fayetteville, AR 72701

UNIVERSITY OF ARKANSAS
Little Rock, AR 72204-1099

BAYLOR UNIVERSITY
Waco, TX 76798

GRAMBLING STATE UNIVERSITY
Grambling, LA 71245

UNIVERSITY OF HOUSTON
Houston, TX 77204

JACKSON STATE UNIVERSITY
Jackson, MS 39217

LAMAR UNIVERSITY
Beaumont, TX 77710

LOUISIANA TECH UNIVERSITY
Ruston, LA 71272

MCNEESE STATE UNIVERSITY
Lake Charles, LA 70609

MISSISSIPPI VALLEY ST. UNIV.
Itta Bena, MS 38941-1400

NICHOLLS STATE UNIVERSITY
Thibodaux, LA 70310

UNIVERSITY OF NORTH TEXAS
Denton, TX 76203-6737

NORTHEAST LOUISIANA
UNIVERSITY
Monroe, LA 71209-3000

NORTHWESTERN STATE
UNIVERSITY
Natchitoches, LA 71497-0003

PRAIRIE VIEW A&M UNIVERSITY
Prairie View, TX 77446

RICE UNIVERSITY
Houston, TX 77251

SAM HOUSTON STATE
UNIVERSITY
Huntsville, TX 77341

SOUTHERN METHODIST
UNIVERSITY
Dallas, TX 75275

SOUTHERN UNIVERSITY
Baton Rouge, LA 70813

SOUTHWEST TEXAS STATE UNIV.
San Marcos, TX 78666-4615

UNIV. OF SOUTHWESTERN LA.
Lafayette, LA 70504-1008

STEPHEN F. AUSTIN STATE UNIV.
Nacogdoches, TX 75962

UNIVERSITY OF TEXAS
Arlington, TX 76019

UNIVERSITY OF TEXAS
Austin, TX 78712

UNIVERSITY OF TEXAS
San Antonio, TX 78249

TEXAS A&M UNIVERSITY
College Station, TX 77843-1228

TEXAS CHRISTIAN UNIVERSITY
Fort Worth, TX 76129-0001

UNIV. OF TEXAS-PAN AMERICAN
Edinburg, TX 78539-2999

TEXAS SOUTHERN UNIVERSITY
Houston, TX 77004

TEXAS TECH UNIVERSITY
Lubbock, TX 79409

District 7

BOISE STATE UNIVERSITY
Boise, ID 83725

BRIGHAM YOUNG UNIVERSITY
Provo, UT 84602

CALIF. STATE UNIV.-FRESNO
Fresno, CA 93740-0048

COLORADO STATE UNIVERSITY
Fort Collins, CO 80523-0100

IDAHO STATE UNIVERSITY
Pocatello, ID 83209

UNIVERSITY OF IDAHO
Moscow, ID 83843

MONTANA STATE UNIV-BOZEMAN
Bozeman, MT 59717-0338

THE UNIVERSITY OF MONTANA
Missoula, MT 59812-1291

UNIVERSITY OF NEVADA
Reno, NV 89557

UNIVERSITY OF NEW MEXICO
Albuquerque, NM 87131

NORTHERN ARIZONA UNIVERSITY
Flagstaff, AZ 86011

SOUTHERN UTAH UNIVERSITY
Cedar City, UT 84720

UNIVERSITY OF TEXAS-EL PASO
El Paso, TX 79968

UNIVERSITY OF UTAH
Salt Lake City, UT 84112

WEBER STATE UNIVERSITY
Ogden, UT 84408-2701

UNIVERSITY OF WYOMING
Laramie, WY 82071

District 8

ARIZONA STATE UNIVERSITY
Tempe, AZ 85287-2505

UNIVERSITY OF ARIZONA
Tucson, AZ 85721

UNIV. OF CALIFORNIA-BERKELEY
Berkeley, CA 94720

UNIV. OF CALIF.-LOS ANGELES
Los Angeles, CA 90095-1405

CALIF. STATE UNIV.-NORTHRIDGE
Northridge, CA 91330

CALIF. STATE UNIV.-SACRAMENTO
Sacramento, CA 95819

EASTERN WASHINGTON
UNIVERSITY
Cheney, WA 99004

UNIVERSITY OF NEVADA
Las Vegas, NV 89154

UNIVERSITY OF OREGON
Eugene, OR 87403-1226

UNIVERSITY OF PORTLAND
Portland, OR 97203-5798

STANFORD UNIVERSITY
Stanford, CA 94305

UTAH STATE UNIVERSITY
Logan, UT 84322-7400

WASHINGTON STATE UNIVERSITY
Pullman, WA 99164

UNIVERSITY OF WASHINGTON
Seattle, WA 98195

NCAA PROVISIONAL MEMBERS
District 6

UNIV. OF ARKANSAS-PINE BLUFF
Pine Bluff, AR 71601

DIVISION II
District 1

BENTLEY COLLEGE
Waltham, MA 02154-4705

BRYANT COLLEGE
Smithfield, RI 02917-1284

KEENE STATE COLLEGE
Keene, NH 03431-4183

UNIV. OF MASSACHUSETTS-
LOWELL
Lowell, MA 01854

SACRED HEART UNIVERSITY
Fairfield, CT 06432-1000

SOUTHERN CONNECTICUT ST.
UNIV.
New Haven, CT 06515

STONEHILL COLLEGE
North Easton, MA 02357

District 2

STATE UNIV. OF N.Y. AT ALBANY
Albany, NY 12222

CHEYNEY UNIVERSITY
Cheyney, PA 19319

EAST STROUDSBURG UNIVERSITY
East Stroudsburg, PA 18301

EDINBORO UNIVERSITY
Edinboro, PA 16444-0001

INDIANA UNIV. OF PENNSYLVANIA
Indiana, PA 15705

KUTZTOWN UNIVERSITY
Kutztown, PA 19530-0721

LOCK HAVEN UNIVERSITY
Lock Haven, PA 17745

LONG ISLAND U./C.W. POST
CAMPUS
Brookville, NY 11548

MANSFIELD UNIVERSITY
Mansfield, PA 16933

MILLERSVILLE UNIVERSITY
Millersville, PA 17551-0302

NEW YORK INSTITUTE OF TECH.
Old Westbury, NY 11568-8000

PACE UNIVERSITY
New York, NY 10038-1502

UNIVERSITY OF PITTSBURGH
Johnstown, PA 15904-2990

QUEENS COLLEGE (NY)
Flushing, NY 11367

SHIPPENSBURG UNIVERSITY
Shippensburg, PA 17257

SLIPPERY ROCK UNIVERSITY
Slippery Rock, PA 16057

THE COLLEGE OF ST. ROSE
Albany, NY 12203

STATE UNIV. OF N.Y. at STONY
BROOK
Stony Brook, NY 11794

WEST CHESTER UNIVERSITY
West Chester, PA 19383

District 3

ALABAMA A&M UNIVERSITY
Normal, AL 35762

BOWIE STATE UNIVERSITY
Bowie, MD 20715-9465

ELIZABETH CITY STATE UNIV.
Elizabeth City, NC 27909

KENTUCKY STATE UNIVERSITY
Frankfort, KY 40601

LANE COLLEGE
Jackson, TN 38301

MISSISSIPPI COLLEGE
Clinton, MS 39058

MORRIS BROWN COLLEGE
Atlanta, GA 30314

NORFOLK STATE UNIVERSITY
Norfolk, VA 23504

NORTH CAROLINA CENTRAL
UNIV.
Durham, NC 27707

UNIVERSITY OF NORTH FLORIDA
Jacksonville, FL 32224-2645

SHAW UNIVERSITY
Raleigh, NC 27611

ST. AUGUSTINE'S COLLEGE
Raleigh, NC 27610

ST. PAUL'S COLLEGE
Lawrenceville, VA 23868

VIRGINIA STATE UNIVERSITY
Petersburg, VA 23806

District 4

ASHLAND UNIVERSITY
Ashland, OH 44805

BEMIDJI STATE UNIVERSITY
Bemidji, MN 56601-2699

FERRIS STATE UNIVERSITY
Big Rapids, MI 49307-2295

GRAND VALLEY STATE
UNIVERSITY
Allendale, MI 49401

HILLSDALE COLLEGE
Hillsdale, MI 49242-1298

UNIVERSITY OF INDIANAPOLIS
Indianapolis, IN 46227

LAKE SUPERIOR STATE UNIV.
Sault Sainte Marie, MI 49783

LEWIS UNIVERSITY
Romeoville, IL 60441

UNIV. OF MINNESOTA-DULUTH
Duluth, MN 55812

UNIV. OF MINNESOTA-MORRIS
Morris, MN 56267

MOORHEAD STATE UNIVERSITY
Moorhead, MN 56563-2996

NORTHWOOD UNIVERSITY
Midland, MI 48640

SAGINAW VALLEY STATE UNIV.
University Center, MI 48710

SOUTHERN ILLINOIS UNIVERSITY
Edwardsville, IL 62026

UNIV. OF SOUTHERN INDIANA
Evansville, IN 47712

SAINT JOSEPH'S COLLEGE
Rensselaer, IN 47978

WINONA STATE UNIVERSITY
Winona, MN 55987-5838

UNIV. OF WISCONSIN-PARKSIDE
Kenosha, WI 53141-2000

District 5

AUGUSTANA COLLEGE
Sioux Falls, SD 57197

CENTRAL MISSOURI STATE UNIV.
Warrensburg, MO 64093

CHADRON STATE COLLEGE
Chadron, NE 69337

EMPORIA STATE UNIVERSITY
Emporia, KS 66801-5087

LINCOLN UNIVERSITY
Jefferson City, MO 65102-0029

MANKATO STATE UNIVERSITY
Mankato, MN 56002-8400

MISSOURI SOUTHERN ST.
COLLEGE
Joplin, MO 64801-1595

UNIVERSITY OF MISSOURI
Rolla, MO 65401

MORNINGSIDE COLLEGE
Sioux City, IA 51106-1751

UNIV. OF NEBRASKA at KEARNEY
Kearney, NE 68849

UNIV. OF NEBRAKSA at OMAHA
Omaha, NE 68182

NORTH DAKOTA STATE
UNIVERSITY
Fargo, ND 58105

UNIVERSITY OF NORTH DAKOTA
Grand Forks, ND 58202

NORTHEAST MISSOURI STATE
UNIV.
Kirksville, MO 63501

UNIV. OF NORTHERN COLORADO
Greeley, CO 80639

NORTHERN STATE UNIVERSITY
Aberdeen, SD 57401

NORTHWEST MISSOURI STATE
UNIV.
Maryville, MO 64468-6001

PITTSBURG STATE UNIVERSITY
Pittsburg, KS 66762

SOUTH DAKOTA STATE
UNIVERSITY
Brookings, SD 57007

UNIVERSITY OF SOUTH DAKOTA
Vermillion, SD 57069-2390

SOUTHWEST BAPTIST
UNIVERSITY
Bolivar, MO 65613

ST. CLOUD STATE UNIVERSITY
St. Cloud, MN 56301-4498

WAYNE STATE COLLEGE
Wayne, NE 68787-1172

District 6

ABILENE CHRISTIAN UNIVERSITY
Abilene, TX 79699

UNIVERSITY OF CENTRAL
OKLAHOMA
Edmond, OK 73034

District 7

ADAMS STATE COLLEGE
Alamosa, CO 81102

COLORADO SCHOOL OF MINES
Golden, CO 80401

FORT HAYS STATE UNIVERSITY
Hays, KS 67601

GRAND CANYON UNIVERSITY
Phoenix, AZ 85017

U.S. AIR FORCE ACADEMY
USAF Academy, CO 80840-5461

WESTERN STATE COLLEGE
Gunnison, CO 81231

District 8

UNIV. OF CALIFORNIA-DAVIS
Davis, CA 95616

UNIV. OF CALIFORNIA-RIVERSIDE
Riverside, CA 92521

CALIF. STATE UNIV.-BAKERSFIELD
Bakersfield, CA 93311-1099

CALIF. STATE UNIV.-LOS ANGELES
Los Angeles, CA 90032-8240

PORTLAND STATE UNIVERSITY
Portland, OR 97207-0751

SEATTLE PACIFIC UNIVERSITY
Seattle, WA 98119

NCAA PROVISIONAL MEMBERS
District 2

UNIVERSITY OF VIRGIN ISLANDS
St. Thomas, VI 00802

District 3

COLUMBIA UNION COLLEGE
Takoma Park, MD 20912

District 6

HARDING UNIVERSITY
Searcy, AR 72149-0001

WOMEN'S TRACK, OUTDOOR

DIVISION I
District 1

BOSTON COLLEGE
Chestnut Hill, MA 02167-3934

BOSTON UNIVERSITY
Boston, MA 02215

BROWN UNIVERSITY
Providence, RI 02912

CENTRAL CONN. STATE UNIV.
New Britain, CT 06050-4010

UNIVERSITY OF CONNECTICUT
Storrs, CT 06269

DARTMOUTH COLLEGE
Hanover, NH 03755

UNIVERSITY OF HARTFORD
West Hartford, CT 06117-1599

HARVARD UNIVERSITY
Cambridge, MA 02138-3800

COLLEGE OF THE HOLY CROSS
Worcester, MA 01610-2395

UNIVERSITY OF MAINE
Orono, ME 04469

UNIVERSITY OF MASSACHUSETTS
Amherst, MA 01003

UNIVERSITY OF NEW HAMPSHIRE
Durham, NH 03824

NORTHEASTERN UNIVERSITY
Boston, MA 02115-5096

PROVIDENCE COLLEGE
Providence, RI 02918

UNIVERSITY OF RHODE ISLAND
Kingston, RI 02881

UNIVERSITY OF VERMONT
Burlington, VT 05405

YALE UNIVERSITY
New Haven, CT 06520-7398

District 2

BUCKNELL UNIVERSITY
Lewisburg, PA 17837

STATE UNIV. OF N.Y. at BUFFALO
Buffalo, NY 14260

CANISIUS COLLEGE
Buffalo, NY 14208-1098

COLGATE UNIVERSITY
Hamilton, NY 13346-1304

COLUMBIA UNIV.-BARNARD
COLLEGE
New York, NY 10027

CORNELL UNIVERSITY
Ithaca, NY 14853

DELAWARE STATE UNIVERSITY
Dover, DE 19901

UNIVERSITY OF DELAWARE
Newark, DE 19716

DUQUESNE UNIVERSITY
Pittsburgh, PA 15282

FAIRLEIGH DICKINSON-TEANECK
Teaneck, NJ 07666

FORDHAM UNIVERSITY
Bronx, NY 10458-5155

GEORGE MASON UNIVERSITY
Fairfax, VA 22030

GEORGETOWN UNIVERSITY
Washington, DC 20057

HAMPTON UNIVERSITY
Hampton, VA 23668

HOWARD UNIVERSITY
Washington, DC 20059

JAMES MADISON UNIVERSITY
Harrisonburg, VA 22807

LA SALLE UNIVERSITY
Philadelphia, PA 19141-1199

LAFAYETTE COLLEGE
Easton, PA 18042

LEHIGH UNIVERSITY
Bethlehem, PA 18015-3089

LONG ISLAND UNIV.-BROOKLYN
Brooklyn, NY 11201

MANHATTAN COLLEGE
Riverdale, NY 10471

MARIST COLLEGE
Poughkeepsie, NY 12601-1387

UNIV. OF MARYLAND-BALT. CO.
Baltimore, MD 21228-5398

U. OF MARYLAND-EASTERN
SHORE
Princess Anne, MD 21853-1299

MONMOUTH UNIVERSITY
West Long Branch, NJ 07764

MORGAN STATE UNIVERSITY
Baltimore, MD 21239

MOUNT ST. MARY'S COLLEGE
Emmitsburg, MD 21727-7799

PENNSYLVANIA STATE UNIV.
University Park, PA 16802

UNIVERSITY OF PENNSYLVANIA
Philadelphia, PA 19104-6380

UNIVERSITY OF PITTSBURGH
Pittsburgh, PA 15260

PRINCETON UNIVERSITY
Princeton, NJ 08544

RIDER UNIVERSITY
Lawrenceville, NJ 08648-3099

ROBERT MORRIS COLLEGE
Coraopolis, PA 15108-1189

RUTGERS UNIVERSITY
New Brunswick, NJ 08903

SETON HALL UNIVERSITY
South Orange, NJ 07079

ST. FRANCIS COLLEGE
Brooklyn Heights, NY 11201

ST. FRANCIS COLLEGE
Loretto, PA 15940-0600

ST. JOHN'S UNIVERSITY
Jamaica, NY 11439

ST. JOSEPH'S UNIVERSITY
Philadelphia, PA 19131-1395

ST. PETER'S COLLEGE
Jersey City, NJ 07306

SYRACUSE UNIVERSITY
Syracuse, NY 13244

TEMPLE UNIVERSITY
Philadelphia, PA 19122

TOWSON STATE UNIVERSITY
Towson, MD 21204

U.S. MILITARY ACADEMY
West Point, NY 10996

U.S. NAVAL ACADEMY
Annapolis, MD 21402

VILLANOVA UNIVERSITY
Villanova, PA 19085

WAGNER COLLEGE
Staten Island, NY 10301-4495

WEST VIRGINIA UNIVERSITY
Morgantown, WV 26505-6201

COLLEGE OF WILLIAM & MARY
Williamsburg, VA 23187

District 3

ALABAMA STATE UNIVERSITY
Montgomery, AL 36101-0271

UNIV. OF ALABAMA at
TUSCALOOSA
Tuscaloosa, AL 35487

UNIV. OF ALABAMA at
BIRMINGHAM
Birmingham, AL 35294-0110

APPALACHIAN STATE UNIVERSITY
Boone, NC 28608

AUBURN UNIVERSITY
Auburn University, AL 36849-5113

AUSTIN PEAY STATE UNIVERSITY
Clarksville, TN 37044-4576

BETHUNE-COOKMAN COLLEGE
Daytona Beach, FL 32114-3099

CAMPBELL UNIVERSITY
Buies Creek, NC 27506

UNIVERSITY OF CENTRAL
FLORIDA
Orlando, FL 32816-0002

CHARLESTON SOUTHERN UNIV.
Charleston, SC 29423-8087

CLEMSON UNIVERSITY
Clemson, SC 29634-000

COASTAL CAROLINA UNIVERSITY
Conway, SC 29526

COPPIN STATE COLLEGE
Baltimore, MD 21216

DAVIDSON COLLEGE
Davidson, NC 28036

DUKE UNIVERSITY
Durham, NC 27708-0555

EAST CAROLINA UNIVERSITY
Greenville, NC 27858-4353

EAST TENNESSEE STATE UNIV.
Johnson City, TN 37614

EASTERN KENTUCKY UNIVERSITY
Richmond, KY 40475-3101

FLORIDA A&M UNIVERSITY
Tallahassee, FL 32307

FLORIDA INTERNATIONAL UNIV.
Miami, FL 33199

FLORIDA STATE UNIVERSITY
Tallahassee, FL 32306

UNIVERSITY OF FLORIDA
Gainesville, FL 32604

FURMAN UNIVERSITY
Greenville, SC 29613

GEORGIA INSTITUTE OF TECH.
Atlanta, GA 30332

UNIVERSITY OF GEORGIA
Athens, GA 30613

JACKSONVILLE UNIVERSITY
Jacksonville, FL 32211-3394

UNIVERSITY OF KENTUCKY
Lexington, KY 40506-0032

LIBERTY UNIVERSITY
Lynchburg, VA 24506

LOUISIANA STATE UNIVERSITY
Baton Rouge, LA 70803

UNIVERSITY OF LOUISVILLE
Louisville, KY 40292

MARSHALL UNIVERSITY
Huntington, WV 25755

UNIVERSITY OF MARYLAND
College Park, MD 20740

UNIVERSITY OF MEMPHIS
Memphis, TN 38152

UNIVERSITY OF MIAMI
Coral Gables, FL 33124-6710

MIDDLE TENNESSEE STATE UNIV.
Murfreesboro, TN 37132

MISSISSIPPI STATE UNIVERSITY
Mississippi State, MS 39762-5509

UNIVERSITY OF MISSISSIPPI
University, MS 38677

MURRAY STATE UNIVERSITY
Murray, KY 42071-0009

UNIVERSITY OF NEW ORLEANS
New Orleans, LA 70148

UNIVERSITY OF NORTH CAROLINA
Asheville, NC 28804-3299

UNIVERSITY OF NORTH CAROLINA
Chapel Hill, NC 27514

UNIVERSITY OF NORTH CAROLINA
Charlotte, NC 28223

UNIVERSITY OF NORTH CAROLINA
Wilmington, NC 28403-3297

NORTH CAROLINA A&T ST. UNIV.
Greensboro, NC 27411

NORTH CAROLINA STATE UNIV.
Raleigh, NC 27695-7001

OLD DOMINION UNIVERSITY
Norfolk, VA 23529

UNIVERSITY OF RICHMOND
Richmond, VA 23173-1903

SAMFORD UNIVERSITY
Birmingham, AL 35229

UNIVERSITY OF SOUTH ALABAMA
Mobile, AL 36688

SOUTH CAROLINA STATE UNIV.
Orangeburg, SC 29117-0001

UNIVERSITY OF SOUTH CAROLINA
Columbia, SC 29208

UNIVERSITY OF SOUTH FLORIDA
Tampa, FL 33620

SOUTHEASTERN LOUISIANA UNIV.
Hammond, LA 70402

UNIV. OF SOUTHERN MISSISSIPPI
Hattiesburg, MS 39406-5001

TENNESSEE STATE UNIVERSITY
Nashville, TN 37209-1561

TENNESSEE TECHNOLOGICAL UNIV.
Cookeville, TN 38505-0001

UNIVERSITY OF TENNESSEE
Chattanooga, TN 37403-2598

THE UNIVERSITY OF TENNESSEE
Knoxville, TN 37996

UNIV. OF TENNESSEE at MARTIN
Martin, TN 38238-5021

TROY STATE UNIVERSITY
Troy, AL 36082

TULANE UNIVERSITY
New Orleans, LA 70118

VANDERBILT UNIVERSITY
Nashville, TN 37212

VIRGINIA COMMONWEALTH UNIV.
Richmond, VA 23284-2003

VIRGINIA POLYTECHNIC INSTITUTE
Blacksburg, VA 24061

UNIVERSITY OF VIRGINIA
Charlottesville, VA 22903

WAKE FOREST UNIVERSITY
Winston-Salem, NC 27109

WESTERN CAROLINA UNIVERSITY
Cullowhee, NC 28723

WESTERN KENTUCKY UNIVERSITY
Bowling Green, KY 42101-3576

WINTHROP UNIVERSITY
Rock Hill, SC 29733

WOFFORD COLLEGE
Spartanburg, SC 29303-3663

District 4

UNIVERSITY OF AKRON
Akron, OH 44325

BALL STATE UNIVERSITY
Muncie, IN 47306

BOWLING GREEN STATE UNIV.
Bowling Green, OH 43403

BUTLER UNIVERSITY
Indianapolis, IN 46208

CENTRAL MICHIGAN UNIVERSITY
Mount Pleasant, MI 48859

CHICAGO STATE UNIVERSITY
Chicago, IL 60628-1598

UNIVERSITY OF CINCINNATI
Cincinnati, OH 45221

CLEVELAND STATE UNIVERSITY
Cleveland, OH 44115

UNIVERSITY OF DAYTON
Dayton, OH 45469

DE PAUL UNIVERSITY
Chicago, IL 60604-2287

UNIVERSITY OF DETROIT-MERCY
Detroit, MI 48219-0900

EASTERN ILLINOIS UNIVERSITY
Charleston, IL 61920-3099

EASTERN MICHIGAN UNIVERSITY
Ypsilanti, MI 48197

ILLINOIS STATE UNIVERSITY
Normal, IL 61761

UNIVERSITY OF ILLINOIS
Champaign, IL 61820

INDIANA UNIVERSITY
Bloomington, IN 47405

UNIVERSITY OF IOWA
Iowa City, IA 52242

KENT STATE UNIVERSITY
Kent, OH 44242

LOYOLA UNIVERSITY
Chicago, IL 60626

MARQUETTE UNIVERSITY
Milwaukee, WI 53201-1881

MIAMI UNIVERSITY
Oxford, OH 45056

MICHIGAN STATE UNIVERSITY
East Lansing, MI 48824

UNIVERSITY OF MICHIGAN
Ann Arbor, MI 48109-2201

UNIV. OF MINNESOTA-TWIN
CITIES
Minneapolis, MN 55455

UNIVERSITY OF NOTRE DAME
Notre Dame, IN 46556

OHIO STATE UNIVERSITY
Columbus, OH 43210

OHIO UNIVERSITY
Athens, OH 45701

PURDUE UNIVERSITY
West Lafayette, IN 47907

UNIVERSITY OF TOLEDO
Toledo, OH 43606

VALPARAISO UNIVERSITY
Valparaiso, IN 46383-6493

WESTERN ILLINOIS UNIVERSITY
Macomb, IL 61455

WESTERN MICHIGAN UNIVERSITY
Kalamazoo, MI 49008-5134

UNIVERSITY OF WISCONSIN
Madison, WI 53711

UNIVERSITY OF WISCONSIN
Milwaukee, WI 53201

YOUNGSTOWN STATE
UNIVERSITY
Youngstown, OH 44555-0001

District 5

BRADLEY UNIVERSITY
Peoria, IL 61625

UNIVERSITY OF COLORADO
Boulder, CO 80309

DRAKE UNIVERSITY
Des Moines, IA 50311-4505

INDIANA STATE UNIVERSITY
Terre Haute, IN 47809

IOWA STATE UNIVERSITY
Ames, IA 50011

KANSAS STATE UNIVERSITY
Manhattan, KS 66506

UNIVERSITY OF KANSAS
Lawrence, KS 66045

UNIVERSITY OF MISSOURI-
COLUMBIA
Columbia, MO 65211

UNIV. OF MISSOURI-KANSAS CITY
Kansas City, MO 64110

UNIVERSITY OF NEBRASKA
Lincoln, NE 68588

UNIVERSITY OF NORTHERN IOWA
Cedar Falls, IA 50614

OKLAHOMA STATE UNIVERSITY
Stillwater, OK 74078

UNIVERSITY OF OKLAHOMA
Norman, OK 73019

ORAL ROBERTS UNIVERSITY
Tulsa, OK 74171

SOUTHEAST MISSOURI STATE
UNIV.
Cape Girardeau, MO 63701-4799

SOUTHERN ILLINOIS UNIVERSITY
Carbondale, IL 62901

SOUTHWEST MISSOURI STATE
UNIV.
Springfield, MO 65804

UNIVERSITY OF TULSA
Tulsa, OK 74104

WICHITA STATE UNIVERSITY
Wichita, KS 67260

District 6

ALCORN STATE UNIVERSITY
Lorman, MS 39096-9402

ARKANSAS STATE UNIVERSITY
State University, AR 72467

UNIVERSITY OF ARKANSAS
Fayetteville, AR 72701

UNIVERSITY OF ARKANSAS
Little Rock, AR 72204-1099

BAYLOR UNIVERSITY
Waco, TX 76798

GRAMBLING STATE UNIVERSITY
Grambling, LA 71245

UNIVERSITY OF HOUSTON
Houston, TX 77204

JACKSON STATE UNIVERSITY
Jackson, MS 39217

LAMAR UNIVERSITY
Beaumont, TX 77710

LOUISIANA TECH UNIVERSITY
Ruston, LA 71272

MCNEESE STATE UNIVERSITY
Lake Charles, LA 70609

MISSISSIPPI VALLEY ST. UNIV.
Itta Bena, MS 38941-1400

NICHOLLS STATE UNIVERSITY
Thibodaux, LA 70310

UNIVERSITY OF NORTH TEXAS
Denton, TX 76203-6737

NORTHEAST LOUISIANA
UNIVERSITY
Monroe, LA 71209-3000

NORTHWESTERN STATE
UNIVERSITY
Natchitoches, LA 71497-0003

PRAIRIE VIEW A&M UNIVERSITY
Prairie View, TX 77446

RICE UNIVERSITY
Houston, TX 77251

SAM HOUSTON STATE
UNIVERSITY
Huntsville, TX 77341

SOUTHERN METHODIST
UNIVERSITY
Dallas, TX 75275

SOUTHERN UNIVERSITY
Baton Rouge, LA 70813

SOUTHWEST TEXAS STATE UNIV.
San Marcos, TX 78666-4615

UNIV. OF SOUTHWESTERN LA.
Lafayette, LA 70504-1008

STEPHEN F. AUSTIN STATE UNIV.
Nacogdoches, TX 75962

UNIVERSITY OF TEXAS
Arlington, TX 76019.

UNIVERSITY OF TEXAS
Austin, TX 78712

UNIVERSITY OF TEXAS
San Antonio, TX 78249

TEXAS A&M UNIVERSITY
College Station, TX 77843-1228

TEXAS CHRISTIAN UNIVERSITY
Fort Worth, TX 76129-0001

UNIV. OF TEXAS-PAN AMERICAN
Edinburg, TX 78539-2999

TEXAS SOUTHERN UNIVERSITY
Houston, TX 77004

TEXAS TECH UNIVERSITY
Lubbock, TX 79409

District 7

BOISE STATE UNIVERSITY
Boise, ID 83725

BRIGHAM YOUNG UNIVERSITY
Provo, UT 84602

CALIF. STATE UNIV.-FRESNO
Fresno, CA 93740-0048

COLORADO STATE UNIVERSITY
Fort Collins, CO 80523-0100

IDAHO STATE UNIVERSITY
Pocatello, ID 83209

UNIVERSITY OF IDAHO
Moscow, ID 83843

MONTANA STATE UNIV-BOZEMAN
Bozeman, MT 59717-0338

THE UNIVERSITY OF MONTANA
Missoula, MT 59812-1291

UNIVERSITY OF NEVADA
Reno, NV 89557

UNIVERSITY OF NEW MEXICO
Albuquerque, NM 87131

NORTHERN ARIZONA UNIVERSITY
Flagstaff, AZ 86011

SAN DIEGO STATE UNIVERSITY
San Diego, CA 92182

SOUTHERN UTAH UNIVERSITY
Cedar City, UT 84720

UNIVERSITY OF TEXAS-EL PASO
El Paso, TX 79968

UNIVERSITY OF UTAH
Salt Lake City, UT 84112

WEBER STATE UNIVERSITY
Ogden, UT 84408-2701

UNIVERSITY OF WYOMING
Laramie, WY 82071

District 8

ARIZONA STATE UNIVERSITY
Tempe, AZ 85287-2505

UNIVERSITY OF ARIZONA
Tucson, AZ 85721

UNIV. OF CALIFORNIA-BERKELEY
Berkeley, CA 94720

UNIV. OF CALIF.-LOS ANGELES
Los Angeles, CA 90095-1405

UNIV. OF CALIF-SANTA BARBARA
Santa Barbara, CA 93106

UNIV. OF CALIFORNIA-IRVINE
Irvine, CA 92717

CALIF. POLYTECHNIC STATE UNIV.
San Luis Obispo, CA 93407

CALIF. STATE UNIV.-FULLERTON
Fullerton, CA 92634-9480

CALIF. STATE UNIV.-NORTHRIDGE
Northridge, CA 91330

CALIF. STATE UNIV.-SACRAMENTO
Sacramento, CA 95819

EASTERN WASHINGTON
UNIVERSITY
Cheney, WA 99004

LONG BEACH STATE UNIVERSITY
Long Beach, CA 90840-0118

UNIVERSITY OF NEVADA
Las Vegas, NV 89154

NEW MEXICO STATE UNIVERSITY
Las Cruces, NM 88003

UNIVERSITY OF OREGON
Eugene, OR 87403-1226

UNIVERSITY OF PORTLAND
Portland, OR 97203-5798

UNIV. OF SOUTHERN CALIFORNIA
Los Angeles, CA 90089-0012

STANFORD UNIVERSITY
Stanford, CA 94305

UTAH STATE UNIVERSITY
Logan, UT 84322-7400

WASHINGTON STATE UNIVERSITY
Pullman, WA 99164

UNIVERSITY OF WASHINGTON
Seattle, WA 98195

NCAA PROVISIONAL MEMBERS
District 6
UNIV. OF ARKANSAS-PINE BLUFF
Pine Bluff, AR 71601

DIVISION II
District 1
BENTLEY COLLEGE
Waltham, MA 02154-4705

BRYANT COLLEGE
Smithfield, RI 02917-1284

KEENE STATE COLLEGE
Keene, NH 03431-4183

UNIV. OF MASSACHUSETTS-
LOWELL
Lowell, MA 01854

SACRED HEART UNIVERSITY
Fairfield, CT 06432-1000

SOUTHERN CONNECTICUT ST.
UNIV.
New Haven, CT 06515

STONEHILL COLLEGE
North Easton, MA 02357

District 2
STATE UNIV. OF N.Y. AT ALBANY
Albany, NY 12222

AMERICAN UNIV. OF PUERTO RICO
Bayamon, PR 00960-2037

BLOOMSBURG UNIVERSITY
Bloomsburg, PA 17815

CALIFORNIA UNIVERSITY
California, PA 15419

CHEYNEY UNIVERSITY
Cheyney, PA 19319

CLARION UNIVERSITY
Clarion, PA 16214

EAST STROUDSBURG UNIVERSITY
East Stroudsburg, PA 18301

EDINBORO UNIVERSITY
Edinboro, PA 16444-0001

GLENVILLE STATE COLLEGE
Glenville, WV 26351

INDIANA UNIV. OF PENNSYLVANIA
Indiana, PA 15705

KUTZTOWN UNIVERSITY
Kutztown, PA 19530-0721

LOCK HAVEN UNIVERSITY
Lock Haven, PA 17745

LONG ISLAND U./C.W. POST
CAMPUS
Brookville, NY 11548

MANSFIELD UNIVERSITY
Mansfield, PA 16933

MILLERSVILLE UNIVERSITY
Millersville, PA 17551-0302

NEW YORK INSTITUTE OF TECH.
Old Westbury, NY 11568-8000

PACE UNIVERSITY
New York, NY 10038-1502

UNIVERSITY OF PITTSBURGH
Johnstown, PA 15904-2990

QUEENS COLLEGE (NY)
Flushing, NY 11367

SHIPPENSBURG UNIVERSITY
Shippensburg, PA 17257

SLIPPERY ROCK UNIVERSITY
Slippery Rock, PA 16057

THE COLLEGE OF ST. ROSE
Albany, NY 12203

STATE UNIV. OF N.Y. at STONY
BROOK
Stony Brook, NY 11794

WEST CHESTER UNIVERSITY
West Chester, PA 19383

WEST LIBERTY STATE COLLEGE
West Liberty, WV 26074

WEST VIRGINIA WESLEYAN
COLLEGE
Buckhannon, WV 26201

WHEELING JESUIT COLLEGE
Wheeling, WV 26003-6295

District 3

ALABAMA A&M UNIVERSITY
Normal, AL 35762

ALBANY STATE COLLEGE
Albany, GA 31705

BELLARMINE COLLEGE
Louisville, KY 40205-0671

BOWIE STATE UNIVERSITY
Bowie, MD 20715-9465

CARSON-NEWMAN COLLEGE
Jefferson City, TN 37760

CLARK ATLANTA UNIVERSITY
Atlanta, GA 30314

ELIZABETH CITY STATE UNIV.
Elizabeth City, NC 27909

FORT VALLEY STATE COLLEGE
Fort Valley, GA 31030

FRANCIS MARION UNIVERSITY
Florence, SC 29501-0547

JOHNSON C. SMITH UNIVERSITY
Charlotte, NC 28216

KENTUCKY STATE UNIVERSITY
Frankfort, KY 40601

LANE COLLEGE
Jackson, TN 38301

LE MOYNE-OWEN COLLEGE
Memphis, TN 38126

LIVINGSTONE COLLEGE
Salisbury, NC 28144

MILES COLLEGE
Birmingham, AL 35208

MISSISSIPPI COLLEGE
Clinton, MS 39058

MORRIS BROWN COLLEGE
Atlanta, GA 30314

NORFOLK STATE UNIVERSITY
Norfolk, VA 23504

NORTH CAROLINA CENTRAL
UNIV.
Durham, NC 27707

UNIVERSITY OF NORTH FLORIDA
Jacksonville, FL 32224-2645

PAINE COLLEGE
Augusta, GA 30901-3182

PEMBROKE STATE UNIVERSITY
Pembroke, NC 28372-1510

SHAW UNIVERSITY
Raleigh, NC 27611

ST. ANDREWS PRESBYTERIAN
COLL.
Laurinburg, NC 28352-5598

ST. AUGUSTINE'S COLLEGE
Raleigh, NC 27610

ST. PAUL'S COLLEGE
Lawrenceville, VA 23868

VIRGINIA STATE UNIVERSITY
Petersburg, VA 23806

VIRGINIA UNION UNIVERSITY
Richmond, VA 23220-1790

WEST GEORGIA COLLEGE
Carrollton, GA 30118

District 4

ASHLAND UNIVERSITY
Ashland, OH 44805

BEMIDJI STATE UNIVERSITY
Bemidji, MN 56601-2699

FERRIS STATE UNIVERSITY
Big Rapids, MI 49307-2295

GRAND VALLEY STATE
UNIVERSITY
Allendale, MI 49401

HILLSDALE COLLEGE
Hillsdale, MI 49242-1298

UNIVERSITY OF INDIANAPOLIS
Indianapolis, IN 46227

LAKE SUPERIOR STATE UNIV.
Sault Sainte Marie, MI 49783

LEWIS UNIVERSITY
Romeoville, IL 60441

MICHIGAN TECHNOLOGICAL
UNIV.
Houghton, MI 49931-1295

UNIV. OF MINNESOTA-DULUTH
Duluth, MN 55812

UNIV. OF MINNESOTA-MORRIS
Morris, MN 56267

MOORHEAD STATE UNIVERSITY
Moorhead, MN 56563-2996

NORTHWOOD UNIVERSITY
Midland, MI 48640

SAGINAW VALLEY STATE UNIV.
University Center, MI 48710

SOUTHERN ILLINOIS UNIVERSITY
Edwardsville, IL 62026

UNIV. OF SOUTHERN INDIANA
Evansville, IN 47712

SAINT JOSEPH'S COLLEGE
Rensselaer, IN 47978

WINONA STATE UNIVERSITY
Winona, MN 55987-5838

UNIV. OF WISCONSIN-PARKSIDE
Kenosha, WI 53141-2000

District 5

AUGUSTANA COLLEGE
Sioux Falls, SD 57197

CENTRAL MISSOURI STATE UNIV.
Warrensburg, MO 64093

CHADRON STATE COLLEGE
Chadron, NE 69337

EMPORIA STATE UNIVERSITY
Emporia, KS 66801-5087

LINCOLN UNIVERSITY
Jefferson City, MO 65102-0029

MANKATO STATE UNIVERSITY
Mankato, MN 56002-8400

MISSOURI SOUTHERN ST.
COLLEGE
Joplin, MO 64801-1595

UNIVERSITY OF MISSOURI
Rolla, MO 65401

MORNINGSIDE COLLEGE
Sioux City, IA 51106-1751UNIV. OF
NEBRASKA at KEARNEY
Kearney, NE 68849

UNIV. OF NEBRAKSA at OMAHA
Omaha, NE 68182

NORTH DAKOTA STATE
UNIVERSITY
Fargo, ND 58105

UNIVERSITY OF NORTH DAKOTA
Grand Forks, ND 58202

NORTHEAST MISSOURI STATE
UNIV.
Kirksville, MO 63501

UNIV. OF NORTHERN COLORADO
Greeley, CO 80639

NORTHERN STATE UNIVERSITY
Aberdeen, SD 57401

NORTHWEST MISSOURI STATE
UNIV.
Maryville, MO 64468-6001

PITTSBURG STATE UNIVERSITY
Pittsburg, KS 66762

SOUTH DAKOTA STATE
UNIVERSITY
Brookings, SD 57007

UNIVERSITY OF SOUTH DAKOTA
Vermillion, SD 57069-2390

SOUTHWEST BAPTIST
UNIVERSITY
Bolivar, MO 65613

ST. CLOUD STATE UNIVERSITY
St. Cloud, MN 56301-4498

WAYNE STATE COLLEGE
Wayne, NE 68787-1172

District 6

ABILENE CHRISTIAN UNIVERSITY
Abilene, TX 79699

ANGELO STATE UNIVERSITY
San Angelo, TX 76909

UNIVERSITY OF CENTRAL
OKLAHOMA
Edmond, OK 73034

EAST TEXAS STATE UNIVERSITY
Commerce, TX 75429-3011

TARLETON STATE UNIVERSITY
Stephenville, TX 76402

TEXAS A&M UNIV.-KINGSVILLE
Kingsville, TX 78363

District 7

ADAMS STATE COLLEGE
Alamosa, CO 81102

COLORADO SCHOOL OF MINES
Golden, CO 80401

FORT HAYS STATE UNIVERSITY
Hays, KS 67601

GRAND CANYON UNIVERSITY
Phoenix, AZ 85017

U.S. AIR FORCE ACADEMY
USAF Academy, CO 80840-5461

WESTERN STATE COLLEGE
Gunnison, CO 81231

District 8

UNIV. OF CALIFORNIA-DAVIS
Davis, CA 95616

UNIV. OF CALIFORNIA-RIVERSIDE
Riverside, CA 92521

CALIF. STATE POLYTECHNIC UNIV.
Pomona, CA 91768

CALIF. STATE UNIV.-BAKERSFIELD
Bakersfield, CA 93311-1099

CALIF. STATE UNIV.-CHICO
Chico, CA 95929-0300

CALIF. STATE UNIV.-LOS ANGELES
Los Angeles, CA 90032-8240

CALIF. STATE UNIV.-STANISLAUS
Turlock, CA 95382

HUMBOLDT STATE UNIVERSITY
Arcata, CA 95521

COLLEGE OF NOTRE DAME
Belmont, CA 94002-9974

PORTLAND STATE UNIVERSITY
Portland, OR 97207-0751

SAN FRANCISCO STATE UNIV.
San Francisco, CA 94132

SEATTLE PACIFIC UNIVERSITY
Seattle, WA 98119

NCAA PROVISIONAL MEMBERS
District 2

UNIV. OF PUERTO RICO-
MAYAGUEZ
Mayaguez, PR 00709

UNIV. OF PUERTO RICO-BAYAMON
Bayamon, PR 00619-1919

UNIVERSITY OF VIRGIN ISLANDS
St. Thomas, VI 00802

WEST VIRGINIA STATE COLLEGE
Institute, WV 25112-1000

District 3

COLUMBIA UNION COLLEGE
Takoma Park, MD 20912

District 5

LANGSTON UNIVERSITY
Langston, OK 73050

NORTHWESTERN OKLAHOMA
ST. UNIV.
Alva, OK 73717

SOUTHEASTERN OKLA. ST. UNIV.
Durant, OK 74701

SOUTHWESTERN OKLAHOMA ST.
UNIV.
Weatherford, OK 73096

District 6

HARDING UNIVERSITY
Searcy, AR 72149-0001

SOUTHERN ARKANSAS
UNIVERSISTY
Magnolia, AR 71753-5000

District 8

CENTRAL WASHINGTON UNIV.
Ellensburg, WA 98926

WESTERN WASHINGTON UNIV.
Bellingham, WA 98225

WOMEN'S SKIING

DIVISION I

District 1

BOSTON COLLEGE
Chestnut Hill, MA 02167-3934

BROWN UNIVERSITY
Providence, RI 02912

DARTMOUTH COLLEGE
Hanover, NH 03755

HARVARD UNIVERSITY
Cambridge, MA 02138-3800

UNIVERSITY OF MASSACHUSETTS
Amherst, MA 01003

UNIVERSITY OF NEW HAMPSHIRE
Durham, NH 03824

UNIVERSITY OF VERMONT
Burlington, VT 05405

District 4

UNIVERSITY OF WISCONSIN
Green Bay, WI 54311-7001

District 5

UNIVERSITY OF COLORADO
Boulder, CO 80309

District 7

MONTANA STATE UNIV-BOZEMAN
Bozeman, MT 59717-0338

UNIVERSITY OF NEVADA
Reno, NV 89557

UNIVERSITY OF NEW MEXICO
Albuquerque, NM 87131

UNIVERSITY OF UTAH
Salt Lake City, UT 84112

DIVISION II

District 1

ST. ANSELM COLLEGE
Manchester, NH 03102-1310

ST. MICHAEL'S COLLEGE
Colchester, VT 05439

District 4

NORTHERN MICHIGAN
UNIVERSITY
Marquette, MI 49855-5391

District 7

UNIVERSITY OF DENVER
Denver, CO 80208

WESTERN STATE COLLEGE
Gunnison, CO 81231

District 8

UNIVERSITY OF ALASKA-
ANCHORAGE
Anchorage, AK 99508

UNIVERSITY OF ALASKA-
FAIRBANKS
Fairbanks, AK 99775-7500

WOMEN'S WATER POLO

DIVISION I

District 1

HARVARD UNIVERSITY
Cambridge, MA 02138-3800

UNIVERSITY OF MASSACHUSETTS
Amherst, MA 01003

District 2

ST. FRANCIS COLLEGE
Brooklyn Heights, NY 11201

VILLANOVA UNIVERSITY
Villanova, PA 19085

District 7

SAN DIEGO STATE UNIVERSITY
San Diego, CA 92182

District 8

UNIV. OF CALIFORNIA-BERKELEY
Berkeley, CA 94720

UNIV. OF CALIF.-LOS ANGELES
Los Angeles, CA 90095-1405

UNIV. OF CALIF-SANTA BARBARA
Santa Barbara, CA 93106

UNIVERSITY OF THE PACIFIC
Stockton, CA 95211

UNIV. OF SOUTHERN CALIFORNIA
Los Angeles, CA 90089-0012

STANFORD UNIVERSITY
Stanford, CA 94305

DIVISION II

District 2

SLIPPERY ROCK UNIVERSITY
Slippery Rock, PA 16057

WOMEN'S CREW

DIVISION I

District 1

BOSTON UNIVERSITY
Boston, MA 02215

BROWN UNIVERSITY
Providence, RI 02912

DARTMOUTH COLLEGE
Hanover, NH 03755

HARVARD UNIVERSITY
Cambridge, MA 02138-3800

COLLEGE OF THE HOLY CROSS
Worcester, MA 01610-2395

UNIVERSITY OF MASSACHUSETTS
Amherst, MA 01003

UNIVERSITY OF NEW HAMPSHIRE
Durham, NH 03824

NORTHEASTERN UNIVERSITY
Boston, MA 02115-5096

YALE UNIVERSITY
New Haven, CT 06520-7398

District 2

BUCKNELL UNIVERSITY
Lewisburg, PA 17837

COLUMBIA UNIV.-BARNARD
COLLEGE
New York, NY 10027

CORNELL UNIVERSITY
Ithaca, NY 14853

DUQUESNE UNIVERSITY
Pittsburgh, PA 15282

GEORGE WASHINGTON
UNIVERSITY
Washington, DC 20052

GEORGETOWN UNIVERSITY
Washington, DC 20057

IONA COLLEGE
New Rochelle, NY 10801

LA SALLE UNIVERSITY
Philadelphia, PA 19141-1199

MARIST COLLEGE
Poughkeepsie, NY 12601-1387

UNIVERSITY OF PENNSYLVANIA
Philadelphia, PA 19104-6380

PRINCETON UNIVERSITY
Princeton, NJ 08544

RUTGERS UNIVERSITY
New Brunswick, NJ 08903

ST. JOSEPH'S UNIVERSITY
Philadelphia, PA 19131-1395

SYRACUSE UNIVERSITY
Syracuse, NY 13244

TEMPLE UNIVERSITY
Philadelphia, PA 19122

U.S. NAVAL ACADEMY
Annapolis, MD 21402

District 3

UNIVERSITY OF CENTRAL
FLORIDA
Orlando, FL 32816-0002

JACKSONVILLE UNIVERSITY
Jacksonville, FL 32211-3394

UNIVERSITY OF MIAMI
Coral Gables, FL 33124-6710

STETSON UNIVERSITY
De Land, FL 32720

THE UNIVERSITY OF TENNESSEE
Knoxville, TN 37996

UNIVERSITY OF VIRGINIA
Charlottesville, VA 22903

District 4

UNIVERSITY OF IOWA
Iowa City, IA 52242

OHIO STATE UNIVERSITY
Columbus, OH 43210

UNIVERSITY OF WISCONSIN
Madison, WI 53711

District 5

CREIGHTON UNIVERSITY
Omaha, NE 68178-0001

UNIVERSITY OF KANSAS
Lawrence, KS 66045

UNIVERSITY OF TULSA
Tulsa, OK 74104

District 7

GONZAGA UNIVERSITY
Spokane, WA 99258

District 8

UNIV. OF CALIFORNIA-BERKELEY
Berkeley, CA 94720

UNIV. OF CALIFORNIA-IRVINE
Irvine, CA 92717

CALIF. STATE UNIV.-SACRAMENTO
Sacramento, CA 95819

LOYOLA MARYMOUNT
UNIVERSITY
Los Angeles, CA 90045-2699

OREGON STATE UNIVERSITY
Corvallis, OR 87331

UNIVERSITY OF SAN DIEGO
San Diego, CA 92110-2492

SANTA CLARA UNIVERSITY
Santa Clara, CA 95053

UNIV. OF SOUTHERN CALIFORNIA
Los Angeles, CA 90089-0012

ST. MARY'S COLLEGE
Moraga, CA 94556

STANFORD UNIVERSITY
Stanford, CA 94305

WASHINGTON STATE UNIVERSITY
Pullman, WA 99164

UNIVERSITY OF WASHINGTON
Seattle, WA 98195

DIVISION II

District 1

ASSUMPTION COLLEGE
Worcester, MA 01615-0005

UNIV. OF MASSACHUSETTS-
LOWELL
Lowell, MA 01854

SACRED HEART UNIVERSITY
Fairfield, CT 06432-1000

District 2

THE UNIVERSITY OF
CHARLESTON
Charleston, WV 25304

MERCYHURST COLLEGE
Erie, PA 16546

District 3

BARRY UNIVERSITY
Miami Shores, FL 33161

ROLLINS COLLEGE
Winter Park, FL 32789

District 8

HUMBOLDT STATE UNIVERSITY
Arcata, CA 95521

SEATTLE PACIFIC UNIVERSITY
Seattle, WA 98119

NCAA PROVISIONAL MEMBERS
District 8

WESTERN WASHINGTON UNIV.
Bellingham, WA 98225

WOMEN'S SYNCHRONIZED SWIMMING

DIVISION I
District 2
CANSIUS COLLEGE
Buffalo, NY 14208-1098

District 3
UNIVERSITY OF RICHMOND
Richmond, VA 23173-1903

District 4
OHIO STATE UNIVERSITY
Columbus, OH 43210

District 8
STANFORD UNIVERSITY
Stanford, CA 94305

WOMEN'S SQUASH

DIVISION I
District 1
BROWN UNIVERSITY
Providence, RI 02912

DARTMOUTH COLLEGE
Hanover, NH 03755

HARVARD UNIVERSITY
Cambridge, MA 02138-3800

YALE UNIVERSITY
New Haven, CT 06520-7398

District 2
UNIVERSITY OF PENNSYLVANIA
Philadelphia, PA 19104-6380

PRINCETON UNIVERSITY
Princeton, NJ 08544

Index